NATIONS APART

ALSO BY COLIN WOODARD

Ocean's End

The Lobster Coast

The Republic of Pirates

American Nations

American Character

Union

NATIONS

APART

HOW CLASHING
REGIONAL CULTURES
SHATTERED AMERICA

Colin Woodard

VIKING

Maps on pages 13, 15, and 16–17 drawn by Sean Wilkinson, Sean Wilkinson Design.

All other maps and illustrations by John Liberty, Motivf Corporation.

Portions of this work originally appeared, in significantly different form, in publications by Nationhood Lab, as well as in the "The Surprising Geography of Gun Violence" and "America's Surprising Partisan Divide on Life Expectancy" in *Politico* (2023); in "The Perplexing Geography of Abortion Opinion" in *Talking Points Memo* (2024); and in "How Joe Biden Can Help Forge a New National Narrative" in *Washington Monthly* (2021).

DESIGNED BY MEIGHAN CAVANAUGH

LIBRARY OF CONGRESS CONTROL NUMBER: 2025025225
ISBN 9780593833407 (hardcover)
ISBN 9780593833414 (ebook)

Printed in the United States of America
2nd Printing

The authorized representative in the EU for product safety and compliance is Penguin Random House Ireland, Morrison Chambers, 32 Nassau Street, Dublin D02 YH68, Ireland, https://eu-contact.penguin.ie.

For Sarah, Henry, and Sadie,

who put up with this writing thing

CONTENTS

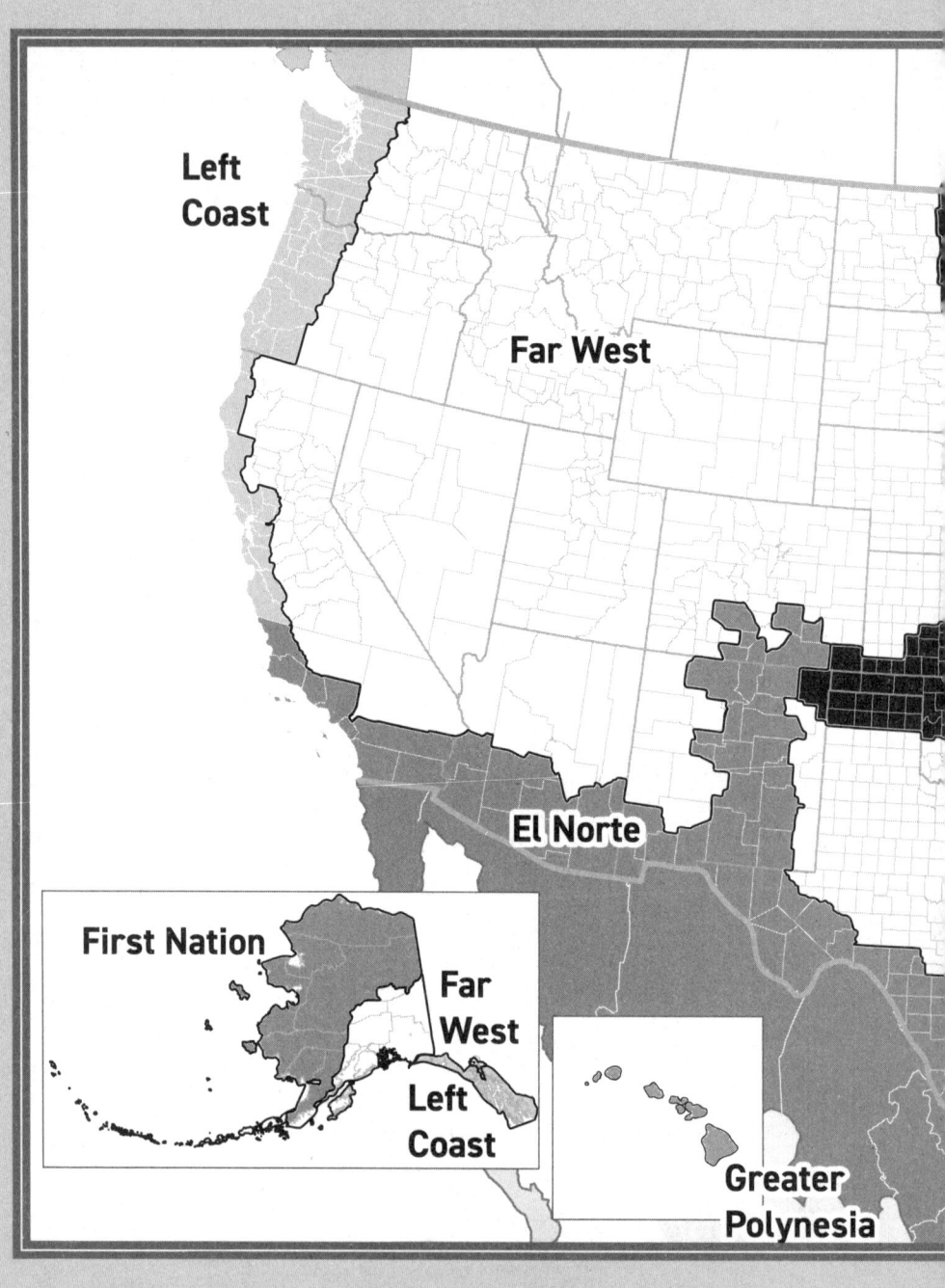

NATIONS APART

INTRODUCTION

D emocratic collapses, like bankruptcies, happen gradually and then all at once. So do collapses of countries. Americans are experiencing what it's like when both are happening at the same time.

The United States is an awkward federation of distinct regional cultures, created as an ad hoc alliance to resist a common, British, opponent. At the moment of this creation, a handful of the most eloquent Founders proposed its ideals: to create a place where all people could live in freedom.

We've been fighting over these ideals ever since, yet, ironically, they are the one thing that can hold us together.

To achieve these ideals, Americans fought for and slowly built a liberal democracy, a form of government where people have both civil and political rights. Across a large swath of the country, this required a revolution, the civil rights movement of the 1960s, to overthrow what had been illiberal, authoritarian regimes under which a person's rights depended on their bloodlines. When those former Confederate states became liberal democracies, America finally did, too.

Now that's all coming apart. Politicians no longer respect election results and have taught their followers not to believe them. Federal judges routinely make nakedly partisan rulings. Supreme Court justices have put the state in charge of women's bodies and put presidents above the law, subject to only their very subjective review. Elected officials, poll workers, public health officials, reporters, and even the grieving parents of murdered children face mob violence and intimidation. An outgoing president encouraged a violent coup attempt at the Capitol to keep himself in power; Republican senators couldn't bring themselves to impeach him, a Democratic attorney general failed to bring him to justice, and voters saw fit to restore him to the presidency in 2024, despite his promises to imprison his enemies, deploy active-duty troops against protesters, round up "vermin" into concentration camps, and pardon convicted insurrectionists en masse.

Our democracy is backsliding. Both the Economist Intelligence Unit and Freedom House—organizations that tourists and businesspeople once looked to for information on the state of democracy in developing countries—reclassified the United States as a flawed democracy years ago and warn that we continue moving in the wrong direction.

The authoritarian movement threatens the federation, too, because it is far stronger in some regions of the country than others, creating increasingly unmanageable political, legal, and constitutional tensions. There are swaths of the U.S. where there are political leaders who push for total abortion bans, who argue that climate change is a natural phenomenon and that transgender people should be driven underground, and who want to deploy Jesus Christ and firearms in every classroom. In other regions, political leaders think reproductive rights are sacrosanct, climate change is a pressing issue requiring immediate redress, church and state are to be kept apart, guns should kept securely at home and far from schools, and more transgender people should hold public office. There are giant blocks of the country that overwhelmingly support an authoritarian ethnonationalist's presidential bids and other blocks where the same man is overwhelmingly reviled. Everywhere there's a growing share of the population that says we'd all be better off if we broke apart; in early 2024, nearly a quarter of American adults and about three in ten Californians, New Yorkers, and Texans said they'd support their state seceding from the United States. Of Republicans surveyed in 2022, 54 percent thought it was likely the country would descend into civil war in the next decade.[1]

How did this happen? What can we do to reverse it?

This book seeks to answer those questions using original data and polling results interpreted through the work of historians, political scientists, social psychologists, health researchers, and other scholars. It concludes with an evidence-based strategy for bringing America's people and regional cultures together around the ideals in our original mission statement, the Declaration of Independence. It reveals the depth and contours of the challenge, but also that the American people are not nearly as polarized as our political leaders on the hot-button issues, and are remarkably united around our ideals.

We can save our democracy, our country, and ourselves. It will take hard work and sound strategy by millions of us over many years, but I believe we'll succeed.

I'M A SCHOLAR OF NATIONALISM, nationhood, and democracy, a historian of North American regionalism, and a former foreign correspondent who spent years reporting from countries that had descended into civil war or overthrown dictatorships or became authoritarian states after one or both of these events had taken place. I've covered atrocities, ethnic riots, war crimes trials, and peace and reconciliation efforts from the Balkans to Bikini Atoll and from Honduras to The Hague. I did academic work on how and why cynical leaders use lies and provocations to get people to kill one another, and how ethnic conflicts come about, before turning to the question of why my own country, the United States, is and has always been so regionally divided. For the past two decades, I've focused on this problem and how we can fix it before it brings down the republic and shatters our federation.

In a previous book, *American Nations: A History of the Eleven Rival Regional Cultures of North America*, I showed that there has never been one America, but rather several Americas, regional cultures that were founded at different times and by very different people and which expanded across mutually exclusive swaths of the continent, laying down their own institutions, fundamental values, and original intents. I demonstrated that we've never been a nation-state in the European sense, but rather a federation of nations, more akin to the European Union than the Republic of France. I showed how this fundamental fact has complicated efforts to find common ground, be it in a policy issue like social spending, gun control, abortion, or the environment, or in more fundamental ideas, like where our society comes from, who can truly belong, and even whether we should be a democracy at all.[2]

In a sequel, *American Character: A History of the Epic Struggle Between Individual Liberty and the Common Good*, I explored how these "American Nations" have fought with one another over the best way to achieve the liberal democracy envisioned in the Declaration. Some regions have always emphasized maximizing the freedom and autonomy of individual citizens (though not everyone could be one), while others have championed the creation and maintenance of a free society, a social project to cultivate a republican citizenry and to ensure that individuals can be meaningfully free even if they are born poor and powerless. I warned that over a half century, our federation had drifted so far into individualism that the social contract had come apart, with a growing gulf between haves and have-nots and fewer ways for people to cross it. I warned that if we didn't change course, people would turn against democracy. The book was released in 2016, a few weeks before Trump secured the Republican Party's nomination for president.

AFTER TRUMP'S INAUGURATION, I started thinking a lot about my time in Yugoslavia before, during, and especially after its civil war. I kept coming back to a day in Bosnia in September 1996, not long after the war had ended. It was election day, actually, and under the watchful eyes of NATO troops and international administrators, Bosnians were voting for the first time since ethnic Serbs had started shelling the capital and murdering their Croat and Bosniak neighbors before a world television audience. I'd hitched a ride with a Canadian election observer to Sokolac, a large village deep in the hills above the burned-out skyscrapers, bullet-ridden Olympic stadiums, and grave-filled city parks of Sarajevo. We drove through unlit road tunnels, past a Bosnian Serb checkpoint and fields marked with minefield warning signs and then, beyond the former front, into forests, mountains, roadside sawmills, and compact lumber towns that looked much like northwestern Maine, where I grew up. Instead of rounding the bend into Farmington or Rangeley, we'd confront an armored column of French peacekeepers or a billboard plastered with pictures celebrating the Bosnian Serb leader Radovan Karadžić, who was later convicted of genocide by an international court.

We'd come to Sokolac to see if any of the ethnic Croats and Bosniaks who'd been forced from their homes by the Serbs' ethnic cleansing campaign had returned to vote under international protection. There was no line at the polling station set up for them, but we found a big crowd at the one for Serbs across town. One of the men in the crowd marched up to me, surrounded by curious onlookers. He was well-dressed and self-assured and had an aggressive manner accentuated by a menacing smile. He'd just returned from Switzerland, where he'd spent most of the war in comfort and, in those pre-internet days, completely outside the Serbian propaganda bubble, where up was down, night was day. Within this bubble, the Bosnian Serbs' rape camps didn't exist and their execution of thousands of civilian men and children at Srebrenica was a heroic act to defend Christendom from Bosniaks, Bosnia's largest ethnic group, whose ancestors had converted to Islam when the region was part of the Ottoman Empire. "Why does the world tell such lies about the Serbs?" the man demanded to know. "All these stories about concentration camps and mass graves—these never existed! Nobody was killed in Srebrenica, and yet you journalists show pictures of corpses they are digging up. Is this any way for democratic countries to behave?" He patted my shoulder with theatrical warmth. "We're saving Europe from the Muslims and you treat us like criminals?"

I spent many hours trying to understand how Karadžić and his mentor, the Serbian dictator Slobodan Milošević, had convinced this guy and millions like him that what they saw with their own eyes never happened, that the most indisputably evil and despicable acts were the work of heroes, that the victims were aggressors and the aggressors were victims. I'd by then spent years in Eastern Europe and the Balkans and had witnessed the collapse of Communism and the withdrawal of Soviet troops, the rise of demagogues, and what raw animal instinct wrought in the trenches and villages on the Slavonian front between Croatia and Serbia. Years of disruption, decades of dictatorship, and centuries of despotism had done something to the people of this unlucky region, I told myself. These lies would never take root in a free society like my own.

Yet they have. And my work now focuses on ensuring that we remain a free society, one that never goes down Bosnia's path.

OUR DIVISIONS FLARE UP over policy flashpoints. In this book, I'll show that the great hot-button political issues of our times have been shaped and are largely explained by the presence of the "American Nations," our underlying regional cultures. Covering topics from abortion and health to gun violence and immigration, this book presents the hard data illustrating just how profoundly settlement patterns from two, three, and four centuries ago shape the world we live in today. This knowledge helps us to understand not only how and why these divisions exist but also the historical and sociocultural forces behind those differences, enabling us to find solutions that can bridge these divides.

The extensive powers our constitution reserves for the states have given us "laboratories of democracy" that allow us to experiment with different approaches. Our data delivers some inescapable verdicts on which experiments are working and which are not. There is a clear pattern. Individualistic policy approaches—financing tax cuts by reducing public services, for instance—have reduced our health, safety, happiness, wealth, and longevity. Communitarian ones, which presume that social investments in shared goods like public parks, libraries, schools, universities, health insurance, or basic scientific research grants can improve individual lives, have had the opposite effect. Deteriorating social conditions, especially in regions with highly individualistic cultures, have created precisely the sort of environment where demagogues thrive. Here's how my fellow Mainer Heather Cox Richardson, professor of history at Boston College, puts it, distilling the essence of Hannah Arendt's *The Origins of Totalitarianism*:

> Authoritarians rise when economic, social, political or religious change makes members of a formerly powerful group feel as if they have been left behind. Their frustration makes them vulnerable to leaders who promise to make them dominant again. A strongman downplays the real conditions that have created their problems and tells them that the only reason they have been dispossessed is that enemies have cheated them of power.[3]

As I write later in this book, the single-minded pursuit of individual freedom is driving us to the brink of despotism. Chapters 2, 3, 5, 6, and 7 show how as they parse regional differences across five emotive issues: gun control, social and health spending, immigration and belonging, abortion, and climate change.

Regional cultural and political traditions also differ on democracy itself. It's not fully appreciated that some regions of our country were governed by ethnonationalist authoritarian regimes until the late 1960s—the Jim Crow South was a racial apartheid system backed by formal law and extrajudicial death squads—and, like fragile democracies the world over, are susceptible to counterrevolution. Chapter 4 reveals the mythic histories of the respective regions, which have differing implications regarding democracy, equality, diversity, and belonging. Chapters 8 and 9 relate the role the "American Nations" have played in the current authoritarian crisis, which started with the shock of the 2008 financial collapse, years before Trump stepped onto the political stage.

Holding this Balkanized federation together has always required a shared vision, a national story of purpose and belonging. Ours is a truly amazing story, a people engaged in a common effort to create and maintain a society where humans can be truly and sustainably free.

The American Experiment is the quest to ensure, in Abraham Lincoln's words, that government of the people, by the people, for the people, shall not perish from the Earth. It includes the American Promise, that we are all created equal and should be treated as such. It's also been contested from the outset by champions of a counternarrative that holds people as inherently unequal and believes that a superior subset should have dominion over all. After the end of the Cold War, many of our leaders told us history had ended, that America had "won," and that, in a sense, the Experiment had come to a successful, triumphant conclusion. We stopped talking about it, stopped acting on its principles, and the Promise began to wither. We need that story now, in a form that speaks to twenty-first-century life. Chapter 10 provides an answer, informed by original research, polling, and in-depth qualitative interviews. We can fix our country and find a new birth of freedom.

MUCH OF THIS WORK was undertaken at Nationhood Lab, the project I founded at the end of 2022 at the Pell Center for International Relations and Public Policy, the think tank at Salve Regina University in Newport, Rhode Island. Broadly speaking, Nationhood Lab studies the problems of U.S. nationhood and how to solve for them. In practice, we use the American Nations model to analyze past and present phenomena where regionalism is important in an effort to better describe and improve the situation. Ahead of the Semiquincentennial, the 250th birthday of the United States and the Declaration in 2026, we've focused on developing, testing, and deploying a renewed civic national story for the country, backed by historical understanding and hard, present-day data.

For data analysis and visualizations, we've partnered with Motivf, an Alexandria, Virginia–based geospatial consultancy that incorporates cultural factors into its work; they created many of the maps and graphics within these covers. On health and social issues, I've collaborated with a shifting team of academic researchers across the country led by Ross Arena, a physiologist at the University of Illinois Chicago, and Nicolaas Pronk, president of the Minneapolis-based HealthPartners Institute, to produce an expanding corpus of peer-reviewed studies driven by the American Nations model. While we strive to maintain standards of academic rigor, Nationhood Lab is primarily focused on driving constructive change outside the academy's walls, and I've shared portions of the research and analysis in articles in *Politico*, *Smithsonian*, the *Washington Monthly*, and other media outlets. If you find this book useful, I encourage you to follow our work online.

1

NATIONS

"W e in America are in reality a federation of sections rather than of states," the eminent historian Frederick Jackson Turner concluded in a book he was still working on when his struggling heart finally gave out in 1932.

In his youth, Turner had become perhaps the most famous academic on the continent on account of his frontier thesis of national unity, an essay that "went viral" in 1893 because it had offered Americans a story they wanted to hear. The frontier environment of the middle and, later, far west had remade those who settled it into Americans, an equality- and democracy-loving people with a can-do attitude and republican spirit. Not long after publishing his thesis, however, Turner realized there was something wrong. His research of county-level data—on economic activity, ethnic geography, church membership, and election returns—showed the various parts of the middle west had been settled by distinct streams of settlers—"'bowie knife southerners,' 'cow-milking Yankee Puritans,' 'beer-drinking Germans,' 'wild Irishmen'"—and they hadn't become more alike over time. In fact, they'd remained noticeably different in their political behavior, ideological outlook, and social organization.

This perplexed Turner, who, like most academics of the age, was a devotee of Charles Darwin's exciting theories about environmental selection. Surely there must be a hidden geographical or ecological explanation for these persistent differences, Turner thought, and he spent the last thirty years of his life trying unsuccessfully to find them.[1]

In the end, he'd begun to accept what the facts had been telling him. The primitive conditions of the North American interior hadn't broken down the varied cultural heritages of the old colonies to the east. The settlers had very much retained their habits, beliefs, customs, values, and ideals. They'd reproduced their political and social institutions on "the frontier," expanding their cultures across the continent and assimilating those who came later. The regions, he wrote at one point, "may be likened to the shadowy image of the European nation, to the European state denatured of its toxic qualities." In that, he was half right.[2]

As *AMERICAN NATIONS* DEMONSTRATED, our abiding divisions stem from the fact that the original clusters of North American colonies were settled by people from distinct regions of the British Isles—and from France, the Netherlands, and Spain—each with their own religious, political, and ethnographic characteristics. For generations, these discrete Euro-American cultures developed in remarkable isolation from one another, consolidating their own cherished principles and fundamental values and expanding across the eastern half of the continent in nearly exclusive settlement bands.[3]

Some of these "nations" championed individualism, others utopian social reform. Some believed themselves guided by divine purpose, others espoused freedom of conscience and inquiry. Some embraced an Anglo-Protestant identity, others ethnic and religious pluralism. Some valued equality and democratic participation, others deference to a traditional aristocratic order modeled on the slave states of classical antiquity. Throughout the colonial period and the Early Republic, they saw them-

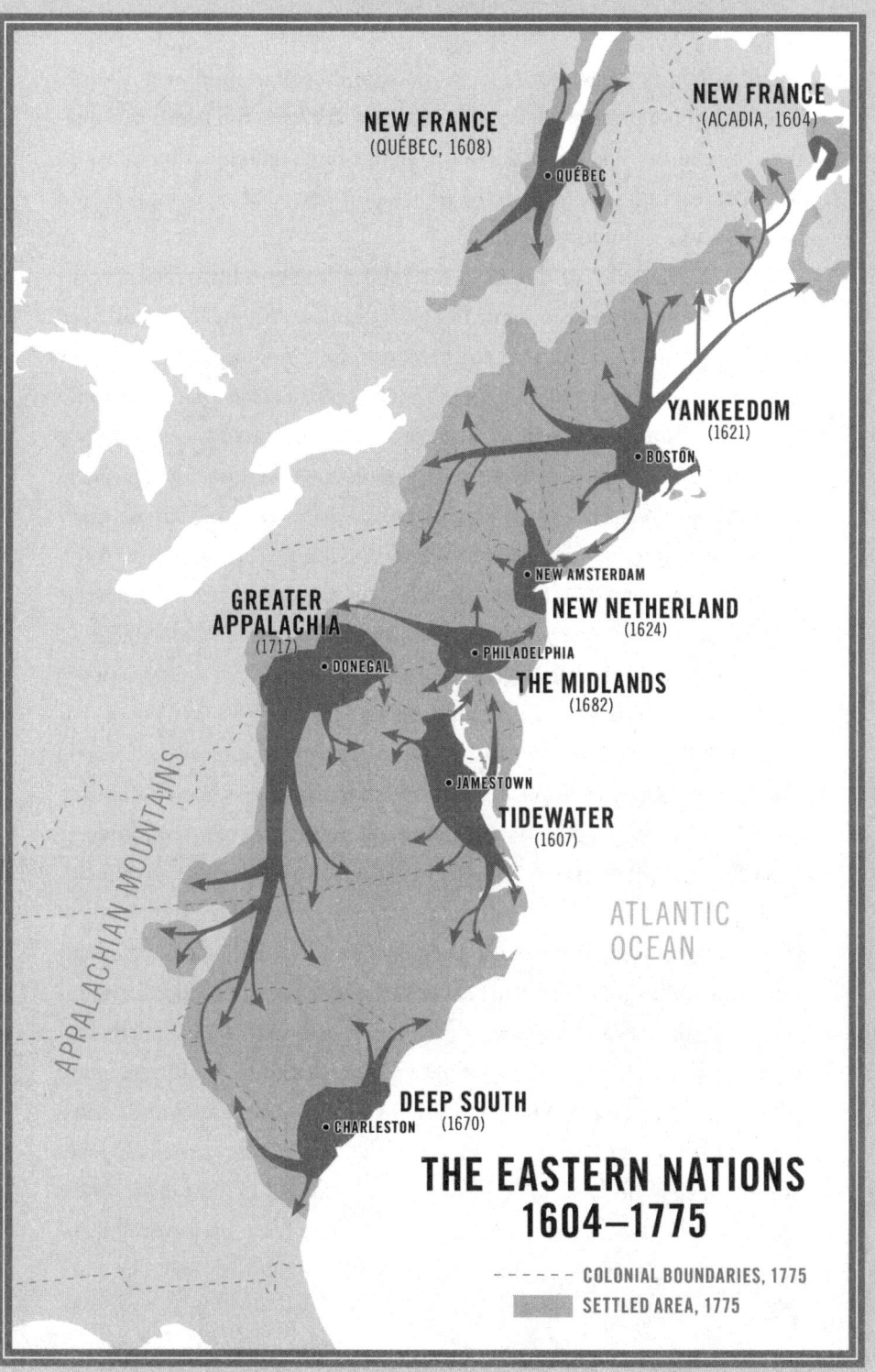

NEW FRANCE
(QUÉBEC, 1608)

NEW FRANCE
(ACADIA, 1604)

• QUÉBEC

YANKEEDOM
(1621)

• BOSTON

• NEW AMSTERDAM

NEW NETHERLAND
(1624)

GREATER
APPALACHIA
(1717)

• DONEGAL

• PHILADELPHIA

THE MIDLANDS
(1682)

APPALACHIAN MOUNTAINS

• JAMESTOWN

TIDEWATER
(1607)

ATLANTIC
OCEAN

DEEP SOUTH
(1670)

• CHARLESTON

THE EASTERN NATIONS
1604–1775

- - - - - - COLONIAL BOUNDARIES, 1775

▬▬▬ SETTLED AREA, 1775

selves as competitors—for land, settlers, and capital—and even as enemies, taking opposing sides in the English Civil War, the American Revolution, and the War of 1812. Nearly all of these regional cultures would consider leaving the Union in the eighty-year period after Yorktown, and two went to war to do so in the 1860s.

Despite centuries of domestic migration, foreign immigration, technological change, and economic integration, these regional cultures' deep underlying characteristics remain with us today. You might well ask how that could possibly be when it would make perfect sense that they would have blended together by now, or been diluted or erased by later migration and immigration patterns and populations. Cultural geographers were asking precisely the same questions decades ago. Wilbur Zelinsky of Pennsylvania State University provided a compelling answer in 1973, when he formulated a theory he called the Doctrine of First Effective Settlement. "Whenever an empty territory undergoes settlement, or an earlier population is dislodged by invaders, the specific characteristics of the first group able to effect a viable, self-perpetuating society are of crucial significance for the later social and cultural geography of the area, no matter how tiny the initial band of settlers may have been," Zelinsky wrote. "Thus, in terms of lasting impact, the activities of a few hundred, or even a few score, initial colonizers can mean much more for the cultural geography of a place than the contributions of tens of thousands of new immigrants a few generations later." Founding settler-colonizers lay down the cultural DNA for the society, the core ideas, practices, and institutions, the historical and mythic memories, symbols, and beliefs that together constitute what anthropologists define as culture. Cultures change over time, to be sure, but broad outlines remain over decades and centuries, be it a nation of Japanese or Icelanders, Zulu or Marshallese, Québécois or Deep Southerners. The Dutch may be all but extinct in the lower Hudson Valley—and the landed aristocracy may have lost control of the Chesapeake country—but their legacy remains, built into social and political institutions and the fabric of daily life.[4]

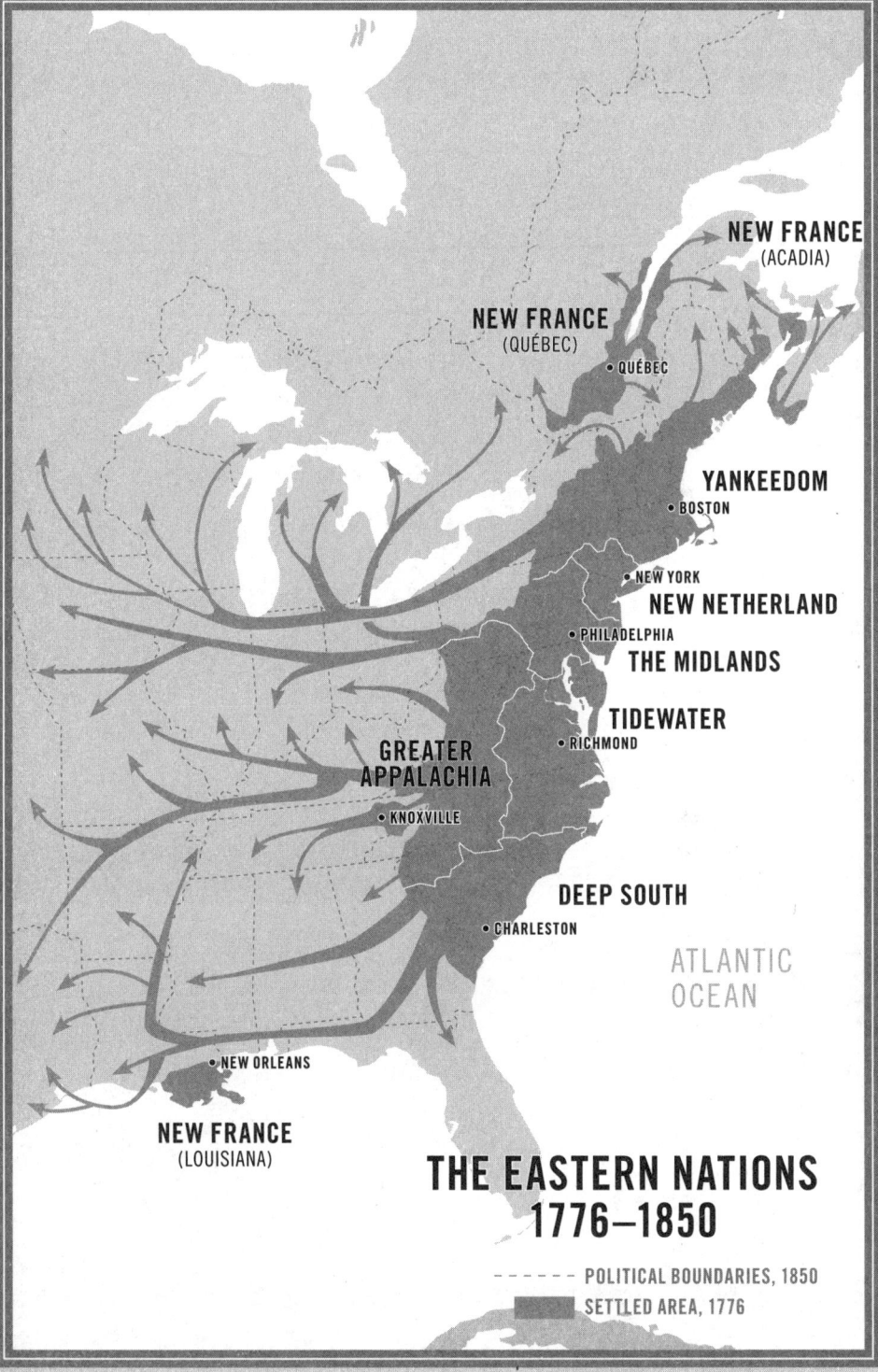

NEW FRANCE
(ACADIA)

NEW FRANCE
(QUÉBEC)

• QUÉBEC

YANKEEDOM

• BOSTON

• NEW YORK

NEW NETHERLAND

• PHILADELPHIA

THE MIDLANDS

TIDEWATER

• RICHMOND

GREATER
APPALACHIA

• KNOXVILLE

DEEP SOUTH

• CHARLESTON

ATLANTIC
OCEAN

• NEW ORLEANS

NEW FRANCE
(LOUISIANA)

THE EASTERN NATIONS
1776–1850

- - - - - - POLITICAL BOUNDARIES, 1850
SETTLED AREA, 1776

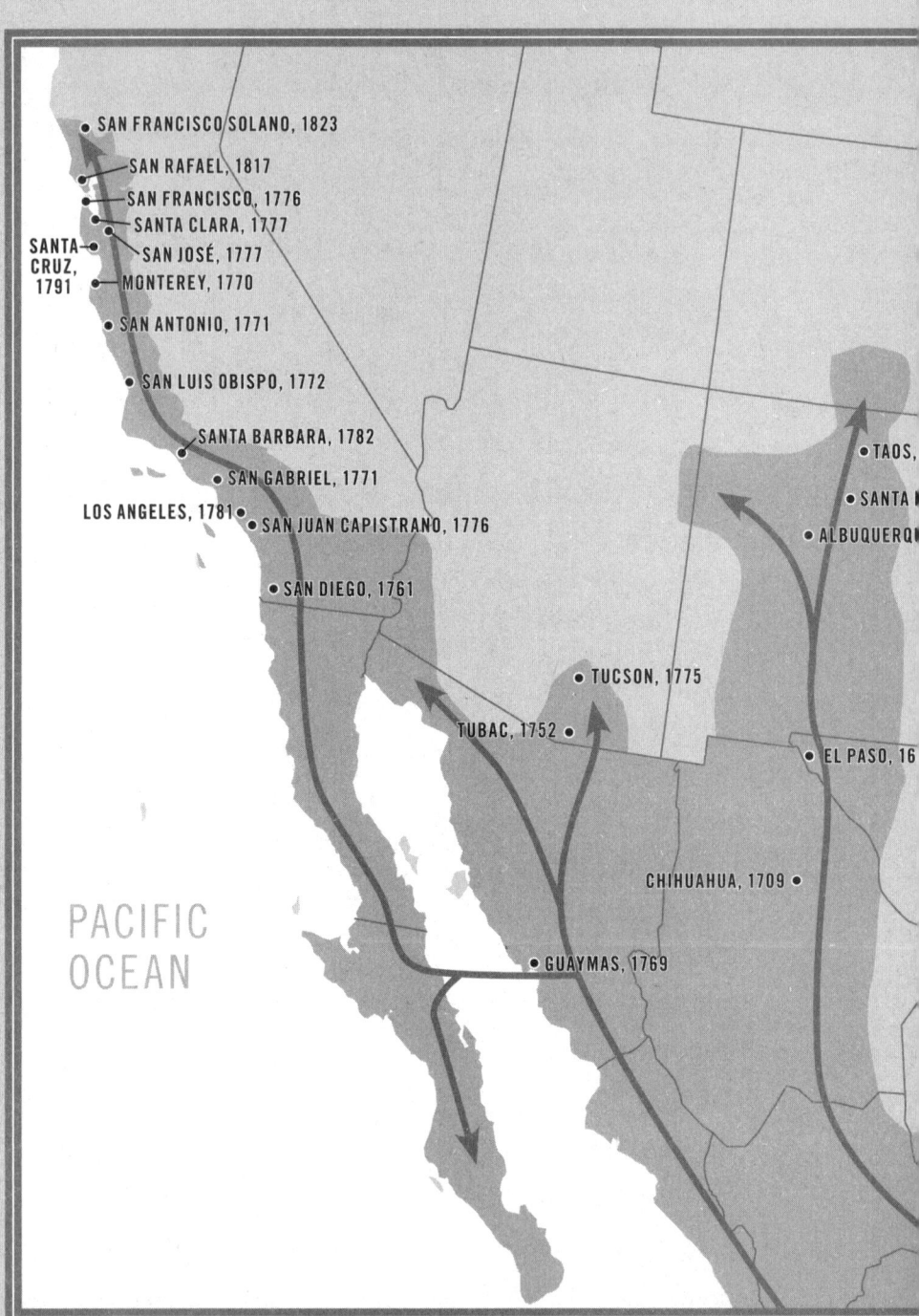

SAN FRANCISCO SOLANO, 1823

SAN RAFAEL, 1817

SAN FRANCISCO, 1776

SANTA CLARA, 1777

SAN JOSÉ, 1777

SANTA CRUZ, 1791

MONTEREY, 1770

SAN ANTONIO, 1771

SAN LUIS OBISPO, 1772

SANTA BARBARA, 1782

SAN GABRIEL, 1771

LOS ANGELES, 1781

SAN JUAN CAPISTRANO, 1776

SAN DIEGO, 1761

TUCSON, 1775

TUBAC, 1752

TAOS,

SANTA

ALBUQUERQ

EL PASO, 16

CHIHUAHUA, 1709

GUAYMAS, 1769

PACIFIC OCEAN

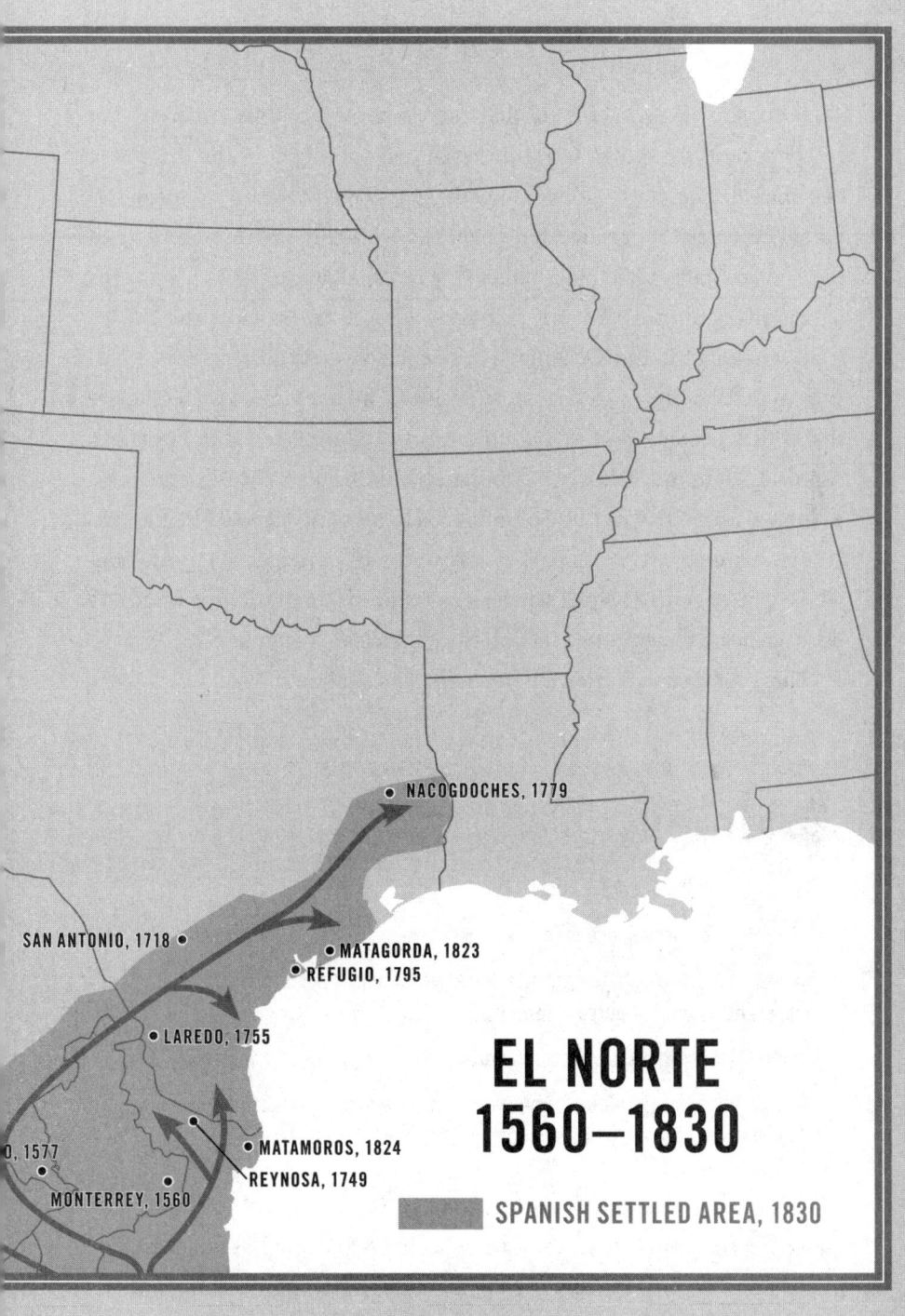

NACOGDOCHES, 1779

SAN ANTONIO, 1718

MATAGORDA, 1823
REFUGIO, 1795

LAREDO, 1755

MATAMOROS, 1824
REYNOSA, 1749

0, 1577

MONTERREY, 1560

EL NORTE
1560–1830

SPANISH SETTLED AREA, 1830

THE POINT OF ALL THIS is that there's never been an America, but rather several Americas, wrestling with one another over the destiny of our shared federation. Today's North America includes nine major regional cultures that are located primarily within the current borders of the United States plus four smaller "enclaves" that are the U.S. portions of regional cultures that are primarily located in Canada, the Caribbean, Greenland, and Oceania. These enclaves have had far less influence over the course of U.S. history—indeed, all are located on territories that didn't become part of the union until the nineteenth or twentieth centuries—but they're essential to understanding state-level phenomena. There's also the District of Columbia itself, an entity created by the federal government that isn't part of any of the other regional cultures but whose presence has helped trigger the rapid disintegration of what had once been the most powerful of all these stateless "nations."

These American Nations, if you will, are as follows:

YANKEEDOM

POPULATION (2020): 55 million

DENSITY: 157 per square mile

DEMOGRAPHICS: 72 percent white, 9 percent Black, 9 percent Hispanic, 4 percent Asian; 9.3 percent foreign-born

ORIENTATION: Aggressively communitarian

STATES DOMINATED: Maine, New Hampshire, Vermont, Massachusetts, Connecticut, Rhode Island, Michigan, Wisconsin, Minnesota

Founded on the shores of Massachusetts Bay by radical Calvinists as a new Zion, since the outset, the nation I call Yankeedom has put great emphasis on perfecting earthly society through social engineering, individual self-denial for the common good, and the aggressive assimilation of outsiders. It has prized education, intellectual achievement, community (rather than individual) empowerment, and broad citizen participation in politics and government, the latter viewed as the public's shield against the machinations of grasping aristocrats, corporations, and would-be tyrants. From its New England core, it has spread with its settlers westward across upper New York State; the northern strips of Pennsylvania, Ohio, Illinois, and Iowa; parts of the eastern Dakotas; northward into the upper Great Lakes states; and eastward across much of the Canadian Maritimes.

The early Puritans believed they had a covenant with God, that they were a chosen people tasked with creating a more perfect society here on Earth, a "city upon a hill," a beacon for humanity to follow in troubled times. From the beginning, they attempted to accomplish this through collective institutions, with the common good invariably taking precedence over individual freedom when the two came into conflict. The point of the New England experiment was to maintain the freedom of the community, which to the region's founders meant remaining ever vigilant against the formation of an aristocracy, which in turn demanded restraint on the avarice of individuals.

Early Yankees tended to settle areas not as individuals, but as family units traveling in groups of friends and neighbors, sometimes as a "village on the move," often led by their Puritan, Congregational, or Presbyterian preacher. On arriving at the frontier—eastern Massachusetts in the early seventeenth century, western New York a half-century later, the Western Reserve of Ohio in the late eighteenth century, or Michigan in the early nineteenth—they divided the land nearly equally among themselves, levied taxes, and promptly constructed a public school, meetinghouse, and common pasture. Each town was, from the outset, a tiny republic unto itself, wherein elected committees decided everything from where the public roads, churches, town greens, and schoolhouses would be located to how to levy, collect, and spend taxes, and how best to raise and organize the militia. The local church congregation was also completely self-governing, with no external hierarchy to which to report. Whereas in other regions, counties held considerable power and towns had little if any, in New England and much of Yankeedom, counties had few powers at all so as to confound the emergence of unaccountable political forces. To this day, many small towns in New England maintain a town-meeting form of government, where the people themselves assemble as a legislature to vote on all substantive decisions directly. Government, to the Yankee mind, was conceived not as the enemy, but rather as an extension of its citizenry.

Indeed, Yankees would come to have faith in government and public institutions to a degree that was unimaginable to the people of other regions. Government, New Englanders believed from the outset, could defend the public good from the selfish machinations of moneyed interests. It could enforce community standards through the prohibition or regulation of undesirable activities, from adultery and swearing in the sixteenth century to slavery and drinking in the nineteenth. It could create a better society through public spending on infrastructure and schools. Even the pursuit of profit—a subject with which the Yankee elite was obsessed—was conceived as being not a private endeavor but a civic responsibility, part of the continuing duty of building the New Zion promised by the Puritan founder John Winthrop in the sermon he gave on his people's departure from England in 1630. "We must be knit together in this work as one man," Winthrop preached. "We must be willing to abridge ourselves of our superfluities, for the supply of other's necessities . . . uphold a familiar Commerce together . . . delight in each other, make other's conditions our own, rejoice together, mourn together, labor and suffer together, always having before our eyes our Commission and Community in the work, our Community as members of the same body."[5]

Here was a society that prized the common good, distrusted the selfish motivations of individuals, and aspired to lead America and the world.

NEW NETHERLAND

POPULATION (2020): **18.8 million**

DENSITY: **3,430 per square mile**

DEMOGRAPHICS: **43 percent white, 25 percent Hispanic, 15 percent Black, 12 percent Asian; 28 percent foreign-born**

ORIENTATION: **Aggressively communitarian**

STATES DOMINATED: **New Jersey**

STATES CONTROLLED: **New York**

Established by the Dutch at a time when the Netherlands was the most sophisticated society in the western world, the regional culture I call New Netherland has displayed its salient characteristics throughout its history: a global commercial trading culture—multiethnic, multireligious, and materialistic—with a profound tolerance for diversity and an unflinching commitment to the freedom of inquiry and conscience. Today it comprises greater New York City, including northern New Jersey, western Long Island, and the Lower Hudson Valley. Like seventeenth-century Amsterdam, it emerged as a leading global center of publishing, trade, and finance; a magnet for immigrants and a refuge for those persecuted by other regional cultures, from Sephardim who moved there in the seventeenth century to gays, feminists, and bohemians in the early twentieth. Not particularly democratic or concerned with great moral questions—it tolerated slavery and defended the Deep South until the 1861 attack on federal troops at Fort Sumter—it nonetheless has found itself in alliance with Yankeedom in defense of a shared commitment to public-sector institutions and a rejection of Evangelical prescriptions for individual behavior.

The early New Netherlanders, to a remarkable degree, struck a balance between individualistic aspirations and the common good. Theirs was a colony founded, owned, and ruled by a corporation, the Dutch West

India Company, and it was organized to earn profits for its shareholders. When some of its early directors tried to rule as authoritarian bosses, treating its polyglot inhabitants as employees, the citizenry would have none of it. The "establishment of an arbitrary government among us," nineteen leading residents wrote in a 1653 protest, "crushed our spirits and disheartened us in our labors and our callings so that we, being in a wilderness, are unable to promote the good of the country with the same zeal and inclination as before." Dutch authorities, they insisted, had the duty "to promote the welfare of their subjects" and, therefore, had to uphold the civil liberties of "every freeborn man" against the company's governor.[6] They won the day.

Unlike the Puritans of New England, the New Netherlanders didn't expect much self-government. There were no representative assemblies and, for much of the Dutch period, no municipal governments. But they did insist that whatever government they did have should provide for the common good. Their successful protest against the authoritarian rule of the West India Company argued that without change "this country will never flourish." In 1653, they won the right to establish a municipal government and immediately undertook a series of public works projects, including building a wall against the English (where Wall Street now lies), paving the streets with cobblestones, digging a proper canal through the middle of the settlement, and constructing a wharf to serve the ocean-going ships upon which the colony's prosperity depended. A series of laws were passed that coerced individuals on behalf of the common good: Thatch roofs had to be replaced with tiles (to prevent major fires in the densely packed town), and street-front chicken coops and pig sties had to be removed (for aesthetic and health reasons). As New York grew in the late eighteenth and early nineteenth centuries, public works and ordinances became all the more essential to maintaining safety and prosperity in an increasingly crowded city.

More important, they constrained their government with strong and explicit protections of individual liberties, which they believed to be their birthright. The 1653 protesters asserted their rights as "freeborn" men to assemble and to protest against the company boss's violations of property rights. When England conquered New Netherland—first in 1664 and permanently in 1674—its people managed to negotiate guarantees for a long list of individual liberties: protections against the arbitrary seizure of property and the quartering of troops in homes, guarantees of trial by jury, and freedom of religion. In the aftermath of the American Revolution, residents of the New Netherland section of New York spearheaded the passage of a state law granting additional rights, including free elections, freedom of speech for legislators, and the guarantee that any new taxes could be imposed by only the people's legislative representatives. Not surprisingly, it was New York's representatives that insisted on the inclusion of a Bill of Rights in the proposed U.S. Constitution. A multireligious society with a tradition of free presses and a historical experience of foreign occupation and authoritarian-minded corporate governors, New Netherlanders were—and remain—attuned to the importance of protecting civil liberties in maintaining a free society.

Finally, New Netherland was, perhaps more than any other colonial culture, a socioeconomically mobile society. At a time when social status in most colonies was largely determined by birth, mid-seventeenth-century New Netherland's local elite were self-made men. The first Vanderbilt (Jan Aertsen Van der Bilt) was an indentured servant, but he begat one of the wealthiest families in history. The founder of the Van Cortlandt dynasty arrived as a soldier, took up carpentry, and eventually became the city's mayor. The Van Burens started as tenant farmers. Frederick Philipse rose from humble butcher to the city's richest man, with a slave plantation in Barbados and a land holding encompassing much of Westchester County. The notion that, with hard work and dedication, any white male might climb to the top of the heap in a single lifetime took hold in the colony's capital and never let go.[7]

As members of a highly mobile, outwardly oriented trading society, New Netherlanders have long recognized the need to have both a competent government that looked out for the common good and clear protections for the freedom of the individuals living under it. Do "not force people's consciences, but allow everyone to have his own belief, as long as he behaves quietly and legally, gives no offense to his neighbors and does not oppose the government," Governor Peter Stuyvesant was directed in 1663 by his superiors in Holland. "Your province . . . would be benefited by it."[8]

MIDLANDS

POPULATION (2020): **38.4 million**

DENSITY: **128 per square mile**

DEMOGRAPHICS: **69 percent white, 12 percent Black, 10 percent Hispanic, 4 percent Asian; 9 percent foreign-born**

ORIENTATION: **Passively communitarian**

STATES DOMINATED: **Pennsylvania, Iowa, Nebraska, Kansas**

STATES CONTROLLED: **Maryland, Delaware, Missouri**

The Midlands, America's great swing region, was founded by English Quakers, who believed in humans' inherent goodness and welcomed people of many nations and creeds to their utopian colonies on the shores of Delaware Bay. Pluralistic and organized around the middle class, the Midlands spawned the culture of Middle America and the Heartland, where ethnic and ideological purity have never been a priority, government has been seen as an unwelcome intrusion, and political opinion has been moderate, even apathetic. An ethnic mosaic from the start—it had a German, rather than British, majority at the time of the Revolution—it shares the Yankee belief that society should be organized to benefit ordinary people, but rejects top-down government intervention. From its cultural hearth in southeastern Pennsylvania, southern New Jersey, and northern Delaware and Maryland, Midland culture spread through central Ohio, Indiana, and Illinois; northern Missouri; most of Iowa; Southern Ontario; and the eastern halves of South Dakota, Nebraska, and Kansas, sharing the border cities of Chicago (with Yankeedom) and greater St. Louis (with Greater Appalachia).

Like Yankeedom, the Midlands got its start as a utopian project, but one with an entirely different character. With their optimistic take on human nature, William Penn and the early Quaker founders saw little need to coerce individuals to act for the greater good. Indeed, the Quakers themselves were opposed to authority and hierarchy, refusing to address gentlemen and nobles with their honorific titles or to doff their hats to them. As pacifists, they would eventually lose control of the colony's government for their refusal to undertake the most basic of government functions: the defense of the colony from destruction (in their case, from an Indian attack that threatened Philadelphia itself). Whereas early Yankee towns were nucleated to buttress community unity, cohesion, and discipline, Penn allowed colonists to settle in separate tracts, resulting in a dispersed pattern of farms. Settlers from a particular religious sect or part of the world—Welsh, Mennonites, or German Palatines—were allowed to form their own communities and actively practice and preserve their separate ways. In his original constitution for Pennsylvania, Penn vested great power in a large annual legislative assembly and very little in the governor, reflecting the egalitarian structure of the Quakers' meetings. Order was expected to come naturally as the result of each person observing the Golden Rule: to do unto others as you would have done to yourself. Government was relatively weak, and Pennsylvania's taxation rates were among the lowest in colonial America.[9]

The underlying ethos of the Midlander colonies was egalitarian. Family farms were the primary driver of their rapidly growing economy and the home to most of their population. There were very few large-scale farms. In the 1760s, the average farm size was just 125 acres in southeastern Pennsylvania and in New Jersey, the southern half of which was settled by Midlanders, during a time when most plantations in the South Carolina lowlands measured between 500 and 1,000 acres. Laws encouraged equal partition of estates, discouraging the formation of a Midlander aristocracy.[10]

Here was a community-minded society distrustful of strong government, a nation where people assumed the best in others and, therefore, could do without one. If the Midlander ethos were to be stated in a single sentence, it would be: "Government, leave our communities alone to get on with building a better place together."

TIDEWATER

POPULATION (2020): **13.2 million**

DENSITY: **293 per square mile**

DEMOGRAPHICS: **52 percent white, 25 percent Black, 12 percent Hispanic, 6 percent Asian; 12.5 percent foreign-born**

ORIENTATION: **Aggressively communitarian (today)**

STATES DOMINATED: **Virginia**

Built by the younger sons of southern English gentry, Tidewater was meant to reproduce the semifeudal manorial society of the countryside they'd left behind, where economic, political, and social affairs were run by and for landed aristocrats. These self-identified "Cavaliers" largely succeeded in their aims, turning the lowlands of Virginia, Maryland, southern Delaware, and northeastern North Carolina into a country gentleman's paradise, with indentured servants and, later, slaves taking the role of the peasantry. Tidewater was, for the first 350 years of its existence, fundamentally conservative, with a high value placed on respect for authority and tradition and very little on equality or public participation in politics.

The society that took hold in the Chesapeake country in the aftermath of the English Civil War is best described as hierarchically libertarian, a liberal autocracy not unlike that which was taking shape back in England as the divine right of kings was discredited. Landed gentlemen—many aspiring to nobility—had a near-monopoly control over property, power, religious institutions, and the law. They were the masters of their estates, the "heads" with the intellect and wisdom to control the "hands" of their lessers: wives and children, laborers and servants, paupers and slaves. They enjoyed "liberties"—that is, privileges—that others did not, including the avoidance of taxes and corporal punishment and the ability to stand for public office. These came, however, with the responsibility to guide society, to provide for one's inferiors, and, later, to uphold liberal republican principles. Fast forward to the Early Republic, and the region was crawling with gentlemen aristocrats—Thomas Jefferson, George Washington, and James Madison among them—whose educations had inculcated them with Enlightenment ideas about rational inquiry, the universalism of humanity, and the natural rights of humans, sitting on their English-style manor estates worked by enslaved people.

Tidewater was the most powerful nation in the seventeenth and eighteenth centuries, the birthplace of eight of our first twelve presidents and the source of many of the aristocratic inflections in our constitutional arrangements, from the Electoral College to the U.S. Senate (whose members were chosen by legislators, not the people, until 1913). Today it is a nation in rapid decline, its distinctiveness vanishing at an accelerating speed since the mid-1960s. Cultures have incredible staying power—Byzantium collapsed in 1453 and the Ottoman Empire in 1922, but their religious, civil, and sociological influences can be felt across a great swath of Eurasia today—but Tidewater's may not be with us much longer. This is a result of two developments. First, in the late colonial era, Tidewater was boxed out of westward expansion by its boisterous Appalachian neighbors, leaving it sandwiched between regions whose relative power and influence grew over time. Then, in December 1800, in an interregional compromise, Congress moved the seat of the federal government from Philadelphia to a new federal zone straddling the Tidewater-Midlands border.

At first, Washington, a sad, artificial city laid out on the swampy shores of the Potomac, was no threat to its cultural surroundings, and the U.S. Navy's presence at the old Royal Navy anchorage in Hampton Roads, Virginia, even less so. But the federal government and national security establishment grew dramatically during the New Deal, World War I, and, especially, the Cold War, sucking in hundreds of thousands and eventually millions of people from other regions of the country to the Tidewater suburbs surrounding the District of Columbia and Norfolk and Newport News, the site of what had become the world's largest naval base. Trillions of dollars in annual federal spending have allowed millions of people to live economic, social, and cultural lives without reference to Tidewater norms for several generations. Over the past twenty years, it has reached a tipping point. Tidewater—wealthy, diverse, and highly educated—is now a progressive region, and not just in the deep "blue" suburbs around DC but, in recent years, across southern Maryland, suburban Richmond, southeastern Virginia, northwestern North Carolina, and even the lower Delmarva Peninsula, the conservative bastion from which Frederick Douglass and Harriet Tubman escaped slavery.

Throughout *Nations Apart*, you'll see evidence of this profound cultural shift in polls, election results, and other data. I doubt anyone will recognize Tidewater at the end of this century. Something new will have taken its place.

GREATER APPALACHIA

POPULATION (2020): **61.5 million**

DENSITY: **117 per square mile**

DEMOGRAPHICS: **68 percent white, 12 percent Hispanic, 11 percent Black, 3 percent Asian; 8.2 percent foreign-born**

ORIENTATION: **Aggressively individualistic**

STATES DOMINATED: **West Virginia, Kentucky, Tennessee, Arkansas, Indiana, Oklahoma**

Founded in the early eighteenth century by wave upon wave of rough, bellicose settlers from the war-ravaged borderlands of Northern Ireland, northern England, and the Scottish Lowlands, Greater Appalachia has often been lampooned as the home of rednecks, hillbillies, and white trash. In reality, it is a transplanted culture that formed in a state of near-constant warfare and upheaval, characterized by a warrior ethic and a deep commitment to personal sovereignty and individual liberty. From southwestern Pennsylvania, its bearers spread down the Appalachian Mountains and out into the southern tiers of Ohio, Indiana, and Illinois, the Arkansas and Missouri Ozarks, the eastern two-thirds of Oklahoma, and on down to the Hill Country of Texas, clashing with Indians, Yankees, and Mexicans along the way. Intensely suspicious of lowland aristocrats and Yankee social engineers alike, Greater Appalachia's people have shifted alliances based on whoever appeared to be the greatest threat to their freedom; since Reconstruction and, especially, the upheavals of the 1960s, the region has been in alliance with the Deep South in an effort to undo the federal government's ability to overrule local preferences.

Generations of Americans have been raised with the myth that our country was founded by highly individualistic frontiersmen, men in coonskin caps and—later—cowboy hats who survived and prospered based on their bravery, hard work, and self-sufficiency. Living in log cabins, defending their families from Indians with their own weapons and courage, they neither sought nor relied on government assistance or the comforts of cities. While this account is entirely untrue for much of what is now the United States, it is an accurate description of much of the Greater Appalachian frontier, which was dangerous, far removed from the centers of government, and populated by people who treasured their individual liberty and were suspicious of ordering institutions of any kind.

The Scots-Irish and other borderland settlers embraced an extreme libertarian definition of freedom: the right to rule oneself with as little intrusion by law enforcement, courts, and other political institutions as possible. They practiced an "eye for an eye" form of justice in which a wronged party was expected to punish his transgressor himself. As a backcountry proverb brought from North Britain put it, "Every man should be a sheriff on his own hearth"; the corollary to this, as historian David Hackett Fischer has pointed out, was that government institutions, including the actual sheriffs, had relatively little to do. Vigilantes and lynch mobs—the latter named for one Charles Lynch, who dispensed frontier justice upon loyalists in Virginia's Appalachian region in 1789—were socially accepted well into the mid-twentieth century. Settlements were few and far between for much of the colonial period—the settlers preferring to live on isolated homesteads—and schools, courts, libraries, and other public institutions were correspondingly rare. Leaders—the local elite—relied on their reputations rather than social rank to attract a personal following, usually by having displayed bravery and decisiveness. The inhabitants of this region neither sought nor received much from their governments, and wished to keep it that way.

Moreover, Greater Appalachians were willing to stand up for their rights, even against powerful opponents. Throughout the colonial era, much of the region was part of one or another colony controlled by the Tidewater or Deep Southern aristocracies. These oligarchs—hierarchical in their thinking and contemptuous of the "baser people" of the mountainous backcountry—refused to give their Appalachian subjects proper representation in the legislatures and passed taxation policies that shifted the burden from wealthy planters to impoverished farmers and herdsman. In North Carolina during the 1760s, Tidewater counties received ten times the per capita legislative representation as the state's ample and rapidly growing Appalachian sections; the backcountry settlers reacted by forming bands of "Regulators" who seized control of their region for three years, beating lawyers, sacking courthouses, and expelling tax collectors, until they were put down in a pitched battle with Tidewater militia. Similar resistance movements formed across the Appalachian frontier, and during the Revolution, pent-up grievances fueled a horrific civil war in the Carolinas and Georgia with frequent atrocities on both sides. Life on the frontier was, right into the nineteenth century, strikingly reminiscent of that of the war-torn British borderlands from which the region's settlers had come.

The region's religious heritage buttressed its individualism. When the Second Great Awakening spread across the American frontiers in the years after the American Revolution, millions of Americans embraced novel religious forms, inventing new Protestant sects and weakening the established churches—Anglican, Puritan Congregational, Presbyterian, and Quaker—that had been brought from Europe. But while Yankee frontiersmen created collectivist religions aiming to fashion more perfect earthly societies—Millerism, Mormonism, Seventh-Day Adventism—Greater Appalachia's people embraced individualistic creeds—Southern Baptist, Southern Methodist, and a wide range of other iconoclastic evangelical Christian forms—whereby each person might meet God personally, be spoken to by Him or his son, and be guided without the mediation of institutions, a clerical hierarchy, or literary interpretation. In Greater Appalachia—and indeed among the non-elite of the Deep South—the emphasis has been not on improving this world, but on one's personal salvation in the hereafter.

Unruly, populist, and highly libertarian, Greater Appalachia has historically been a cauldron for individualistic political efforts, be it in the Regulator movement or the Tea Party one.

DEEP SOUTH

POPULATION (2020): **45.6 million**

DENSITY: **148 per square mile**

DEMOGRAPHICS: **52 percent white, 24 percent Black, 16 percent Hispanic, 3 percent Asian; 10.4 percent foreign-born**

ORIENTATION: **Aggressively individualistic**

STATES DOMINATED: **South Carolina, Alabama, Mississippi**

STATES CONTROLLED: **Georgia, Florida**

Established by English slave lords from Barbados as a West Indies–style slave society, the Deep South has been a bastion of white supremacy, aristocratic privilege, and a version of classical Republicanism modeled on the slave states of the ancient world, where democracy was the privilege of the few and enslavement the natural lot of the many.

The Barbadians who landed in the 1670s in what was then still called Carolina in the West Indies cherished their own individual liberty and maximized it by taking freedom away from most everyone else. They loved John Locke, the seventeenth-century philosopher who made his mark providing a theory that justified aristocratic rebellions to protect their interests from the Crown at a time when the latter was the only real force standing in the way of the gentry's effort to end medieval obligations to the commoners who had worked their manors. Indeed, Locke wrote the first Carolina constitution, which stipulated that "every freeman of Carolina shall have absolute power and authority over his negro slaves" and created a hereditary serf caste obliged to obey a hereditary titled nobility. It was an oligarchy, a government by and for those on top, and has remained so to one degree or another ever since.[11]

"It is a great and dangerous error to suppose that all people are equally entitled to liberty," the South Carolina Senator John C. Calhoun proclaimed in 1851, summing up the Deep Southern elite's point of view. "It is a reward to be earned, not a blessing to be gratuitously lavished on all alike—a reward reserved for the intelligent, the patriotic, the virtuous and deserving—and not a boon to be bestowed on a people too ignorant, degraded and vicious, to be capable either of appreciating or of enjoying it." This system didn't betray republican values, the South Carolina Governor James Henry Hammond asserted in 1845. "In the slave-holding States, however, nearly one-half of the whole population and those the poorest and most ignorant, have no political influence whatever, because they are slaves," he wrote. "Hence, slavery is truly the 'cornerstone' and foundation of every well-designed and durable 'Republican edifice.'"[12]

From its Charleston beachhead, the Deep South spread apartheid and authoritarianism across the Southern lowlands, ultimately encompassing most of South Carolina, Georgia, Alabama, Mississippi, Florida, and Louisiana, plus western Tennessee and southeastern Arkansas, Texas, and North Carolina. In the antebellum period, its leaders had extensive territorial ambitions in Latin America, wanting to annex most of Mexico, Central America, and the Spanish Caribbean to form a slaveholding empire. When these ambitions were frustrated and it became clear the population of the antislavery regions would continue to outpace theirs, they created their own slaveholder's confederation, fired on federal troops, and, backed by reluctant allies in Tidewater, led Americans into a horrific civil war that left 700,000 people dead.

Even after its slave and caste systems were dismantled by outside intervention and internal uprisings, its leaders have continued to fight for rollbacks of federal power, reductions of taxes on capital and the wealthy, and diminished environmental, labor, and consumer safety protections. It is the least democratically minded of the regions, with a history of authoritarian one-party rule and the suppression of dissent. It forged an uneasy "Dixie" coalition with Appalachia and Tidewater in the 1870s and has remained locked in an epic battle with Yankeedom and its Left Coast and New Netherland allies for the future of the continent.

EL NORTE

POPULATION (2020): **34.4 million**

DENSITY: **147 per square mile**

DEMOGRAPHICS: **47 percent Hispanic, 34 percent white, 9 percent Asian, 5 percent Black; 23.1 percent foreign-born**

ORIENTATION: **Passively communitarian**

STATES DOMINATED: **Arizona**

STATES CONTROLLED: **New Mexico, California**

The oldest of the Euro-American nations, El Norte dates back to the late sixteenth century, when the Spanish Empire founded Monterrey, Saltillo, and other outposts in what are now the Mexican-American borderlands. Today this resurgent culture spreads from the current frontier for a hundred miles or more in both directions, taking in south and west Texas, southern California and the Imperial Valley, southern Arizona, most of New Mexico, parts of Colorado, and the six northernmost Mexican states. Most Americans are aware that the region is a place apart, where Hispanic language, culture, and societal norms dominate; few realize that among Mexicans, *norteños* have a reputation for being more independent, self-sufficient, adaptable, and work-centered than their central and southern countrymen. Long a hotbed of democratic reform and revolutionary settlement, various parts of the region have tried to secede from Mexico to form independent buffer states between the two federations. Today it has come to resemble Germany during the Cold War: a single people with a common culture separated from one another by a large wall.

Seventeenth- and eighteenth-century Spain, unlike England and the Netherlands, was an unenlightened, unreconstructed despotism, a centralized monarchy wherein neither the mother country nor its staggering array of American colonies had any representative legislative bodies of any sort. Trade and manufacturing were highly regulated, with special licenses required to engage in most activities—if they were permitted at all—and prices were fixed by central officials. Most of El Norte, the far-flung frontier of New Spain's already far-flung Mexican viceroyalty, was settled as if it were a lunar base: by militarized missions of farmers, ranchers, servants, and soldiers sent to establish remote installations. Most of the region was ruled by military officers or other outsiders appointed by the distant bureaucracy.[13]

Even when Mexico became independent in 1821, the parts of El Norte that are now in the United States all lacked full statehood and, thus, institutions of self-government. Under Mexico's 1836 constitution, state legislatures were eliminated, state governors were appointed in Mexico City, and only the wealthy were allowed to stand for office. In Alta California, a Mexican cavalry officer reported that "allowances should be made" because not a single person had "the capital indicated by law in order to become governor, senator, or deputy." Courts remained physically out of reach to the region's people, as serious cases could only be heard by making a journey of several weeks, and local judicial bodies were handicapped by a lack of literate lawyers or judges. "The government of California," an American visitor reported in the 1840s, was "very lax and inefficient . . . and infinitely worse than none." The region's political heritage, right up to the U.S. annexations, was of centralized yet completely ineffective government.[14]

More than any other part of Mexico, however, the North aspired to a more democratic future. Life on the arid frontier was less stratified than in central Mexico, and individuals had greater opportunities to engage in entrepreneurship, even if they had to do so through illicit trade with their Deep Southern neighbors over the U.S. border. Disgusted with the centralized authoritarianism of central Mexico, parts of the region attempted to secede to form the Republic of the Rio Grande and, later, the Republic of Texas, intended to be buffer states between the U.S. and Mexican federations. The parts of El Norte that remained in Mexico provided the resistance to the turn-of-the-twentieth-century dictator Porfirio Díaz, and many exiles fled over the U.S. border to foment radical left-wing ideas of revolution among working-class Hispanics who were, by then, exploited by a racial caste system imposed by the new American state governments, many of which were dominated by newcomers from the Deep South and Appalachia.[15]

Since the 1960s, El Norte's Spanish-speaking majority has reasserted itself, helping topple the region's caste system and reclaiming its political rights. Its inherited legacy, as Chicano scholar Juan Gómez-Quiñones once put it, is of being both "leery of government" while also maintaining "the fairly continuous expectation that government should provide for the general welfare, combined with the practical awareness that it provides for a select number." In El Norte, where family and church ties are strong, and the collectivist impulses of the Catholic Church remain influential, government is seen as an agent of the common good, even if there is little expectation that it will be able to perform its role without prejudice in favor of the region's elites. In political terms, El Norte is theoretically a swing region, but only if its Hispanic cultural legacy is accepted and respected by both the Democratic and Republican parties.[16]

TWO OTHER REGIONAL CULTURES were established much later—in the mid- and late nineteenth century—and were founded not by European-American colonizers but by people from the older, aforementioned regional cultures. The histories of these areas are much shorter and, until the twentieth century, settler populations were sparse, resulting in a lighter cultural footprint. That footprint does, however, exist, and it exerts a powerful influence on the political ideals of half of what is now the United States.

LEFT COAST

POPULATION (2020): **20.9 million**

DENSITY: **170 per square mile**

DEMOGRAPHICS: **52.2 percent white, 19 percent Hispanic, 17 percent Asian, 4 percent Black; 21.4 percent foreign-born**

ORIENTATION: **Aggressively communitarian**

STATES DOMINATED: **Oregon, Washington**

The first of these areas to be settled was the Left Coast, a Chile-shaped nation wedged between the Pacific Ocean and the Cascade and Coast Mountain ranges and stretching from Monterey to Juneau. This region was originally colonized by two distinct groups: merchants, missionaries, and woodsmen from New England (who arrived by sea and dominated the towns) and farmers, prospectors, and fur traders from Greater Appalachia (who generally arrived by wagon and controlled the countryside). Yankee missionaries expended considerable effort to try to make it "a New England on the Pacific", but were only partially successful: The Left Coast remains a hybrid of Yankee idealism, faith in good government, and social reform and the Appalachian commitment to individual self-expression and exploration.

The Left Coast culture defines the common good differently from Yankeedom, as its project was to create a nurturing support system for individual actualization rather than to create an ordered community that can keep individual avarice in check. This has proven to be a profoundly successful strategy for economic innovation. The region has a population only the size of Romania's, and yet it's the birthplace and headquarters of most of the tech giants that dominate early twenty-first-century life on this planet: Apple, Amazon, Google, Meta, Microsoft, HP, and Nvidia among them. It is, nonetheless, a highly communitarian culture, the driving force behind the hippie side of the 1960s cultural revolution and the U.S. and international environmental movements.

Since its foundation, it has been Yankeedom's staunchest ally on the federal political stage, while locked in a constant battle with the Far Western sections in the interiors of its home states.

FAR WEST

POPULATION (2020): **30.5 million**

DENSITY: **25 per square mile**

DEMOGRAPHICS: **57 percent white, 26 percent Hispanic, 5 percent Asian, 4 percent Black; 12.6 percent foreign-born**

ORIENTATION: **Passively individualistic**

STATES DOMINATED: **Colorado, Wyoming, Montana, Idaho, Utah, Nevada, Alaska**

The Far West, the other "second-generation" nation, is the one part of the continent where environmental and geographic factors trumped ethnographic ones. High, dry, and remote, the Far West stopped the expansions of the eastern nations in their tracks and, with minor exceptions, was colonized only via the deployment of vast industrial resources: railroads, heavy mining equipment, ore smelters, dams, and irrigation systems. As a result, settlement was largely directed and controlled by large corporations headquartered in distant New York, Boston, Chicago, or San Francisco or by the federal government itself, which controlled much of the land. Because the region was exploited as an internal colony for the benefit of the seaboard nations, its political leaders have focused public resentment on the federal government (on whose infrastructure spending they depend) while avoiding challenges to the region's corporate masters, who retain near Gilded Age influence. The Far West encompasses nearly all of the North American interior west of the 100th meridian, from the northern boundary of El Norte to the southern frontier of First Nation, including much of California, Washington, Oregon, British Columbia, Alaska, Colorado, and Canada's Prairie provinces, and all of Idaho, Montana, Utah, and Nevada.

The Far West's much-discussed libertarian streak—celebrated in the image of the cowboy individualist, alone against nature and the corruption of distant urban interests—is tempered by the region's dependence on gigantic public works projects and government-supported industries. Massive irrigation, dam, and water transfer projects enabled cities and water-intensive farms to exist in an arid region. Federally subsidized railroads and, later, highways and airports, linked it to distant markets. World War II and Cold War military spending—from the nuclear weapons labs of Los Alamos, New Mexico, and Hanford, Washington, to the aircraft plants of Wichita, Kansas, and dozens of military bases in between— became vital to its economy. From the early colonization period onward, the harsh realities of the western environment required people to cooperate and depend on one another to a far greater degree than the earlier Appalachian frontier environment had. "What really allowed the West to be settled was the wagon train, where everyone is organized, working together, and has their own chores and tasks. That's how individuals survived," the former Colorado Governor John Hickenlooper, who is fond of noting that barn raisings were more common than shootouts, told me. "People have a broader self-interest than they often think they do."[17]

There's also the influence of the Mormons—the followers of a Yankee-led utopian creed with its origins in Vermont and Upstate New York—who, mirroring the early Puritans, sought to build a promised land in the American wilderness. With central planning, a communal mindset, and intense group cohesion, Utah's Mormon pioneers succeeded in building and maintaining their own irrigation projects and other infrastructure, allowing them to colonize their Far Western homeland themselves. "There's been this interesting dynamic in Utah's history between individualism and communitarianism," said Alan Matheson, a gubernatorial aide who headed that state's massive and highly effective long-term land use and transportation planning project. "All these people come to an area with a harsh environment and had to pull together to survive, but they also had the tension with the idea of the rugged individual on the Western frontier."[18]

The Far West is also a region whose exploiters have been private as well as public. In the nineteenth and early twentieth centuries, Anaconda Copper literally ran Montana, buying off judges and public officials and dictating rules and regulations that enriched its owners and executives; at one point it employed three-quarters of that state's wage earners and owned five of Montana's six daily newspapers, which suppressed news unfavorable to the company. Logging interests clear-cut the region's federally owned forests for next to nothing, while oil and gas companies prospected on federally administered Indian reservations, often without ever paying the required royalties to the tribes.[19]

Having been so badly exploited, Far Westerners have been highly attuned to issues of economic fairness. Thus, this individualistic frontier culture was also a hotbed of economic populism, labor unionism, and other "common good" concerns right up until World War II. It elected progressive senators like Burton K. Wheeler of Montana or Idaho's William Borah and enthusiastically endorsed FDR and the New Deal. Today the region's people are mobilized against another perceived tormenter, the federal government, an effort led by regional politicians who promise to get the government out of the way of prosperity and self-reliance by reducing regulations and oversight.

It is, in short, a conflicted political culture shaped by colonial exploitation, one that seeks a fair shake for individuals and values civil liberties but also a level playing field and an open public purse for spending that buttresses the economy. Egalitarian and individualistic—but not strenuously so—culturally pluralistic and lacking a dominant ethnic group, it is in many ways the analog of the Midlands, only with libertarian rather than communitarian leanings.

NEW FRANCE

POPULATION (2020): **2.9 million**

DENSITY: **169 per square mile**

DEMOGRAPHICS: **57 percent white, 12 percent Black, 10 percent Hispanic, 4 percent Asian; 5.4 percent foreign-born**

ORIENTATION: **Aggressively individualistic (U.S. portion today)**

STATES DOMINATED: **Louisiana**

Founded in the early 1600s, New France blends the folkways of ancien régime northern French peasantry with the traditions and values of the aboriginal people they encountered in northeastern North America. Down-to-earth, egalitarian, and consensus-driven, since emerging from imperial rule with Québec's Quiet Revolution in the 1960s, they've imparted many of their attitudes on the Canadian federation, where interculturalism, social justice, and negotiated consensus are treasured. Polls consistently show the New French of Québec and the Canadian Maritimes to be far and away the most liberal people on the continent within their society (but not so in regards to, say, the use of English in Montreal).

Its enclave in Louisiana—founded by refugees ethnically cleansed from Acadia after the British victory in the French and Indian War—was until relatively recently distinct and politically opposed to the state's Protestant, Deep Southern section. But the Acadians, a term that morphed into "Cajun" over time, had fled to a French colony that embraced West Indies–style slavery. Before the United States purchased the colony, the area around New Orleans was run by aristocratic French slave plantation owners. After the French Revolution inspired enslaved Haitians to seize control of their island in 1803, ten thousand French-speaking Afro-Creoles moved into the city and nearby Cajun Country. (For these reasons, Orleans Parish, where the city is located, is one of only two U.S.

counties that are equally shared by two American Nations, in this case the Deep South and New France.) As in other parts of New France, Euro-American Cajuns blended their cultures and families with other people, including Indigenous and Creole neighbors, creating a rich cultural mélange bonded by French language and, often, Catholicism. But over time, Cajun culture also adopted practices from their Deep Southern and French "Bourbon" slave lord neighbors, including slavery, the racial caste system, and reactionary economic and cultural attitudes.[20]

In the early twenty-first century, New France's enclave in Louisiana has become the most conservative and authoritarian of all the United States's culture regions, transforming Louisiana from a swing state to a bastion of individualistic and ethnonationalist sentiment.

FIRST NATION

POPULATION (2020): **68,000**

DENSITY: **0.2 per square mile**

DEMOGRAPHICS: **76 percent Native, 13 percent white, 2 percent Asian, 2 percent Hispanic; 2.9 percent foreign-born**

ORIENTATION: **Aggressively communitarian**

STATES DOMINATED: **None**

Like the Far West, First Nation encompasses a vast region with a hostile climate: the boreal forests, tundra, and glaciers of the far north. The difference is that its indigenous inhabitants still occupy the area in force, most tribal groups having never given up their land by treaty or trickery, while retaining the cultural practices and knowledge that allow them to survive in the region on its own terms. First Nation's people have recently begun reclaiming their sovereignty and have won considerable autonomy in Alaska and Nunavut, considerable say in the affairs of northern Canada via landmark constitutional rulings there, and a self-governing nation-state in Greenland, which stands on the threshold of full independence from Denmark. A new, yet very old nation, First Nation's people have a chance to put Native North America back on the map: culturally, politically, and environmentally. It's a highly communitarian society—many groups don't recognize private ownership of land—and a place where women often dominate cultural and political leadership.

First Nation has rapidly reasserted control of much of Yukon, the Northwest Territories, and Labrador, the entirety of Nunavut and Greenland, the northern tier of Ontario, Saskatchewan, Alberta, and British Columbia, and the northern two-thirds of Québec. Its U.S. portion lies in northern and western Alaska, where Alaska Native people form more than three-quarters of the population. As we will show, it is also far and away the most impoverished of the regional cultures, with terrifying life expectancy, preventable disease, and high suicide rates, the product of centuries of imperial oppression and federal neglect.

GREATER POLYNESIA

POPULATION (2020): **1.5 million**

DENSITY: **423 per square mile**

DEMOGRAPHICS: **37 percent Asian, 22 percent white, 20 percent multiracial, 19 percent Hispanic, 10 percent Native; 18 percent foreign-born**

ORIENTATION: **Aggressively communitarian**

STATES DOMINATED: **Hawaii**

The Hawaiian Islands are the U.S. portion of the vast Polynesian cultural space, the legacy of the great Pacific celestial navigators who colonized an ocean area larger than the North American continent between 1000 BCE and 900 CE. Polynesians reached Hawaii by 800 CE when Europe was in the Early Middle Ages, and controlled these islands until very recently. The islands' rival chiefdoms were united under Kamehameha the Great, who established a sovereign kingdom in 1795 that was recognized by all the world's major powers by the 1870s. Nature and landscapes were often sacred—the domains of gods and spirits—and the concept of private property didn't exist until the late 1840s. Everything changed in 1893, when the Hawaiians' country was illegally seized by the United States. U.S. Marines surrounded the royal palace on Oahu to back a coup led by western expatriates, establishing a regime that promptly pushed Native Hawaiians out of government, seized Native lands, and repressed their language and cultural practices. The U.S. Congress formally apologized for "the illegal overthrow of the Kingdom of Hawaii" in 1993, but the position and influence of the island chain's indigenous people has little improved since.[21]

A white business oligarchy effectively controlled Hawaii into the second half of the twentieth century and brought large numbers of laborers from Japan, China, and the Philippines to tend the extensive sugar and pineapple plantations they'd established on the islands. As a result, today it's the only region with an Asian plurality and where there are about as many people identifying as multiracial as there are who identify as white or Hispanic. This has meant the enclave has had no choice but to embrace a multicultural identity, which has led sociologists to hold it up as a model for better race relations in America, though it obscures the marginalization and displacement of Native Hawaiians on their own islands. Today the region is politically progressive, communitarian in orientation, and environmentally minded, with little tolerance for either laissez-faire economics or white ethnonationalism.[22]

SPANISH CARIBBEAN

POPULATION (2020): **8.2 million**

DENSITY: **623 per square mile**

DEMOGRAPHICS: **39 percent Hispanic, 39 percent white, 16 percent Black, 12 percent Asian; 35.2 percent foreign-born**

ORIENTATION: **Passively communitarian**

STATES DOMINATED: **None**

South Florida is the northernmost extension of New Spain's maritime cultural space, a commercial society that developed as a key link in imperial commerce, plugged into the communications and economic networks of the world's greatest sixteenth- and seventeenth-century power. Its hub is Cuba, the largest and richest island in the Caribbean, and it also includes Puerto Rico and the Dominican Republic. The colonial Spanish Caribbean was a society of trading ports and aristocratic plantations closely modeled on those of Iberian Spain, which it was in constant contact and communication with. Like Iberia—where Christian Spaniards and Muslim Moors jostled for centuries—the region was characterized by the forging of family and kinship ties across ethnic and racial lines, European, African, and indigenous, though these arrangements were often far from equal. Right into the second half of the nineteenth century, the Spanish islands were sugar plantation economies powered by African and Indian slaves, and although after abolition the region did not institute racial caste and apartheid systems like the Deep South and Tidewater did, racial hierarchies persisted.[23]

While the Spanish had short-lived military outposts and Jesuit missions in South Florida in the sixteenth and early seventeenth centuries, the region wasn't successfully settled until the 1895 completion of a railroad line to Biscayne Bay by tourism speculators, more than sixty years after

Spain surrendered it to the United States. This transportation link spawned the little tourist town of Miami, which slowly grew into a small city by the 1930s, with immigrants from Cuba—which was closer and far easier to travel from than Tampa or Jacksonville—forming a neighborhood called Little Havana. Shortly after communists seized power in Cuba in 1959, two hundred thousand middle- and upper-class Cubans fled to South Florida, staying there because of its proximity to Cuba and the presence of the Cuban-owned bodegas, drugstores, and shops of Little Havana. Because they thought their exile was temporary, they didn't try to assimilate to "American" culture but instead used their wealth and business acumen to create Cuban schools, churches, theaters, bars, newspapers, radio stations, and community organizations, which served as a magnet to draw hundreds of thousands more Cuban and other Latino exiles and migrants to the region. They became city councilors, mayors, legislators, and Congressmen and transformed the city into an alternate-reality Havana in which Fidel Castro had never taken power. By the early 1990s, academic geographers were categorizing South Florida as a Cuban American "homeland," the place an ethnonationalist group imagines as their native land. "Cubans are probably the only people who really do feel comfortable in Dade County these days," the cultural analyst David Rieff wrote in a book on the enclave back in 1987. "Miami is their town now."[24]

Today, South Florida is the de facto capital of the Spanish Caribbean, the financial, transportation, and economic hub of the entire Caribbean basin. Cuban Americans account for a fifth of the region's eight million people—and people with ancestry in other parts of the Spanish Caribbean number in the hundreds of thousands—but, in accord with its regional legacy, it is a multicultural, multiracial mélange, tolerant of diversity and oriented toward commerce.

THE SETTLEMENT STREAMS that created these regional cultures rarely respected state or even international boundaries. Sometimes this was because those borders didn't exist or were in a different location at the time of initial colonization. In other instances, it was because the borders had little meaning to the farmers, ranchers, slave lords, or miners who chose their new homes for their ecological or geographic attributes. As a result, many states are riven into two, three, or even four discordant sections by these tectonic cultural fault lines. This explains the eternal rivalries between Upstate and Downstate Illinois and New York, among Northern, Southern, and mountain California, between coastal and intermountain Oregon and Washington, between lowland and upland Virginia and North Carolina, or among the various squabbling regions of Maryland, Ohio, and Texas.

This book uses data to analyze the political, cultural, sociological, and medical differences between the regional cultures. To accomplish this, we seek county- rather than state-level data to power our research, whether it's on elections, gun deaths, or life expectancy. Often, however, that data just hasn't been collected or isn't available at the county or even congressional district level, forcing us to try to discern what might be going on from statewide metrics. But how do we evaluate how much power a given region has in a divided state?

To solve for this, we calculated the population of every section of each of the fifty states from the 2020 Census. The results are in the following table, which we reproduce here for readers to cross-reference whenever their curiosity grabs them:

The American Nations: Population Share in the 50 States (2020)

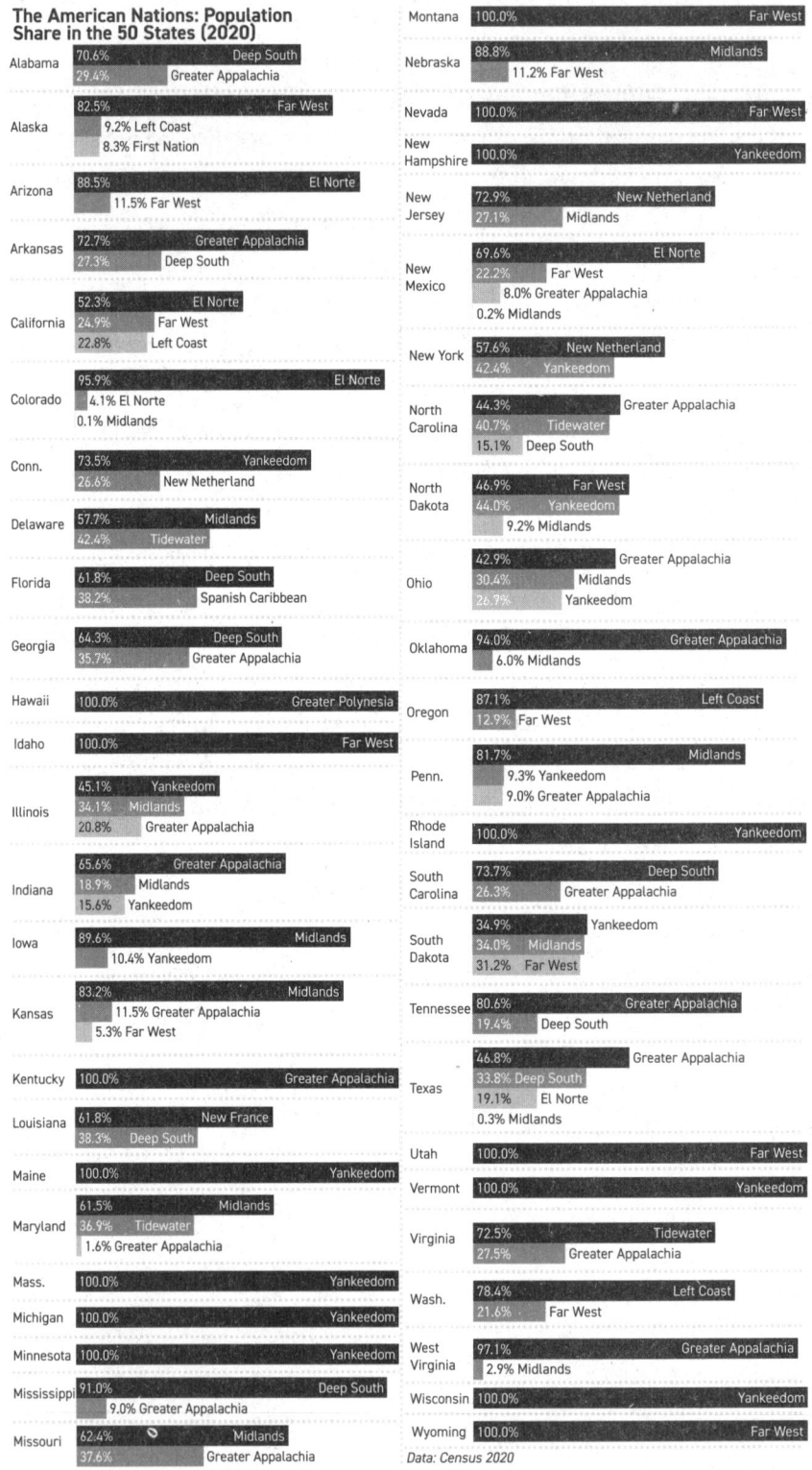

Alabama
70.6% Deep South
29.4% Greater Appalachia

Alaska
82.5% Far West
9.2% Left Coast
8.3% First Nation

Arizona
88.5% El Norte
11.5% Far West

Arkansas
72.7% Greater Appalachia
27.3% Deep South

California
52.3% El Norte
24.9% Far West
22.8% Left Coast

Colorado
95.9% El Norte
4.1% El Norte
0.1% Midlands

Conn.
73.5% Yankeedom
26.6% New Netherland

Delaware
57.7% Midlands
42.4% Tidewater

Florida
61.8% Deep South
38.2% Spanish Caribbean

Georgia
64.3% Deep South
35.7% Greater Appalachia

Hawaii
100.0% Greater Polynesia

Idaho
100.0% Far West

Illinois
45.1% Yankeedom
34.1% Midlands
20.8% Greater Appalachia

Indiana
65.6% Greater Appalachia
18.9% Midlands
15.6% Yankeedom

Iowa
89.6% Midlands
10.4% Yankeedom

Kansas
83.2% Midlands
11.5% Greater Appalachia
5.3% Far West

Kentucky
100.0% Greater Appalachia

Louisiana
61.8% New France
38.3% Deep South

Maine
100.0% Yankeedom

Maryland
61.5% Midlands
36.9% Tidewater
1.6% Greater Appalachia

Mass.
100.0% Yankeedom

Michigan
100.0% Yankeedom

Minnesota
100.0% Yankeedom

Mississippi
91.0% Deep South
9.0% Greater Appalachia

Missouri
62.4% Midlands
37.6% Greater Appalachia

Montana
100.0% Far West

Nebraska
88.8% Midlands
11.2% Far West

Nevada
100.0% Far West

New Hampshire
100.0% Yankeedom

New Jersey
72.9% New Netherland
27.1% Midlands

New Mexico
69.6% El Norte
22.2% Far West
8.0% Greater Appalachia
0.2% Midlands

New York
57.6% New Netherland
42.4% Yankeedom

North Carolina
44.3% Greater Appalachia
40.7% Tidewater
15.1% Deep South

North Dakota
46.9% Far West
44.0% Yankeedom
9.2% Midlands

Ohio
42.9% Greater Appalachia
30.4% Midlands
26.7% Yankeedom

Oklahoma
94.0% Greater Appalachia
6.0% Midlands

Oregon
87.1% Left Coast
12.9% Far West

Penn.
81.7% Midlands
9.3% Yankeedom
9.0% Greater Appalachia

Rhode Island
100.0% Yankeedom

South Carolina
73.7% Deep South
26.3% Greater Appalachia

South Dakota
34.9% Yankeedom
34.0% Midlands
31.2% Far West

Tennessee
80.6% Greater Appalachia
19.4% Deep South

Texas
46.8% Greater Appalachia
33.8% Deep South
19.1% El Norte
0.3% Midlands

Utah
100.0% Far West

Vermont
100.0% Yankeedom

Virginia
72.5% Tidewater
27.5% Greater Appalachia

Wash.
78.4% Left Coast
21.6% Far West

West Virginia
97.1% Greater Appalachia
2.9% Midlands

Wisconsin
100.0% Yankeedom

Wyoming
100.0% Far West

Data: Census 2020

Only fifteen states belong entirely within a single regional culture. Another twenty are overwhelmingly dominated by a single region that comprises more than 70 percent of the population; in these places, the dominant culture rarely has to compromise or negotiate with the others to set statewide policies, though there may be sectional variations in local policy and in legislative and Congressional delegations. (In the descriptions of the "nations" you just read, these were listed as "States Dominated" by a given regional culture.) Nine states are weakly controlled by a single section where between 50 and 69 percent of the state's people live, necessitating frequent cross-regional negotiation to get things accomplished. (These are the ones listed earlier as "States Controlled" by a given region.) The remaining six—Ohio, Illinois, North Carolina, Texas, and the Dakotas—are truly divided, with none of the American Nations constituting a majority. Obviously, in each of these cases the mix makes a great difference to the comity of state politics. In the current political environment, there isn't a wide gulf between the dominant policy preferences of the Deep South and Greater Appalachia—which together have a supermajority in Texas—while there is a yawning one between North Carolina's Tidewater and Greater Appalachian sections, which makes for an incredibly volatile political environment.[25]

Bear in mind these are the power ratios in 2020 based on population. In the past these balances of power were sometimes quite different. In the seventeenth century, Maryland was dominated by Tidewater, and on the eve of the Civil War, New York's Yankee upstate was more populous than downstate New Netherland. To get a better handle on change over time, we repeated our power calculations using the 1900 and 1950 censuses. I was surprised to find that, despite massive population growth, urbanization, and immigration, the ratios in most states were much the same in 1900 and in 2020, with a couple of important exceptions. The Left Coast dominated California at the start of the twentieth century; now it's the smallest of the Golden State's three sections. Illinois has shifted dramatically since 1950, with the Yankee north—which includes half of Cook

County, where Chicago is located—going from the smallest to the largest of the state's three sections, while Greater Appalachia experienced just the opposite. Virginia went from being just barely under Tidewater control in 1900 and 1950 to being overwhelmingly dominated by that section today. Both Dakotas have seen a shift toward the Far West and away from the Yankee and Midlands portions, which helps to explain their rightward drift over the same time period.[26]

We'll be referring to state-level data here and there in the chapters that follow, unpacking why it is that the states are so different from one another, some "red," some "blue," and some "purple," but all tinted by their underlying regional cultural heritage.

So THOSE ARE THE STATELESS nations of North America. Their effects on American history and society have been profound. You will find the American Nations map echoed in the battle lines of the English Civil War of the 1640s, the War of 1812, and the American Revolution, in the key Congressional debates leading up to the U.S. Civil War, and in the Culture Wars of the 1960s, stories told in *American Nations* and its sequel, *American Character*. You see them in the cultural geographer's maps of the continental dissemination of different vernacular-building traditions, in maps plotting the distribution of Quaker meetinghouses in the 1770s, Congregational churches in the 1860s, and Baptist or German Reformed churches in 1890, or in social scientists' plotting of where every lynching and deadly race riot took place between 1835 and 1964. You can see their broad outlines in linguists' maps of American dialects, such as this map:[27]

American Dialect Regions

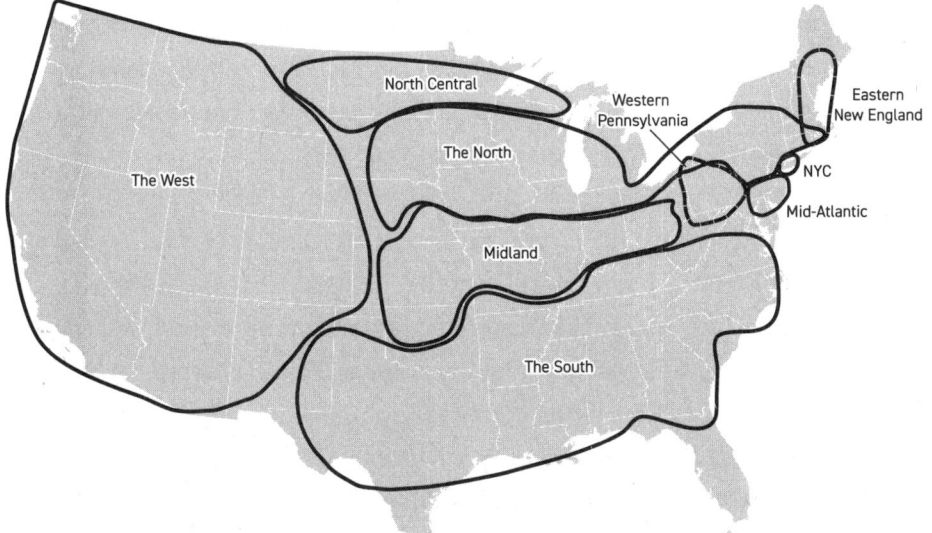

Data: William Labov, Sharon Ash, and Charles Boberg, The Atlas of North American English (2005)

In 2017, scientists at Ancestry published research findings in the journal *Nature Communications* that revealed that the regional cultures left a significant genetic imprint, as well. This surprised me, because *American Nations* is decidedly about cultural transmission, not genetics, and immigration, internal migration, and the slave trade presumably would have all but erased the continuity of family lines. The Ancestry researchers had probed the DNA sequencing of 770,000 Americans who'd taken their mail-in tests and fed them all into supercomputers to identify clusters of people who were subtly more related to one another. They then cross-referenced the results to the birth and death places in the genealogies those individuals had posted on Ancestry.com, and mapped the resulting migration patterns dating back as far as ten generations. The cluster patterns match the *American Nations* map to a remarkable degree, revealing the Greater Appalachians' division into separate streams on either side of the namesake mountains; the New Englanders' imprint on Michigan and Upstate New York; the Midlanders' spread from Pennsylvania to eastern Nebraska; the extension of the Deep Southern influence to East Texas and

Central Florida; and that the *Norteños* who spread into South Texas were distinct from the Central Mexicans, who did not. The implication is that members of a regional culture tended to form families with one another, rather than with people from rival areas, even when those rivals lived close at hand, in the very same colony or state.[28]

Then there's politics.

We started talking about "red" and "blue" states only during the disputed election of 2000, but the regional divides behind them have been affecting our politics since before any of our current political parties existed. You can see the pattern in almost any hotly contested presidential election in our history, from the 1860 election that narrowly brought Abraham Lincoln to power to the 1916 contest between the incumbent Deep Southern white supremacist Woodrow Wilson and the Yankee-born Supreme Court Justice Charles Evans Hughes, for which the county-level results are depicted here:

1916 Presidential Election

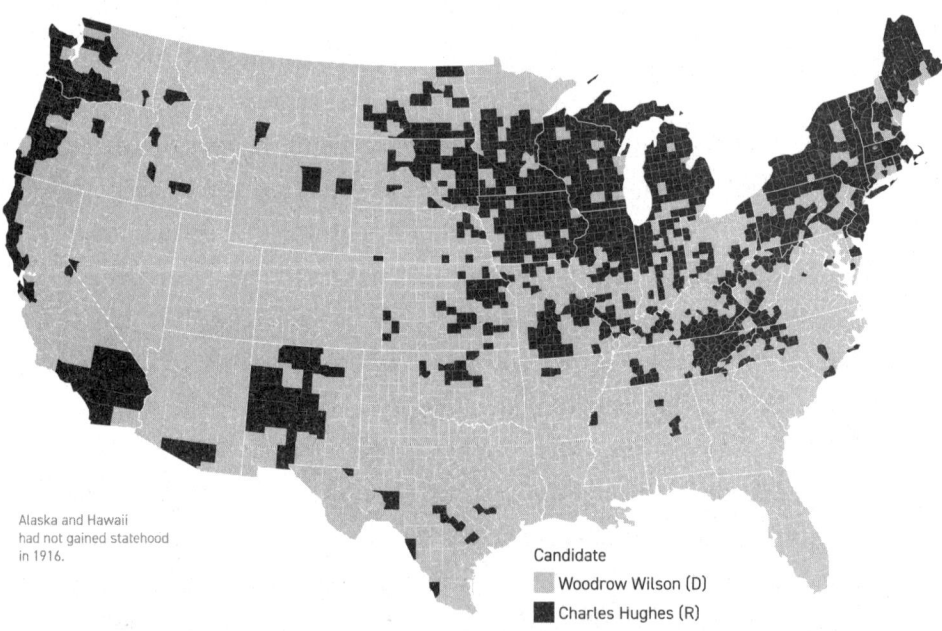

Alaska and Hawaii
had not gained statehood
in 1916.

Candidate
Woodrow Wilson (D)
Charles Hughes (R)

Data: MIT Election Data and Science Lab, "County Presidential Election Returns 2000–2020" + Census Bureau, 1920 Census (via University of Minnesota-IPUMS)

Compare those results with this map, the results of the 2008 presidential contest between Barack Obama and John McCain:

2008 Presidential Election

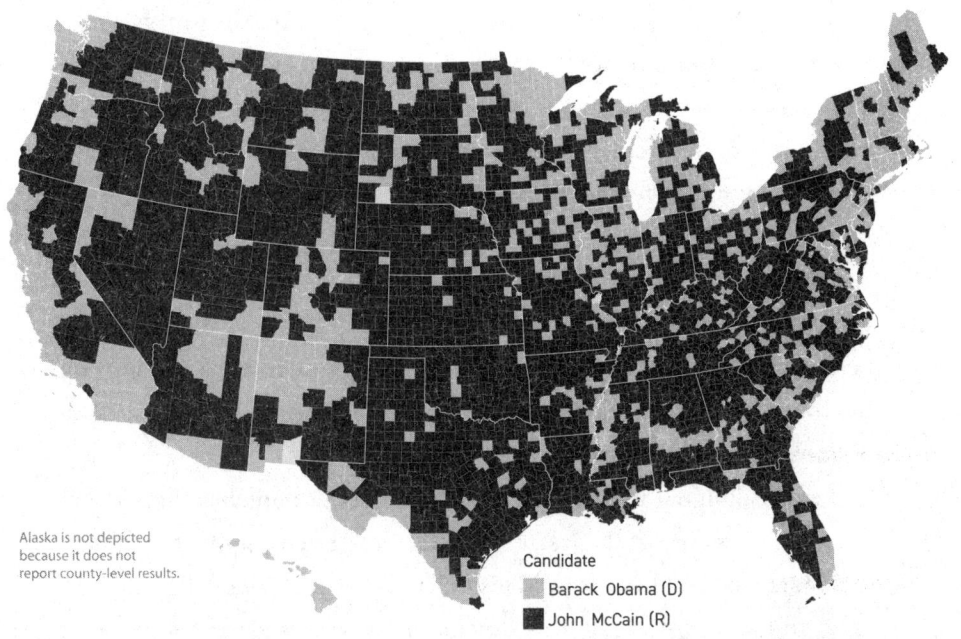

Alaska is not depicted
because it does not
report county-level results.

Candidate

Barack Obama (D)

John McCain (R)

Data: MIT Election Data and Science Lab, "County Presidential Election Returns 2000–2020"

You'll notice the patterns are almost the same, except the partisan alignments of the regions have flipped. This is why trying to understand U.S. political history through a partisan lens is a fool's errand. Political parties come and go; where are the Whigs, Federalists, or the Democratic-Republicans today? But over time they can also completely swap their ideologies, policy platforms, and regional constituencies, as the Democrats and Republicans have since 1960. In 1916, the Republicans were the party of communitarianism, increased federal power, and civil rights, the Democrats the party of white supremacy, racial apartheid, and individual liberty. By the early twenty-first century, laissez-faire business conservatives and white supremacists overwhelmingly voted for Republicans, while activists for racial justice, greenhouse gas regulations, and the taxation of the rich voted Democratic. (Notice the biggest changes in the map—the visibility of El Norte and African American majority counties in the Deep South and Tidewater—are largely due to Black and Latino Americans being able to vote, which was nearly impossible in those regions back in 1916.) As we'll show in the chapters that follow, it's no accident that our ideological voting blocs are regionally maldistributed. The parties can swap places, but the geographical fissures of our politics have remained remarkably stable.

IN *AMERICAN NATIONS*, I sought to explain our past so that we might better comprehend the present. In the remainder of *this* book, we're going to probe how these regional cultures explain our present, in the hopes we might shape our collective futures.

Before plunging in, here are a few notes about nomenclature. When referring to people from Greater Appalachia, I often use the term "Borderlander" within these pages. This is because "Greater Appalachian" is a mouthful and shortening it to "Appalachian" is confusing because that term is already in use for describing people from the Appalachian uplands, and the region we're talking about includes the Ozarks, southern Indiana, the Texas Hill Country, and other places far from that mountain range. Brandeis University historian David Hackett Fischer, writing about the origins of this culture in a book that helped inspire my work, *Albion's Seed: Four British Folkways in North America*, described them as "borderers" because they'd come from the contested Borderlands of Scotland, England, and Ulster. In North America, they settled on the borderlands of the European colonies, the "backcountry" frontier still contested by the Native peoples the colonists were displacing, an experience that reinforced the settlers' cultural norms.[29]

When referring to the Deep South and Tidewater collectively—and they were closely allied from the 1850s to the 1990s—I use the word "lowland," as in "lowland southerners," to make clear we're not including Greater Appalachia, which in the southern context occupies the hilly, "upland" terrain. For the period after 1877, I sometimes use "Dixie" or "Dixie Alliance" in reference to these three regions together. Greater Appalachia was really on the Union side in the Civil War, but that's not how many latter day Borderlanders would wind up remembering it. As we'll see, historical memory is a funny thing.

But that's enough about words. Let's get on with the show.

2

GUNS

Whenever it is that you happen to be reading this book—months, years, even decades after I've written these words—a chilling mass shooting has probably been in U.S. news headlines recently. When I started writing out our initial Nationhood Lab analysis of gun violence in the spring of 2023, it was the murder of three nine-year-olds, their principal, their teacher, and their custodian at a small Christian school in a comfortable Nashville neighborhood by a former student with an AR-15 rifle. By the time I finished, less than four weeks later, five more people had been killed at a Louisville, Kentucky, bank, including a close friend of that state's governor; thirty-two had been shot—four fatally—at a Zumba studio in rural Alabama where a sixteen-year-old girl was celebrating her birthday; teenagers had been shot after accidentally ringing the wrong doorbell in Kansas City and approaching the wrong car after cheerleading practice in suburban Texas; a twenty-year-old woman had been killed after turning into the wrong driveway in Hebron, New York; and a young man executed his parents and two family friends in rural Maine and then shot two random people on a stretch of highway I drive regularly because he wrongly thought they were pursuing him. Six months later my peaceful Maine town went on lockdown for two days while authorities hunted for a fugitive gunman who'd murdered eighteen and injured more than a dozen at a family bowling alley and a friendly neighborhood pub just up the road in Lewiston.[1]

Wherever you live in the United States, there's the numbing certainty that someone somewhere soon will enter a shopping mall, concert venue, restaurant, lawn party, university campus, or school and start shooting people. It can—it has—happened just about everywhere: places rich and poor; in big cities, leafy suburbs, and tiny towns; in schools in Newtown, Connecticut, and Columbine, Colorado, and Parkland, Florida; in the shadow of a Las Vegas skyscraper and on the altar of a Charleston church and on the steps of a Chicagoland synagogue.

It's not just mass shootings. Our country as a whole is marked by staggering levels of deadly violence, much of it committed with firearms. Our death rate from assault is many times higher than that of highly urbanized countries like the Netherlands or South Korea; sparsely populated nations with plenty of forests and game hunters like Sweden, Finland, or New Zealand; and large, populous ones like the United Kingdom, Germany, and Japan. There's state-sponsored violence, too: In 2022, we executed eighteen times as many prisoners as other advanced industrialized democracies combined, which is less surprising when you realize that Japan is the only other such country that allows the practice. Our gun homicide rate is nearly seven times that of Canada's, eighty-nine times greater than the United Kingdom's, and 4,382 times Japan's.[2]

What's much less appreciated is how much the incidence of deadly violence generally—and gun violence in particular—varies by region. It's as if we live in separate countries, some of which have gun violence profiles that look like Canada's, others that resemble the Philippines', Panama's, or Peru's. The reasons for this go back centuries—before the advent of shotguns, revolvers, ammunition cartridges, breach-loaded rifles, and the American Republic itself. Once you take the American Nations into account, a number of insights into the problem are revealed.

——————

AT NATIONHOOD LAB, we knew decades of scholarship showed that there were large regional variations in levels of violence and gun violence and that the dominant values in those regions likely played a significant role. Working with our partners at Motivf, we ran the data for the period from 2010 to 2020 using the American Nations model. As expected, the disparities between the American regions are stark, but even I was shocked at just how wide the differences were, and also by some unexpected revelations.[3]

The best available data is from the U.S. Centers for Disease Control's National Vital Statistics System. It's superior to other sources because health care providers and law enforcement agencies are required to report to it and because it collects and presents gun death data by the race and ethnicity of the victim and other factors. But the CDC doesn't make it easy to probe data at the county level, which you need to do to reveal the American Nations patterns because our regional cultures often don't respect state boundaries. Being a public health agency, they've made the unfortunate decision to treat gun deaths as if they were medical diagnoses requiring careful protection of patient privacy, rather than events where the identities of the victims are almost always public and where privacy laws do not apply because the victims are dead. They will give researchers access to state-level data, but when it comes to counties, they suppress any data request that would yield fewer than ten victims in the relevant time period. To minimize data suppression, we sought aggregate data for the eleven-year period from 2010 through 2020, but that still left the data suppressed for more than 900 out of the 3,144 U.S. counties extant in this period. Most of the censored counties were rural, but there were some larger (unusually safe) ones as well. In any case, it was clear the suppression would throw off our results, potentially hiding high per capita rates in small, dangerous counties and very low rates in large, safe ones.

We found a way around the problem, though. The CDC will share "smoothed" rates for the suppressed counties. This means they've smudged the data in spatial terms—like making a high-resolution image a little pixilated—to try to make it impossible for a victim to be personally identified. That makes it a reliable depiction of geographic patterns and of the risks of living in a given area, but it is, by design, not the precise rate of the county itself. To mitigate the distortions that could occur when dangerous and safe counties are smudged together, we "unsmoothed" the data by reverse engineering the CDC's smoothing process* before calculating the rates of each American Nation. The end result was perfect for our purposes of comparing regional differences.

What we found was pretty shocking.

The map on the next page shows the annual per capita intentional gun death rates—both suicides and homicides—for each regional culture. The Deep South is the deadliest of the large regions at 15.6 per 100,000 residents, followed by Greater Appalachia at 13.5. That's quadruple and triple the rate of New Netherland—the most densely populated part of the continent—which has a rate of 3.8, which is comparable to that of Switzerland. Yankeedom is the next safest at 8.6, which is about half the rate of the Deep South, despite being home to Detroit, Milwaukee, and half of Chicago, cities often associated with gun violence in the popular mind. The Left Coast follows closely behind at 9 per 100,000, a rate comparable to Panama's. Among the large regions, El Norte, the Midlands, Tidewater, and the Far West fill out the middle.

Most of the smaller "enclave" regions are outliers. New France (in

---

*In each exercise, we calculated the rates for our regions by taking the CDC's smoothed death rate for each county and dividing them by the smoothed population. To do the latter calculation, we reverse engineered what the CDC did to create their rate: We added together the population of the target county's "neighborhood"—that county and the counties it bordered on. The figure we used was the average of each county's 2010 and 2020 census population—in other words, its average population during the eleven-year study period. As a test, we also calculated statewide rates based on our "unsmoothed" data and compared them to the official (uncensored) state-level CDC data and found them to be about 90 percent accurate.

Gun Deaths per 100,000 Residents (2010–2020)

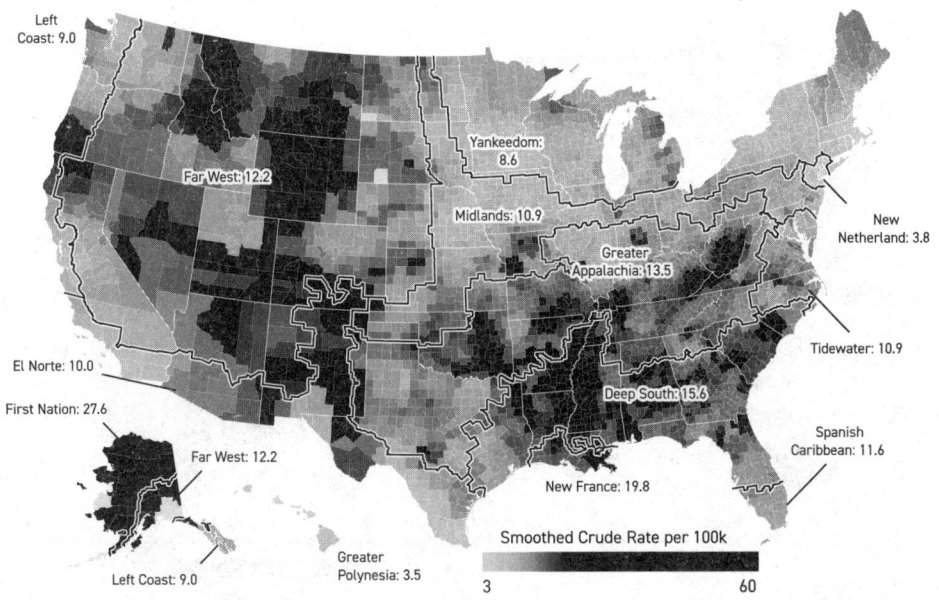

Left Coast: 9.0

Far West: 12.2

Yankeedom: 8.6

Midlands: 10.9

Greater Appalachia: 13.5

New Netherland: 3.8

El Norte: 10.0

First Nation: 27.6

Far West: 12.2

Tidewater: 10.9

Deep South: 15.6

Spanish Caribbean: 11.6

New France: 19.8

Left Coast: 9.0

Greater Polynesia: 3.5

Smoothed Crude Rate per 100k

3   60

Data: CDC - National Center for Injury Prevention and Control

southern Louisiana) and First Nation (in northern and western Alaska) have staggeringly high rates—19.8 and 27.6 deaths per 100,000 people respectively. Hawaii—part of the truly sprawling Greater Polynesia region in the Pacific—has a very low rate of 3.5, making it the safest culture region of the country. The Spanish Caribbean—that's southern Florida—is in the middle of the pack at 11.6 deaths per 100,000.

Here is the same data, but just for gun suicides:

Gun Suicides per 100,000 Residents (2010–2020)

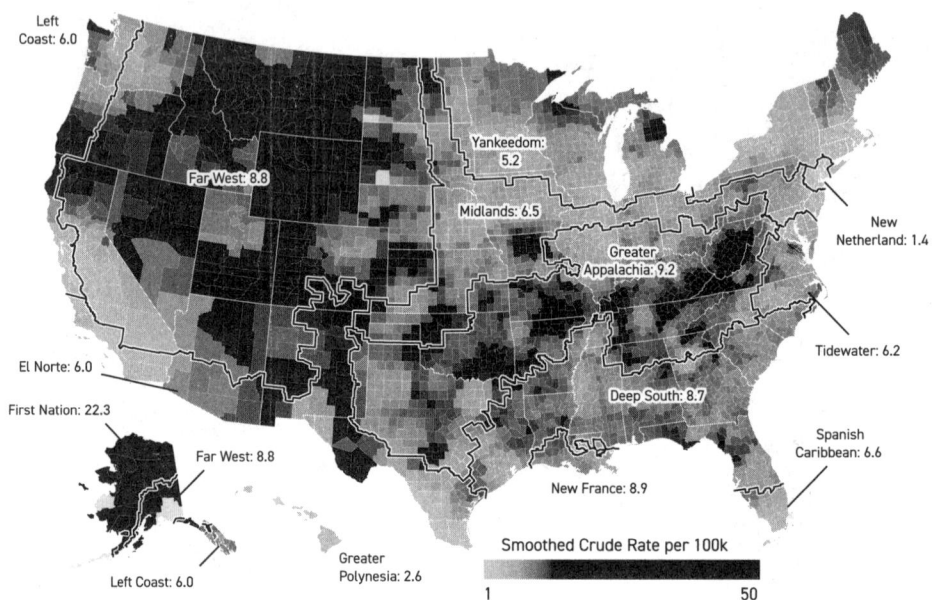

Left Coast: 6.0

Yankeedom: 5.2

Far West: 8.8

Midlands: 6.5

New Netherland: 1.4

Greater Appalachia: 9.2

El Norte: 6.0

First Nation: 22.3

Tidewater: 6.2

Deep South: 8.7

Far West: 8.8

Spanish Caribbean: 6.6

New France: 8.9

Smoothed Crude Rate per 100k

Greater Polynesia: 2.6

Left Coast: 6.0

1   50

Data: CDC - National Center for Injury Prevention and Control

The pattern is similar: New Netherland is the safest big region, with a rate of just 1.4 gun suicide deaths per 100,0000, which makes it safer in this respect than Canada, Sweden, or Switzerland. Yankeedom and the Left Coast are also relatively low risk, but Greater Appalachia surges to be the most dangerous with a rate of 9.2, or more than six times higher than the Big Apple. The Far West becomes a danger zone, too, with a rate just slightly better than its libertarian-minded Appalachian counterpart.

Compare this with the regions' gun homicide rates:

Gun Homicides per 100,000 Residents (2010–2020)

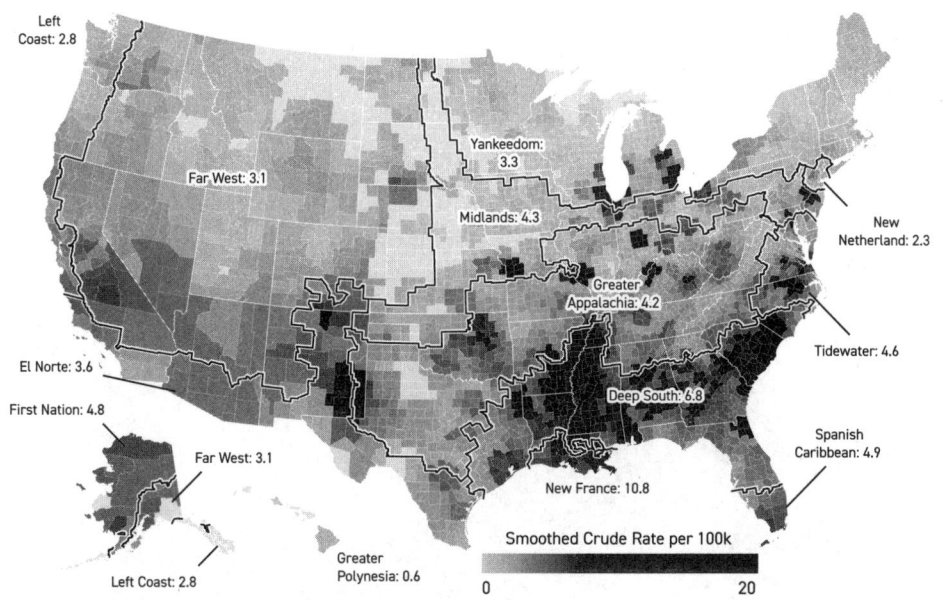

Data: CDC - National Center for Injury Prevention and Control

Note that the Far West goes from being the second worst of the large regions for suicides to the second safest for homicides, a stark disparity not seen anyplace else. New Netherland is once again the safest large region, with a rate about a third that of the Deep South, the nation's deadliest save for New France, whose 10.8 rate is comparable to that of Barbados. Two other "blue" regions, the Left Coast and Yankeedom, are also extremely safe, as is Greater Polynesia, with a homicide rate of just 0.6 per 100,000, or one-*eighteenth* that of New France.

WE ALSO COMPARED THE GUN homicide and suicide rates across these categories for just white Americans—the only ethnoracial group tracked by the CDC whose numbers were numerous enough to get accurate results, because of that agency's aforementioned county-level data suppression.

The pattern is essentially the same, except that Greater Appalachia—middle-of-the-road for overall gun homicides—becomes a hot spot when looking at whites only, with a rate of 2.2 per 100,000. The Deep South is again the worst at 2.8, and New Netherland is the safest at just 0.5, a rate comparable to the gun homicide rate of Canada. Yankeedom's is just 0.8, which is just twice that of Belgium.

White Gun Homicides per 100,000 Residents (2010–2020)

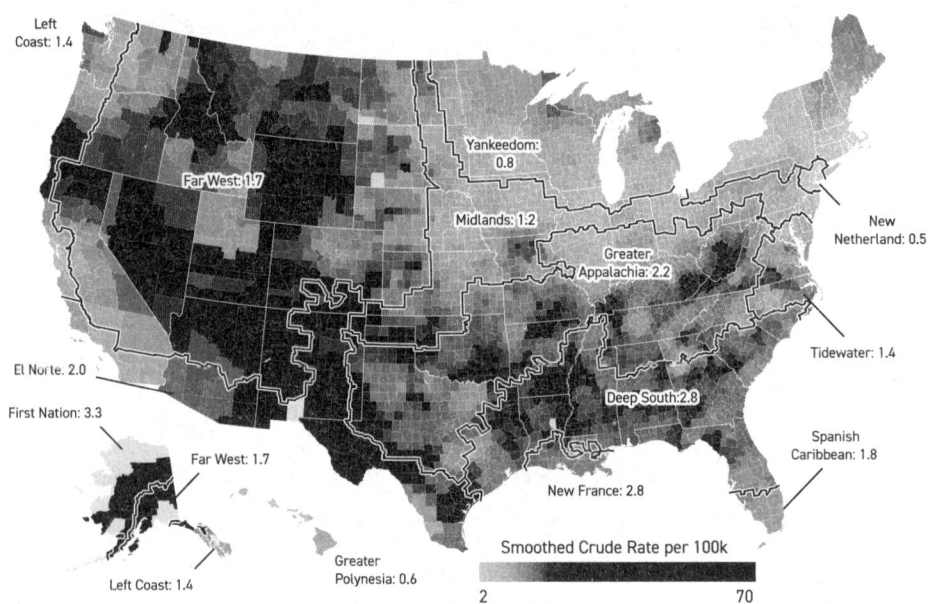

Left Coast: 1.4
Far West: 1.7
Yankeedom: 0.8
Midlands: 1.2
Greater Appalachia: 2.2
New Netherland: 0.5
Tidewater: 1.4
El Norte. 2.0
First Nation: 3.3
Deep South: 2.8
Spanish Caribbean: 1.8
Far West: 1.7
New France: 2.8
Left Coast: 1.4
Greater Polynesia: 0.6

Smoothed Crude Rate per 100k
2   70

Data: CDC - National Center for Injury Prevention and Control

The data was robust enough to allow us to do a comparison of rates among white and Black people living in the 466 most urbanized U.S. counties, where 55 percent of all Americans live. In these "big-city" counties, there is a racial divergence in the regional pattern for homicides. The regional pattern for "big-city" whites is very similar to that for whites overall.

But for big-city African Americans, the regional picture changes completely. The Deep South and Greater Appalachia become relatively safe—

both overall and for gun homicides—even as they are the deadliest for white people. The most dangerous large regions for African American big-city residents are the Left Coast, Yankeedom, and the Midlands, where the per capita smoothed homicide rates hit a shocking 24.5, 26.6, and 29.5 per 100,000, respectively—figures more than twice Mexico's national rate. (Some context: For many decades, Black Americans have faced far-higher gun homicide rates than white Americans, but they have roughly half the gun suicide risk.) New Netherland remains the safest region, though, with a rate of 11.1.

A look at the CDC's county-level smoothed rates shows that Black homicide rates are driven by a handful of large metro hot spots: the Bay Area in the Left Coast; Chicago, which is shared between Yankeedom and the Midlands; Detroit and Milwaukee in Yankeedom; and the Kansas City, St. Louis, Pittsburgh, Philadelphia, and Baltimore metro areas in the Midlands. Other large metros have relatively low rates, including Boston, Hartford, New York, Minneapolis, Seattle, and Portland. It's not immediately clear why some of these cities are safer for Black people than others.

The data suppression issue prevented us from calculating the regional rates for just rural counties, but a glance at a map of the CDC's smoothed county rates indicated that rural Yankeedom, El Norte, and the Midlands are very safe (even in terms of suicide), while rural areas of Greater Appalachia, Tidewater, and (especially) the Deep South are quite dangerous.

So, to summarize the situation by region:

The **Deep South** is the most dangerous large region in almost every respect, except if you are African American, where it becomes one of the safer regions on a per capita basis.

Greater Appalachia is one of the most dangerous places if you are white, especially for gun homicides, but the overall homicide rate ranks it in the middle of the other large regions.

The **Far West** is very safe, relative to the rest of the United States, in terms of gun homicide risk, but very dangerous in regards to suicide. No other region shows this degree of polarization.

The **Midlands** is generally in the middle of the pack, except for gun homicides, where it is one of the most dangerous places to be Black and one of the safer places to be white. A glance at the smoothed rate county map indicates that there is a strong difference between rural and urban areas, with the latter more dangerous. (The Midlands is also the only region with strong, persistent urban-rural divides in political behavior.[4]) It's also one of the most dangerous places to be a Black city dweller.

El Norte generally ranks in the middle of the other regions in terms of gun violence, too. It's fairly safe in terms of gun homicides (3.6 per 100,000) and suicides (6.0 per 100,000), where it ties the Left Coast as the third safest of the large regions. The white homicide rate is relatively high at 2.0 per 100,000, making it the third most dangerous of the large nations (after the Deep South and Greater Appalachia) in this respect. It's one of the safer nations for Black big-city dwellers.

Tidewater historically had very high indices of violence, but today it's one of the safer regional cultures. This change has happened in tandem with the accelerating disintegration of its hierarchical, aggressively individualistic legacy culture over the past few decades in the face of the massive federal government presence around the District of Columbia and Hampton Roads. Note that the most dangerous counties are those in the Piedmont, approaching Greater Appalachia, where the "federal halo effect" is weakest.

Yankeedom is also one of the safest regions, with the second-lowest per capita deaths of any of the large regions from gun suicide overall and also for suicide and homicide for city dwellers, whites, and white city dwellers. The exception: It's one of the most dangerous places to be a Black city dweller in regards to homicides. There is a more than thirty-three-fold difference between the African American and white homicide rate in the "big-city" urban counties*, 0.8 and 26.6 per 100,000. (For comparison, there is "only" a eight-to-one difference between these populations in Deep Southern big-city counties, where the figures are 2.4 and 19.0.) This, as with the Midlands, appears to be driven by a handful of metro areas: Chicago (shared with the Midlands), Detroit, Milwaukee, Cleveland, and Buffalo.

The **Left Coast**, as with so many things, displays a similar pattern as Yankeedom. It's the second-safest large region in terms of overall homicide and third for overall suicide. It also has a wide white/Black disparity among city dwellers—1.3 to 24.5—due almost entirely to the high African American homicide risk in the Bay Area.

New Netherland is far and away the safest of the large regions, and often safer even than Hawaii, despite being the most densely populated part of our continent. This applies to gun homicides and suicides and for both white and Black Americans. The white gun homicide rate, as mentioned before, rivals Canada's all-population rate, while the region's African American rate (which is twenty-eight times higher) is less than half the corresponding rate for Yankeedom or Left Coast. (Because all of New Netherland's counties are highly urbanized, we know this region's overall Black rates,

---

*When analyzing phenomena through an "urban-rural" lens, we categorize counties using the six-tier coding system developed by the National Center for Health Statistics. The "big-city" counties referred to in this chapter are those in NCHS Categories 1 and 2 from the federal agency's 2013 schema.

whereas in other regions, data suppression made calculating these figures in smaller counties too imprecise.)

In regards to the four smaller "enclave" regions, **First Nation** is the riskiest place in terms of deadly gun violence, with a calculated smoothed rate of 27.6 per 100,000. This figure is overwhelmingly driven by a catastrophic gun suicide rate of 22.3 per 100,000, a rate more than double that of its nearest rival (Greater Appalachia at 9.2) and quadruple that of Yankeedom. A word of caution on these numbers: While First Nation is, geographically, the largest North American regional culture examined in *American Nations*, it is sparsely populated (the U.S. section has just 68,000 residents) and several of its enormous counties border on more populous Far Western ones, so smoothing could have an unusually distorting effect. But the overall picture is correct, as the suicide crisis within these Alaska Native communities—which bears heaviest on very young men—is well documented.[5]

New France is overwhelmingly the most dangerous part of the United States for gun homicides, with a smoothed rate roughly triple that of the northeastern fifth and western half of the country. Gun suicides are also high and Black and white big-city homicide rates are the highest in the country (a tie with the Deep South in the case of white deaths). Orleans Parish (home to New Orleans and shared with the Deep South) is the epicenter in all cases, but rates are also high in the Cajun country parishes.

Hawaii, the U.S. portion of **Greater Polynesia**, is by many metrics even safer than New Netherland. This is a state with strong gun control policies that are easy to enforce because most people travel to these islands via security-screened transport: commercial aircraft and ships. The **Spanish Caribbean** is roughly in the middle in most categories.

So why the stark contrast between the regions, with some displaying characteristics approaching those in parts of western Europe, others comparable to those of many Central and South American countries? Cultural attitudes toward violence play an enormous role and shape the policy environment as well.

In a classic 1993 study of the geographic gap in violence, the social psychologist Richard Nisbett of the University of Michigan noted that the regions initially "settled by sober Puritans, Quakers and Dutch farmer-artisans"—that is, Yankeedom, the Midlands, and New Netherland—were organized around a yeoman agricultural economy that rewarded "quiet, cooperative citizenship, with each individual being capable of uniting for the common good." Much of the South, he wrote, was settled by "swash-buckling Cavaliers of noble or landed gentry status, who took their values . . . from the knightly, medieval standards of manly honor and virtue" (by which he meant Tidewater and the Deep South) or by Scots and Scots-Irish Borderlanders who hailed from one of the most lawless parts of Europe and relied on "an economy based on herding," where one's wealth is tied up in livestock, which is far more vulnerable to theft than grain crops.[6]

These southern cultures developed what anthropologists call a "culture of honor tradition," in which males treasure their honor and believe it can be diminished if an insult, slight, or wrong is ignored. "In an honor culture you have to be valiant about people impugning your reputation and part of that is to show that you can't be pushed around," says Dov Cohen, a psychologist at the University of Illinois Urbana-Champaign who conducted a series of experiments demonstrating the persistence of these quick-to-insult characteristics. White male students from the Greater Appalachian section of his state lashed out in anger at insults and slights that those from the Midlands and Yankee parts ignored or laughed off. "Arguments over pocket change or Popsicles in these Southern cultures can result in people getting killed, but what's at stake isn't the Popsicle, it's personal honor," Cohen notes.[7]

Pauline Grosjean, an economist at Australia's University of New South Wales, found strong statistical relationships between the presence of Scots-Irish settlers in the 1790 U.S. census and early *twenty-first-century* homicide rates, but only in southern areas "where the institutional environment was weak"—which is the case in almost the entirety of Greater Appalachia. She further noted that in areas where Scots-Irish were dominant, settlers of other ethnic origins—Dutch, French, and German—were also more violent, suggesting that they had acculturated to Appalachian norms. The effect was strongest for white offenders and persisted even when controlling for poverty, inequality, demographics, and education. "Cultural norms have persisted as a private justice system, which substituted for formal law enforcement," she concluded.[8]

In another study, Robert Baller of the University of Iowa and two colleagues looked at late-twentieth-century white male "argument-related" homicide rates, comparing those in counties that, in 1850, were dominated by Scots-Irish settlers with those in other parts of the "Old South." In other words, they teased out the rates at which white men killed one another in feuds and compared those with rates in Greater Appalachia, the Deep South, and Tidewater. The result: Appalachian areas had significantly higher homicide rates than their lowland neighbors—"findings [that] are supportive of theoretical claims about the role of herding as the ecological underpinning of a code of honor," the researchers wrote.[9]

Another research team, from the University of Oklahoma's psychology department in 2009, examined the 108 prototypical school shootings that occurred in the U.S. between 1990 and 2008 and found that 75 percent occurred in "culture of honor" states, those controlled by Greater Appalachia, the Deep South, and the Far West. They also found that 80 percent of rampage shootings—those in which the shooter is lashing out at the school, community, or teenage pecking order as an institution, killing victims at random—occurred in the honor culture states, even though those states comprised less than 57 percent of the U.S. population in this period. "The state-level demographic variables that we examined—which included temperature, rurality, social composition, and indices of economic and social insecurity—were unable to account for the association between culture of honor and our school-violence indicators," the researchers wrote. "School violence might be partially a product of long-term or recent experiences of social marginalization, humiliation, rejection, or bullying, all of which represent honor threats with special significance to people (particularly males) living in culture-of-honor states."[10]

In 2014, that study's lead author, Ryan P. Brown, also probed if higher white gun suicide rates in the honor culture states might be higher simply because those states had higher firearm ownership rates. But even after controlling for this—and for temperature (because statistics show hot places tend to be more violent), access to medical care, and social deprivation—"honor" states still had significantly higher white firearm suicide rates, creating what they termed the "gun access gap." (This gap between gun suicide ratios and gun ownership rates did not exist among people of color.) The researchers concluded that the cause and effect were likely reversed: That is, the white "gun access gap" was likely explained at least in part by the culture of honor, and they suggested that scholars might even consider using it "as a statistical signal for the influence of honor ideology within a state."[11]

In the southern regions, this proclivity for aggression is coupled with the violent legacy of having been slave societies. Before 1865, enslaved people were kept in check through the threat and application of violence including whippings, torture, and often gruesome executions. For nearly a century thereafter, similar measures were used by the KKK, off-duty law enforcement, and thousands of ordinary white citizens to enforce a racial caste system. The Monroe & Florence Work Today project mapped every lynching and deadly race riot in the United States between 1848 and 1964 and found that more than 90 percent of the incidents occurred in the former slaveholding regions and El Norte, where Deep Southern "Anglos" enforced a caste system on the region's Hispanic majority. In places with a legacy of lynching—which is only now starting to pass out of living memory—SUNY Albany sociologist Steven Messner and two colleagues found a significant increase in one type of homicide that isn't explained by other factors: the argument-related killing of Black people by white people.[12]

The southern regions and the Far West are also those where capital punishment is fully embraced. The states they control account for more than 95 percent of the 1,594 executions in the United States from 1976 to 2023. In the same period, the twelve states definitively controlled by Yankeedom and New Netherland—states that account for almost a quarter of the U.S. population—have executed just one person. New Hampshire, the last Yankee-dominated state to allow executions, ended the practice in 2019.[13]

The Deep South and Greater Appalachia have also most enthusiastically embraced "stand-your-ground" laws, which waive a citizen's duty to try and retreat from a threatening individual before killing the person. Of the thirty states that have such laws, only two, New Hampshire and Michigan, are within Yankeedom, and only two others—Pennsylvania and Illinois—are controlled by a Yankee-Midlands majority. By contrast, every one of the Deep South– or Greater Appalachia–dominated states has passed such a law, and almost all the other states with similar laws are in the Far West.[14]

By contrast, the Yankee and Midland cultural legacies featured factors that dampened deadly violence by individuals. The Puritan founders of Yankeedom promoted self-doubt and self-restraint, and their Unitarian and Congregational spiritual descendants believed vengeance would not receive the approval of an all-knowing God (though there were plenty of loopholes in regards to Indigenous peoples and others being seen as outside the community). This region was the center of the nineteenth-century death penalty reform movement, which began eliminating capital punishment for burglary, robbery, sodomy, and other nonlethal crimes, and today none of the states it controls permits executions. The Midlands was founded by pacifist Quakers and attracted likeminded immigrants who set the cultural tone. "Mennonites, Amish, the Harmonists of Western Pennsylvania, the Monrovians in Bethlehem, and a lot of German Lutheran pietists came who were part of a tradition which sees violence as being completely incompatible with Christian fellowship," says Joseph Slaughter, an assistant professor at Wesleyan University's Religion Department and codirector of the school's Center for the Study of Guns and Society.[15]

In rural parts of Yankeedom—like the northwestern foothills of Maine where I grew up—gun ownership is widespread and hunting with them is a habit and passion many parents instill in their children. But fetishizing guns is not a part of that tradition. "In Upstate New York, where I live, there can be a defensive element to having firearms, but the way it's ingrained culturally is as a tool for hunting and other purposes," says Jaclyn Schildkraut, executive director of the Rockefeller Institute of Government's Regional Gun Violence Consortium, who formerly lived in Florida. "There are definitely different cultural connotations and purposes for firearms depending on your location in the country."

If herding and frontier-like environments with weak institutions create more violent societies, why is the Far West so safe in regards to gun homicide and so dangerous for gun suicides? Carolyn Pepper, professor of clinical psychology at the University of Wyoming, is one of the foremost experts on the region's suicide problem. She says here, too, the root causes appear to be historical and cultural. "If your economic development is based on boom-and-bust industries like mineral extraction and mining, people come and go and don't put down ties," she told me. "And there's lower religiosity in most of the region, so that isn't there to foster social ties or perhaps to provide a moral framework against suicide. Put that together and you have a climate of social isolation coupled with a culture of individualism and stoicism that leads to an inability to ask for help and a stigma against mental health treatment." Another association that can't be dismissed: Suicide rates in the region rise with altitude, even when you control for other factors, for reasons that are unclear. (The firearm suicide rate steadily increases with mean altitude in U.S. counties, starting at about 1000 feet.)[16] But while this pattern has been found in South Korea and Japan, Pepper notes, it doesn't seem to exist in the Andes, the Himalayas, or the mountains of Australia, so it would appear unlikely to have a physiological explanation.

As for the Far West's low gun homicide rate? "I don't have data," she says, "but firearms out here are seen as for recreation and defense, not for offense."

Gun policies, I argue, are downstream from culture, so it's not surprising that the regions with the worst gun problems are the least supportive of restricting access to firearms. A 2011 Pew Research Center survey asked Americans what was more important, protecting gun ownership or controlling it. The Yankee states of New England went for gun control by a margin of 61 to 36, while those in the poll's "southeast central" region—the Deep South states of Alabama and Mississippi and the Appalachian states of Tennessee and Kentucky—supported gun rights by exactly the same margin. Far Western states backed gun rights by a proportion of 59 to 38. After the Newtown school shooting, not only Connecticut but also neighboring New York and nearby New Jersey tightened gun laws. By contrast, after the recent shooting at a Nashville Christian school, Tennessee lawmakers ejected two of their (young, Black, male, and Democratic) colleagues from the chamber for participating in a protest for tighter gun controls; then the state senate passed a bill to shield gun dealers and manufacturers from lawsuits. In Greater Appalachia, protecting gun owners and manufacturers is simply more important to voters and politicians than protecting schoolchildren from being shot.[17]

Gun ownership is also regionally varied, with the least safe places being the most heavily armed. We probed the massive Democracy Fund + UCLA Nationscape dataset, a series of detailed surveys conducted every week between late 2019 and early 2021 that polled half a million Americans about their opinions on a wide range of attitudes and issues and practices, including if anyone in their household owned a firearm. New Netherland, the safest large region in the country, had the lowest owner-ship level at 17.6 percent. Two other regions with low per capita gun deaths, El Norte and the Left Coast, also had low gun ownership, at 29.2 and 29.3 percent of households, respectively. Yankeedom and the Midlands were only slightly more armed with 30.6 and 33.8 percent. By contrast, the three large nations with the highest per capita gun deaths—Greater Appalachia, the Deep South, and the Far West—had the most armed households at 46.0, 44.0, and 39.2 percent respectively.[18]

Gun Ownership in the American Nations

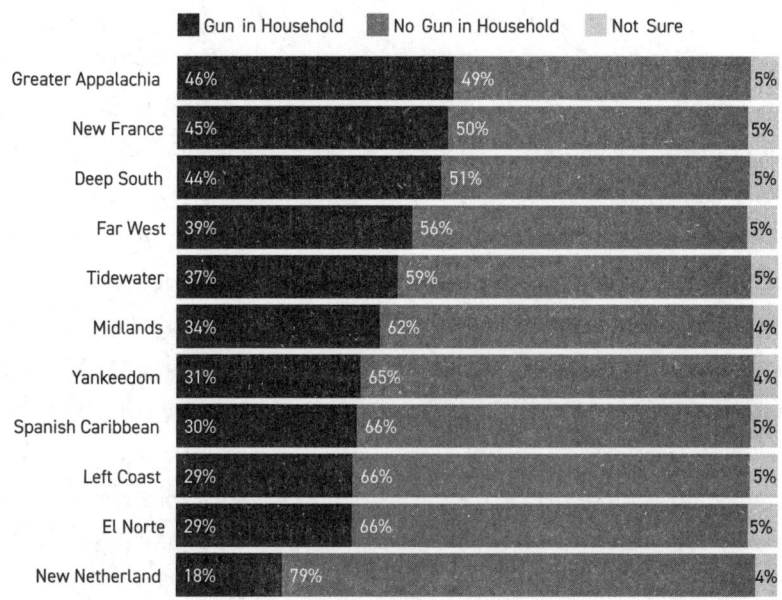

Data: Democracy Fund + UCLA Nationscape Survey (2019–2021)

But I expected, when I turned to New York–area criminologists and gun violence experts, to be told the more restrictive gun policies in New York City, and in New York State and New Jersey, largely explained why New Netherland is so remarkably safe compared with other U.S. regions, including Yankeedom and the Midlands. Instead, they pointed to regional culture. "New York City is a very diverse place. We see people from different cultural and religious traditions every moment and we just know one another, so it's harder for people to foment intergroup hatreds," says Jeffrey Butts, director of the research and evaluation center at the John Jay College of Criminal Justice in Manhattan. "Policy has something to do with it, but policy mainly controls the ease to which people can get access to weapons. But after that you have culture, economics, demographics and everything else that influences what they do with those weapons."[19]

Jaclyn Schildkraut emphasized that there are clear regional patterns in how state governments react to mass shootings. "When Newtown happened, Connecticut and nearby New York and New Jersey passed incredibly comprehensive gun control packages," she said. "But while New York was trying to close gun loopholes, Texas has been trying to put more guns out there, making changes that would make it easier for something like Uvalde to happen."

With such sharp regional differences, it is unlikely that the United States will ever reach a federation-wide consensus on gun control. The cultural gulf between Appalachia and Yankeedom or the Deep South and New Netherland is simply too large. But, as with so many things in the history of U.S. federal politics, it's conceivable that a multiregional political consensus could form to push for limited gun safety measures that might have a modest effect, such as banning high-capacity magazines or creating truly universal background checks. In regional terms, that would mean finding common ground between the "nations" that are already eager to act—Yankeedom, the Left Coast, and New Netherland—and those where a large proportion of the population are willing to consider it: the Midlands, El Norte, Tidewater, and, yes, the Far West.[20]

The Nationscape surveys asked more than 465,000 people between 2019 and early 2021 if they supported different levels of gun control. The encouraging news is that majorities in every region support the gun control measures described above, though by completely different margins. New

Netherlanders, for instance, supported banning high-capacity gun magazines by a whopping 38 points (58–20), with the Left Coast, Yankeedom, and El Norte following with decisive 27-, 25-, and 24-point margins. But that margin dropped to 11 points in the Deep South, 9 points in the Far West, and a mere 8 points in Greater Appalachia (42–36). Tidewater and the Midlands were in the middle on this measure, at +16 and +20 percent.

Support was somewhat stronger in all the regions for banning assault rifles, but followed essentially the same pattern. New Netherland again had the highest margin of support at +49, followed by the Left Coast, Yankeedom, and El Norte at +36, +34, and +32 points, respectively. Support was most tepid in Greater Appalachia (+13), the Deep South (+17), and the Far West (+17). The Midlands (+27) and Tidewater (+26) were again in the middle of the pack.

One measure had overwhelming and essentially undifferentiated support in every regional culture: requiring background checks for all gun purchases. Support ranged from 75 to 81 percent in every region, which in this polarized age amounts to virtual unanimity. Those are higher percentages than the share of Americans that believe NASA really did land on the moon (71 percent) and comparable to the percentage who agree that the Earth is round (80 percent). And contrary to what the gun lobby has said, nobody wants to ban all firearms. Respondents rejected this most draconian of measures by between 17- (New Netherland) and 66-point (Greater Appalachia) margins.[21]

But none of these reforms are going to get our country's gun death rates down to the levels of the United Kingdom, New Zealand, Germany, or Japan. "There was a time in my lifetime when Gallup showed sixty percent of Americans supported banning handguns, a measure that wasn't thought of as extreme and would have a dramatic effect," Carl T. Bogus, a second amendment scholar at the Roger Williams School of Law, says. "Today it's probably in the single digits and that's because the gun control movement let gun activists shift the Overton window" of what is acceptable to contemplate. That, in turn, created the environment that facilitated a 2008 Supreme Court decision that found, for the first time in American history, an individual constitutional right to firearm ownership separate from one's role in a regulated militia, a decision that would have to be overturned if Americans are to become safe from gun violence.[22]

"Culture drives politics, law, and policy," Bogus adds. "Somebody has got to be working on shifting the Overton window back so we can have effective gun control. Not next year or in five years, but eventually."

Knowing these regional cultural effects and characteristics can help craft better gun control strategies. Bogus is likely right about the effectiveness of the policies that are implementable in the current environment, but whether you're aiming for a paradigm shift or just trying to build support for popular policies that may improve matters only at the margins, successful advocates will frame their arguments differently depending on what regional population they're trying to persuade. In honor cultures like Greater Appalachia, for instance, one's pitch for a given reform would be that it "will help you better protect your friends and family." In a more communitarian, non-honor culture like Yankeedom, the pitch for the very same reform would instead argue that it "will help keep your community safe." The messages ultimately mean the same thing, but if you swapped them between these audiences, neither would be as effective. It all comes down to ideas of agency. In Greater Appalachia, security is seen as the individual's responsibility; in Yankeedom, it's the responsibility of the community and thus is delegated to shared institutions.

This is far from the only realm where this is so.

3

HEALTH AND SURVIVAL

From the outset, the American political conversation has centered on how to protect and further our liberal democratic experiment—the aspirational pursuit of a society where all individuals can be free. The problem is that we've never agreed on how to do that, not just as individuals but as regional cultures, with Yankeedom and the Deep South having contradictory traditions that have kept them at loggerheads throughout our history. The argument is as follows:

Is freedom ultimately about maximizing the autonomy of the individual, about personal sovereignty and a lack of restraints—especially (but not exclusively) from government? If we had less government, fewer taxes, and less regulation, is it not axiomatic that each of us would be more free?

Or is it that freedom is about building and maintaining the infrastructure and institutions of a free society, the enabling and leveling mechanisms that ensure that each person has a fair shot at achieving their potential, at being meaningfully free, regardless of the circumstances of their birth? Is it a shared endeavor, a social project, the cultivation of a republican citizenry?

Is freedom, in other words, best achieved by maximizing individual liberty—the laissez-faire, libertarian, or "individualistic" approach—or the common good, the building and maintenance of a free society, which is the "communitarian" strategy?

I argued in my 2016 book, *American Character*, that these two sides of freedom are both essential components of a liberal democracy, in moderation. If you stray too far toward one or the other, you wind up in tyranny. On the individualistic end, tyranny takes the oligarchic form found in late twentieth-century Honduras or El Salvador, where the Five Families or the Fourteen Families (which were always capitalized) had maximized their freedom and killed anyone who wanted some for themselves. In the communitarian direction, it's the Orwellian form of Hitler's Germany or Stalin's Soviet Union, where the keepers of the "common good" criminalized dissent and "wrong" thinking and murdered millions in an attempt to cleanse the nation of the disloyal. Optimizing a free society for the long haul isn't about one of these aspects of freedom conquering the other; it's about keeping the two in equilibrium so individuals are neither tyrannized nor deprived of a decent chance at pursuing their freedom and happiness. Different cultures will choose different equilibrium points— Japan is not Australia, and vice versa—which makes things particularly difficult for the U.S., as the centuries-old regional cultures that make up our unwieldy federation don't agree on these things.[1]

We have regions like the Deep South and Greater Appalachia, where the common good has few friends, and others like Yankeedom, which prize it. Then there are swing regions that fall in between, like the Midlands, where the ethos is communitarian, but people are also skeptical of top-down government intervention. Far Westerners are more individualistic, but the extremities of their settlement environment forced a reckoning with their interdependencies, both with one another and with the federal government and corporate masters. Getting balance in this very individualistic federation of ours at the federal level has, in large part, been about getting the swing regions aboard a "soft communitarian" regional coalition.

But we live in a federation of states with broad powers over most aspects of our lives, from education funding and teaching standards to the regulation of health insurance companies, the construction of highways, the funding of libraries and public health clinics, and the setting of eligibility requirements for Medicaid or welfare benefits. Our constitution, written to keep the southern regions in the nascent federation, requires most federal programs and standards to operate through state governments—usually in the form of grants—allowing the states to shape how they are implemented and for whose benefit. In addition, states often further devolve powers to county and municipal governments, which, in states with divided initial settlement histories, often reflect distinct regional ideologies. It is often said that this system provides the United States with "laboratories of democracy," where disparate ideas can be tried out at the state level and the successful ones replicated. This is too optimistic. As we'll delve into in chapter 8, some of our regions have a history of oligarchy and authoritarianism, others of direct democracy and an intrusive state. They tend to operate laboratories that aim to optimize their regional proclivities, resulting in wildly divergent levels of health, well-being, and social resilience across our federation. The performance of these laboratories also gives us valuable insights into the policies that make for a healthy society and the ones that don't.

In chapter 1, I outlined the regional cultures' various stances vis-à-vis the individual and the collective, the libertarian ethos and the communitarian one. You could organize them into four camps: *aggressively individualistic* (the Deep South and Greater Appalachia), *passively individualistic* (the Far West), *passively communitarian* (the Midlands, El Norte, the Spanish Caribbean), and *aggressively communitarian* (Yankeedom, New Netherland, the Left Coast, Greater Polynesia, and First Nation). As noted in that first chapter, two regions have undergone dramatic cultural change over the past four decades: New France has gone from passively communitarian to aggressively individualistic, while Tidewater has done precisely the opposite. In the "aggressively" individualistic or communitarian regions, these philosophies have always been central drivers of the policy and judicial decisions taken by regional elites. In the "passive" regions, those stances exist but have not had the same level of influence over such decisions, which have been subject to other considerations. For instance, in the pioneer-era Far West, individualism was tempered by the need to rely on one another in an extreme and often perilous environment. In preconquest El Norte, a communitarian-leaning society with strong family, social, and patron-peon obligations and a collective-minded church also had little expectation that governing institutions would solve or improve conditions.

The aggressively communitarian regions have built strong institutions, social services, and regulatory environments paid for by higher taxes on wealth, income, property, and business, while the passively communitarian ones did so to a lesser degree. The aggressively individualistic regions have fewer and weaker institutions, regulatory regimes, and taxes and provide markedly fewer public services. The Far West, the passively individualistic region, is less rigid on these matters but still seeks to have a lean public sector.

The results of these differences are dramatic and, in some cases, dire.

LET'S START WITH the bottom line: life and death.

Public health researchers have long known that health and longevity at the population level are closely related to socioeconomic status and access to quality food, exercise opportunities, clinical care, and social supports. Given that America's regional cultures have always had strongly divergent views on the desirability of social spending, equality, government regulation, and investment in public goods, it stands to reason that they would have similarly divergent health outcomes, including the bottom-line statistic of how long the average person will live.

With our partners at Motivf, the Alexandria, Virginia–based cultural consulting firm, we crunched the numbers and found big life expectancy gaps between the American Nations regions: three-, four-, and nearly five-year differences between the regions for the period from 2018 to 2020. That might not sound that large, but at population levels these are dramatic gaps, comparable to those separating the United States from Bulgaria, Libya, and the Philippines respectively. The life expectancy difference between the Left Coast and First Nation was more than a decade, comparable to the gulf between Japan and Peru. The Deep South and Greater Appalachia had an overall life expectancy of 77 years during this period, similar to Albania's in 2020, while in the Left Coast the figure was 81.6 years, which was about the same as Canada's. The differences between some of the enclave regions were even greater, with the gap between Hawaii (part of Greater Polynesia) and First Nation standing at a staggering 10.8 years. As with deadly gun violence, it's as if we're living in different countries.[2]

Life Expectancy (2018–2020)

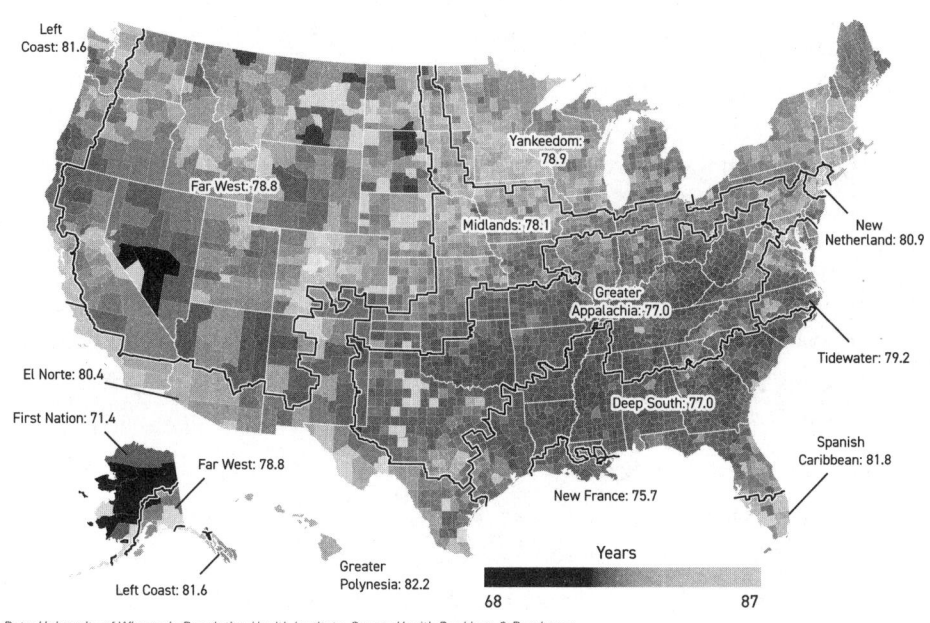

Data: University of Wisconsin Population Health Institute, County Health Rankings & Roadmaps

We thought this might just be a reflection of wealth. Some American regions have always had lower or higher standards of living than others because of how their culture values the relative importance of individual liberty versus the common good, economic freedom versus social equality, and low taxes versus quality services. From their arrival in the late seventeenth century, the Deep Southern oligarchy didn't value shared prosperity, public education, or ordinary people's participation in public affairs; for theological and political reasons, Yankeedom's Puritan founders valued all three. Urbanized New Netherlanders—inhabitants of the Dutch-founded area around New York City—couldn't avoid realizing their dependency on shared infrastructure, while the Scots and Scots-Irish founders of Greater Appalachia had historic reasons for equating government with tyranny. As a result, a much greater share of people are poor in the Deep South and Greater Appalachia than in Yankeedom or New Netherland. States controlled by those regions account for eleven of the twelve states with the highest poverty rates between 2016 and 2020, according to the Census Bureau, with Mississippi and Louisiana at the top of the list. (New Mexico, in El Norte, was number three.) Of the twelve best-performing states, nine are run by communitarian regional cultures—New Hampshire and Maryland topped the list—and the other three were in the passively individualistic Far West. So maybe the differences between the regions would go away if you just compared life expectancy of rich counties and poor ones? We did just that.[3]

Researchers at the University of Wisconsin's County Health Rankings & Roadmaps project (or CHR&R)—from which we got our life expectancy estimates—calculated the percentage of children living in poverty in each county and then sorted those figures into quartiles. We compared the results between regions using just the least impoverished quartile of U.S. counties—the "richest" ones. As you can see in the table on the next page, the gaps persisted: There was a 4.6-year difference in life expectancy between the *rich* counties in the Left Coast and Deep South, for instance. And they got even wider when we looked at just the counties in the bottom quartile, those with the most childhood poverty: There was a staggering 6.7-year difference between those same two regions, which is like the difference between the United States and Uzbekistan. Further, the gaps between these rich and poor counties within the American Nations was more than twice as wide in Greater Appalachia (3.4 years) and the Deep South (4.3 years) as in Yankeedom (1.7 years.)[4]

Life Expectancy by County Poverty Level (2018–2020)

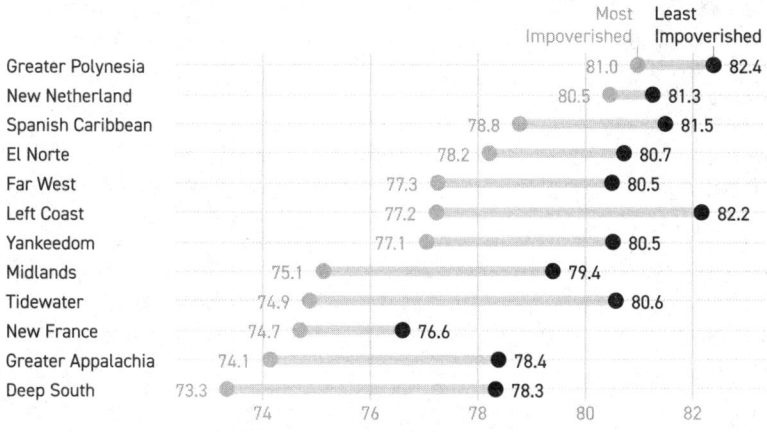

Data: University of Wisconsin Population Health Institute, County Health Rankings & Roadmaps

And consider this: The poorest quartile of U.S. counties that happen to be in Yankeedom have a *higher* life expectancy than the richest quartile of U.S. counties that happen to be in the Deep South, by 0.3 years. Remember, those are both big regions (more than 50 million people each) with a wide mix of counties: rural, urban, rich, poor, blue and white collar, agricultural and industrial. If you compare the poorest category of counties in (completely urbanized) New Netherland to the richest ones in the Deep South, the former have a 0.4-year *advantage* in life expectancy, despite their relative poverty. And people in the Left Coast's poorest quartile of counties live *2.4 years longer* than those in the richest quartile counties in the Deep South. Even the "have" communities are not doing better in the laissez-faire regions.

We repeated the exercise for education, comparing CHR&R's top- and bottom-quartile counties for the percent of the adult population with at least some college education. The patterns were very similar to the childhood poverty ones, as shown in the following table:

Life Expectancy by County Education Level (2018–2020)

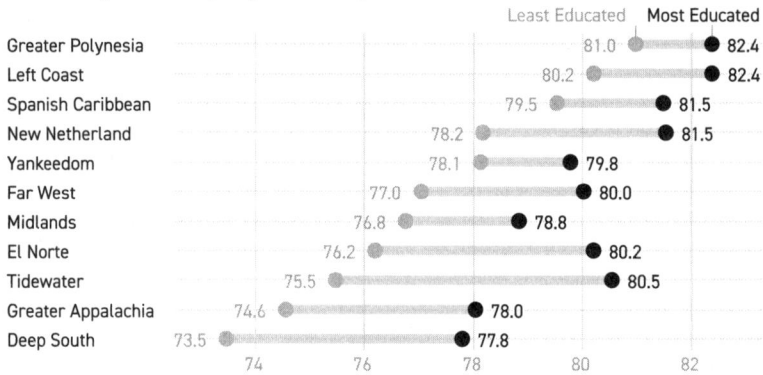

	Least Educated	Most Educated
Greater Polynesia	81.0	82.4
Left Coast	80.2	82.4
Spanish Caribbean	79.5	81.5
New Netherland	78.2	81.5
Yankeedom	78.1	79.8
Far West	77.0	80.0
Midlands	76.8	78.8
El Norte	76.2	80.2
Tidewater	75.5	80.5
Greater Appalachia	74.6	78.0
Deep South	73.5	77.8

Data: University of Wisconsin Population Health Institute, County Health Rankings & Roadmaps

So maybe this is a rural versus urban phenomenon? In the United States, metropolitan places tend to be richer and more educated and have been demonstrated to have higher life expectancy, so it stands to reason the regional gaps might close if you compared just urban counties or just rural ones. So we calculated that too, using the National Center for Health Statistics' six-tiered categorization system for U.S. counties,[5] which sorts them from urban cores of megacities to counties so rural there isn't a single town of 10,000 people within them. The gaps persisted. Here's just urban counties across the American Nations:

Life Expectancy: Urban Counties (2018–2020)

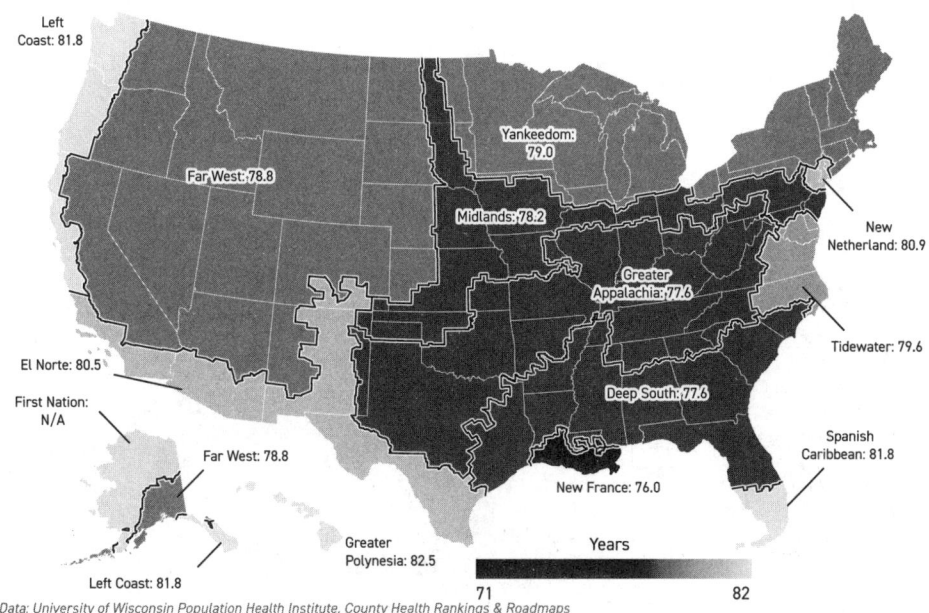

Data: University of Wisconsin Population Health Institute, County Health Rankings & Roadmaps

And on the next page are just the rural counties. Life expectancy is lower in almost every nation, but rural people live 4.7 years longer in the Left Coast or Yankeedom than in the Deep South (and 9.9 years longer in Hawaii than in First Nation). And the gap between rural and urban health almost vanishes in Yankeedom (where municipalities have wide powers) and the Far West (for reasons less clear), but remains about three or four years wide in most of the other big regions. When it comes to life and death, some regions are less equal than others.

The same went for relative access to quality clinical care. CHR&R assigns every U.S. county a ranking for this based on a combination of ten factors, including the number of doctors, dentists, mental health professionals, mammography screens, flu vaccinations, and uninsured people per capita, as well as how often Medicare enrollees wind up admitted to

Life Expectancy: Rural Counties (2018–2020)

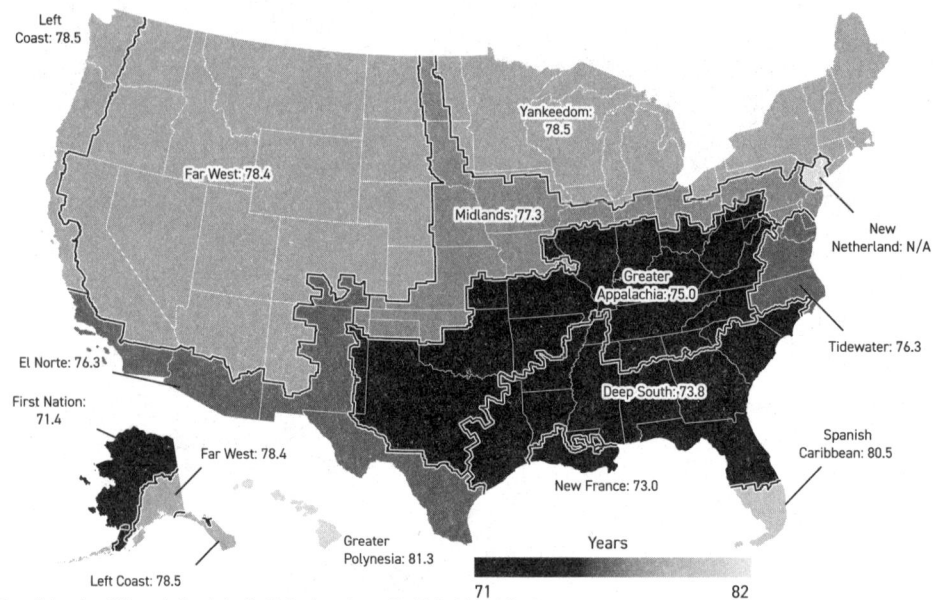

Data: University of Wisconsin Population Health Institute, County Health Rankings & Roadmaps

hospitals with conditions that should have been treatable on an outpatient basis, an indication that the latter services weren't available. We compared those counties in the top quartiles of this ranking system to one another across the regions and found that the gap between them not only persisted, it actually widened, with the Deep South falling about 2.5 years behind Yankeedom, El Norte, and the Far West, 4.4 years behind New Netherland, and 5.1 years behind the Left Coast.

We repeated the experiment using counties that fell in the worst quartile for clinical care and saw the gap grow even wider, with Greater Appalachian (74.6 years) and Deep Southern (74.7 years) life expectancy in those communities lagging Yankeedom by about 3 years and New Netherland by about 5.5 years. That there are fewer counties where most people can afford and access top-notch clinical care in these southern regions than the northern and Pacific coast ones isn't really a surprise:

laissez-faire political leaders tend to create systems that have looser health insurance regulations, leaner Medicaid programs, and fewer public and nonprofit hospitals. That those which do manage to have decent services nonetheless underperform suggests that reversing these gaps won't be easy.

MAYBE, WE THOUGHT, it might be a matter of racial disparities. The lifespans of Black Americans are about 3.5 years shorter than those of white Americans, so it's logical that the regional differences could simply be a statistical artifact of the proportion of African Americans living in each. (The Deep South, for instance, is just shy of 25 percent Black, while Yankeedom is only 9 percent.) But when we looked at white-only life expectancy across the regions, the pattern and gaps remained. Whites in Greater Appalachia are dying 3.6 years sooner than whites in the Left Coast and 4.4 years sooner than those in New Netherland. In the Deep South, the region that had the continent's most repressive slave and racial caste systems, the gap with the three aforementioned regions was almost identical—just a tenth of a year better than Greater Appalachia. Three centuries of formal white supremacy hasn't served whites very well.

Five years ago, University of Cincinnati sociologist Jennifer Malat and two colleagues probed a related question: Given the legacy of white privilege in American society, why do white people have lower life expectancy than their counterparts in Canada and Western Europe, as well as per capita suicide and psychiatric disorder rates far higher than their Black, Asian, or Latino peers? Their conclusion: "Whiteness encourages whites to reject policies designed to help the poor and reduce inequality because of animosity toward people of color as well as being unaware that the poor include a great many white people." Other wealthy countries, they noted, produce poverty rates similar to or greater than ours, but they have stronger welfare systems that buffer much of the population from the health problems that often flow from poverty. Whatever the reason, our data definitely shows a relationship between social spending and health outcomes for white people across regions.[6]

Life Expectancy: Racial Differences Across the American Nations

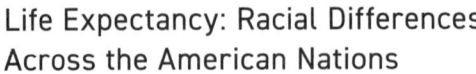
▲ Overall ● Black ● Hispanic ● White

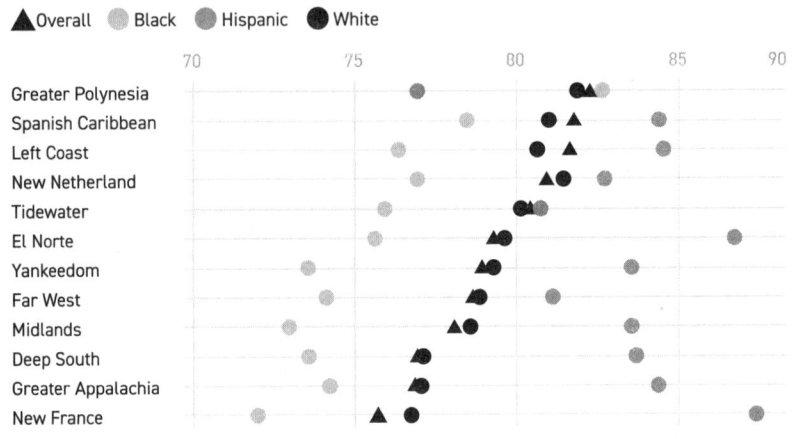

Data: University of Wisconsin Population Health Institute, County Health Rankings & Roadmaps

We repeated this exercise for Black American life expectancy and the gaps persisted, although there was a little shift in the ranking of the regional cultures. On average, Black people live longer in Greater Appalachia than in Yankeedom or the Far West (which isn't true of whites or the overall population). And—in a pattern we also saw with gun deaths—the Midlands moves from the middle of the pack to the worst large region, with Black life expectancy about 5 months shorter than in the Deep South and 3.9 years less than in New Netherland. Yankeedom isn't much better, with a Black life expectancy of 73.6, the same as in the Deep South. Tidewater, which like the Deep South is about a quarter Black, has one of the best Black life expectancies (75.6), while in the Left Coast—where Black people are just 4 percent of the population—it's 76.3. In Hawaii (part of Greater Polynesia), the data has Black life expectancy higher than that for whites, though that could be a statistical anomaly as there are only about 10,000 Black people living there. Among the biggest drivers of Black life expectancy, according to the Brookings Institution's Andre M. Perry, developer of the Black Progress Index, are the percentages of the community that are foreign born, have college degrees, and have higher incomes, as well as the gun violence rate where they live. His data shows that all of these metrics are unusually good across the regions where we found the best Black life expectancy: New Netherland, the Left Coast, and the Spanish Caribbean, as well as in the major population centers of the next best after that—Tidewater and El Norte.[7]

The bottom line is that health disparities between Black and white Americans are real and enormous, but they don't really explain the big life expectancy gaps we see between U.S. regions.

We weren't able to confidently do a cross-regional comparison of Asian American life expectancy as this group constitutes less than 5 percent of the population in most of the American Nations. But given that the average Asian American lives more than seven years longer than other Americans, the fact they constitute 16.5 percent of the population of the Left Coast—and 36.5 percent of Hawaii's—is likely part of the reason those two regions outperform most of the rest of the country.

Hispanic Americans also have much better life expectancy than whites, and we found that was true in every region, save Hawaii. Researchers call this the Hispanic Paradox, because it confounds the usual associations between socioeconomic status and life expectancy, and they've spent considerable time trying to understand why without finding solid consensus. It has been established—by demographers Alberto Palloni and Elizabeth Arias—that Cuban and Puerto Rican Americans don't have better life expectancy than whites, but Mexican Americans do.[8]

I share this background because, curiously, we found that Hispanic life expectancy is relatively poor in El Norte (80.7 years) and the Far West (81.1), the two regions where people of Mexican descent presumably form a supermajority of the Hispanic population. New Netherland—home to the second-largest concentration of Puerto Ricans on Earth—isn't that great, either, at 82.7. Surprisingly, Hispanic Americans in southern regions do really well, with Tidewater and New France hitting the upper 80s to top the list (though you may want to take the latter finding with a grain of salt, as the number of Hispanic Americans there is pretty small).

Keith Gennuso of the University of Wisconsin's Population Health Institute—which hosts CHR&R—has studied border life expectancy issues. He says the reason Hispanic life expectancy is worse in El Norte is likely linked to centuries of discrimination against them. "Unjust housing policies and forced land dispossessions, immigration enforcement, racial profiling, taxation laws, and historical trauma, among numerous other issues, all act as barriers to equal health opportunities for these populations at the border, with known impacts across generations," he notes. Other researchers have found that the mortality advantage is greatest among Mexican migrants who'd moved to places with few longstanding Mexican residents and suspect that these newer immigrant communities are more insulated from less-healthy U.S. dietary and lifestyle choices than those that have been in the United States for decades or centuries.[9]

First Nation's life expectancy rates are catastrophically bad however you look at them, a well-documented legacy of exploitation, ethnic cleansing, and—in many cases—attempted genocide. Native Americans and Alaska Natives in the United States are disadvantaged in access to safe drinking water, nutritional food, health care, educational opportunities, and jobs and have higher exposure to disease, drugs, alcohol, tobacco, and violence. This can also be seen in the "Lower 48" county map—where some of the worst life expectancy "hot spot" islands are Indian reservations—as well as in parts of First Nation lying outside the United States, such as Greenland, which, despite benefiting from some of the vigorous social welfare provisions of the Kingdom of Denmark, has a life expectancy of just 71.6 years. Inuit born in Canada have a life expectancy of just over 72 years, which, as in Denmark and the U.S., is a decade less than their fellow nationals. We do note, however, that the total population of the U.S. portion of First Nation is only 68,000, so there's a greater margin of error in life expectancy estimates, and one should doubt the highly unlikely white life expectancy figure there of 98 years.[10]

I asked CHR&R's codirector, Marjory Givens, for her reaction to the life expectancy gaps we found between the American Nations regions, and she wasn't surprised. "This is logical considering the overall values and variation in health and opportunity of Yankeedom are more favorable than the Deep South or Greater Appalachia," she told me. "There are regions of the country with structural barriers to health, where types of long-standing discrimination and disinvestment have occurred through policies and practices applied and reinforced by people with more power. . . . Counties in these regions have fewer social and economic opportunities today."[11]

One example: States that have expanded Medicaid eligibility have seen significant reductions in premature deaths, while those that have not have seen increases. As of 2024, ten states still hadn't expanded this state-implemented program even though almost the entire cost burden of doing so is borne by the federal government. All but three of those states are controlled by the Deep South and Greater Appalachia. Just one—Wisconsin—is in Yankeedom, and its Democratic governor has been trying to expand it through a Republican legislature. Expansion was a no-brainer for Republican administrations in Michigan, Ohio, New Jersey, New Hampshire, and Vermont, but a bridge too far for their colleagues farther south.[12]

Or take New Netherland. Despite its density, diversity, and income inequalities, it's one of the healthiest places to live in the United States, with an overall life expectancy of 80.9 years. "You can have policies that can meaningfully change life expectancy: reduce drug overdoses, expand Medicaid, adopt gun control, protect abortion and maternal health," the data scientist Jeremy Ney, author of the American Inequality data project, told me after looking at our results. "That New Netherland region ticks the box on all five of those."[13]

Jeanne Ayers is the executive director of Healthy Democracy Healthy People, a collaboration of eleven national public health agencies that probes the links between political participation and health. "We don't have these differences in health outcomes because of individual behaviors; it's related to the policy environments people are living in," Ayers, who was Wisconsin's top public health official during the Covid-19 pandemic, said after looking at maps of Nationhood Lab's data. "Your health is only ten percent influenced by the medical environment and maybe twenty or thirty percent in behavioral choices. The social and political determinants of health are overwhelmingly what you're seeing in these maps."[14]

REGIONAL DIFFERENCES PERSIST IN other measures of health outcomes. With my colleagues, the health scientists Ross Arena and Deepika Laddu of the University of Illinois Chicago and Nicolaas Pronk of the Minneapolis-based HealthPartners Institute, I looked at county-level data from 2020 to 2022 to examine rates of obesity and diabetes and also the self-reported prevalence of exercise and the availability of exercise opportunities. (A lack of exercise is one of the key factors leading to obesity, diabetes, and ultimately heart disease.) Our findings, published in the academic journal *Progress in Cardiovascular Diseases*, revealed the familiar regional patterns, with poor outcomes concentrated in the Deep South, Greater Appalachia, and New France, and with First Nation at the bottom of the list for all four. The diabetes rates in the Deep South and New France (12 percent of adults aged twenty and older have the disease) were a quarter higher than that of the four aggressively communitarian nations (where only 9 percent have it). The obesity rates in the Deep South, Greater Appalachia, and New France were almost a third higher than that of New Netherland. On the Left Coast, 18 percent of adults reported that they get no leisure-time physical activity, compared to 25 percent of Greater Appalachian respondents, 27 percent of Deep Southerners, and 30 percent of First Nation residents.[15]

Obesity Prevalence (2020–2022)

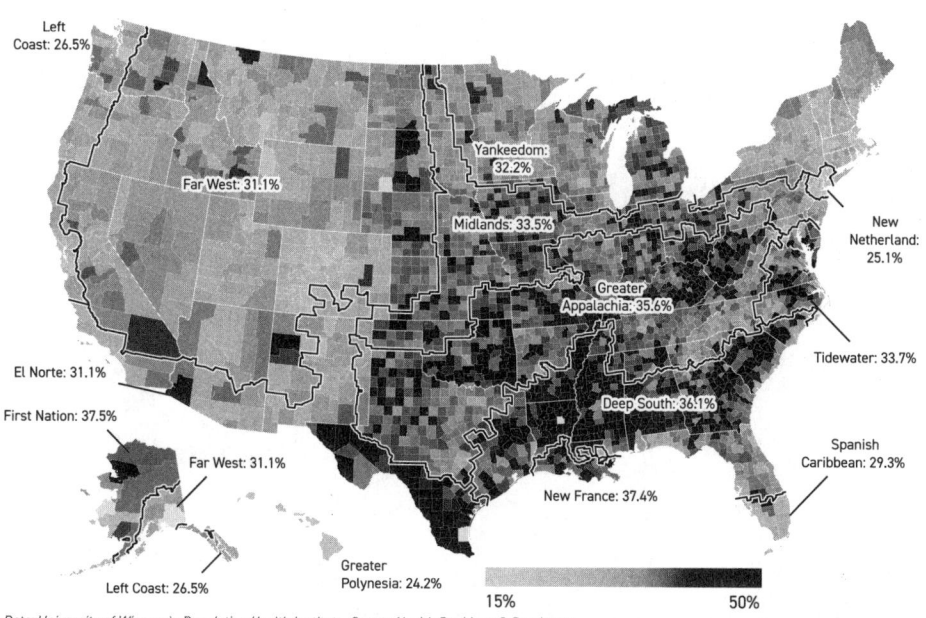

Data: University of Wisconsin Population Health Institute, County Health Rankings & Roadmaps

"The difference between eighteen percent of people being inactive and twenty-seven percent makes a really big difference, and on a population level small improvements in those numbers can equate to big changes in health outcomes," Arena, a physiologist who studies the effect of exercise, tells me.[16]

With that in mind, our research team also parsed CHR&R's county-level data on access to adequate exercise opportunities, defined as living in a census block less than half a mile from a park and either one or three miles from a recreational facility, depending on whether the area is urban or rural. The same patterns held, with more than 90 percent of residents of New Netherland, the Left Coast, Greater Polynesia, and El Norte living

Diabetes Prevalence (2020–2022)

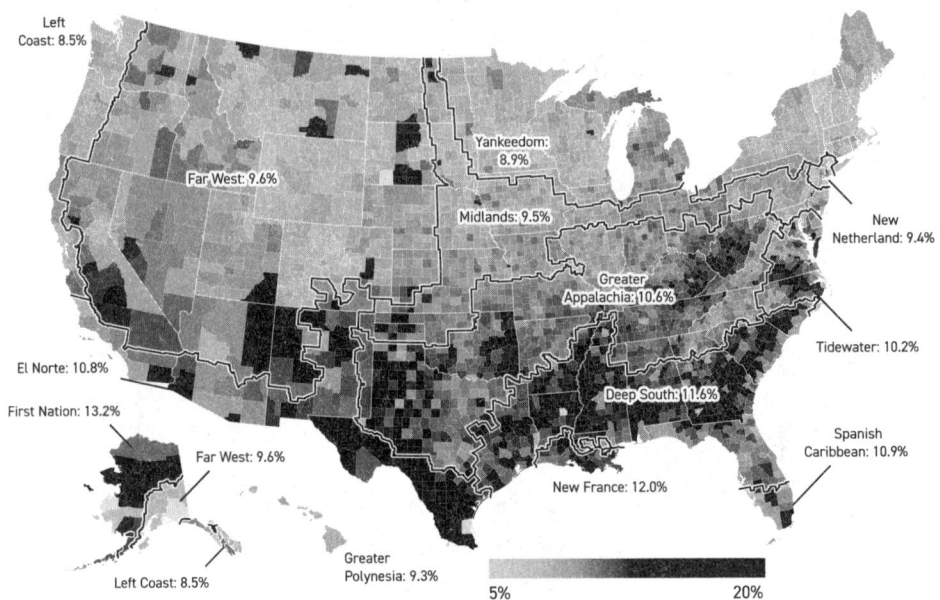

Data: University of Wisconsin Population Health Institute, County Health Rankings & Roadmaps

near such exercise resources compared to only 75 percent in Greater Appalachia and the Deep South and 80 percent in New France. The aggressively libertarian regions haven't created adequate physical infrastructure to allow people to exercise, while the communitarian ones have. The exception and outlier, as in far too many phenomena we've looked at, is First Nation, where only 46 percent have access to exercise opportunities.

Another reason people don't exercise: They're afraid of being harmed or shot in many of the places where they might do so. Knowing the massive regional differences in deadly gun violence, Arena, Pronk, HealthPartners Institute physician Thomas Kottke, and I merged the county-level data on physical inactivity and firearm fatalities. Our results, published in the *American Journal of Medicine,* found counties with poor physical activity metrics had significantly higher firearm death rates, and this was consistent for victims across races. The aggressively individualistic regions—plus El Norte and First Nation—had the strongest associations, suggesting violence is increasing nonviolent deaths. "Gun violence in itself may be directly impacting physical inactivity patterns or potentially serves as a surrogate marker of perceived community safety that influences physical inactivity patterns," Kottke, the paper's lead author, concluded.[17]

We found the same patterns when we looked at people's dietary patterns. The aggressively individualistic regions had the highest prevalence of food insecurity—13 percent of households in the Deep South and Greater Appalachia and 14 percent in New France—save for First Nation, again an outlier at 17 percent. The least food insecure were the Left Coast and Tidewater (at 10 percent). Using data derived from the U.S. Department of Agriculture's Food Environment Atlas for 2019, we also determined the percentage of people with limited access to healthy foods. The three southern regions were again at the bottom of the heap (at 8 to 10 percent each), save for First Nation, at a frightening 21 percent. The communitarian regions had far lower rates of food insecurity, ranging from 6 percent of residents in El Norte to just 1 percent in New Netherland. "The cultural context and historical background of a region . . . play a pivotal role in shaping food-related practices, preferences, and the availability of resources," lead author Deepika Laddu, a population health and risk management researcher, wrote in our research paper in *Current Problems in Cardiology*. "Recognizing that the complexity and heterogeneity of food insecurity is perpetuated by a history of discriminatory policies and practices embedded in cultural and socioeconomic systems, applying the American Nations model may be an essential approach in informing discussions on how policies can be effectively revised."[18]

We also did separate peer-reviewed studies on the prevalence of disabilities, sleep disturbances, and arthritis. Again, we saw the same regional patterns. There was what our team described as a "disability belt" across the three southern, aggressively libertarian regions, plus First Nation, which again had the worst metrics in the country; the other aggressively communitarian regions had fewer disabilities per capita, with New Netherland's rate (23.4 percent of its population) less than three-quarters of the Deep South's (32.1 percent). At a county level, the disability patterns very closely matched those for age-adjusted physical inactivity—a statistical technique for measuring correlations revealed this relationship accounted for 87 percent of the variations, a far stronger association than our team expected. Arthritis prevalence, adjusted for age, showed a very similar pattern, with the condition most prevalent in Greater Appalachia and the Deep South and least so in Greater Polynesia, New Netherland, El Norte, and the Left Coast; the other regions were in between, including Yankeedom (where arthritis is most prevalent in rural counties), the Far West, and First Nation, which for once wasn't an extreme outlier. For insufficient sleep, adjusted for age and defined as less than seven hours a night on average, the aggressively individualistic nations were again clustered at the top of the list, with the communitarian ones at the bottom, save that this time Greater Polynesia was the extreme outlier, with 40.8 percent of residents not getting enough rest, compared to 30 percent in the most well-slept region, the Left Coast. Sleep researchers have found no evidence that sleep differs across ethnicity, race, or countries, but they have found that sleep deprivation hot spots have high rates of obesity, diabetes, and cardiovascular diseases. Poor wellness has cascading effects.[19]

"It's no big surprise when you look at county-level data that the southern regions have higher prevalence of these things, but never has the relationship been so clean as with the American Nations settlement maps," Arena tells me. "The gaps you see in life expectancy are just the tip of the iceberg because our health system is really good at keeping unhealthy people alive through medications and surgeries. The regional gap in people's health span—how many years of your life are you living with a high quality of life with independence and functionality—is probably even greater because it lines up with smoking, access to healthy foods, and these other factors."[20]

Led by Ross Arena in 2024, our team developed a multifactor metric to allow researchers to develop comparisons of the lifestyle behaviors, chronic conditions, and self-reported health statuses between populations. This Lifestyle Health Index (or LHI) uses age-adjusted data collected by the CDC to generate an index score for every county based on the prevalence of binge drinking, smoking, physical inactivity, insufficient sleep, high blood pressure, cancers (excluding skin cancers), coronary heart disease, diabetes, kidney disease, chronic obstructive pulmonary disease, stroke, and self-reported physical and mental health. For a paper in the *Journal of Cardiopulmonary Rehabilitation and Prevention*, we calculated the LHI for each of the American Nations, which once again produced the familiar pattern. First Nation was the unhealthiest region, followed by the three aggressively individualistic regions. The aggressively communitarian Left Coast, Greater Polynesia, and New Netherland were the three healthiest, followed by the passively individualistic Far West, passively communitarian El Norte, and aggressively communitarian Yankeedom. At a county level, the divides between the regions were stark, with almost all the counties in the three southern regions falling into the least-healthy categories and every county in the Left Coast and New Netherland (save the Bronx) outperforming the national average. While most of western and central El Norte was healthy, almost every county that fell inside (Appalachia and Deep South–controlled) Texas was in crisis. The least-healthy stretches of the Midlands were in Ohio and Missouri, while in the Far West, many of the worst LHI scores were for counties dominated by American Indian reservations, where state governments have little involvement or responsibility for infrastructure, health-related or otherwise.[21]

You could argue that the reason the aggressively individualistic regions perform so badly across these health metrics is that they're poor. I would counter that the reason they're poor is precisely because they're aggressively individualistic, with centuries of underinvestment in their people, institutions, and infrastructure, a choice made by generations of elites so they would have low taxes, cheap labor, and uncontested political control. International development experts have learned what makes countries wealthy or not, and it boils down to having built equitable education, health, sanitation, transportation, and legal systems. It's how you unlock individual potential, keep markets competitive, and, yes, allow people to live longer, happier lives. If laissez-faire economics was a panacea, the Deep South would be the wealthiest region in the country and Honduras would be among the world's wealthiest nations. If high taxes and expansive services were destructive to economic performance, New Netherland, Yankeedom, and the Left Coast would be the country's poorest regions and Scandinavia the world's worst. It's just not the case.

THE INDIVIDUALISTIC WORLDVIEW is poorly suited to collective action problems, such as confronting and containing a deadly airborne virus. During the terrifying first year of the Covid-19 pandemic, regional differences—and the abdication of federal leadership by then President Trump—made the United States ground zero for the global crisis, as elected officials and large numbers of citizens across the aggressively libertarian regions mobilized not against the deadly virus but against public health measures meant to contain it.

In the first weeks of the pandemic, Arkansas Governor Asa Hutchinson prohibited town and city mayors from imposing stay-at-home orders, which were saving lives across Yankeedom and the Midlands. As a deadly new strain spread in the pandemic's second spring, Texas Governor Greg Abbott prohibited cities, counties, school districts, public health authorities, and other state entities from requiring people to wear masks in their buildings, including public school teachers and students, a move the chief executive of Travis County—where the state capital, Austin, is located—called "irresponsible at best and dangerous at worst." Abbott responded a few weeks later by prohibiting the same entities from requiring that their employees or students be vaccinated. At the same time, Hutchinson, in Arkansas, prohibited mask mandates, a move that triggered a spike in cases so severe he was soon calling for their reinstatement. Florida Governor Ron DeSantis also forbade compulsory masking in schools and other public places while, at the same time, ordering the state health department to stop informing the public about new Covid cases, deaths, and vaccinations; he would later advise Floridians not to get vaccine boosters, contradicting the medical community, and dismissed masking advice as "medical authoritarianism."[22]

These attitudes contributed to enormous regional disparities in the public response to the pandemic, starting with adherence to the initial lockdown recommendations, and even to compliance in states where lockdowns had been imposed. In the first, frightening months of the pandemic in the early spring of 2020, the *New York Times* analyzed anonymized cell phone tracking information to see how far people in each county traveled each day on average, and then compared how far they went in the first weeks of the crisis. The difference was acute, with the people in almost all of the counties in the Deep South and Greater Appalachia making little reduction in travel, while the people in the vast majority of counties in Yankeedom, New Netherland, the Midlands, Tidewater, and the Left Coast complied with lockdown advice. (The Far West and El Norte were less-coherent patchworks.) At the time, I was reporting on the pandemic at Maine's *Portland Press Herald*, and my colleagues and I tracked weekly new infections in each of the American Nations. In the communitarian nations—which had been hit hardest in the initial wave because of commercial air links with primary infection sites in China and northern Italy—infections had peaked by the end of April and fell dramatically by midsummer. In the nations where people didn't stop moving around, the infection rate skyrocketed over the same time period.[23]

Then, in a triumph of scientific research and technological knowhow, highly effective vaccines were created, manufactured, and widely distributed during the first half of 2021. By that summer, any adult who wished to be vaccinated had ample opportunity to do so, greatly reducing the chance of dying, as some 600,000 Americans already had. By then, a new and more deadly mutation, the Delta variant, had been spreading across the country, increasing the urgency of becoming vaccinated. Yet tens of millions refused to take the free, lifesaving vaccinations, the vast majority of them residing in the libertarian regions. With the help of our partners at Motivf, we calculated the per capita vaccination rates in each of the American Nations as of August 15, 2021, which we mapped here:

COVID-19 Vaccination Rates (as of August 15, 2021)

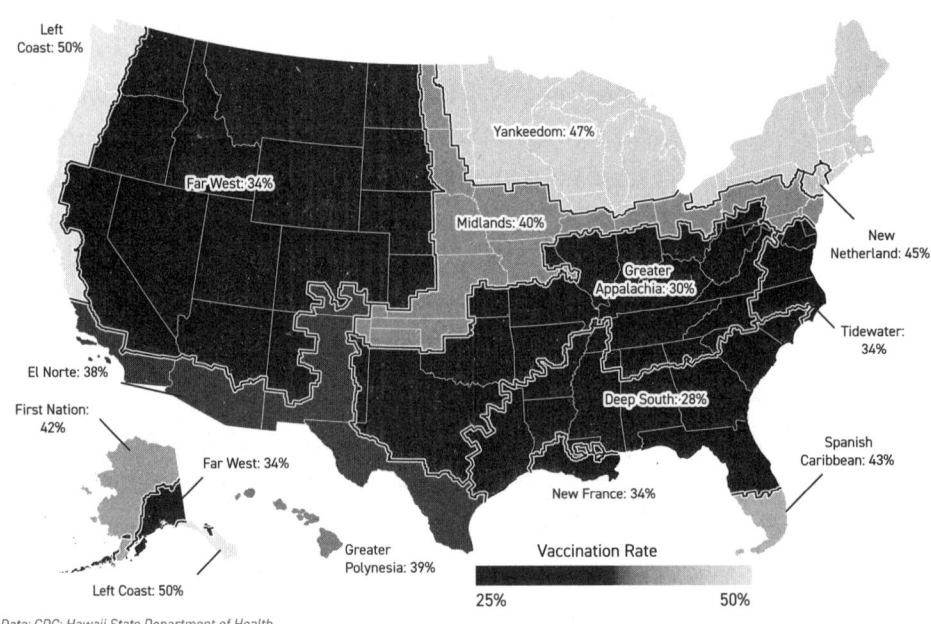

Data: CDC; Hawaii State Department of Health

The Left Coast had vaccinated 50 percent of all its citizens (regardless of age), New Netherland 45 percent, Yankeedom 47, and the Midlands and First Nation 49. These communitarian nations included or controlled all the states with the best full vaccination rates at that time as well. These were, in order, Connecticut, Vermont, Maine, Massachusetts, Rhode Island (all Yankeedom), New Jersey (Midlands/New Netherland), Maryland (Midlands dominating Tidewater), and Washington (Left Coast dominating the Far West), as per the *New York Times* trackers.[24] In Yankeedom in particular, even Republican governors had behaved in a broadly communitarian manner, supporting public health advice and ordering lockdowns in their states, including the chief executives of Vermont, Massachusetts, and New Hampshire. This is because they are all *Yankee* Republicans. The passively communitarian nations were generally in between, with El Norte, a region where the old patron-peon system bound communities together in frontier conditions, at 51, and Tidewater—once individualistic, now not so much—at 41.

The individualistic cultures performed the worst, with the Deep South trailing the nation with an overall vaccination rate of just 38 percent and Greater Appalachia at 39 percent. The Far West, where a libertarian ethos is often tempered by the need to cooperate in frontier conditions—and by the presence of the highly communitarian Mormon enclave—the rate was 45 percent, just a few points under the worst performing of the communitarian nations. The Deep South was where you found governors like Florida's Ron DeSantis, Texas's Greg Abbott, and Tate Reeves in Mississippi trying to stop school districts, localities, and/ or businesses from imposing mask or vaccine mandates. Their declared reasoning: protection of personal freedom. "This is still America, and we still believe in freedom from tyrants," Reeves said at the end of the summer of 2021 after the Biden administration imposed a vaccination mandate for federal contractors and large employers in an effort to end the crisis, which had by then become a pandemic of the unvaccinated. His state, which had the lowest vaccination rate in the nation that summer, had also been hit the hardest, the University of Mississippi Medical Center having been forced to erect a field hospital in its parking garage to treat the critically ill.[25]

By the crisis's end, the toll of such policies was clear. For a joint research project we did on the pandemic, Ross Arena obtained the final county-level death tallies generated by the federal government's interagency task force, which had its last update on February 23, 2023. The

Deep South had lost 505 people per 100,000 residents to Covid-19—nearly a quarter million dead. That's more than 2.5 times the proportion who died in the Left Coast (195 per 100,000), nearly 3 times that in First Nation (174 per 100,000), and about 5 times the rate in Greater Polynesia (104 per 100,000), which had the benefit of being able to effectively quarantine itself from the other regions. New Netherland had 17 percent fewer per capita Covid deaths than Greater Appalachia, despite having a population density 30 times higher and having been one of the places hardest hit in the entire world by the initial infection wave. Yankeedom, with a population density of 157 people per square mile, had fewer per capita deaths than the Far West, with a density of just 25 per square mile. Of the passive communitarian nations, only El Norte rivaled the southern regions, with 471 deaths per 100,000, most of them in the Texas portion that suffered the consequences of Governor Abbott's coronavirus-friendly policies. Individualistic ideologies almost certainly resulted in the preventable deaths of tens of thousands of people.[26]

AT THE OUTSET I argued that individual liberty and the common good are both important, but that they need to be in equilibrium. The data presented here makes clear that our aggressively individualistic nations have moved way beyond that healthy balance point, making societies more dangerous, sickly, vulnerable, and short-lived. What it doesn't tell us is whether or not our most communitarian regions have yet reached the tipping point in the other direction. The United States, as a whole, is an unusually individualistic country, so it's entirely possible that even our most communitarian regions might have to get *more* communitarian to hit the sweet spot, at least insofar as health, wellness, and, yes, even happiness are concerned. To test that hypothesis, you would have to look beyond our borders to countries that have strong welfare states, with generous universal benefits; free or highly subsidized health care, child care, and higher education; and expansive public infrastructure, from public transit to community recreation centers. That all costs a lot of money, which generally means people and private businesses are heavily taxed to pay for it. Does the tradeoff make their people happier and healthier than countries that don't have such an orientation?

The RAND Corporation, a think tank created by the Pentagon to use systems-scale analyses to help the United States outcompete the Soviet Union, looked at this very question in regards to health outcomes in an international study completed in 2016. They found that countries with more expansive government social expenditures—welfare programs—had substantially better health outcomes than those that did not. The United States, they noted, spent far more on medical care and substantially less on social programs than the original fifteen European Union member states did; the latter countries had much healthier populations, with better life expectancy, lower infant mortality, fewer low-birth-weight babies, and lower risk of death from illness or injury. "Countries with greater social expenditure have better health outcomes," their report concluded. "It seems sensible that US policymakers consider rebalancing health and social spending."[27]

Health statistics capture an aspect of well-being, but maybe people in individualistic nations are happier than their overtaxed, communitarian-led counterparts? Using their network of local offices, Gallup—the multinational research Goliath—has surveyed 1,000 citizens in each of 160 countries every year since 2005 on a wide range of questions, including measures of the respondent's own assessments of their life satisfaction. This has allowed them to compile a "happiness" index that powers the World Happiness Reports they produce in conjunction with the University of Oxford and the United Nations. Kelsey J. O'Connor, a behavioral economist at the University of Southern California, examined the relationship between a country's Gallup happiness score and the percentage of their gross domestic product spent on public social protection, including welfare payments, unemployment, sickness, disability, workplace injury, and old-age benefits. He found that citizens in countries that spent more on social protection reported higher levels of life satisfaction, and that the relationship was just as powerful as how rich or poor the country was, as measured by per capita GDP. The countries that have the highest life satisfaction scores year after year—Denmark, Finland, the Netherlands, Iceland, Switzerland, and Sweden—are social democracies with strong welfare states, several of them spending a third more of their GDP on social protection than the United States. In the 2024 World Happiness Report, the U.S. ranked twenty-third, trailing Slovenia, Israel, and Costa Rica.[28]

The data shows that our society, at least in terms of health, wealth, and resilience, would be demonstrably better off with more social investments, especially in the aggressively individualistic regions. As with gun policies, if this is to happen, arguments for doing so will need to be tailored by region. In Greater Appalachia and the Far West, for instance, these investments should be touted as ways to free individuals from tyrannical, oligarchical forces like drug and health insurance companies, the lobbyists rigging the tax code for fat cats, or the out-of-touch coastal charlatans trying to take away the proverbial weapons your family needs to protect themselves from deadly diseases, toxic spills, and natural disasters. In Yankeedom and the Midlands, the very same investments would be framed as ways to make the community safer, healthier, happier, and wealthier. Both approaches tell a story that's accurate and true, but each works in some regions and not others.

As we will see in the chapters that follow, this is not a lesson that's limited to health and happiness.

4

HISTORY WARS

How to hold a nation together? This is a question people have been asking since humans started trying to construct nation-states in the late eighteenth century out of sometimes arbitrary collections of people who'd previously been ruled by whichever king, prince, duke, or emperor had inherited the land they lived on. Through much of human history up to that point, dynastic states had been held together by allegiance to a sovereign who, it was said, had been chosen by God or the gods to rule. National states, because their legitimacy is built on representing a community with a shared identity, need a shared past. "Every nation needs a history," Yale University historian Edmund Morgan wrote in 1978. "Without the collective memory embodied in a history, a people would lose their collective identity in the same way an individual suffering from amnesia loses his personal identity." This collective memory, he said, "is apt to be faulty; it suppresses some events and reshapes others, and because it fades with the passage of time, it often needs refreshing."[1]

This task is much harder for a federation like the United States because it is made up of nations that have their own pasts. Most of them had their own state-building intellectuals and national mythologies, and some of them believed their history provided the real origin story of the young United States. As a result, Americans have frequently been battered by "history wars," bitter intellectual and political fights that, in the 1860s, contributed to a catastrophic military conflict. It's as if half a dozen countries were fighting over the nation's steering wheel, while half a dozen others were protesting from the back seat that they'd been forced into the car against their will.

The stakes are enormous. In the end, collective memory isn't about the past; it's about controlling a nation's future. Effective autocrats have always focused on controlling historical memory. To help consolidate his dictatorship, Vladimir Putin created a self-serving official version of Russian history and passed a series of draconian "memory laws" that allow his regime to imprison anyone who writes, speaks, or teaches forbidden facts, such as that Nazi Germany and the USSR allied to invade Poland together at the start of World War II.[2] Pol Pot's genocidal regime took this concept to its illogical extreme upon seizing power in Cambodia, declaring April 17, 1975, to be the first day of Year Zero and ordering the complete erasure of all knowledge of events preceding that date; 1.1 to 2.2 million Cambodians met a violent death in the four years of repression that followed, including many tens of thousands of intellectuals executed for their potential ability to preserve and someday retell the forbidden memories.[3]

The American Nations regional cultures have their received stories, and few of them stand up to careful scrutiny. In the past, some of them have used both the law and vigilante mob violence to ensure they were not challenged. Political leaders in some of the same regions are doing so again in an effort to suppress truths about the present. Understanding these narratives and what sort of future each endorses is vital to understanding the ongoing battles over what can be taught, celebrated, said, or acted upon in our pasts. It's the only way we can forge a workable American story, the subject of the last chapter of this book. It's *e pluribus unum*, with a healthy dose of humility.

These are *mythic* stories, first created by regional elites for the purpose of identity formation and adopted and revised as needed in the decades or centuries that have followed. None of these stories are necessarily true and all of them demand certain things be forgotten because they undermine or spoil the overarching story of peoplehood each seeks to propagate. In most cases, these stories were created by intellectuals from the region in question, individuals with their own biases and agendas, but whose story took hold and, rightly or wrongly, shaped the way the region's people thought of themselves and their place in the world.

In this chapter we're focusing on the large regions because, unlike the enclaves, they have the size, means, and predilection to try to shape or even dictate the content of our shared American historical memory. Let's start with the historical take that had a head start and dominated the early conversation about who we are and where we came from: the Yankee story.

THE PURITANS WHO FOUNDED **YANKEEDOM** had big ideas. They believed themselves a covenanted people, like the Old Testament's Hebrews, chosen by God to create a Calvinist utopia in the New England wilderness. On their departure from England in 1630, their leader, John Winthrop, said, "We shall be as a city upon a hill; the eyes of all people are upon us." Theirs was, as the Puritan divine Samuel Danforth put it in 1670, "an errand into the wilderness" to create a more Godly society here on Earth.

Whatever story the Yankees had come up with was bound to have had an outsize influence because in the late eighteenth, the nineteenth, and much of the twentieth centuries, their region had a massive cultural and logistical advantage over the others when it came to creating and promoting ideas. This was an unintended by-product of a core early Puritan theological belief, that people had to read the Bible themselves, which prompted them to deploy compulsory, taxpayer-financed public schools in every town and village from the beginning of colonization. This, in turn, begat what was probably the world's most literate population in the late seventeenth century, which in turn fostered the creation of publishing houses, newspaper presses, research collections, lending libraries, and colleges at a per capita density unmatched anywhere on the continent. (Only nineteenth-century New Netherland, which had emerged as the continent's center of book publishing, would come close.) For the first century and a half of the United States's existence, Yankeedom largely set and controlled the national "media conversation." Its culture produced highly effective thought leaders and communicators like George Bancroft, Henry David Thoreau, Theodore Parker, William Lloyd Garrison, Daniel Webster, and Susan B. Anthony and gave them the means of spreading their ideas. (Another beneficiary of this cultural and institutional heritage was Frederick Douglass, who was based in Yankeedom for most of his career and adopted much of its vision for the country.) Yankees—especially the Harvard- and Yale-educated elites—believed they spoke for all of America in saying we were a people on a divine mission to achieve the natural rights in the Declaration, setting an example for the world.

Yankeedom's Puritan founders not only believed God had chosen them to create a more perfect society but that they would be collectively punished or rewarded by Him based on their performance. "God may justly leave off a people and unchurch a nation," the Puritan divine Thomas Hooker, founder of Connecticut, warned in 1639. "God will [not] cast off his Elect eternally, but those that are only in outward covenant with him he may." These beliefs made for a culture that was constantly monitoring its own performance, where self-interest was wrapped up in the pursuit of ideals. Also buried deep in the Yankee psyche was the idea that the "New England errand" was of importance to the whole of humanity, that the world's people were tracking the new Israelites' progress. "Our American Republic exists not for herself alone," William Plumer, a Baptist preacher who'd served New Hampshire as governor and U.S. senator, told an Independence Day crowd in 1828. "She is a city set upon a hill that cannot be hid: a beacon kindled upon the mountain top to which the nations look for light and guidance . . . from every quarter of this benighted globe."[4]

It probably comes as no surprise that the Yankees were the first to offer a story to define the newly created United States, and that it so happened to also be *their* story. Starting in the 1820s, New England intellectuals dedicated themselves to promoting a historical narrative that established New England as the birthplace of America and the wellspring from which American culture, political ideals, and character sprang. Plymouth Rock, a large boulder dropped in Plymouth Harbor by retreating ice sheets 20,000 years ago, was proclaimed the birthplace of America by dint of the Pilgrims perhaps having used it to help unload the *Mayflower*. The Pilgrims and the notoriously intolerant Puritans were recast as freedom-loving republicans committed to spreading the ordered, deferential liberty of the New England town, with its strong institutions and equitable division of property. In the Virginia tidewater, they argued, Jamestown's settlers had been motivated by greed, been cursed with laziness, and collapsed into anarchy. New England was the cradle of American values.[5]

The battlefields at Lexington, Concord, and Bunker Hill were consecrated in solemn ceremonies and marked with grand monuments as the birthplaces of the Revolution. "It will be hallowed by the gratitude of mankind, as among the most precious and beneficent contests ever waged in behalf of human rights and human happiness," the historian William Tudor wrote in 1828 of the New Englanders at Bunker Hill. In these battles, the Yankees claimed, New Englanders won their independence and became the first Americans, an act of bravery that inspired the other colonies to join their project. "To the Puritans of New England," John Quincy Adams pronounced, "this continent owes its independence and its freedom."[6]

The historian-statesman George Bancroft, the son of a famous Massachusetts Unitarian preacher and graduate of Phillips Exeter and Harvard, took this project several steps further in the 1830s and 1840s, asserting that America was traveling on a historical path set forth by God, with New Englanders leading the way. We'll be returning to Bancroft again in chapter 10, which deals with the fight over our story of national purpose, as his mythmaking skills were so powerful and effective he was able to birth a civic national story for the United States that's still with us today. He was able to do this because of his unusual intellectual experiences as a very young man in the late 1810s. Nearsighted, bookish, and pinched, Bancroft had been such a promising student at Harvard that, upon graduating at age seventeen, the college's president sent him on an epic study-abroad trip to get his doctorate in the German Confederation shortly after the end of the Napoleonic Wars. There he studied under the very men who were developing the ideas of Germanic Romantic nationalism: Arnold Heeren, Georg Hegel, and the von Humboldts among them. He chummed around with the Marquis de Lafayette, Washington Irving, Lord Byron, and Goethe; backpacked from Paris to Rome; danced with princesses and Napoleon's niece; and returned home with his head churning with ideas about his country's place in the world. His vision—laid out in his epic ten-volume *History of the United States of America*—combined his Puritan ancestors' ideas about divine mission with his German mentors' notion that nations developed like organisms and from a plan history had laid out for them.

If you closely studied history, Bancroft argued, the direction of God's plan for his chosen people could be detected, like we might guess where an airplane overhead might be bound based on the contrails of an aircraft. The mission was to promote orderly freedom. The direction was forward, across the continent, an idea that prompted one of his fans, the journalist John L. O'Sullivan, to opine about America's "manifest destiny." Which raises a dangerous aspect of this Yankee vision of our history: the notion that the United States, being the object of God's special favor, does not operate under the same constraints as all the others. We're excepted from those limits, and thus "exceptional," and the things we do in the world are good simply by virtue of it being us who has done them.

But Bancroft had also placed the principles of the Declaration of Independence at the center of the Yankee mission, a pledge to honor the inherent equality of humans, to give them life and liberty and the ability to pursue their own happiness. America, Yankees came to argue by the middle of the nineteenth century, should be defined by its devotion to these principles and judged by how they fared. Americans, Yankees believed, had been charged with this world-historical task, and American history was rightly the story of the country's progress toward its completion.

Deep Southerners disagreed.

THE DEEP SOUTH and Tidewater had their intellectuals, too, but they were almost exclusively the privileged sons of the great aristocratic families that controlled those regions' political, economic, and social lives, men educated by private, live-in tutors and at elite boarding schools and colleges in Yankeedom, New Netherland, and Great Britain. This was because these regions had no public education to speak of and discouraged or even criminalized providing such to the people they'd enslaved, who composed a majority of the population in large swaths of their territory. Consequently, there were few readers in these regions and, thus, few lending libraries or book publishers or institutions of higher education. Particularly in the Deep South, where leaders' greed was untampered by any notion of aristocratic responsibility, newspapers and intellectual journals struggled to find enough paying subscribers to survive. When antebellum Southern intellectuals wanted to get their ideas out, they had to do so via New Netherland publishers. But they had ideas to get out, and the cultural and financial capital to help do so.

The Deep Southern slave lords' mythic story was based on precisely the opposite assumption as the Yankee one. The Declaration was wrong, they explicitly argued. Not only were humans not seen as equal, it was believed that most of those deemed to belong to the lower orders should be enslaved for the benefit of "civilization," which is best understood as a fancy word for the oligarch's interests. "Of what benefit would have been the discovery of Columbus if slavery had not been introduced to render the newly found countries profitable," asked the Charleston attorney Edward Brown in a proslavery essay written in 1826. "Slavery has ever been the step-ladder by which civilized countries have passed from barbarism to civilization. History, both ancient and modern, fully confirms this position."[7]

The bearers of this civilization were the aristocratic planters. In the 1820s, the Deep Southern and Tidewater gentry discovered *Waverley*, *Ivanhoe*, and the other novels of the English Romantic writer Sir Walter Scott. Scott's wildly popular books featured chivalric knights—brave in battle, noble and commanding at home. Like the southern plantation lords, Scott's characters cared about horsemanship, upholding their honor, and defending their homes, and they naturally ruled over the lesser orders. The lowland aristocrats didn't just love the books; they seized on them to create a mythic history for themselves. They decided they were descended from the Norman aristocrats who had invaded England in 1066, conquered the Anglo-Saxon commoners, and established the nobility that had led Britian to greatness. There was a kernel of truth in this story in regards to the Tidewater gentry, many of whom really were descended from high-born Cavaliers who had fought on the king's side in the English Civil War in the 1640s and, in defeat, fled to Tidewater to establish feudal estates. But regarding most of the Deep Southern oligarchs who became its greatest proponents, it was total bollocks: Most were the descendants of lowborn English and Irish sugar farmers who'd built their fortunes from nothing, working slaves to death in seventeenth-century Barbados. Plantation owners in both regions even started calling themselves "Southrons," a term in Sir Walter's novels that Scots characters used when referring to the English. "It was he that created rank and caste down there, and also reverence for rank and caste, and pride and pleasure in them," Mark Twain recalled in 1883. "Sir Walter had so large a hand in making Southern character, as it existed before the war, that he is in great measure responsible for the war."[8]

William Gilmore Simms, South Carolina author, editor, politician, and slave plantation owner, further developed these ideas in his role as the antebellum South's leading man of letters. Simms is largely forgotten today, but in the first half of the nineteenth century he was one of the United States's most successful novelists, compared favorably with Edgar Allan Poe and James Fenimore Cooper. His historical novels were set on the Deep Southern frontier, where well-bred lowland leaders forced civilization on barbarous inferiors, Black and white alike. Hierarchy brought order and from order came civilization, he argued in essays, speeches, and poems. "Pity it is, that the louzy and lounging lazzaroni [the underclass] of Italy cannot be made to labor in the fields under the whip of a severe task-master," he wrote in an 1853 essay. "They would then be a much freer—certainly a much nobler animal—than we can possibly esteem them now." Native Americans, he added, had "needed nothing but an Egyptian bondage of four hundred years to have been saved for the future."[9]

Simms was joined by his friend and neighbor, James Henry Hammond, South Carolina governor and U.S. senator, who argued in the antebellum period that slavery was the foundation of any "well-designed and durable Republican edifice" and should therefore be extended to poor whites as well. *De Bow's Review*, the Deep South's leading intellectual journal, saw the Civil War as a struggle to reverse the ill-conceived American Revolution, restoring "the natural reverence of the Cavalier for the authority of established forms over mere speculative ideas." The Confederate Vice President Alexander Stephens, explaining his new country's purpose, said the Declaration and U.S. Constitution had been constructed on the faulty premise of human equality. "Our new government is founded upon exactly the opposite idea; its foundations are laid, its corner-stone rests, upon the great truth that the negro is not equal to the white man; that slavery subordination to the superior race is his natural and normal condition," he proclaimed in his famous March 1861 speech. "This, our new government, is the first, in the history of the world, based upon this great physical, philosophical, and moral truth."[10]

This was the core story of the Deep South and one also embraced by Tidewater's leaders during the Civil War and Reconstruction. The Southern elite were chivalric civilizers, saving their region from barbarism through the subjugation and enslavement of inferior beings and building a fine and genteel society atop their corpses.

THE MIDLANDS'S MYTHIC STORY was the legacy of William Penn's Holy Experiment. Like the Early Puritans, Penn linked his colonial project with Biblical prophecy, in his case Daniel's interpretation of King Nebuchadnezzar's dream. Daniel said four kingdoms will rise and fall because of their flaws, but that God would then lay down the foundation of an enduring fifth kingdom. Penn believed that Babylon, Persia, Greece, and Rome had fallen, but that God had planted the fifth kingdom on the shores of Delaware Bay. He named the new colony's capital Philadelphia, the name of the prophesied city of God in the third chapter of the Book of Revelation, described there as "the New Jerusalem which comes down from my God out of heaven." Pennsylvania (which then included Delaware) and Penn's other Quaker colony, West Jersey (the southern and western parts of what's now New Jersey), were biblically inspired in their founder's minds. But for what purpose?[11]

Penn's colonies were to be refuges for the economically oppressed and a sanctuary of religious toleration. "Mine eye is to a blessed government and a virtuous, ingenious and industrious society," Penn wrote from London to a colleague as Pennsylvania was taking shape, "so that people may live well and have more time to serve the Lord then in this crowded land." The Quaker elite who controlled the colony in the colonial period had experienced persecution in England and took the then radical step of prohibiting an official, government-supported church in Pennsylvania, West Jersey, or what became Delaware. Because they believed humans were inherently good—possessed with an "inner light"—they welcomed people of many creeds and ethnicities to their utopian colonies, which quickly became among the most diverse places in the British colonies, as described in chapter 1.[12]

The most significant aspect of "the Midlands story" wasn't merely the tolerance of diversity; it was the total embrace of a pluralistic, multicultural social model that created the notion that the United States was a "nation of immigrants." Midlanders didn't just welcome immigrants; they encouraged them to maintain their own cultural practices, languages, and lifeways forever. People were to share a political identity as Americans but maintain their cultural distinctiveness. This became an obvious fact on the ground by the end of the seventeenth century, by which time the Midland settlement zone was a patchwork of distinct ethnoreligious communities: Amish, Mennonite, and Shaker villages; German catholic, Protestant Dutch, and Ashkenazi Jewish towns and urban neighborhoods; Swiss Calvinists, Scots-Irish Presbyterians, and English Quakers and Anglicans. And by the early twentieth century, Midlander and German-American intellectuals were touting this system as a positive role model for the United States at large.[13]

One of these intellectuals, the Prussian-born Jewish social philosopher Horace Kallen, coined the term "cultural pluralism" as an alternative to the aggressive "melting pot" assimilation model he'd witnessed as a student in Boston. The promises in the Declaration could be achieved only, he argued, if people were able to maintain their cultural identities through which their understanding of the pursuit of happiness was tied. The United States, he wrote in a widely read 1915 essay titled "Democracy Versus the Melting Pot," should be "a democracy of nationalities, cooperating voluntarily and autonomously in the enterprise of self-realization through the perfection of men according to their kind."

The common language of the commonwealth would be English, but each nationality would have for its emotional and involuntary life its own peculiar dialect or speech, its own individual and inevitable esthetic and intellectual forms. The political and economic life of the commonwealth is the single unit and serves as the foundation and background for the realization of the distinctive individuality of each nation that composes it. . . . As in an orchestra, every type of instrument has its specific timbre and tonality, founded in its substance and form; as every type has its appropriate theme and melody in the whole symphony, so in society each ethnic group is the natural instrument, its spirit and culture are its theme and melody, and the harmony and dissonances and discords of them all make the symphony of civilization.[14]

The Midlander myth envisioned America as a mosaic of peoples, a salad bowl, a federation of cultures, but this vision had its limits. The peoples and "races" it contemplated were European in origin. Slavery was controversial in this region—the Quakers inveighed against it—but in the eighteenth, nineteenth, and early twentieth centuries, people of African descent were rarely included in its multicultural tapestry. "'American civilization' may come to mean the perfection of cooperative harmonies of 'European civilization,'" Kallen had argued in his famous essay, which repeatedly embraced Germans, Jews, Poles, Frenchmen, and Scandinavians but never once mentioned African Americans at a time when there were more than a quarter million living in Pennsylvania alone.[15] The racial barrier remains to this day, but the broader model of cultural pluralism is still in operation, from the now seventy-five-year-old Puerto Rican communities embedded in Pennsylvania Dutch country to the Mexican and Central American enclaves scattered across rural Iowa and West-Central Kansas.[16]

Despite its shortcomings, the Midlands story has played a vital role in our battle over our nation's meaning and identity. It has been an important counterweight to efforts to define the United States as a British Protestant culture, and it has offered a template for cultural pluralism and civic identity that resonates powerfully in our globalized age.

THE MYTHIC TRADITION that came out of **New Netherland** was similar in many respects to the Midlands one, but with an important twist: an almost religious faith in the promise of upward mobility.

As mentioned in chapter 1, the seventeenth-century Dutch colony was at its core a commercial trading hub and, for a time, the wholly owned subsidiary of a global corporation. Tolerance and the freedom of inquiry and conscience were the signature traits of Golden Age Amsterdam and the namesake village its leaders spawned on the tip of Manhattan; under the rule of the Dutch West India Company, these values were adopted and adapted to maximize profits. The company was never able to convince enough people to trade lives in their prosperous, tolerant home country for the uncertain, uncomfortable, and isolated conditions of the Lower Hudson Valley, so they welcomed immigrants from other nations and nationalities. When the colony's antisemitic governor, Peter Stuyvesant, tried to expel Jewish refugees from Portuguese-conquered Dutch Brazil, his superiors overruled his actions, noting that profits were dependent on an increasing population. From a very early date, the colony relied on enslaved Africans—indeed, it's the Dutch who sold Tidewater Virginians their first slaves in 1619—but allowed them to negotiate all sorts of business deals with their masters, so long as the latter saw marginal benefit, leading to various kinds of what was called "half freedom." As the historian Joyce Goodfriend once aptly put it: "Expediency rather than devotion to principle dictated the tolerance of diversity in New Amsterdam."[17]

Nevertheless, the society that emerged in the eighteenth and nineteenth centuries had many parallels to that of the Midlands. It was pluralistic, with many people of many ethnicities, races, and religions living side by side with no group in either the majority or accepted as being the one in charge. When England seized control of the colony in 1664, the majority of its inhabitants weren't ethnic Dutch—there were Africans, French Huguenots, Sephardic Jews, English Puritans, Belgian Catholics, and at least one Muslim farmer—but the Dutch ethos of tolerance was well entrenched. Unlike the Quaker experiment, Dutch tolerance was based not on morality but rather practicality: intolerance, ethnic cleansing, and religious persecution were seen as simply being bad for business.

If the Midlands offered refuge and cultural freedom, the New Netherland cultural zone became the place where one tried to "make it." Russell Shorto, the writer who has done the most to place New Netherland's story back in the national consciousness, puts it this way: "The first Manhattanites didn't arrive with lofty ideals. They came—whether as farmer, tanner, prostitute, wheelwright, barmaid, brewer or trader—because there was a hope for a better life."[18] In the Dutch colonial period, the largest number of settlers—Dutch or not—arrived via the Netherlands, which at the time was the wealthiest country in the world, its multinational trading corporations linking its colonies and trading posts in the East and West Indies, Africa, and the Americas. Its capital, Amsterdam, was experiencing explosive economic and population growth and a staggering degree of social mobility. Hundreds of thousands of impoverished immigrants found stable incomes as soldiers, sailors, and factory workers. Humble merchants rose to the heights of national power in a single generation. "The prevailing mindset: economically speaking, the sky was the limit," historian Benjamin Roberts writes of this era. "Everybody could become rich and move up the social ladder." These were the assumptions emigrants brought with them to New Amsterdam, with ramifications that reverberate to this day.[19]

Thus, it's no accident that New York City became the primary port of entry for nineteenth- and early twentieth-century immigrants and a beacon to fortune and adventure seekers from across the continent. It's freewheeling, materialistic, porous culture offered unparalleled opportunities for success and failure. After the Civil War, champions of laissez-faire economics started gleefully misapplying Charles Darwin's observations about the evolution of species to human society, shorthanded as the "survival of the fittest," and a mythos emerged out of New York City that was soon applied to the country at large.

Three New Yorkers provided its central tropes. The novelist Horatio Alger was perhaps the most influential. Born in Massachusetts, Alger moved to New York in 1866 after losing his posting as the pastor of the First Unitarian Parish Church for "the abominable and revolting crime of gross familiarity with boys." At the time, Gotham was home to tens of thousands of street urchins, many of them Civil War orphans or children of foreign immigrants whose families had collapsed under the pressures of alcohol, opium, and poverty. Alger was drawn to them, studying their hustles, personalities, speechways, and survival strategies. He raised money for shelters and the Children's Aid Society and took some boys in to live with him. And he wrote stories about them, works of young adult fiction in which plucky, hardworking street children of frugal and honest character have their merits recognized and mentored by benevolent members of the upper classes.[20]

Alger's *Ragged Dick: Or, Street Life in New York* (1867) set the template. Dick, one of tens of thousands of orphaned children surviving in the rough streets of Manhattan in the aftermath of the Civil War, catches the eye of the narrator through his pluck, good looks, and refusal to cheat, lie, or steal. As he passes a series of moral tests, Dick's benefactors give him small rewards that allow him to climb the next rungs of the city's social ladder, eventually becoming a clerk in a counting house and rebranding himself as "Richard Hunter, Esq." The book was a commercial success, prompting Alger to write a whole Ragged Dick series and then, with diminishing returns, dozens more books rehashing the same themes. But it wasn't until the early twentieth century that Alger's books became a phenomenon, selling millions of copies and making the phrase

"Horatio Alger story" a nationwide shorthand for by-your-bootstraps upward mobility. It always played best, however, in the metropolitan region in which it was born, New Netherland.

Another New Yorker, the poet Emma Lazarus, channeled her city's multicultural, immigrant character to write a sonnet to raise money for the construction of a pedestal for the Statue of Liberty to rest on. Lazarus, a descendent of the Portuguese Jewish refugees Stuyvesant had tried to deport in 1655, was an activist for Jews trying to escape murderous pogroms in Imperial Russia and was moved to write the verses for arriving immigrants. "'Keep, ancient lands, your storied pomp!,' cries she with silent lips," "The New Colossus" read:

> Give me your tired, your poor,
> Your huddled masses yearning to breathe free,
> The wretched refuse of your teeming shore.
> Send these, the homeless, tempest-tost to me,
> I lift my lamp beside the golden door!

The sonnet was written in 1883, but it wasn't included in the opening ceremonies for the statue on Liberty Island held three years later. After Lazarus's death, her friend Georgina Schuyler—great-granddaughter of Alexander Hamilton and the New Netherland Dutch heiress Eliza Schuyler—successfully lobbied to have the famous stanzas added to the pedestal, where they've been since 1903. In our national mythology, they are the most powerful evocation of the idea that we're a refuge and place of opportunity for those oppressed elsewhere—an idea with its footings in the culture of the Golden Age Dutch Republic and its fledgling colony at the mouth of the Hudson.

These New Netherlander ideas—that America is a land of opportunity, upward mobility, and ethnocultural diversity—infected the national discourse because New Amsterdam grew to be the continent's most important city, the center of publishing and media, and the main port of entry for immigrants. But it remained very much at odds with the historical narratives of some of the country's other regional cultures.

FOR MUCH OF THE EIGHTEENTH and nineteenth centuries, **Greater Appalachia** had few means of asserting its take on regional and national history. An oral culture with low literacy rates and few libraries, colleges, universities, publishing houses, and other units of cultural production, a "national story" didn't emerge from this massive region until the end of the nineteenth century. But it's had an enormous and growing influence on the history wars ever since.

Greater Appalachia's mythic narrative was crafted by a handful of intellectuals from or based in the region at the turn of the twentieth century, a time when the country's white Protestant establishment was fearful and angry about the massive wave of non-Protestant immigrants that were arriving by the millions from southern and eastern Europe, Mexico, and Asia. Many Americans were documenting and celebrating their "old stock" status as "Anglo-Saxons," the people whose alleged genius, values, and character formed the template of the American "race." They were founding new genealogical societies like the Mayflower Society, the Daughters of the American Revolution, Colonial Dames, and Daughters of the Confederacy, all aiming to buttress the influence of this imagined British cultural wellspring.

Amid this anxious white Protestant quest for its taproots, the Appalachian intellectuals offered their region as a cultural treasure trove. The hills and mountain valleys that formed its core—isolated, inaccessible, and untouched—had captured tens of thousands of eighteenth-century Protestant settlers from the British Isles and sealed them in amber. Their descendants, now numbering in the millions, lived much as their pioneering great-great-great-grandparents had. For a century and a half they slept unnoticed, Rip Van Winkle–like, until the Civil War mobilizations awoke them to fight for the liberties of a freeborn people, unsullied by slaveholding, uncompromising in their British entitlement to liberty.

"Conceive of a shipload of emigrants cast away on some unknown island, far from the regular track of vessels, and left there for five or six generations, unaided and untroubled by the growth of civilization," Horace Kephart, a Pennsylvania-born research librarian who moved to North Carolina's Great Smokies, wrote in his influential 1913 book on the region, *Our Southern Highlanders*. "Among the descendants of such a company we would expect to find customs and ideas unaltered from the time of their forefathers. And that is just what we do find today among our castaways in the sea of the mountains. . . . The mountain folk still live in the eighteenth century . . . still thinking essentially the same thoughts, still living in much the same fashion, as did their ancestors in the days of Daniel Boone."[21]

In 1855, Yankee abolitionists founded Berea College in the Kentucky town of the same name, tasking it with uplifting the region and its people, Black and white. William Goodell Frost, Berea's president from 1893 to 1920, wrote one of the most famous articles about Appalachia for *The Atlantic Monthly*, emphasizing its people's "Saxon" heritage and "pioneer" lifestyle. "It is a longer journey from northern Ohio to eastern Kentucky than from America to Europe, for one day's ride brings us into the eighteenth century," Frost explained in this 1899 essay. The people there were still cutting wood with whipsaws, grinding grain with hand-mills, making clothes with spinning wheels and hand looms, and speaking with the "startling survivals of Saxon speech . . . a vocabulary of Chaucer's words."[22]

For a predominantly northern audience, the Appalachian mythmakers emphasized the Borderlanders' supposedly freedom-loving nature, noting the region's opposition to the creation of the Confederacy, which several states refused to join and which triggered Unionist insurrections in the Appalachian sections of states that did. "These people were driven here by persecution at home," Protestant missionary Mrs. S. M. Davis said of the region's Scots-Irish colonizers in 1895. "But they would have no complicity with slavery and hence the slaveocracy would have nothing to do with them and consequently they were crowded into the mountains, which became their fastnesses." She told fellow missionaries they might be "a reserve force that God will bring out of these mountains, saved by Christ, for the coming crisis of conflict, a stalwart band to stand with us in defense of Protestantism!" Frost, with a secular lens, emphasized the fact that unlike many urban Protestants, these people of "native born" stock had extremely large families, the national value of which was "sufficiently evident."[23]

"In these isolated communities . . . we find the purest Anglo-Saxon stock in all the United States," Ellen Churchill Semple, Louisville native and president of the Association of American Geographers, wrote in 1901. "They are the direct descendants of the early Virginia and North Carolina immigrants, and bear about them in their speech and ideas the marks of their ancestry as plainly as if they had disembarked from their eighteenth-century vessel but yesterday. . . . The stock has been kept free from the tide of foreign immigrants which has been pouring in recent years into the States."[24]

During the twentieth century, Appalachia was cast as being a preserve of untainted "American Christian" values, as well. After the American Revolution, evangelical denominations spread rapidly in this previously Presbyterian-dominated region, triggering massive, emotional outdoor Christian revivals. Emphasizing personal rebirth and each person's direct contact with God—and spurning calls to remake the existing world—regional variants of Baptism and Methodism opposed modernism, liberal theology, and scientific discoveries like evolution, the age of dinosaur fossils, and the origins of competing versions of scripture that made it clear that not every passage of the Bible could be literally true in every detail. The region became synonymous with "fundamentalism," an insistence on the total inerrancy and authority of the Bible that took its name from a series of pamphlets—"The Fundamentals," edited by pastor A. C. Dixon of Shelby, North Carolina, brother of white supremacist Thomas Dixon Jr., a coproducer of *The Birth of a Nation*. Appalachia was where the infamous 1925 Scopes Trial took place, in which a Tennessee high school biology teacher was found guilty of teaching evolution. The prosecuting attorney was William Jennings Bryan, the Scots-Irish presidential candidate from the Appalachian Egypt District of Illinois. It was the base of fundamentalist institutions, from Appalachian Indiana-born William Bell Riley's World Christian Fundamentals Association in the 1910s, to the segregation-minded Bob Jones University founded in the Appalachian section of South Carolina in 1927, to Jerry Falwell's Liberty University and Moral Majority in the 1970s and '80s.

The Appalachian Myth holds that there was a genuine, unadulterated American ethnicity that practiced a pure form of Protestant Christianity and preserved and defended American moral and political traditions from unsavory aliens and corrupted cosmopolitans. It's the foundation of the Christian Nationalist's argument that "real Americans" have to rise up and save the country from newcomers who have stolen it. "I hope to see the day when as in the early days of our country there were no public schools," Falwell once said, redacting the Yankee cultural model from historical memory in favor of the Appalachian colonial world. "The churches will have taken them over again and Christians will be running them. . . . We must never allow our children to forget we are a Christian nation. We must take back what is rightfully ours."[25] White Protestant supremacy and Christian nationalism have ample adherents outside this region, but this is where their historical narrative comes from.

AROUND THE SAME TIME AMERICANS were discovering the forgotten Appalachian frontier, another set of mythmakers were constructing a national story out of the experience of the **Far West**.

By the 1890s it was clear the "frontier" was coming to a close. For three centuries, the Euro-American colonial project had pushed its line of settlement across the continent, seizing Indigenous lands and adding them to "western civilization." Now it was over. The West was won and Americans wondered what they were to do now. In 1883, Buffalo Bill Cody, a retired Pony Express rider and celebrated army scout, created a circus-like theatrical show that toured the country, spreading a mythic version of the West that presented the settlers and U.S. army as noble, peaceable civilization-bringers weathering senseless attacks by inexplicably hostile Indians. The show's enormous cast included Sitting Bull and numerous other Indians who had actually fought Colonel Custer at the Battle of Little Big Horn; white and Latino men who had worked as cowboys or army scouts; the celebrated markswoman Annie Oakley; and Cody himself, who brought to life an imagined version of the Western frontier just as the real one vanished. The show toured across the United States and did eight stints in Europe, including a performance for Queen Victoria and other European royalty in London, a show in Verona's Roman amphitheater, and others as far east as Galicia in today's Poland. By the turn of the century, Cody was arguably the most famous American on Earth and his productions had shaped how Americans saw the Far West and themselves.[26]

But it was an academic who would perfect the Far Western myth and try to make it serve for the United States as a whole.

Frederick Jackson Turner was born in Portage, Wisconsin, in November 1861 when it was still very much a frontier settlement. He played in the ruins of an old wooden fort, worked in his father's newspaper office, attended the local high school, and then studied history at the nascent University of Wisconsin. There, his mentor, the Massachusetts Yankee William Francis Allen, introduced him to the conflicting social science currents of the day, including the Bancroftian Yankee thesis of Americans as a chosen people on a mission and the new Darwinian-inspired notion that societies, like organisms, adapted themselves to the environments they encountered. Scientific laws, not divine will, he had advised young Turner, guided the course of nations.[27]

As a young academic, Turner was invited to present a paper on the influence of "the West" on the direction of the nation at the 1893 Chicago World's Fair. The resulting essay, "The Significance of the Frontier in American History," argued that the West, not New England or the Chesapeake Country, was the real place of America's birth. He told an audience containing many who had lived through the Civil War that the slavery question itself, when "right viewed," became but "an incident" in the nation's story. The real action had happened when westward-bound settlers poured over the Appalachian Mountains and into the "frontier" of the vast Mississippi River watershed. There the environment they encountered forced them to finally leave the fingerprints of the Old World behind, to embrace self-reliance and independence, qualities Turner argued fostered democracy, democratic constitutional arrangements, and the vigorous local civics he had grown up with in Portage.

The "West," he thought, was an Eden that had forced Americans to adapt to primitive conditions, a return to innocence and virtue that shaped the U.S. character. As they traveled westward, Turner imagined, settlers had been taken "from the railroad car," stripped of "the garments of civilization," and found themselves "in the birch bark canoe" and "the hunting shirt and the moccasin." They were soon "planting Indian corn and plowing with a sharp stick" and shouting war cries. Faced with Native American resistance—Turner never much considered their part in the story or what their extirpation might say about the American character—the settlers looked to the U.S. government for protection, fostering loyalty to the nation, and not to their half-forgotten state of origin.

His thesis statement would be quoted in a thousand future textbooks and academic papers: "The existence of an area of free land, its continuous recession, and the advance of American settlement westward explain American development." Much as the varying conditions on the Galápagos Islands had shaped the evolution of the subspecies of finches Charles Darwin had observed there, the allegedly uniform conditions of the western frontier had shaped diverse Americans into one democracy-loving people.

His idea spread like wildfire, because he'd presented it when an industrializing, urbanizing, continent-spanning, immigrant-attracting Goliath of a country needed a new origin story that could explain how it had gotten where it was and where it might be going. Americans, having weathered the Civil War and its untidy aftermath, were reassured that their nation's destiny was to be the torch bearer of freedom in the world, and Turner had provided a rationale that relied on the latest scientific ideas—Darwinism—rather than the fuzzy metaphysics of Puritan theology. Academics, journalists, teachers, and textbook writers embraced it and propelled it into the popular psyche, where it remains. Within a few years, Turner had realized the data contradicted his theory, and pivoted his focus to understanding the persistence of regional differences. But like a band that can't escape the shadow of an early hit song, Turner couldn't get Americans interested in his new argument, which he was still trying to put into book form upon his death in 1932.

But the frontier thesis lived on. The myth of American exceptionalism, innocence, and unity proved far more appealing than Turner's less-than-reassuring alternative. It would inform and inspire the history textbooks the Silent Generation and Baby Boomers grew up with and, together with Buffalo Bill's more combat-oriented view of the Far West, the "cowboy and Indian" movies and television shows of the second half of the twentieth century. Americans were a tough, individualistic people engaged in battles pitting civilization against nature and barbarism, and the Far West had made them so.

EL NORTE'S MYTHIC HISTORY was crafted much later, from the 1960s onward. The region's Spanish colonial backstory had been suppressed for generations, as if nothing important had occurred prior to America's mid-nineteenth-century annexations. As more and more "Anglo" people colonized the region in the 1880s, they found they didn't feel like Midlanders or Yankees, Deep Southerners, or Appalachians and started looking for a myth to call their own. What they settled on was a nostalgic and picturesque imagining of what life in Spanish America was like: an Edenic world of gracious *rancheros*, captivating *señoritas*, and devoted *padres* who lovingly worked to civilize their Indigenous wards within elegant mission complexes. The master mythmaker was Los Angeles–based journalist and librarian Charles Fletcher Lummis, who fought to preserve the then decaying mission complexes and urged newcomers to investigate "the glamour made by histories you did not know, by people whose language you can't understand." In his books, magazine articles, and speeches, Lummis painted a picture of a pre-annexation utopia in the El Norte sections of California, Arizona, and New Mexico, one he wrongly thought would influence the whole of the United States. "The missions of California are already making as deep an impression on American life as did the Puritans and the impression is deepening faster and will last longer," he wrote in 1920, five years after being knighted by the Spanish King Alfonso XIII, who adored his work. "It is more in tune with our day, for it is gentler, more human, more tolerant, more unselfish."[28]

Powered by real estate developers, novelists, and artists, the Spanish fantasy dominated popular conceptions of the region, but it largely omitted the region's residents who were actually descended from the Spanish colonizers. Rather than being revered, ethnic Mexicans were subjected to a caste system that operated with varying degrees of intensity throughout the region, and forced them into designated neighborhoods and rural *colonias*. "They seemed to gradually disappear from the landscape," University of California San Diego historian David Gutiérrez noted, "thereby fulfilling the prophesies of those proponents of Manifest Destiny who had predicted the West's Indigenous peoples would 'recede' or 'fade away' before the advance of American civilization."[29] But in the 1960s and 1970s,

Norteño activists challenged this narrative, led by militant Chicanos who emphasized the Indigenous (rather than the Spanish) side of their ancestry. They agreed the region was a place apart, but instead of looking to Iberia (*Hispania* in Latin) for the source of its historical origins, they looked to Aztec folklore.

Aztec sources encountered by the Spanish conquistadors spoke of their people having migrated to Central Mexico centuries earlier from a homeland somewhere to the north called Aztlán. Chicano activists said Aztlán was located in the southwestern United States, which made El Norte (and much of the Far West and the Left Coast) their ancestral homeland, predating Spanish and American colonization alike. At its height, the Chicano movement was calling for national independence, seeking to create a new nation where their people could be reunited and regenerated after the terrible invasions. "We are a Bronze People with a Bronze culture," their 1969 manifesto, *El Plan Espiritual de Aztlán*, declared. "We are a Nation, We are a Union of free pueblos. We are Aztlán."[30] Today, statehood is a fringe position, but the idea that El Norte is a place apart, where newcomers ought to adapt to Hispanic or Chicano or Tejano culture, not the other way around, is a powerful force in the fight over history and meaning in this part of the continent.

THE OTHER REGIONS have their stories, but they're no longer significant to the national history debate. The **New France** enclave's is that of a people cleansed from Acadia by British forces, relegated to the swamps at the mouth of the Mississippi, and discriminated against by the Deep Southern Protestant establishment that arrived after the U.S. annexation. The **Left Coast**'s was an origin myth tied to ancestor worship of early pioneers and settlers that was then subsumed by Yankee-born elites into the Yankee "mission" story, with the Left Coast as a Pacific outpost of a utopian American mission. As we've seen, **Tidewater**'s story was subsumed into that of the Deep South in the run-up to the Civil War, then lost in recent decades as that regional culture has disaggregated under pressure from the expanding "federal zones" around DC and Hampton Roads. The people of **First Nation** and **Greater Polynesia** have their origin stories, but for generations they were ignored or marginalized by Alaska and Hawaii's state governments, and barely known by Americans living in other states.

THOSE ARE THE AMERICAN NATIONS' mythic narratives, key to understanding regional self-conceptions. They also explain our past and present history wars.

The most explosive struggle for collective memory comes out of the Confederacy's military defeat, which Deep Southern and Tidewater political, religious, and intellectual leaders promptly set about spinning into a moral and cultural victory. According to their "Lost Cause" myth, the South hadn't seceded to protect slavery but rather to uphold noble principles about the rights of individual states (to allow humans to own other humans). Slavery, it argued, was actually a good thing, as masters and slaves loved one another and the latter were happy with their lot in life, contrary to the "lies" of the Yankees. In fact, Southern society had been the perfect model of Christian goodness, and the Confederate army had been led and manned by Christian knights gallantly martyred for man's sins. "Jesus was in our camps with wonderful power," former Confederate Army chaplain John William Jones wrote after the war. "No army in all history—not even Cromwell's 'Roundheads'—had in it as much real, evangelical religion and devout piety."[31]

According to the Lost Cause myth, the greatest outrage came after the war, when a Yankee-dominated occupation forced the Deep South, Tidewater, and Confederate parts of Greater Appalachia to grant political, economic, and educational rights to African Americans. These initiatives were part of what historians call Reconstruction, which was an effort to reconstruct the occupied South along Yankee-Midlander lines, including limited acceptance of the Declaration's tenets of human equality. In states and districts with Black majorities, African Americans were elected to mayorships, the state legislatures, and to both the U.S. House and Senate, while their children enrolled at previously segregated universities and colleges. Many whites in the Deep South, Tidewater, and Greater Appalachia hated all of this and organized violent terrorist campaigns to kill, torture, and intimidate anyone who supported Reconstruction's aims. Members of the Ku Klux Klan and other terrorist groups burned people alive and laid entire neighborhoods to waste, sometimes killing hundreds of people in a single day, and often with the active participation of local officials and law enforcement. But in the Lost Cause version of the story, the KKK were painted as heroes, nobly fighting "savage" Blacks and tyrannical Unionists to protect the purity of white women, the rightful rule of the noble plantation families, and a system that kept "inferior" races subjugated.

After the North gave up on Reconstruction in 1877, southern officials, educators, and religious leaders took decisive action to ensure that the Lost Cause story was the only version of history white Southerners ever heard about. "The world must be made to know that Confederate soldiers are not ashamed of the great struggle they made for constitutional liberty," General Jubal A. Early told his fellow Confederate veterans in 1870, "and regret nothing, in that respect, except that they failed to accomplish their great purpose." They set up institutions devoted to propagating the myth: the United Confederate Veterans, the Southern Historical Society, the Daughters of the Confederacy, the University of the South, and Washington and Lee College. They wrote novels celebrating a "moonlight and Magnolias" vision of life on a slave plantation and eventually wildly popular plays and movies celebrating the KKK's terrorism, like the evangelical preacher Thomas Dixon Jr.'s *The Clansman*, the basis of the film that created both Hollywood and the Second KKK, *The Birth of a Nation*. ("The former enemies of the north and south are united again in common defense of their Aryan birthright," the 1915 film concludes.[32])

Most of all, however, the history warriors focused on textbooks. Every state controlled by Greater Appalachia, the Deep South, and Tidewater centralized the approval of textbooks at the state level and carefully screened the history their students received. At the turn of the century, the Daughters of the Confederacy—led by their "historian general," Mildred Lewis Rutherford of Athens, Georgia—became the enforcers of Lost Cause compliance. "We are absolutely powerless if we permit ourselves to . . . allow Northern publishing houses to place books unfair to us in our schools," Rutherford proclaimed in 1915.[33] They were outraged at references to Lincoln or the Emancipation Proclamation being good or slavery or the rebellion bad and forced textbook publishers to apologize and create special "southern" editions. Most important, they started creating their own.[34]

The resulting schoolbooks cast Lincoln as a tyrant, the North as aggressors, and the South as noble defenders of constitutional norms. *New School History of the United States*, published in Richmond in 1900 and written by Susan Pendleton Lee, wife and daughter of slaveholding Confederate generals, was typical of the genre and one of the most popular. "The kindest relations existed between the slaves and their owners," Lee's text told generations of schoolchildren:

> A cruel and neglectful master or mistress was rarely found. The sense of responsibility pressed heavily on the slave-owners, and they generally did the best they could for the physical and religious welfare of their slaves. The bondage in which the negroes were held was not thought a wrong to them, because they were better off than any other menial class in the world.[35]

Reconstruction, Lee wrote, caused much more suffering in the South than the war itself. "The enormous negro majorities were the principal cause of the misrule, and dishonesty prevailing throughout the Southern

States, and the Ku Klux devoted itself to keeping the negroes from voting," her textbook stated approvingly. "Sometimes negroes and Northern whites, who stirred up others to deeds of violence against the harassed and exasperated Southerners, received severe whippings." The Klan had been created "to protect white women and defenceless families" and was made up of "high-spirited, courageous people . . . the best men in the south."[36] Also popular was Woodrow Wilson's *A History of the American People* (1902), which depicted freed slaves as "dupes," Chinese immigrants as "evil spirits," and the KKK as a group created "for the mere pleasure of association." Wilson, the son of the Confederate Presbyterian Church's leading white supremacist thinker, certainly knew the violent truth about the Klan, having grown up in wartime Georgia and the capital city of Reconstruction-era South Carolina.[37]

Textbooks published in Yankeedom, New Netherland, and the Midlands were eradicated from Deep Southern and Tidewater schools in the opening decades of the twentieth century. Particularly hated was the Massachusetts-born Columbia University professor David Saville Muzzey's *An American History*, a book first published in Boston in 1911 that became the required history text of the majority of American high school students from the mid-1910s to the early 1960s. Though Muzzey accepted the neo-Confederate view of Reconstruction—the project had foolishly tried to "set the ignorant, superstitious, gullible slave in power over his former master"—he also said Lincoln was a hero and accurately described slavery as both evil and the reason for the Confederacy's secession. This put the text—a national bestseller—in the crosshairs of Rutherford's Daughters of the Confederacy and allied groups. "The leaders of the confederacy are put in a certain light of disrespect," one letter writer complained to the *Charlotte Observer* in 1921, adding that if the book continued to be used in North Carolina schools, people would "cease to be true southerners nor true Americans."[38] President John Tyler's son Lyon appeared before the 1932 meeting of the Sons of Confederate Veterans to denounce Muzzey's text for placing Lincoln "on a pedestal higher than Robert E. Lee" and condemned the Virginia Board of Education for not having banned it from classrooms.[39]

As noted earlier, Greater Appalachia fought on the U.S. side in the Civil War, but it did so to protect the union and to spite lowland slave plantation lords, not to fight for Black freedom. Lincoln's 1862 Emancipation Proclamation and 1863 Gettysburg Address pivoted federal war aims from preserving the federation to extending the Declaration's promises to Black men, creating shockwaves not only in the Confederate-controlled parts of the region, but in Kentucky, West Virginia, and Appalachian parts of Missouri. Kentucky's congressional delegation fought against the Thirteenth Amendment, which ended slavery, and the Fifteenth Amendment, which, in 1870, extended voting and political rights to people of color. The KKK and other paramilitaries beat and murdered Black people who attempted to cast ballots, from Missouri's Little Dixie to Asheville, North Carolina, where a white mob attacked Black people attempting to register to vote in 1868. Throughout Greater Appalachia, white Unionists joined their former enemies in an effort to defend white privilege, restoring rebel political rights, raising statues to Confederate generals, and embracing the Lost Cause narrative. One of that narrative's twentieth-century champions, the western North Carolina–born historian E. Merton Coulter, once remarked that Kentucky was the only state to secede after Appomattox, but this was symbolically true of the Appalachian sections of many states.[40]

So successful was the neo-Confederate campaign that the Lost Cause narrative remained embedded in Tidewater, Deep Southern, and Greater Appalachian textbooks right into the 1980s. "Life among the Negroes of Virginia in slavery times was generally happy," South Carolina–born historian Francis Butler Simkins and his colleagues told seventh graders in a textbook commissioned by the state of Virginia in 1950 and used into the 1970s. "The Negroes went about in a cheerful manner making a living for themselves and for those for whom they worked [and] . . . remained loyal to their white mistresses even after President Lincoln promised in his Emancipation Proclamation that the slaves would be freed."[41] In 1975, Mississippi rejected a secondary textbook that accurately described slavery, lynchings, and the perspectives of Black residents in favor of the book the state had been using that reaffirmed all the Lost Cause's tropes, from the happy slave to the heroic Klansmen.

The Lost Cause texts started being challenged only during the Civil Rights era and they persisted in public school curricula for a decade or more. In Mississippi, the more accurate textbook mentioned above became permitted in schools only in 1980 as the result of a lawsuit in federal court. The text's authors proved it had been rejected in an effort to continue the suppression of any discussion of racial injustices in the Magnolia State in violation of their First and Fourteenth Amendment rights.[42] Other states liberalized their schoolbook criteria only under the public and legal pressure of congressional and Justice Department investigations in the 1960s and 1970s.

TODAY'S HISTORY WARS ARE, at their core, a reprise of this struggle between regional narratives. On one side, there's a story of America as a country engaged in a perpetual struggle to achieve the universal natural rights propositioned in the Declaration, not always succeeding, but learning from its mistakes. On the other, there is an assertion that the American founding was sacred and Christian and that racism, intolerance, and institutionalized discrimination were never serious problems and, in any case, no longer exist today. The first of these stories, predominant in the discourse of states controlled by Yankeedom, New Netherland, the Left Coast, Greater Polynesia, and (contemporary) Tidewater, implies America has work to do to achieve its ideals; the second story, dominant in Deep South– and Greater Appalachia–controlled states, holds that we may have stood closer to our ideals in the Early Republic, implying that efforts to further racial, gender, sexual, or religious equality are unnecessary and undesirable.

After the election of Barack Obama, the country's first Black president, Deep Southern and Greater Appalachian states became history battlegrounds. Texas's schoolbook commission in 2012 revised standards for texts and curricula to downplay the importance of the civil rights movement, the violence of the KKK, and the fact that Washington, Jefferson, Madison, and many other Founding Fathers were slaveholders; the transatlantic slave trade was to be renamed the "Atlantic triangular trade"; the Founders' argument for the separation of church and state was deemphasized; and references to the role of "states' rights" in bringing on the Civil War were brought back from exile. Tea Party groups lobbied to implement similar changes in Georgia and Tennessee.

The 2016 election of Donald Trump, who called neo-Nazis "fine people" and denounced the renaming of schools and military bases dedicated to Confederate or KKK leaders, emboldened Lost Cause–style activists. Between 2019 and 2021, every state controlled by the Deep South or Greater Appalachia introduced legislation to curtail the discussion and teaching of racism, not only in primary and secondary schools but in public colleges and universities, as well. The laws typically banned "divisive concepts" and material that might make a student "feel discomfort, guilt, anguish, or any other form of psychological distress on account of that individual's race or sex," language modeled on President Donald Trump's September 2020 executive order restricting what can be taught to soldiers and in training programs for government contractors and federal employees. Such measures—which make it impossible to effectively teach about slavery, the Civil War, Reconstruction, Jim Crow, or the Civil Rights Movement—became law in South Carolina, Texas, Tennessee, and Oklahoma, as well as Idaho in the Far West and Arizona, for which we will have more to say shortly. (North Dakota and New Hampshire instituted bans on "critical race theory," an academic approach to institutional racism that isn't taught at the primary or secondary level, as did local school districts in Kentucky, Georgia, and the Deep Southern portion of North Carolina.) By contrast, Maine, Connecticut, Minnesota, New Jersey, and Washington State all passed laws requiring additional culturally inclusive history courses during this same period.[43]

In 2021, Glenn Youngkin successfully campaigned to be Virginia's governor on a promise to crush discussion of racism in public schools, winning more than 70 percent of the Greater Appalachian and 89 percent of the white evangelical vote; his first act in office was to issue executive orders to prohibit "divisive concepts, including critical race theory" in classrooms. After taking office in 2019, Florida's governor, Ron DeSantis, signed laws banning public school and university teachers from "distorting" historical events and teaching "identity politics" or anything "based on theories that systemic racism, sexism and privilege are inherent in the institutions of the United States." This made it difficult for teachers to explain the existence of slavery and segregation, or early Supreme Court rulings that said only white people could become citizens. The core law was so extreme a federal judge blocked its implementation because "the First Amendment does not permit the State of Florida to muzzle its university professors, impose its own orthodoxy of viewpoints, and cast us all into the dark." Another Florida law barred institutions from "shielding" students from unwelcome or offensive ideas, which the university faculty union took to be intended to prevent curbing of racist or hate speech on campus while disallowing counterarguments.[44]

In this era, North Carolina lieutenant governor Mark Robinson asked parents to report "biased" lessons in their children's classrooms and Oklahoma banned any lessons that caused anyone to "feel discomfort, guilt or anguish" on account of their sex or race, which theoretically made it illegal to teach about the 1921 Tulsa Race Riot on its 100th anniversary. (One Oklahoma teacher expected they would have to stop sharing interviews with ex-slaves recorded during the Great Depression by the Federal Writers Project because students often cried when they heard them.) A Tennessee law, passed in 2021, would cut off funding to districts that taught about "white privilege," which arguably would prevent students from learning about official racism in twentieth-century home mortgage lending or police brutality against minorities in the twenty-first.[45]

"The clear goal of these efforts is to suppress teaching and learning about the role of racism in the history of the United States," a joint statement from the American Association of University Professors, the American Historical Association, the Association of American Colleges & Universities, and the anti-censorship group PEN America noted. "Educators owe students a clear-eyed, nuanced, and frank delivery of history so that they can learn, grow and confront the issues of the day, not hew to some state-ordered ideology."[46]

It was not clear, in the mid-2020s, which approach would carry the day in these regions.

AMID THIS DISCORD, libertarian-minded intellectuals and pro-business fiscal conservatives have poured energy and resources into promoting New Netherland's "American Dream" myth. It's attractive because it suggests that our socioeconomic system is fundamentally just. If honesty and "hard work" are what bring people success, material well-being, and happiness, then prosperity ultimately boils down to individual character. The rich are rich because they worked hard and followed the rules; the poor are poor because they didn't. In 2023, as the United States emerged from the pandemic and the various emergency aid programs of that era expired, the American Enterprise Institute founded an American Dream Initiative. "Work is the key to achieving the American dream," the group's president, Robert Doar, explained at its launch. "If you work hard and play by the rules, you can secure a better life for yourself and your children." Michael Milken, the "junk bond king" who served prison time for securities fraud and was pardoned by President Trump, has spent tens of millions buying and renovating a historic bank bloc opposite the White House and Treasury building to serve as the headquarters and exhibit space for his Milken Center for the Advancement of the American Dream, which seeks to ensure everyone has access to its pathway. "This American dream is a chance based on your ability—what you can achieve," Milken explained.[47]

These are well-intentioned efforts staffed by capable and well-meaning people. In my capacity as a scholar of U.S. nationhood, I've participated in events hosted by both these organizations and I've offered my advice to each. The American Dream of meritocratic upward mobility is predicated on the American Experiment to secure and protect one another's inherent rights, the pursuit of happiness being but one among them. The American Dream is not a substitute; it's a wholly owned subsidiary of this experiment.

EL NORTE'S EXPERIENCE deserves special mention. In a region annexed to the United States via military conquest and where roughly half the population is Hispanic, the passions around how the region's history is taught run particularly high. The region controls only two states, Arizona and New Mexico, and only in New Mexico is there a Latino majority. Because of the massive, Anglo-driven growth of Phoenix—whose population went from 65,000 in 1940 to nearly 1.7 million in 2024—Arizona is only about 30 percent Latino and its state politics are controlled by a white, non-Hispanic majority. Similarly, Tejanos don't control Texas politics and California's Latinos don't hold sway over that state, even if they are a plurality in its largest city and regional section. Only in New Mexico are *Norteños* really in control of state education policies.

The result is a wide difference in the conduct of the history wars in the Southwestern border states. The legacy issue in all of them is how the Spanish and Mexican periods of each state's history are taught, how the annexations are looked upon, and how the region's former Jim Crow–style ethnoracial caste system is discussed. In New Mexico and California (where Left Coasters are allies), the Obama and Trump Eras provoked a dramatic expansion in "ethnic studies," school classes that focus on *Norteño* history and culture. In California, where this academic discipline was founded in 1968, ethnic studies spread to K-12 education after 2010.

But in Texas and Arizona, state officials moved to suppress ethnic studies. Arizona enacted a law in 2010 prohibiting courses that were "designed primarily for pupils of a particular ethnic group" or that "advocated for ethnic solidarity" or promoted "the overthrow of the U.S. government." Tucson's school district refused to comply, forsaking millions in funding; students protested by chaining themselves at a school board meeting. Arizona school chief John Huppenthal declared Tucson's Mexican-American studies course to be a "Ku Klux Klan class . . . in a different color" taught by "skinheads." A federal judge disagreed, striking down the law in 2017 because it had been enacted and enforced with "racist intent."[48]

By contrast, in 2021, California enacted a law requiring all students to take an ethnic studies course in order to graduate from high school and directed school districts to develop coursework on the experiences of Latinos, Asian Americans, Blacks, and Native Americans. The following year, New Mexico revised their standards to require school districts to increase classroom focus on social identities and how the world is shaped by race, class, and privilege. The high school requirements include students having a deep knowledge of exactly the issues Deep Southern and Greater Appalachian states did not want discussed, including how the U.S. government's refusal to accept Article X of the peace treaty with Mexico—a measure which would have required the United States to respect existing land grants—affected New Mexicans.[49]

Again, what's being fought over is the future. Will children in this region grow up understanding it's a place that was conquered and occupied by the United States, where social relations were shaped by an imperial template right into living memory, or will schools try to keep those un-comfortable facts from them? Those who seek to suppress this history may think they're promoting unity, thinking it's better to forget what divides us. But this serves future citizens poorly, because the cover story has huge holes in it. How did *Norteños* somehow lose all their land and disappear from public life after the annexations? Why were there Black slaves in Texas, New Mexico, and Arizona? Why did it take decades for Congress to approve New Mexico and Arizona's admission as states, even though their resource bases and populations were far larger than Midwestern and Western territories were when they'd be admitted?[50]

El Norte's past and present simply can't be understood by pretending it's just another part of the Far West, any more than the Deep South and Tidewater can be understood by making believe they weren't built on systemic, institutionalized atrocities.

OUR HISTORY WARS HAVE BEEN raging for a very long time and show no sign of ending. Some of these stories—Deep Southern ethnonationalist authoritarianism and messianic Yankee civic nationalism, for instance—are impossible to reconcile. Others can coexist or even reinforce one another if people are clear-eyed about how they fit together. The Yankee story that we're a people on a mission to further human freedom is the vital prerequisite to the New Netherlander American Dream and the Far Western frontier myth and the justification for Midlanders' cultural pluralism and Borderlanders' historic defense of individual liberty. It also legitimates the grievances of regions like El Norte, Greater Polynesia, and First Nation that were conquered in contravention of the ideals in the Declaration (due to the Yankees' unfortunate embrace of the idea of divine destiny). We can, in fact, assemble a coherent history—and, with it, a shared peoplehood—but only by recognizing and reckoning with our shortcomings. Hiding or lying about our fractured, complicated past doesn't foster American unity. It helps destroy it.

5

BELONGING

Who are "Americans" supposed to be? Who can be a "real American" and who is just "too different" to count as one? These questions of national identity have haunted humanity's efforts to create and maintain pluralistic, multiethnic liberal democracies. Multiethnic kingdoms and empires didn't have the same pitfalls as today's democracies, Johns Hopkins University political scientist Yascha Mounk has pointed out, precisely because the people had no sovereignty. "So long as you trust the monarch to tolerate your community, you can look upon an influx of people from a different ethnic or religious group with relative equanimity," he wrote. "If you are a citizen of a democracy, by contrast, the relative number of people in your own group directly impacts your ability to shape political outcomes."[1]

In the United States, there have always been movements that seek to define national belonging in narrowed ethnic and racial terms. Our founding documents clearly assert that the people are supposed to ultimately be in charge and that their government is supposed to protect their inborn rights as humans, so the pushback has always been framed around who "the people" are. The answers to these questions have also always varied regionally, with many of the American Nations having distinct attitudes about who among us should have full political rights and who should be allowed to join our peoplehood and on what terms. This has had an enormous influence on where immigrants have and have not settled, and has thus amplified the demographic, religious, economic, and ideological differences between the regional cultures.

It all started with ideas, big ideas about how the world should be run. All the regional cultures had such ideas, but only a handful of them had the power, population, and audacity to actively seek to have their narratives of identity and belonging applied to define the United States as a whole. To understand today's fights over immigration, Christian nationalism, the Great Replacement Theory, and racism itself is to understand our internal clash of civilizations.

YANKEEDOM's PURITAN FOUNDERS didn't let just anyone join their communities. Believing themselves to be in covenant with God to create a more perfect society in the New World, they made little distinction between political and church membership; one joined—or was cast out—from both at the same time. Each church was also a covenant among its members and to join, one had to demonstrate by word, deed, and reputation that you were among the "elect," the subset of humanity the Calvinists' God had already chosen to be saved from eternal hellfire. In a despotic age, New England towns were direct democracies where every adult male citizen could vote, but becoming a citizen required one to be morally upstanding, an adherent to the Puritan religion, and not too ethnographically exotic. Puritan divine Thomas Hooker, who founded the Connecticut colony, was clear about this latter point. If simply living in a town gave someone "right to Church fellowship, then Atheists, Papists, Turks and profane ones, who are enemies to the truth and Church . . . men of strange Nations and languages, who neither know, nor be able to do the duties of Church, members, should be fit matter for a Church, because they have abode in such places," he fumed before his death in 1647. "That all children of all nations, Turks, Pagans etc. should be admitted unto the privilege is absurd." In the late 1650s, Quaker missionaries were legally banned from entering Massachusetts under pain of whipping, imprisonment, and (for repeat offenders) execution. At the end of the seventeenth century—three generations after their arrival—Puritans constituted more than 95 percent of the inhabitants of Boston, New England's primary center of immigration.[2]

Not until the 1720s and 1730s did Yankeedom experience significant non-English immigration and, despite a shortage of servants and farm laborers, a lot of people were upset by it. The immigrants were almost entirely Scots-Irish (who at least were Calvinists) or Celtic Irish (who very much were not) and they were loathed for their looser morals and strange ways. "An endless swarm of refugees, Tag-Rag and Long tails, the Lord knows who . . . thrust themselves in among us, and are ready to devour us, and eat one another," Boston's *New England Courant* complained at the end of 1724. "I know not how we shall easily get rid of them, for they are like ill weeds, not easily rooted out." The newspaper didn't want them killed—"would you knock their brains out or tie them back-to-back and throw them into the sea?"—but wished they could be driven into the countryside to do honest farmwork.[3]

The prevailing stance toward newcomers was that they could come, but with the requirement that they assimilate into Yankee norms. Hector St. John de Crèvecoeur, a French mapmaker and writer who lived in the Yankee upstate of New York from 1759 to 1779, recognized this. "He is an American who leaving behind him all his ancient prejudices and manners receives new ones from the new mode of life he has embraced, the new government he obeys, and the new rank he holds," he famously wrote in 1782. "Here individuals of all nations are melted into a new race of men."[4]

As immigration gained strength in the early nineteenth century, Yankeedom's sophisticated network of public schools was tasked with turning immigrant children into good Protestant Yankees, while adults were expected to learn Yankee ways and leave their own identities behind. Leading this effort was Horace Mann, the head of the first state board of education in the United States in his native Massachusetts, who sought to use government to shape and empower public schools to better assimilate the children of immigrants and the poor into a common "American" culture which, to Mann's thinking, was really Yankee culture. "In order that men may be prepared for self-government, their apprenticeship must commence in childhood," Mann argued in 1847. "A foreign people, born and bred and dwarfed under the despotisms of the Old World, cannot be transformed into the full stature of American citizens, merely by a voyage across the Atlantic, or by subscribing to the oath of naturalization." First in New England and then across the Yankee Northeast, states channeled resources to heretofore locally financed public schools to ensure that immigrant children learned English and were socialized into regional norms. By 1915, the Vermonter John Dewey, the leading education reformer of the era, was pushing states to establish free, compulsory evening schools for the illiterate teenaged children of immigrants, so they could gain an academic—not vocational—education after their factory shifts ended. "There must not be one system for the children of parents who have more leisure and another for the children of those who are wage-earners," Mann warned. Massachusetts, Connecticut, and Wisconsin led the way at a time when most Deep Southern and Greater Appalachian states made such programs illegal. In Michigan, Henry Ford set up a night school of his own to "Americanize" his immigrant workers. At graduation, students dressed in their national garbs marched behind a giant "melting pot," which their teachers stirred with long ladles until they emerged from the other side wearing "American" clothes and waving the U.S. flag. In Yankeedom, newcomers were meant to "melt" into the existing culture.[5]

Racism was rampant everywhere in the antebellum United States, but Yankeedom offered African Americans more rights and opportunities than most other regions. Yankees believed themselves to be a chosen people, but also that they had been charged with a universal mission to improve the world. They generally "tempered their racial views with a moral sense which viewed the whole of mankind as awaiting redemption," as the preeminent historian of American racial Anglo-Saxonism, Reginald Horsman, puts it. "The moral and religious core that persisted in the New England mind made it more difficult for ideas which totally ignored other people to gain acceptance." Thus, in the antebellum period, African American males had the same voting rights as their white counterparts in Maine, Massachusetts, New Hampshire, Rhode Island, and Vermont—the only places in the United States where this was the case—and could vote in most elections in Michigan and New York (which was Yankee-controlled at the time) if they could meet certain requirements. Black men could vote in Wisconsin until 1849 and then again from 1866. Only in one of the Yankee-controlled states, Connecticut, did male Black suffrage have to wait for the passage of the Fifteenth Amendment, and even then it was encumbered by poll taxes and other restrictions until the 1965 Voting Rights Act.[6]

Every African American who earned a college degree in the antebellum period received it from a Yankee institution, starting with Vermonter Alexander Lucius Twilight (Middlebury, 1823) who would go on to be the first Black person elected to a state legislature; South Carolina–born Edward Jones (Amherst, 1826); and John Brown Russwurm (Bowdoin, 1826), who went on to found the first Black-owned-and-operated newspaper in the United States (New York City's *Freedom's Journal*). Oberlin College, in Ohio's Yankee-settled Western Reserve, started admitting Black students in 1835 and, in 1850, awarded the first college degree to an African American woman, schoolteacher Lucy Ann Stanton. All of Yankeedom's Ivy League colleges—Dartmouth, Harvard, Yale, Brown, and Cornell—had issued degrees to Black students by 1892. Edward Alexander Bouchet, the son of the enslaved valet of a South Carolinian Yale undergraduate, attended Yale himself, where he became the first Black person in the United States to be elected to Phi Beta Kappa and, in 1876, the first to earn a PhD (in Physics). In 1849, Charles L. Reason became the United States's first African American professor when he began teaching at Central College in Upstate New York. Frederick Douglass built his speaking, writing, and editing career in Yankeedom in the 1840s and 1850s, while most other nineteenth-century African American intellectuals were educated in the region, including Richard T. Greener (BA, Harvard, 1870), who led the University of South Carolina during Reconstruction; newspaper editor and activist William Monroe Trotter (BA, Harvard, 1895); and sociologist W.E.B. Du Bois (PhD, Harvard, 1895), who became one of the foremost American intellectuals of his generation.[7]

Life in Yankeedom at the start of the twentieth century was by no means easy for immigrants or native-born people of color, but of all the American Nations it was the one that came closest to implementing the civic national ideals its leaders claimed to embrace.

By contrast, the slaveholding oligarchs and aristocrats who ruled the **Deep South** and **Tidewater** saw no need for immigrants to be free and created an economic and social environment that offered few reasons for any to come for a century after slavery was vanquished. As we saw in chapter 4, during the antebellum period they argued that the United States was a collection of ethnostates belonging to the superior "Anglo-Saxon people," and that others were not entitled to full citizenship or—in the case of African Americans—humanity. Like their Yankee counterparts, the Deep Southern and Tidewater elite sought to imprint their regional model on the United States as a whole, and with considerable success.

Theirs was a vision of a Herrenvolk democracy, a homeland by and for the dominant ethnic group. The precise definition of who belonged in this group would evolve over time, starting with Anglos and other "Saxon" people, then extended to white Protestants generally. Those outside this group were to accept that they were mere guests in the society, assumed to be culturally or genetically unfit for democratic self-government, subhuman and barbarous. The states these regional cultures controlled were independent classical republics, like Ancient Greece and Rome, where a small subset of the population had the liberty or privilege to practice democracy, and subjugation and slavery were the natural lot of the many. The United States had existed to protect these Anglo-Saxon ethnostates, South Carolina's William Gilmore Simms and his allies asserted in the 1830s and 1840s, but this function had been frustrated by the fanatic and uncouth Yankees and the faulty, un-Christian heresy of Thomas Jefferson. Deep Southerners, in particular, sought to expand their region southwestward by annexing Texas (and turning it from free to slave) and invading Mexico, Cuba, and other subtropical and tropical regions. When it became clear, in the 1850s, that they were losing this westward race, they created their own country in an effort to uphold and protect this ethnostate model.

The lowland Southerners were not chastened by the Confederacy's defeat. In the half century following the Civil War, this lowland Southern ethnonationalist model was further developed and aggressively propagated by Tidewater and Deep Southern intellectuals, celebrities, and political leaders. In the 1880s, the novelist Thomas Nelson Page, whose aristocratic parents had lost their Virginia slave plantation after the war, created an image of life in the Old South as a genteel civilization where genetically superior families ruled, slaves and masters loved and cared for one another, and everyone knew their place. Slaves, Page told his nationwide fan base, benefited from an "education which comes with daily association with people of culture" and were their master's "faithful guardians, their sympathizing friends, and their shrewd advisors . . . with the devotion not of slaves but of clansmen." In 1905, North Carolina's Thomas Dixon Jr. wrote *The Clansman*, a wildly popular book and subsequent touring theater production that demonized Yankees for trying to dismantle this superior, feudal society and lionized the Ku Klux Klan's deadly Reconstruction Era terrorist campaign to undo the political and economic emancipation of African Americans. Dixon subsequently partnered with D. W. Griffith to bring his story to the cinema, resulting in the first Hollywood blockbuster, *The Birth of a Nation*, the 1915 film that inspired the founding of the second KKK and was used as its primary recruiting tool.[8]

Dixon had dedicated one of his earlier books to his close friend and graduate school classmate, Woodrow Wilson, who became the country's first Deep Southern president in 1913. He and Griffith quoted Wilson's *History of the American People* repeatedly in *Birth of a Nation* to substantiate the film's white supremacist assertions. When an African American–led boycott in Yankeedom and New Netherland threatened to bankrupt the production, Wilson screened the film in the White House, a tacit endorsement that ensured mayors and governors would be unable to censor it as the protesters were demanding. Wilson said it was "like writing history with lightning, and my only regret is that it is all so terribly true." Later, he was asked to condemn the film and refused.[9]

This ethnonationalist definition of the United States was dominant, federation-wide, from the Wilson years through the 1960s. During this era, Congress passed a severe new immigration law that aimed to maintain the "Anglo-Saxon" character of country by severely restricting immigration from eastern and southern Europe, Asia, Africa, and the Middle East. As a result of this 1924 law, total immigration fell from more than 630,000 people a year in the 1910s to 241,000 in 1930. More than a quarter of this flow for the entire world was reserved for British people (27 percent) and another 11 percent for Germans. The annual quota for Swedes (3,314 people) was greater than all of Asia and Africa combined. "No law passed by Congress in the past half century compares with this one in its importance upon the future development of the nation," its cosponsor, Senator David Reed of Pennsylvania, promised readers of the *New York Times*. "Its adoption means that America of our grandchildren will be a vastly better place to live in . . . more homogenous, more self-reliant, more independent, and more closely knit by common purpose and common ideas."[10]

By the time the 1924 Immigration Act passed, Deep Southern and Tidewater oligarchs had been practicing its principles for decades. They, too, needed cheap labor in the 1870s as hundreds of thousands of Black Americans fled the new racial apartheid systems they had set up in their regions at the end of the northern military occupation. They spent millions trying to divert Great Wave immigrants to work on plantations, railroads, and factory floors, but only those from northern Europe. South Carolina legislators in 1904 directed the state's immigration bureau to bring only "citizens of Ireland, Scotland, Switzerland, France, and other foreigners of Saxon origin." North Carolina's bureau sought people from British Canada "and other nations of Teutonic, Celtic or Saxon origin" and was under instructions not to recruit southern Italians to the state's Greater Appalachian section. (Tidewater planters wanted their labor, and secured exceptions.) Alabama Congressman Oscar W. Underwood rejected "the Slav, the Iberic, and the Mongolian" because they would "contaminate our blood with an inferior race" and create a "South American" civilization. "The cry was, on the one hand, for only the highest type of immigrant," South Carolina's immigration commissioner lamented in 1905, "and on the other to secure him at the scale of wages paid the negro."[11]

The few immigrants who did come soon regretted having done so because the white Deep Southern and Tidewater public saw them as a threat to tradition, evangelical Christian hegemony, and cultural purity. The typical European immigrant saw little attraction in southern workplaces where, a British consul in the Deep South observed in 1873, "he is to be housed, fed, and treated just as the black race used to be." Most who did come were peasants from southern Italy, itself a neo-feudal society with patron-peon labor relations, and they were often treated as a subhuman caste. Local white Protestants welcomed Italian farmers who settled undeveloped land in Tontitown, Arkansas, in 1896 by twice burning down their church. When Italian children showed up for school in Sumrall, Mississippi, locals drove their entire families from the town. In 1890s Louisiana, mobs lynched nearly two dozen Italians suspected of crimes. Xenophobia, South Carolina's immigration commissioner admitted, was the greatest obstacle to his efforts to bring foreign workers to the state.[12]

"The South did not want foreign immigration, remaining firm in the idea of ant-bellum days that the social structure was built wholly upon negro labor, and upon that alone," the editors of the monumental pro-Southern history series *The South in the Building of the Nation* concluded in 1909. "The people were proud of their homogeneous population, and felt no desire to introduce alien elements."[13]

This would have longstanding implications for everyone in the United States, with ramifications that shape many aspects of the federation's political life today.

AS DISCUSSED IN CHAPTER 4, two other "northern" regions, the **Midlands** and **New Netherland**, embraced related strains of pluralism and multiculturalism, by which immigrants were not only welcomed but encouraged to retain their cultural practices, identities, and languages. These regions were diverse from the outset, with no one ethnocultural group asserting exclusive ownership and with relatively wide circles of belonging. It's in these two regions that the notion of America as a "nation of immigrants" took root, but over time they would increasingly differ on how "different" those immigrants could be. They also differed in their commitment to racial equality and, by extension, slavery and civil rights.

New Netherlanders, as described in chapter 4, valued cultural pluralism because it was good for business. Not surprisingly, given its commercial emphasis and foreign trade orientation, in the mid-nineteenth century the New York City area surpassed Boston, Philadelphia, and Baltimore to become the largest port in the United States and then, for a time in the mid-twentieth century, the largest in the world. It became far and away the primary gateway for immigrants well before that, with two-thirds of the 5.4 million foreigners who emigrated to the United States between 1820 and 1860 passing through the port, and four-fifths of the million more who arrived in the 1890s. A great many stayed in New Netherland, making New York City more than 40 percent foreign-born by 1910. "New York remains without a doubt the largest and most self-consciously diverse conglomeration of races and tongues ever gathered in one spot on the earth's surface," the Manhattan-born editor of *Foreign Affairs*, Hamilton Fish Armstrong, observed in 1941, noting the presence of artists, singers, cooks, delicacies, and movies from every corner of the world. "By a thousand channels the daily life of New York is exposed for good or ill to the impact of foreign cultures, whether in art, food, music, science, dressmaking or journalism. . . . New York is Cosmopolis. To it nothing anywhere—no event, no idea—is wholly alien."[14]

New Netherland didn't demand the people of the world blend into a "native" race. It simply slammed the entire world together on an archipelago of islands at the mouth of the Hudson and let them all have at it.

For Midlanders, by contrast, cultural pluralism was the central characteristic of their civilization, valued regardless of any possible commercial benefit. By the 1750s, William Penn's Holy Experiment had created a cosmopolitan society that was remarkably tolerant and peaceable for its times. Modern sociologists have developed a "diversity index" that measures the probability of random cross-cultural encounters in a given location. Philadelphia's rate in 1759 was the same as it would be in 2010, and it became considerably more diverse between 1760 and 1810, as French refugees fled the Haitian Revolution with their Afro-Caribbean slaves. Irish and Welsh Catholics, Ulster Scots Presbyterians, English Quakers, Dutch Calvinists, and Swedish Lutherans loosely clustered in overlapping neighborhoods, cross-pollinating them with one another's churches, shops, and gathering places.[15] Germans formed a plurality across Pennsylvania and New Jersey's Midland sections, disturbing the

Yankee-born Benjamin Franklin with their disinterest in giving up their ways. "Few of their children in the Country learn English," he complained to an English friend in 1753:

> They import many Books from Germany; and of the six printing houses in the Province, two are entirely German, two half German half English, and but two entirely English; They have one German News-paper, and one half German. Advertisements intended to be general are now printed in Dutch and English; the Signs in our Streets have inscriptions in both languages, and in some places only German: They begin of late to make all their Bonds and other legal Writings in their own Language, which (though I think it ought not to be) are allowed good in our Courts, where the German Business so encreases that there is continual need of Interpreters; and I suppose in a few years they will be also necessary in the Assembly, to tell one half of our Legislators what the other half say.[16]

After the American Revolution, Midlanders often selected Germans to represent them in Congress. Four of the sixteen members of Pennsylvania's delegation to the first U.S. Congress were of German heritage, including House Speaker Frederick Muhlenberg, the German-educated son of immigrants from the Electorate of Hanover who had already served as speaker of the Pennsylvania house and as a member of the Continental Congress. When Franklin died in 1790, his official eulogy was held in his adopted city's largest German Lutheran Church.[17]

In the Midlands, ethnic communities continued to retain their language and cultural practices for the next century and beyond. Germans, as the largest single ethnic group, were at the vanguard, successfully lobbying to protect German- and other minority-language schools from legal interference in Pennsylvania (1837), Ohio (1838), Illinois (1857), Iowa (1861), and Kansas (1867). Baltimore had a thriving bilingual school system in 1874, while German-language theological and teacher's seminaries popped up in Midland cities in Iowa, Indiana, Missouri, and Nebraska. There were German clubs, newspapers, journals, and publishing houses across the Midland belt right up until the United States declared war on Germany during the First World War, after which anti-German hysteria damaged or destroyed many of these institutions. Iowa had towns that were almost entirely Danish (Elk Horn), Dutch Separatist (Pella), Hessian Pietist (the Amana colonies), or Pennsylvania Quaker (Oskaloosa, which today is home to William Penn University). "Here," the journalist John Gunther remarked of the state in 1944, "is one of the comparatively few places in the United States where, it seems, the melting pot did not quite melt." That was, of course, exactly the point.[18]

As elsewhere in the United States, however, this tolerance did not so easily extend to African Americans or to later immigrants from Asia, Africa, or the Middle East. In the Early Republic and the antebellum period, the region was second only to New England in the presence of abolitionist groups, usually led by Quakers. Most Midland-dominated states (and states that also had large Yankee sections) banned slavery by the early nineteenth century and did not institute formal Jim Crow laws in the early twentieth. Pennsylvania Quakers set up the first U.S. colleges explicitly intended for Black students—what are now Lincoln and Cheyney universities. But the region was also a bastion of the Second Ku Klux Klan in the 1920s, with the Midland sections of Indiana and Illinois matching those state's Greater Appalachian areas in support for what was an anti-Black and anti-Catholic movement. A similar pattern emerges among confirmed "sundown towns," where African Americans were discouraged from entering, especially after dark. Some of the worst pogroms against Black people took place in the region, including those in East St. Louis in 1917 (when hundreds were killed en masse by a white mob, including children thrown into burning buildings), Springfield in 1908 (seventeen were killed and thousands of Black people were driven from the city following a false rape accusation by a white woman), Omaha in

1919 (10,000 whites set the county court house on fire, lynched a Black rape suspect, and hanged the white mayor, who was rescued before death by police), and Chicago in 1919 (twenty-eight were killed in clashes after a white man murdered a Black boy who had drifted while swimming into a "whites only" section of Lake Michigan).[19] A century later, structural racism is especially egregious. A 2019 study of racial disparities confronting Black people revealed Midlands-controlled Pennsylvania, Iowa, Missouri, Nebraska, and Kansas to be among the very worst in the country in terms of disparities in wages, poverty, infant mortality, homeownership, school suspensions, and incarceration. "While many Midwestern cities appear in viral 'best places to live' lists, they are also among the very worst places to live for African Americans," the study's lead author, the University of Iowa historian Colin Gordon, told the *Des Moines Register* after its release.[20]

As we saw in chapter 4, **Greater Appalachia**'s mythic story taught white Borderlanders to regard themselves not just as a separate ethnicity, but as members of a pure, unadulterated *American* ethnicity. Relatively isolated from demographic, intellectual, and technological changes, Revolutionary- and antebellum-era Borderlanders came to think of themselves as the carriers of the traditions, values, folkways, and uncorrupted Protestant faith of the original British-American settlers. They were the "real Americans," the "real Christians," and they felt they had to be vigilant to protect themselves and their ways from corruption. Most were small farmers, a group whose central characteristic was "their sincere belief that the south must be maintained as a one-hundred percent 'Anglo-Saxon' community," the Georgia-born University of North Carolina historian Benjamin Kendrick explained in 1923. "Hence they are anti-negro, anti-Catholic, anti-Jew, anti-foreign and most recently anti-evolution (and) . . . pro-sacredness-of-the-home to the point of acquitting one of their number who commits murder in defense of it." This was not a region that embraced pluralism.

In reality, Greater Appalachia was never monocultural, nor were its multigenerational white inhabitants purely descended from Ulster and Lowland Scots and North English Borderlanders. The original colonizer-settler cohorts that spread south and west from southwestern Pennsylvania typically had clumps of Germans embedded within them who often settled together in their own enclaves in places like Mecklenburg (now Shepardstown, West Virginia), North Carolina's Wachovia Tract (named for Wachau, Austria), Brunerstown (now Jeffersontown) in Kentucky, and New Braunfels in the Appalachian-colonized Texas Hill Country. Euro-American colonizers often formed families with Indigenous Cherokee, Shawnee, and Osage spouses. In 1800, African Americans, most of them enslaved, formed nearly a quarter of Kentucky's population, 15 percent of (then fully Appalachian) Tennessee's, and 11 percent of that of the counties that would one day become West Virginia.[21] To propagate the regional myth, however, all this needed to be forgotten.

Antebellum Appalachia had little to offer early nineteenth-century immigrants: no free or practically free "frontier" land, scant labor-hungry industrial facilities, no cities to rival the attractions of Boston, New York, Baltimore, Cleveland, or Chicago. Wages were low, schools weak, transport difficult, and the popular reception cold. "Leave us in peaceful possession of our slaves and our Northern neighbors may have all the paupers and convicts that pour in upon us from European prisons," said William "Parson" Brownlow, editor of Knoxville's unionist *Whig* newspaper and future Tennessee governor and senator, in 1858.[22]

After the Civil War, however, outside corporations suddenly needed to find armies of laborers to deploy on remote Appalachian mountain coal fields or the expanding railroad lines being built to link them with the industrial centers of Yankeedom, the Midlands, and New Netherland. The Chesapeake & Ohio, Norfolk & Western, and Louisville & Nashville lines advanced into the Pocahontas, Flat Top, and Eastern fields in Virginia, West Virginia, and Kentucky in the 1870s and 1880s, bringing tens of thousands of workers in and millions of tons of coal out. In Tennessee, the owners of iron mines, coal fields, lumber yards, and mills couldn't expand for lack of workers. Seeing the massive wave of immigration pouring into New Netherland, Yankeedom, the Midlands, and the Far West, Appalachian state officials and industry leaders invested in promotional campaigns, subsidized steamship-and-railroad tickets, and supported other schemes in an attempt to divert some of these workers to the region. Few came. Despite concerted efforts, Tennessee's foreign-born population actually fell during the 1870s, while Kentucky's remained flat and shrank as an overall share. The Central Appalachian coal fields relied on trickery to secure foreign labor, offering "free" transportation to newly arrived Italian, Czech, and Hungarian immigrants in New York in exchange for signing a labor contract; upon arrival in the company mining towns they learned they had to pay off the debt for this transport, plus exorbitant prices for food, mining tools, clothing, and lodging. Many found themselves prisoners, prevented from leaving the mines by armed guards and, in at least one instance in West Virginia, shot as they tried to escape.[23]

Unable to sign up enough immigrants, the coal executives sent recruiters to Black farming communities in Tidewater and the Deep South with offers of free transportation and wages five to seven times what they earned as sharecroppers. Tens of thousands of Black men took the offers, with the vast majority moving to West Virginia because it was the only Appalachian state that allowed them to vote. They recognized that the mining camps followed the general outlines of the lowland sharecropping system, but with better and more frequent payouts. Because the camps were in remote, company-owned mountain areas, however, there was little prospect of becoming independent farmers, so the vast majority of the Black workers were seasonal migrants, returning to their families on sharecropped land in Tidewater Virginia and North Carolina or Alabama at harvest time. Jim Crow was alive and well in Greater Appalachia; even the bars, lunch counters, housing, and bathhouses in the mining camps were segregated. When mechanization began reducing labor demands in the second quarter of the twentieth century, many Black migrants left the region for better prospects in the Midlands, Yankeedom, or the Far West.[24]

Despite being a former slaveholding region, Greater Appalachia, in 2020, was the second-whitest region in the country at 68 percent. (Yankeedom was first at 71 percent.) As with the Deep South and Tidewater, the region's exclusive ideas about identity and belonging have massive policy and political implications for all of us today.

THE TWO "NEWER" NATIONS, the Far West and the Left Coast, had ethnographically and racially mixed populations from their foundation in the mid-nineteenth century and much looser ideas about identity and belonging than those to the east.

Recall from chapter 1 that the Euro-American colonization of the **Far West** was largely controlled and directed by railroad, mining, and timber corporations based outside the region. Their business models required they somehow attract and settle huge numbers of workers over a staggeringly large area remote from markets, ports, and major population centers over the resistance of the Indigenous peoples living there. The federal government, which claimed ownership over most of the region while its subdivisions remained federal territories rather than states, subsidized this effort, offering free or nearly free land to colonists, while the railroads did the same for transportation from the East Coast or even Europe. These factors alone convinced a substantial share of the Great Wave immigrants to settle in the Far West, where in 1900 they constituted nearly 18 percent of the population.

By 1900, Far Western regional mythology had adopted Frederick Jackson Turner's frontier thesis, which held that the differences between Euro-

American settlers—and possibly others—were irrelevant because the region's challenging conditions would mold them together into a single "American" people. White Appalachian people believed they were "real" Americans because they were one people who came to the frontier and retained their ways. Far Westerners' claim to uber-Americanness was the reverse: Many peoples had come to the frontier where they became Americans. Unlike the eastern nations, however, the Far West also received streams of East Asian immigrants from across the Pacific, and Latinos from El Norte and Mexico. The region was, and is, sparsely populated, but it is surprisingly diverse. The 2020 census returns show it to be only 57 percent white and more than a quarter Hispanic, with 1 in 19 residents of Asian descent and 1 in 50 of Native American background, far and away the highest proportion in the United States outside of First Nation.[25]

The **Left Coast**, as related in chapter 1, was initially colonized by two rival groups: Yankees in the towns and cities and Borderlanders from the Appalachian Midwest. These regions shared a certain degree of ethnochauvinism, expressed in the late nineteenth century as descending from "Anglo-Saxon stock," though they parted on the question of who else could or should be assimilated into the dominant culture. Not surprisingly, the region has had an inconsistent approach to identity and belonging, ricocheting between New Netherland-like multiculturalism and Yankee-Appalachian nativism. For the most part, however, multiculturalism has dominated, not least because of how far removed the region was from much of the rest of the United States at the time of colonization. (There's a reason the Gold Rush–era 49ers are called Argonauts: They'd crossed oceanic distances to find their gold.) The population of San Francisco increased twenty-five-fold—from 1,000 to 25,000—in just three years, while the Left Coast section grew by a thousand percent. As nearly everyone was a newcomer—virtually all *Californios* lived in the state's El Norte section—there were no "old stock" settlers asserting cultural ownership. One in four Argonauts were foreign-born—British, Irish, French, German, Italian, Anglo-Australian, and Chinese—but they arrived on essentially equal footing with the American-born migrants. In 1852, San Francisco was already like a West Coast version of New Netherland, with thirty houses of worship—Catholic, Jewish, and Protestant—a cacophony of languages, and ships arriving from around the world. "Such an omnium gatherum of humanity," the city's *Alta California* newspaper declared in early 1851, "has never been witnessed before in the world's history." Coastal Oregon and Washington were settled more gradually, but from a similarly diverse set of sources.[26]

The emergent Yankee leadership, which dominated the major towns, sought to make the region a New England on the Pacific. They created colleges, libraries, schools, and other strong public institutions that aimed to improve society, but they were unable to impart Yankee cultural norms on an increasingly un-Yankee population. There were sporadic efforts to impose a "melting pot" model on immigrants, including aggressive "othering" of Japanese and Chinese immigrants and their descendants who, under federal law, were for decades denied birthright citizenship on account of their race. Oregon's territorial and state governments enacted laws barring African Americans from living in the state and, despite the passage of the Fourteenth Amendment, kept those laws on the books until 1926. The first KKK was active in the Bay Area in the aftermath of the Civil War, beating Chinese people and burning down the schools, churches, and factories where they congregated. The second KKK was very strong in both Washington and Oregon in the 1920s, agitating primarily against Catholic schools and Asian immigration. California and Oregon's Left Coast–controlled legislatures refused to ratify the Fourteenth and Fifteenth Amendments in the late 1860s because they feared giving full civil, political, and citizenship rights to East Asians. Ultimately, however, continuing foreign immigration and domestic in-migration would leave Left Coasters to conclude their region had no root stock for outsiders to assimilate into. Theirs would be a goulash, a great mix of people living between the mountains and the sea.[27]

THE REMAINING NATIONS—El Norte, New France, First Nation, Greater Polynesia, and the Spanish Caribbean—are all regional cultures that were conquered and incorporated into the United States. As noted in the previous chapter, their respective stories seek to conserve and strengthen their regional culture and historical memory after decades or a century or more of imperial control. Polynesian Hawaii, Cajun and Bourbon Louisiana, Spanish-legacy South Florida, and the long-oppressed Indigenous peoples of Northern and Western Alaska have their own ideas of identity and belonging. The Spanish Caribbean and Greater Polynesia are liberally minded on immigration, New France deeply reactionary, while few non-Indigenous foreigners have made it as far as First Nation. These four enclaves are also too small to have had meaningful influence over policies on the national stage.

El Norte, however, is both large and at the center of contemporary debates over immigration and identity, so it's worth understanding how the long-suppressed *Norteño* regional culture looks on these issues. Spanish colonizers thought that Indigenous people were inferior but that it was due to their cultural and technological backwardness, not some inherent biological flaw. The Spaniards' rule was horrific—witness their atrocities against the Aztecs and Inca—but they did believe Native people had the potential to be their equals if "civilization" could be brought to them, thus their emphasis on "missions" where this tutelage could take place. They also had fewer qualms about "race mixing" than the English and, because few Iberian women came to New Spain, by the eighteenth century most people in the northern part of what would become Mexico were of mixed or mestizo decent, whereas many people in central Mexico (and most in the South) were entirely Indigenous. In El Norte, frontier conditions (and centuries of warfare with the Apache and Comanche) collapsed hierarchical distinctions between European and mestizo colo-nizers, effectively making all the colonizers "white," and fostering last-ing regional contempt for purely Indigenous Maya and Aztec people in Central and Southern Mexico, who many *Norteños* still regard as lazy and backward. After Mexico became independent in 1821, its Central Mexican–based intellectuals believed a true nation could be formed by continued racial mixing—*mestizaje*—to produce a people with the best cultural attributes of both races, though they bitterly argued over what European immigrants would produce the best admixture. This debate had less relevance in the North because its people already exemplified—in their own minds at least—the mestizo ideal. This Mexican regional dynamic adds additional complexity to identity and immigration atti-tudes among Tejanos and other multigenerational U.S. *Norteños* today who often regard themselves as "white" and therefore reject the Chicano movement's embrace of the Indigenous side of their identity.[28]

Regardless of how they thought of themselves, after the U.S. annexa-tions, whites regarded most *Norteños* in Alta California, Tejas, and Nuevo Mexico as members of an inferior race. They were sent to segregated schools and, in the twentieth century, restricted to certain areas of movie theaters and swim times at public pools. In Arizona, *Norteños* of mes-tizo descent sometimes fell afoul of racial exclusion laws, denying them the ability to vote, run for office, or marry a person legally regarded as "white." Since the 1960s, *Norteños* have reasserted their influence over the politics and culture of the El Norte sections of Texas, New Mexico, and even California. However, Arizona's El Norte section is an exception in this regard because it contains Greater Phoenix, the fastest-growing city on the continent, which was little more than a village a century ago and now dominates the section and state. Most of the city's people are first- or second-generation migrants from other regional cultures and have reinforced "Anglo" imperialistic assumptions about who Arizona belongs to and who it doesn't. While the other parts of El Norte—a re-gion which was 47 percent Hispanic in 2020—have liberal attitudes about immigration, Arizona has some of the most reactionary politics on the issue in the entire federation.[29]

AT NATIONHOOD LAB, we were interested in how these regional ideas might have affected past immigration patterns, present-day immigration policy debates, and the underlying demographics of the country. To explore this, we parsed U.S. census data to determine where the 1880–1924 Great Wave immigrants settled. We used the 1900 census because, unlike in 1910 and 1920, the Census Bureau didn't exclude foreign-born people of color from their tabulations. We then calculated the proportion of foreign-born in each county and American Nations region, presented in this figure:

1900 Foreign-Born (Percent of population)

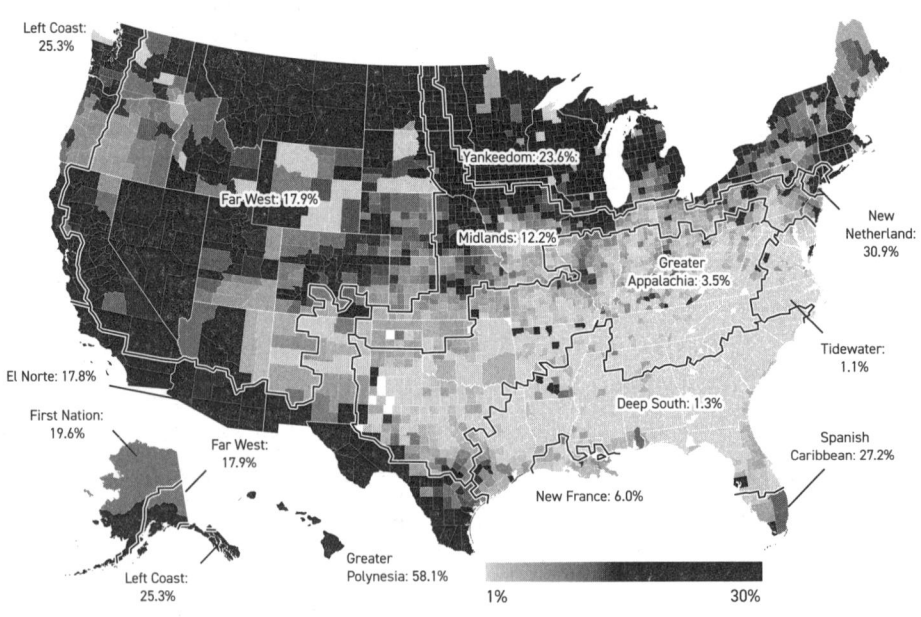

Left Coast: 25.3%

Yankeedom: 23.6%

Far West: 17.9%

Midlands: 12.2%

New Netherland: 30.9%

Greater Appalachia: 3.5%

Tidewater: 1.1%

El Norte: 17.8%

First Nation: 19.6%

Far West: 17.9%

Deep South: 1.3%

Spanish Caribbean: 27.2%

New France: 6.0%

Left Coast: 25.3%

Greater Polynesia: 58.1%

1%   30%

Data: Census Bureau, 1900 Census (via University of Minnesota-IPUMS)

Notice just how few people emigrated to the Deep South, Tidewater, and Greater Appalachia: barely more than 1 percent in the two lowland regions and just 3.5 percent in Appalachia, most of it concentrated in Pennsylvania and Illinois counties adjacent to well-populated Midland urban centers (Pittsburgh and St. Louis) and in the Texas Hill Country where it abuts El Norte. It's also clear few foreigners stuck around Coal Country, as most counties there have less than 1 percent foreign-born.

By contrast, immigrants were a substantial share of the population across Yankeedom, the Left Coast, and New Netherland, regions where they comprised 23.6, 25.3, and 30.9 percent of residents respectively. El Norte and the Far West also had significant foreign influxes, accounting for 17.8 and 17.9 percent of their overall populations, though not in the Southern Rockies or interior Oregon. The Midlands, interestingly, was only 12.2 percent foreign-born in 1900, with the effects concentrated in Central Illinois, northern Iowa, and the eastern half of the Great Plains states. You can see the effect of Japanese- and Filipino-powered plantation agriculture in Hawaii, where nearly six in ten people were immigrants.

This uneven regional distribution—with a more than twenty-fold difference between some of the largest of the American Nations—had massive and lasting effects on intra-regional politics, most immediately in terms of self-conception. Scholars have long recognized that the Great Wave profoundly changed ideas about American identity, forcing legacy Protestant America to accept that Catholics, Orthodox Christians, and Jews—at least—would be regarded as full-fledged Americans. For two generations thereafter—through the Roaring Twenties, the Great Depression, the World War, and the postwar boom—Great Wave immigrants fought their way into American life, forcing the northern and western regional cultures to accept them into the circle of belonging. Yankees and Left Coasters still had largely Anglo-Protestant elites in the mid-1960s, but it was impossible for them to think of their regions as being primarily Anglo or Protestant. The Midlands and New Netherland were more diverse than ever and the possibility of there ever being an Anglo-Protestant-controlled Far West or El Norte had vanished. The nations remained very different cultural and ideological spaces, but it became widely accepted that they weren't and would never be ethnoracially or religiously homogenous and shouldn't try to be, either.

What's gone largely unrecognized is that none of this happened in the Deep South, Tidewater, and Greater Appalachia because the Great Wave immigrants had completely avoided settling in these places. Compared with the other nations, these became homogenous (if racially sorted) cultures where preexisting power structures, family hierarchies, and received ways of life had few challengers. "The long defensive fight against alien-infested Yankeedom had vastly intensified in Southerners generally a feeling . . . that they represented a uniquely pure and superior race, not only against the Negro but as against all other communities of white men as well," W. J. Cash wrote of post-1924 whites in *The Mind of the South*. "They were extraordinarily solicitous for its preservation, extraordinarily on the alert to ward off the possibility that at some future date it might be contaminated by the introduction of other blood-streams than those of the old original stocks."[30]

Of even greater consequence, these three Dixie regions also remained religiously homogenous, the only parts of the continent where evangelical Protestants dominated church life. Being racial caste societies or, in the case of Greater Appalachia, overwhelmingly white, churches were racially segregated with the white evangelical denominations dominant and empowered. These regions became the Bible Belt and remain so today, as you can see from the map on the facing page, which is based on data from the Association of Statisticians of American Religious Bodies' 2020 U.S. Religion Census. It depicts the dominant religion in each county today, and you can see that Catholics, far and away the largest cohort of the Great Wave immigrants, are still the largest denomination across the regions where they settled. Notice the mainline Protestant United Methodists are dominant in scattered parts of the Midlands. Southern Bap-

Dominant Religious Denomination by County (2020)

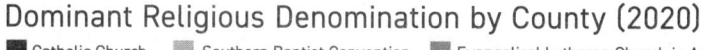

■ Catholic Church   ■ Southern Baptist Convention   ■ Evangelical Lutheran Church in America
▨ United Methodist Church   Nondenominational Christian Churches
▨ Church of Jesus Christ of Latter-day Saints   ■ Other

Data: Association of Statisticians of American Religious Bodies, 2020 U.S. Religion Census

tists, the largest white evangelical grouping, are the largest force in religious life in the Deep South, Tidewater, and Greater Appalachia. Those same three regions are the stronghold of nondenominational Christian churches, as well, the vast majority of which are independent Baptist fundamentalist congregations, which typically regard the Southern Baptist Convention as too "liberal." Notice the remarkable degree of affinity with both the 1900 immigration map displayed earlier in this chapter as well as the borders of the American Nations.[31]

These are also the only regions where white Christian Nationalism—the belief that the United States is a country founded by and for white Christian evangelical Protestants—finds purchase. In all the other regions, white Protestants, whether evangelical or not, haven't been a plurality of the population for decades or even centuries, but in the southern nations, Protestants have always been the dominant force, and evangelicals have been in the driver's seat since the early nineteenth century. A majority of white evangelical Christians hold Christian Nationalist views, with 77 percent in 2014 believing the Founders intended the United States to be a "Christian nation" and more than half saying God intended it to be a promised land for "European Christians." Scholars have shown that white Christian Nationalists define themselves in political, ethnic, and cultural terms much more so than theologically, a people rather than a faith. "It is a particular kind of white Christian ethno-culture," the University of Oklahoma's Samuel Perry, a sociologist who focuses on evangelicals in politics, told the *New Yorker.* "It means pro-Christian and all the other things we assume like [being] natural born citizens instead of immigrants."[32]

White Christian Nationalists as a group have been extremely hostile to immigrants, people of color, and members of other religions. "There is a presumption in contemporary American Christian nationalism that many or most immigrants are not Christian—or not the right kind of Christian," the sociologists Darren Sherkat and Derek Lehman concluded after statistical analysis of data from the 2004–2016 General Social Survey, the National Science Foundation–funded biannual survey of American's social attitudes. "This variant of white Christian nationalism seems inherently 'racialized' in its view of non-white immigrants as a cultural threat to the dominance of white Christianity." These effects are so large that when another team of researchers removed all Christian Nationalists from their survey samples of evangelicals, regular church attenders, and social conservatives, those other groups went from being positively correlated with disliking immigrants to negatively correlated.[33]

In sum, the Great Wave profoundly *increased* the differences between the regions. We're still living in the world that era left behind.

WE WERE INTERESTED IN how the present, post-1965 immigration wave has been regionally distributed. This wave was triggered by the repeal of an ethnoracial quota system, which was replaced with one that prioritized family reunification. When it really got underway in 1970, after decades of severe restrictions, the United States was only 4.7 percent foreign-born, the lowest proportion since official record keeping began in 1850 and probably since the colonial era. As of 2022, more than 60 million new immigrants had arrived. The U.S. population had reached 13.8 percent foreign born, 1 percentage point less than its Great Wave peak in 1890.[34]

Here's what we found, using the Census Bureau's 2020 American Community Survey data:

2020 Foreign-Born (Percent of population)

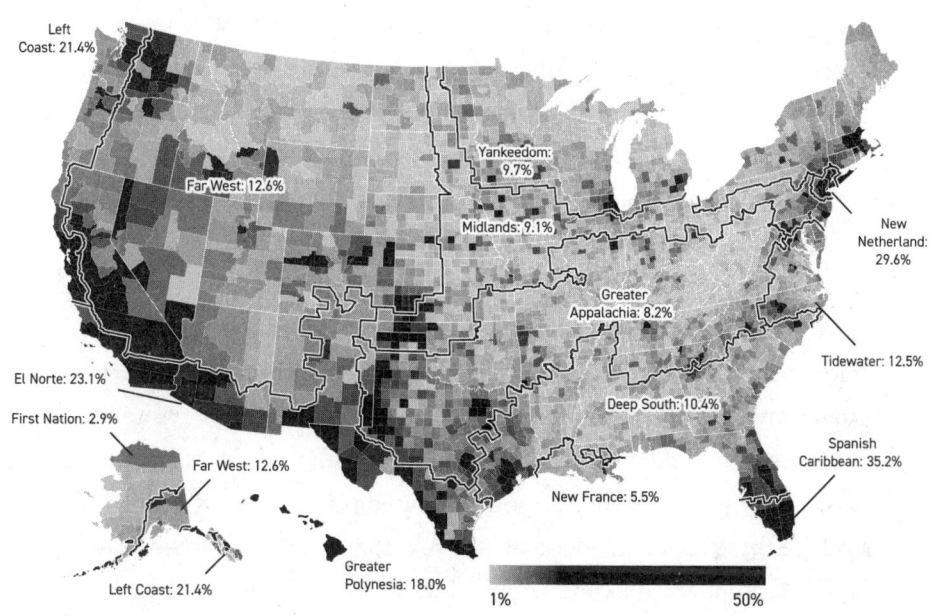

Left Coast: 21.4%

Yankeedom: 9.7%

Far West: 12.6%

Midlands: 9.1%

New Netherland: 29.6%

Greater Appalachia: 8.2%

Tidewater: 12.5%

El Norte: 23.1%

First Nation: 2.9%

Deep South: 10.4%

Spanish Caribbean: 35.2%

Far West: 12.6%

New France: 5.5%

Left Coast: 21.4%

Greater Polynesia: 18.0%

1%   50%

Data: Census Bureau, 2018–2022 Five-Year American Community Survey

Notice that the share of immigrants remains roughly the same now as it was in 1900 in most of the regions that were the primary destinations for the Great Wave immigrants: the Left Coast, New Netherland, the Spanish Caribbean, and El Norte. These four regions remain "nations of immigrants" in a literal sense. By contrast, the Deep South, Tidewater, and Greater Appalachia have seen a substantial increase: roughly tenfold in the case of Tidewater and the Deep South, and a more than doubling in Appalachia. These three nations are new destinations with cultures unaccustomed to foreign residents. Meanwhile, four regions that received large numbers of foreigners during the Great Wave have significantly less now as a share of their overall populations. Compared with 1900, the immigrant share of the population has fallen by a fifth in the Far West, by about a quarter in the Midlands, and more than half in Yankeedom, where the foreign-born have gone from 23.6 percent of residents to just 9.7 percent. In the Hawaiian Islands (Greater Polynesia), it's fallen by more than two-thirds, and the First Nation section of Alaska stands at barely a seventh of its 1900 level. These are the "former destination" regions, places where mass immigration is part of their heritage, but not a present reality. (Louisiana's New France enclave stands alone in having few immigrants both then and now.)

Today the Deep South and Tidewater have a higher proportion of foreign-born people than either Yankeedom or the Midlands. Greater Appalachia isn't far behind these two northern nations, either, and, if current trends continue, may surpass them both when the 2030 census is compiled. In all three of these "Dixie" regions, almost all of the immigrant growth has happened since the late 1990s, the result of the collapse of Yankee-Midland manufacturing and the transfer of factory jobs to low-wage, low-regulation, low-tax jurisdictions like the states controlled by these three regions. Tidewater, as I've emphasized throughout, has experienced fundamental and irreversible cultural change since the 1960s due to the presence of the federal government and its workforce needs; it's essentially ceasing to exist as a distinct regional culture. This is not at all true of the Deep South and Greater Appalachia, and it's fueled anti-immigration sentiment that's been exploited by early-twenty-first-century demagogues.

"Around 2001, Latino children began to enter southern schools in noticeable numbers and Latino families began to buy homes in rural Alabama and Arkansas," Jamie Winders, a geographer at Syracuse University's Maxwell School who studied the issue, concluded in 2007. "In the wake of this collision between the South's emergence as an immigrant-receiving region and the nation's post-9/11 eruption into border hysteria, southern states have scrambled to contain the social, political, and cultural challenges that Latino migrants bring to southern communities from an even deeper 'south.'"[35]

The states controlled by the Deep South and Greater Appalachia—traditionally places people emigrated from—became destinations for Latino migrants at the turn of the twenty-first century, attracted to fill labor shortages in factories and meat and seafood processing plants. Starting from an extremely low baseline, Latino populations grew by hundreds or even thousands of percent in many Southern states during the 1990s and aughts, sprouting new Little Mexico neighborhoods in many cities and spurring migration researchers to start calling the region the *Nuevo* New South.[36] Much of the scholarly research suggests that people in regions that have always been prominent immigrant destinations have positive feelings about immigrants, but people in regions that have recently become such after having few if any foreign-born residents are more likely to see them as invaders. Regions that were once major immigrant destinations but no longer are today are in the middle. This analysis definitely tracks for the behavior of early-twenty-first-century political leaders across the American Nations.

Americans' attitudes toward immigration improved dramatically overall in recent decades, with the proportion of people saying it strengthens (rather than burdens) the United States rising from 31 to 62 percent between 1994 and 2019, according to the Pew Research Center. However, the partisan divide—which didn't exist in 1994—has gotten wider with Democrats and Republicans differing by 20 points on the issue, with only 38 percent of Republicans in 2019 saying immigration strengthens the country compared to 58 percent of Democrats.[37] At the same time, there has been a growing policy gap between the regional cultures, with those historically hostile to immigration leading the charge against immigrants, especially unauthorized ones and others taking steps to help them.

This regional gap first opened up in the early twenty-first century after the Deep South and Greater Appalachia began experiencing their first significant foreign in-migration since the United States banned the import of enslaved people in 1817. Coupled with post-9/11 border security anxiety, in the aughts and 2010s, states controlled by these regional cultures enacted a spate of laws to facilitate the deportation of unauthorized immigrants or to make life so difficult and insecure they would "self-deport." (Ironically, this phrase was first created by Chicano satirist Lalo Alcaraz and his fellow comedian Esteban Zul to mock anti-immigrant campaigners but was then popularized by Republican politicians like Pete Wilson and Mitt Romney, who adopted it in earnest.[38]) Many unauthorized immigrants fled Alabama in 2011 after legislators passed a draconian law that made it illegal for them to reside in the state or for people to give them rides or to rent them homes, while directing law enforcement to screen the immigration status of all public school students.[39] South Carolina and Georgia passed similar laws before the courts overturned most of their provisions as being unconstitutional intrusions on federal authority over immigration.[40] (Arizona, a state split between El Norte and the Far West, had a "check your papers" law that the Supreme Court overturned for the same reason.) When researchers at Queens University of Charlotte in North Carolina analyzed 3,500 state and local immigration policy measures passed across the United States between 2005 and 2017, they found those in Southeastern states—all of which are controlled by the Deep South, Greater Appalachia, Tidewater, or a combination thereof—were significantly more restrictive than those passed in other regions.[41] Another team of researchers, led by Columbia University's Goleen Samari, developed a system to codify the 714 immigration policies adopted by individual states between 2009 and 2019 by the degree to which they furthered the exclusion or inclusion of immigrants.

Their results, expressed in a scale from -12 (most exclusive) to +12 (most inclusive), ranked the three states with significant or dominant Left Coast sections as having adopted the most immigrant-friendly policies (+8.18 to +3.73), and Deep Southern–controlled Georgia (-9.73) and Alabama (-9.64) and Greater Appalachian–run Indiana (-9) at the other, anti-immigrant extreme. Most Yankee- and both New Netherland–controlled states were net inclusive, most Deep Southern and Greater Appalachian states highly exclusive.[42] These were the rankings of the states based on the laws in effect in 2019, the last year of the study period:

Immigration Policies: Hostile or Friendly (2019)

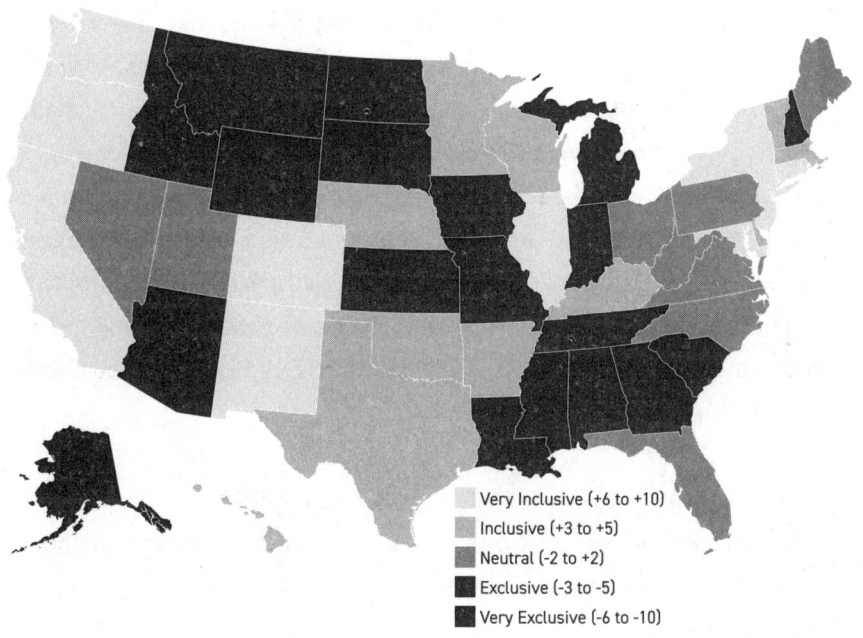

Very Inclusive (+6 to +10)
Inclusive (+3 to +5)
Neutral (-2 to +2)
Exclusive (-3 to -5)
Very Exclusive (-6 to -10)

Data: Goleen Samari, Amanda Nagle, and Kate Coleman-Minahan, "Measuring Structural Xenophobia: U.S. State Immigration Policy Climates over Ten Years," SSM-Population Health, 16 (2021), Table V.

The situation has accelerated since, with the governors of Texas (controlled by Greater Appalachia and the Deep South) and Florida (Deep South) transporting and dumping migrants on the streets of Yankeedom and New Netherland without prior warning. In 2023, Texas adopted a law empowering local and state police to arrest migrants entering its territory, and Louisiana followed suit the following spring. Both states argue these intrusions on federal control are justified because the migrants constitute an "invasion."[43]

States have a choice whether or not they want their agencies and state and local police forces to help federal agents detain or deport migrants. Some state legislatures have passed laws prohibiting cooperation—so-called sanctuary states—while others adopted laws that require local and state officials to cooperate with federal Immigration and Customs Enforcement (ICE), providing them holding cells, jail beds, access to interview detainees, and assistance in apprehension and custody transfer. The Immigrant Legal Resource Center monitors such enforcement policies and provides each state with a pro- or anti-immigrant score. In their 2023 index, the states with the most anti-immigrant policies—Florida, Texas, Iowa, Alabama, and West Virginia—were controlled by the Deep South, Greater Appalachia, and the Midlands. The pro-immigrant states—Oregon, Illinois, New Jersey, Washington, California, Vermont, and Connecticut—were all dominated by the Left Coast, Yankeedom, New Netherland, or, in California's case, El Norte. No Yankee, New Netherland, or Left Coast state had enacted anti-immigrant policies, while almost all Deep Southern and Greater Appalachian states had.[44]

AT NATIONHOOD LAB, we were curious if the gaps seen at the policy level reflected regional differences in public opinion on these issues. We again turned to the Nationscape survey set, that massive polling project that surveyed more than half a million Americans on a broad range of issues and attitudes between mid-2019 and early 2021, including several questions on immigration and border security. As with the other issues that we and other analysts have looked at, the American people are much closer together on the issues than their elected representatives are. In every region, large majorities disapproved of Donald Trump's policy of separating children from their migrant parents (so as to deter would-be asylum seekers via terror) as well as his Muslim ban, which sought to stop people of that religion from entering the country. Everywhere, supermajorities want "Dreamers"—undocumented people brought to the United States as small children—to be allowed to become citizens, and they think there should be a path to citizenship for law-abiding migrants who entered illegally. They also think the immigration system needs a fundamental overhaul, a position everybody who has studied it for more than an hour, agrees with.

There are significant regional differences on several salient issues, however. Trump's promise to build a 2,000-mile-long border wall got plurality support in Greater Appalachia and New France and broke about even with Deep Southerners. Pluralities in all the other regions don't want the wall built, with the net strength of opposition ranging from about 10 points in the Far West to almost 32 points in the Left Coast. El Norte, where the wall would actually be built, rejects it by more than 22 points.

Do You Support "Building the Wall"?

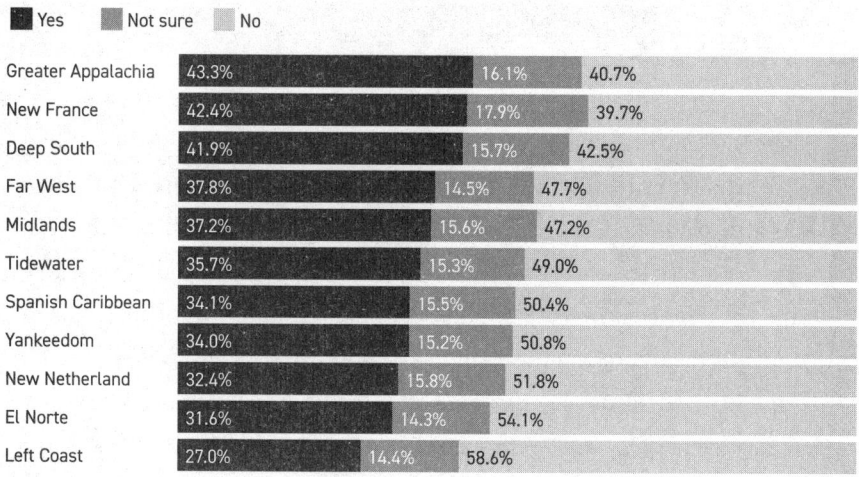

■ Yes ▨ Not sure ▨ No

	Yes	Not sure	No
Greater Appalachia	43.3%	16.1%	40.7%
New France	42.4%	17.9%	39.7%
Deep South	41.9%	15.7%	42.5%
Far West	37.8%	14.5%	47.7%
Midlands	37.2%	15.6%	47.2%
Tidewater	35.7%	15.3%	49.0%
Spanish Caribbean	34.1%	15.5%	50.4%
Yankeedom	34.0%	15.2%	50.8%
New Netherland	32.4%	15.8%	51.8%
El Norte	31.6%	14.3%	54.1%
Left Coast	27.0%	14.4%	58.6%

Data: Democracy Fund + UCLA Nationscape Survey (2019–2021)

There was almost an identical pattern when people were asked if they supported deporting all undocumented immigrants, some 11 million people. Slight pluralities in Greater Appalachia (40–39 percent) and New France (41–38) agreed, while the policy was rejected by huge margins in New Netherland (30–51), El Norte (28–53), the Left Coast (27–54), and Florida's Spanish Caribbean section (30–50). Residents of Tidewater, the Midlands, and Yankeedom disagreed with the policy by closer margins and the Deep South by fewer than 3 points.

All Undocumented Immigrants Should Be Deported

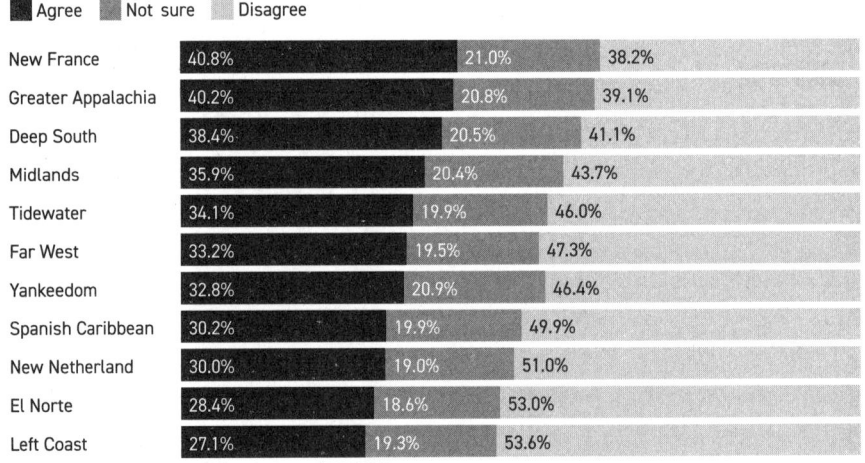

Data: Democracy Fund + UCLA Nationscape Survey (2019–2021)

There was a similar pattern—and even more support—for charging people who enter the country illegally with a federal crime, even though it was already, in fact, illegal to do so. (At the time of this writing, the first offense is a misdemeanor and subsequent one is a felony, but most migrants are deported instead because of the human and financial costs of trying and incarcerating them and caring for minors while they are imprisoned.[45]) Pluralities again agree in Greater Appalachia (44–34) and New France (42–35) and were joined by respondents in the Deep South

(42–37) and the Midlands (41–38). Respondents in the Far West and Tidewater were statistically tied on the issue, while pluralities opposed the measure in Yankeedom (38–40), the Spanish Caribbean (36–43), El Norte (34–45), New Netherland (35–46), and the Left Coast (21–47).

IT WAS CLEAR IN LATE 2024 that Americans, by and large, continue to see the country as a nation of immigrants and reject radical anti-immigrant policies, but that this support was far weaker in the southern regions and not very robust in the Midlands. These regions propelled the reelection of Donald Trump, the country's most dangerous agitator against immigrants and people of color, who made constructing border fortifications and rounding up undocumented migrants a central feature of Trumpism and ordered Congressional Republicans to spike a bipartisan deal that would have addressed many of their longstanding concerns. ("I do not think we should do a Border Deal, at all, unless we get EVERYTHING needed to shut down the INVASION of Millions & Millions of people," Trump wrote on his Truth Social internet platform, "many from parts unknown, into our once great, but soon to be great again, Country!") He and his followers call immigrants—few of whom are white and Protestant—invaders, rapists, criminals, disease-spreaders, and "vermin" who are "poisoning the blood of our country." At the time of this writing, he is about to resume the presidency, where his immigration policies will further drive intra-regional animosity and division.[46]

Data and history tell us that countering the ethnoracial othering of immigrants is possible everywhere, but far easier when the effort can be framed around legal immigrants or the children of undocumented ones who are either birthright citizens or Dreamers who know no other country than this one. In the Midlands, effective counterarguments would embrace and champion the region's fundamental heritage as a culturally pluralistic society of immigrants, while drawing the easy parallels between Trump's xenophobic rhetoric and that of those who attacked seventeenth-century Quakers, eighteenth-century Scots-Irish and Anabaptists, and early twentieth-century Germans, East Europeans, and Jews. Everywhere, one should take up the ideals in the Declaration—the earthly things most sacred to Americans and the subject of chapter 10—as cudgels against racists and xenophobes. Those ideals can help short-circuit the effects of Greater Appalachia's ethnonationalist myth, deploying freedom against heritage, and provide the elemental rebuttal to the Deep South's Herrenvolk tradition. It's a fight Americans can't afford to lose.

6

ABORTION

F ew issues in American life have created the kind of de jure threats to the survival of the federation as abortion has since six conservative Supreme Court justices ended women's half-century-old constitutional right to abort a pregnancy in their June 2022 decision in *Dobbs v. Planned Parenthood.*

States across the South and interior West moved immediately to not only ban abortion, but to try to criminalize their residents obtaining one—or helping someone obtain one—in states where it had been completely legal. Texas allows civil suits against any entity that provides funds or assistance to someone trying to obtain an out-of-state abortion and South Dakota law opens the possibility that out-of-state medical providers could face criminal charges for filling a mail-order prescription for federally approved abortion drugs. Alabama's attorney general says anyone helping an Alabaman obtain an out-of-state abortion has engaged in a criminal conspiracy.

At the same time, states in the Northeast and on the Pacific coast moved to protect reproductive rights and have declared other state's anti-abortion laws to be inapplicable in their courts. Maine, Massachusetts,

Rhode Island, New Jersey, and Delaware now prohibit law enforcement from cooperating with abortion investigations or answering legal summons by pro-life states. Maine Governor Janet Mills—a career state prosecutor and former state attorney general—issued an executive order prohibiting authorities from arresting or surrendering an individual for these new crimes on behalf of an anti-abortion state's government. California legislators passed laws that prohibit companies, tech Goliaths, and government agencies from providing personal data or medical data to out-of-state abortion investigators.

Together, these regional divides amount to what George Washington University law professor Paul Berman has called "the biggest set of nationwide conflicts of law problems since the era of the Fugitive Slave Act before the Civil War," when southern states began forcing northerners to apprehend any Black person they claimed had escaped from slavery and, without due process, return them to bondage.

The distribution of pro- and anti-abortion states is by no means random. Rather, it follows distressingly familiar regional patterns. In the first two years after *Dobbs* was decided, fourteen states fully banned abortion, and seven others had restricted the procedure to earlier in the pregnancy than allowed by *Roe v. Wade*, the 1972 case the Supreme Court had overturned, upending legal precedent. Together, these include every state controlled by the Deep South or Greater Appalachia, plus two Far West–controlled states and four—Missouri, the Dakotas, and Nebraska—with mixed Midlands and Far Western control.

By contrast, abortion remains legal and unchallenged in every state controlled by Yankeedom, New Netherland, Tidewater, the Left Coast, and Greater Polynesia, and most of those states have increased protections since the *Dobbs* ruling. Lawmakers in Ohio, a state with large Yankee and Midlands sections but a Greater Appalachian plurality, tried to ban the procedure as well but were stymied by the public via a ballot measure in November 2022, and the same thing happened in Midlands–controlled Kansas.

At Nationhood Lab, we were curious if public attitudes toward abortion mirrored these patterns. Most sources provide only national- or state-level data, which is unhelpful because America's real cultural regions often ignore state boundaries. We turned again to the Nationscape survey's data, wherein several questions relevant to the issue were posed to about half a million Americans between mid-2019 and early 2021. (Again, two of the smallest nations, Greater Polynesia and First Nation, didn't have enough respondents to parse this data in a reliable way, so we've had to exclude them from this analysis.)

The data confirmed what many others have found: Americans are much closer together on abortion than the actions of their elected leaders would suggest. Supermajorities in every American Nations region reject an outright ban on abortion, and large majorities in each region believe the procedure should be legal for additional reasons beyond incest, rape, and the life of the mother. If public will were followed, no state would have an outright ban. But many do, and this is where margins of opposition and the settlement history of our continent become essential to understanding the situation.

The survey revealed substantial regional differences in the levels of opposition to abortion. Support for a total ban is nearly twice as high in New France (30.9 percent) than in the Left Coast (15.5 percent), and the gaps between the Deep South (25.1 percent) and Greater Appalachia (27.1 percent) on one hand and Yankeedom (17.1 percent), Tidewater, El Norte, New Netherland (all 19.5 percent), the Spanish Caribbean (19.9 percent), and the Far West (19.4 percent) on the other are significant. There's a similar regional pattern—and up to 14-point gaps—in opposition to abortions for reasons other than rape, incest, or saving the life of the mother, what scholars term "traumatic" (as opposed to "elective") reasons.[1]

When it comes to implementing coercive measures to make abortion services harder to access—like imposing mandatory waiting periods or allowing employers to deny insurance coverage for them—the regions are in outright disagreement. Pluralities in those same three conservative

Support for a Total Abortion Ban

■ Support ■ Oppose ░ Don't Know

	Support	Oppose	Don't Know
New France	30.9%	48.9%	20.2%
Greater Appalachia	27.1%	53.9%	19.0%
Deep South	25.1%	55.5%	19.5%
Midlands	20.0%	62.1%	17.9%
Spanish Caribbean	19.9%	62.6%	17.5%
El Norte	19.5%	62.9%	17.5%
New Netherland	19.5%	63.6%	16.9%
Tidewater	19.5%	62.4%	18.1%
Far West	19.4%	63.3%	17.3%
Yankeedom	17.1%	65.1%	17.8%
Left Coast	15.5%	69.4%	15.2%

Data: Democracy Fund + UCLA Nationscape Survey (2019–2021)

Abortion Beyond Rape, Incest, Maternal Life?

■ Oppose ■ Support ░ Don't Know

	Oppose	Support	Don't Know
New France	35.0%	46.1%	18.9%
Greater Appalachia	34.8%	48.0%	17.1%
Deep South	31.3%	51.4%	17.3%
Midlands	28.7%	54.8%	16.5%
Far West	27.8%	56.7%	15.5%
Tidewater	27.3%	56.3%	16.5%
Yankeedom	24.7%	58.8%	16.5%
El Norte	23.5%	60.7%	15.8%
Spanish Caribbean	23.3%	61.4%	15.3%
Left Coast	20.9%	64.4%	14.7%
New Netherland	20.6%	64.5%	14.8%

Data: Democracy Fund + UCLA Nationscape Survey (2019–2021)

nations—the Deep South, Greater Appalachia, and New France—support these measures, while the other nations oppose them, creating a 19-point gap between the Left Coast and New France on the insurance question and a 13.5-point gap on waiting periods.

Mandatory Waiting Periods to Get an Abortion

■ Support ■ Oppose ▫ Don't Know

	Support	Oppose	Don't Know
New France	44.9%	30.8%	24.3%
Greater Appalachia	44.8%	31.4%	23.9%
Deep South	42.9%	32.8%	24.4%
Midlands	38.8%	36.2%	25.1%
Spanish Caribbean	37.0%	40.4%	22.6%
Far West	36.9%	38.8%	24.3%
Tidewater	36.9%	37.6%	25.5%
New Netherland	36.3%	39.3%	24.4%
El Norte	35.6%	39.4%	25.0%
Yankeedom	34.9%	38.6%	26.4%
Left Coast	31.4%	44.9%	23.7%

Data: Democracy Fund + UCLA Nationscape Survey (2019–2021)

Ohio's tripartite regional identity was on stark display in their November 2023 vote on whether to protect abortion rights in their state constitution. Though Ohio voters had consistently elected Republicans in most statewide races for more than a decade, the referendum passed by a statewide margin of 14 percentage points. The vote—together with similar results in Kansas and Kentucky—has rightly been seen as a warning that Republicans in state legislatures, Congress, and on the Supreme Court bench are radically out of step with the citizenry on this issue, even in reliably red states, which is consistent with our data.

However, the vote on Ohio's referendum was geographically split along patterns that would have been familiar to Frederick Jackson Turner back in 1895. Every county in the New England–settled Northeast voted overwhelmingly in favor, rural and urban alike. The middle section of the state, where colonization was led by Pennsylvania "Dutch" and German immigrant farmers from the Midlands, opposed the measure, which only barely passed in its cities. In the Scots-Irish-settled south of the state— first colonized via western Virginia and Kentucky—Columbus, Cincinnati, and Ohio University were islands poking from a sea of opposition.

The results, mapped below, mirror the spatial patterns of another ballot vote a few months earlier in which Ohio voters quashed a Republican effort to make it harder to pass a future referendum.[2]

Ohio Issue 1: Constitutional Right to Abortion (2023)

Ballot question to establish the right to "make and carry out one's own reproductive decisions," including abortion before fetal viability. The measure passed statewide, 56.8 to 43.2.

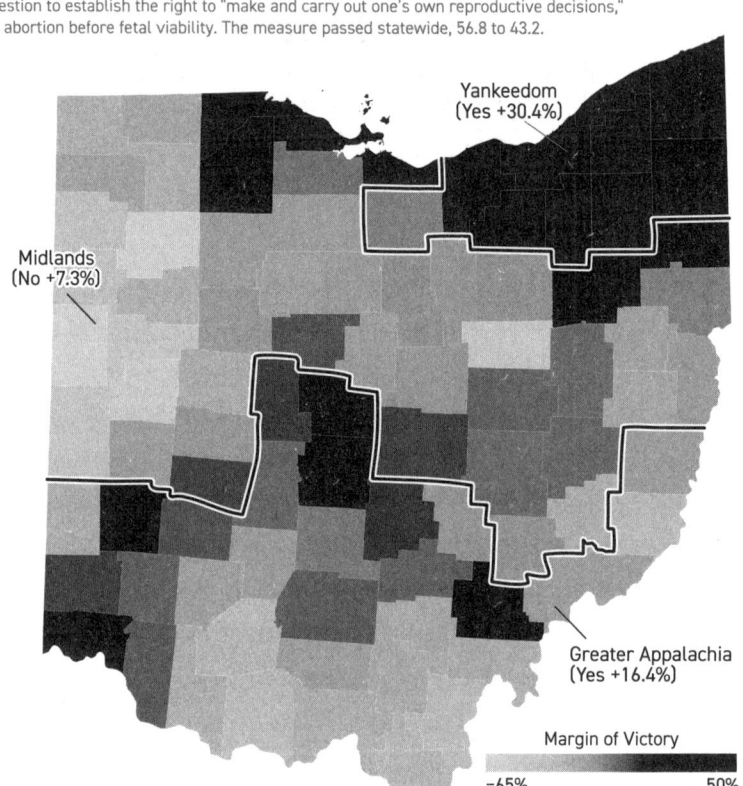

Data: Ohio Secretary of State

There are two takeaways thus far. First, there are big gaps between the three Dixie regions and most everyone else, with the Midlands lying, as per historical form, in between. Second, there's the question as to why pro-life forces have had such an outsize influence over policy in states controlled by the Dixie regions and/or the Midlands and the Far West, given they still represent a minority of the population.

As a cultural historian, one hypothesis I wanted to test was whether pro-life forces were getting a boost in these regions because they might have more patriarchal cultural attitudes. Decades of social science research and polling has shown "Southerners"—male and female alike— to have significantly more conservative attitudes regarding female participation and equality in the work force, economic leadership, and political life. In the early twentieth century, Deep Southern, Tidewater, and Greater Appalachian states were the most resistant to the women's suffrage movement and most of them refused to ratify the Nineteenth Amendment. By contrast, the women's suffrage movement got its start in Yankeedom and New Netherland but came to fruition in the Far West and the Left Coast, where "frontier" realities had given women more equal roles in work, land ownership, and business management. Indeed, there were so few women in the region in the 1860s—men outnumbered women by between three- and twenty-to-one depending on the state—that state and territorial legislators felt they had to go out of their way to make their region attractive for would-be migrants. Wyoming's lawmakers granted women full voting rights a few months after the territory's April 1869 creation, the first state or territory to do so. Utah followed in 1870, though the state's Mormon leadership was primarily motivated by wanting to boost its electoral power to defend polygamy. The next six to do so were all in or controlled by the Far West or the Left Coast and, on the eve of the Nineteenth Amendment's ratification, every state controlled by these regions had granted women the vote, comprising the majority of the states who had done so by choice.[3]

At the turn of the millennium, scholars created a "gender equality index" compiling a wide range of state-level statistics, from the proportion of legislators who were female to gaps in workforce participation, wages, and legal rights; the top six states in equality were all controlled by the Left Coast or Yankeedom, the bottom six consisted of (Mormon) Utah, (Greater Appalachia/Tidewater-controlled) North Carolina, and, at the bottom, four Deep Southern states. The Equal Rights Amendment, an effort in the 1970s and early 1980s to explicitly prohibit gender discrimination, was ratified in time by nearly every Yankee, New Netherland, Midlands, Left Coast, and Far West–controlled state, but the measure failed due to the opposition of most Greater Appalachian– and all Deep Southern– and Tidewater-controlled states. These regional divides suggested a possible explanation for those we see on abortion: If women are expected to stay within the domestic sphere of child rearing and homemaking, perhaps this would negatively impact reproductive freedom, with all of the economic, political, and social implications for gender equality.[4]

The Nationscape surveys asked several questions that get at this, including if respondents would prefer to have a male boss, if they thought women were as capable of "thinking logically as men," and if women who complain about harassment "often cause more problems than they solve." As it turns out, in every region only small minorities reject female equality in these questions, though men are less reliable in this regard everywhere. Intriguingly, the regional gaps that opened up between the genders—think of them as "sexism indicators"—were greatest in New Netherland and the Left Coast. (Yankeedom and the Midlands were the least sexist in this regard.) More men in New Netherland and New France agreed with the statement about women reporting harassment than disagreed, the only regions where that was the case. And there was almost no gender gap at all on abortion in southern regions, but there was a double-digit one in New Netherland, with many more men than women supporting restrictive policies. Are the high-pressure professional environs of the Big Apple, Silicon Valley, and Seattle the most sexist places in the country? This is an avenue for further research, but it's clear from this data that patriarchy, sexism, and abortion opinion have differing regional patterns.

Women Who Complain About Harassment Cause More Problems Than They Solve (Percent Agree)

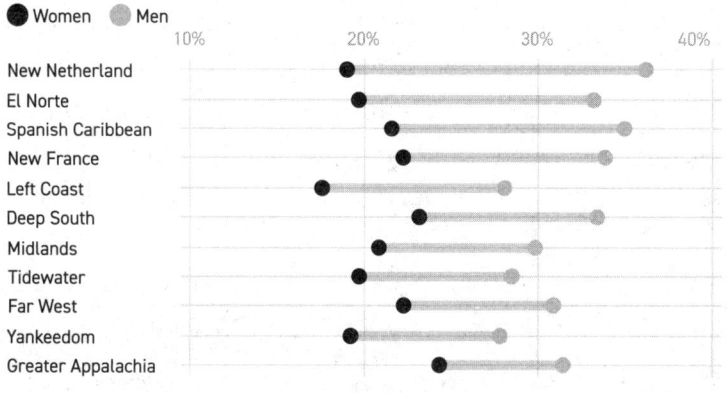

Data: Democracy Fund + UCLA Nationscape Survey (2019–2021)

Support for a Total Abortion Ban by Gender

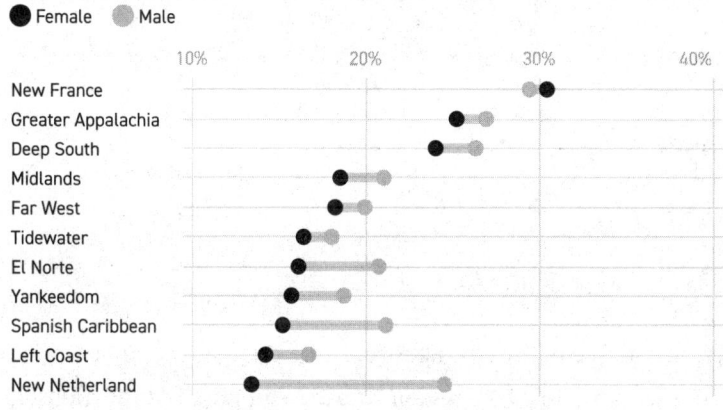

Data: Democracy Fund + UCLA Nationscape Survey (2019–2021)

If patriarchal attitudes don't explain the regional variations, we thought, maybe religious geography does. We segmented the Nationscape respondents by religion and . . . bingo.

The Nationscape surveys asked respondents their religion and whether they considered themselves evangelical or not. This allowed us to compare abortion attitudes across regions for Catholics, mainline (non-evangelical)

Protestants, Evangelical Protestants, and the unchurched, and even to do segmentation for white and (in some regions) Hispanic Catholics and white and Black evangelicals. (Even with 500,000 respondents, the data wasn't rich enough to confidently parse smaller religious groups like Jews, Buddhists, Mormons, Muslims, or Orthodox Christians across the regions.) We found stark, profound, and broadly consistent gaps across the American Nations regions for a wide range of relevant questions.

Abortion Ban Support by Religion (2019–2021)

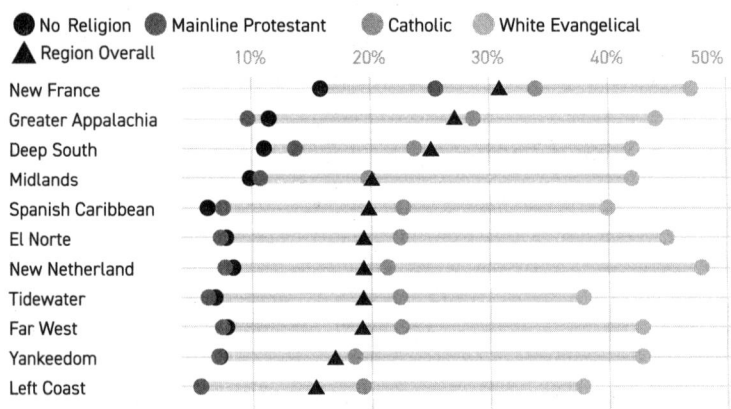

Data: Democracy Fund + UCLA Nationscape Survey (2019–2021)

As you can see in the chart above, white evangelicals are extreme outliers on this issue in every region. Indeed, support for abortion bans is driven almost entirely by this religious group, who are roughly five times more likely to take this hardline position than their mainline Protestant counterparts, who are more pro-choice than even the unchurched in most of the nations. Catholics are in the middle, slightly more pro-choice than the average citizen in the Deep South and the Midlands and slightly more pro-life in the rest of the regions. (Other polls have consistently shown Black Protestants to be pro-choice.)

You'll also notice that within religious traditions there's variation by region, with Catholics more likely to hold pro-choice opinions in the Left Coast, Yankeedom, and the Midlands than in the Deep South or Greater Appalachia. White evangelicals are a bit more moderate in Tidewater and the Left Coast, but most pro-life in New Netherland (where they constitute just 2.8 percent of the population). Louisiana's New France enclave is an outlier across the board, with every group substantially more pro-life than in the other regions. (More on that later.)

Could the regional maldistribution of white evangelicals account for much of the difference in abortion opinion? The Public Religion Research Institute (PRRI)—a Washington, DC–based think tank—has the best county-level estimates of various types of religious adherents and they kindly shared their 2020 Census of American Religion data with us. It turns out the answer is yes.[5]

Here is the percent of the population of each of the American Nations that is white evangelical:

White Evangelicals (Percent of population)

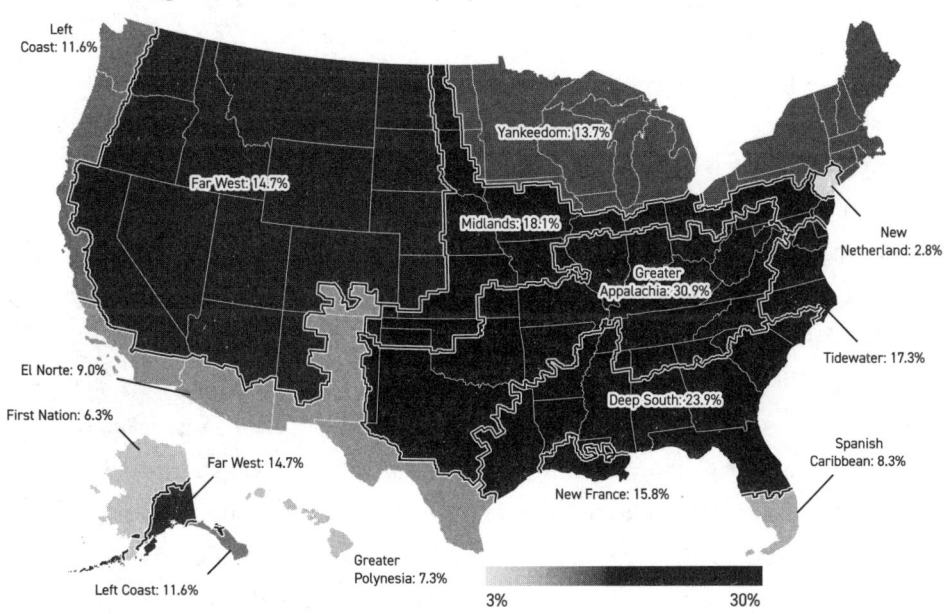

Left Coast: 11.6%

Yankeedom: 13.7%

Far West: 14.7%

Midlands: 18.1%

New Netherland: 2.8%

Greater Appalachia: 30.9%

Tidewater: 17.3%

El Norte: 9.0%

First Nation: 6.3%

Deep South: 23.9%

Spanish Caribbean: 8.3%

Far West: 14.7%

New France: 15.8%

Left Coast: 11.6%

Greater Polynesia: 7.3%

3%   30%

Data: PRRI, 2020 Census of American Religion

Compare this with the table on page 184—Support for a Total Abortion Ban—and notice the similarities. We'd like to have been able to show county-level correlations against the Nationscape data but, alas, the latter is coded only at the congressional district level. But recent abortion-related ballot measures in several states give us an opportunity to test county-level relationships in the post-*Dobbs* world.

In Ohio, where voters were asked in November 2023 to approve a constitutional amendment protecting abortion rights, the county-level correlations between the percent of voters who opposed the measure and the percentage of the population who are white evangelical were very high. We calculated the Pearson correlation coefficients, in which a +1.0 indicates a perfect and complete correlation between two variables, a 0 indicates there is absolutely no relationship, and a -1.0 indicates a perfect negative relationship. In the Yankee-settled Western Reserve, the Pearson bivariate correlation was an extremely robust 0.82, and in Greater Appalachia, it was 0.89. In the Midlands, it was a somewhat weaker 0.49, suggesting additional factors are also at play, which we'll get to in a minute. And white evangelicals are not distributed evenly across the state. Cuyahoga County, where Cleveland is located and the heart of the Yankee Western Reserve, attracted lots of Great Wave immigrants a century ago and today is only 8 percent white evangelical. The big cities in Greater Appalachian Ohio have a significantly larger share—13 percent in Cincinnati, 16 percent in Columbus, and 21 percent in Dayton—but nothing like the counties of the Appalachian and Midland countysides, where they typically constitute at least 30 to 40 percent of the population.

The PRRI's 2020 Census of American Religion estimated the percentage of people adhering to each religious denomination at the county level. In Ohio, Catholics—whose immigrant ancestors were typically attracted by the jobs offered in industrializing Yankeedom—are much more prevalent in the Western Reserve than in Greater Appalachia. White Protestant Evangelicals, who've always faced headwinds in post-Puritan Yankeedom, are few on the ground; in no county do they reach 30 percent. Regionalism profoundly shaped Ohio's religious geography, and when it comes to abortion attitudes, religion is destiny.[6]

The white evangelical factor was similarly robust for the Yankeedom and Greater Appalachian sections of other states that held abortion votes in 2023. In Michigan (which lies entirely within Yankeedom), the white evangelical correlation with casting a pro-life vote was 0.75, while in Kentucky (entirely Greater Appalachian), it was 0.79. When Kansas voted on the issue, the correlation in its Greater Appalachian section—which comprises 11.5 percent of the state's population—was 0.75. (Its populous, largely urbanized Midlands section had a higher correlation, 0.71, than we saw in the more rural Ohio Midlands.)

When California voted on the issue, the white evangelical correlation was 0.74 in the state's Left Coast section, 0.56 in the Far West, and a very weak 0.14 in El Norte. The latter region has very few white evangelicals, so, by way of comparison, we ran the numbers for Hispanic Catholics and also found a weak relationship of 0.29. (In the Left Coast, curiously, this number was 0.74, suggesting regional cultural differences are playing a role.) The Far Western section of Kansas, by the way, had a white evangelical correlation of 0.40, broadly similar to that seen in California, suggesting the evangelical effect on this issue is not as strong in that region; more on that to come.

So, to summarize, the difference in abortion opinion is closely tied to the presence of white evangelicals, who are extreme outliers on the issue. Initial post-*Dobbs* popular votes on the issue suggest this relationship is especially acute in Greater Appalachia, Yankeedom, and the Left Coast; strong in the Midlands and the Far West; but weak in El Norte, possibly because Southern California's white evangelicals are more permissive on the issue, as the data suggests that section's much larger cohort of Hispanic Catholics are. At the time of this writing, there aren't any comparable results for the Deep South (because most states there don't allow citizen ballot initiatives) or New Netherland (because abortion is not under threat within New York, New Jersey, or Connecticut).

RECALL THAT MAJORITIES in every region oppose abortion bans, but that in states controlled by the Deep South, Greater Appalachia, the Midlands, the Far West, or some combination thereof, white evangelicals have gotten their way nonetheless. How?

Academics have been asking this question for decades and have come to some broad conclusions. From their fight against gay marriage in the early 2000s to wanting to ban abortion today, white evangelicals succeed in states where they've been able to capture intermediary institutions like state (Republican) parties, (the Republican caucuses of) state legislatures, or the state executive branch. "Successes have been achieved," the sociologists Rebecca Sager and Keith Bentele concluded in a study of how and where faith-based legislation passed between 1996 and 2009, primarily "through effective utilization of an existing political institution, the Republican Party."[7]

It turns out evangelical churches are excellent training grounds for political organizing. "Places of worship provide a natural foundation for organizing, a place where people are showing up every week and maybe serving on a board or volunteering at all sorts of events," Christopher Scheitle, professor of political science at West Virginia University, says. "And Evangelical churches have this entrepreneurial spirit and they don't have to seek approval from a hierarchy of a bishop to set up associated nonprofits like sports camps or publishing houses, which get people in the pews involved."[8]

An organized minority can get a long way, but numbers still matter. It's one thing to gain control of a state political party, legislative majority, or gubernatorial administration if your group represents 20 or 30 percent of the population, quite another if it's only 2, 8, or 10 percent, which is why white evangelicals are not getting their way in New Netherland and Yankeedom. Allies can help, of course. A 2022 PRRI survey on the issue found Latter Day Saints (LDS, the dominant Mormon denomination) to be the only group whose abortion opinions come close to that of white evangelicals—though their church allows for abortion in traumatic circumstances—and the two Far Western states that have restricted the procedure are also the states with the largest LDS constituencies in the country: 56 percent of Utah's population and 20 percent of Idaho's.[9]

"You have a lot of LDS activists who take up the Catholic belief that life begins at conception, even though the church is less explicit about this," notes the University of Oklahoma historian Jennifer Holland, author of *Tiny You: A Western History of the Anti-Abortion Movement.* Holland discovered the pro-life movement in the interior West was founded and continues to be led by members of the tiny white Catholic minority—even in Mormon Utah. "In the intermountain West, a lot of states aren't like the U.S. South, which has these very strong Evangelical majorities, they're multiracial and multireligious, so the groups have to negotiate with each other."[10]

In chapter 5, I showed how the Great Wave immigrants of the late nineteenth and early twentieth centuries—who were mostly Catholic, Orthodox Christian, or Jewish—actively avoided the Deep South, Tidewater, and Greater Appalachia, leaving those regions—and *only* those regions—homogenously Protestant and evangelical. But why were these regions overwhelmingly evangelical by the 1870s, given that the region was largely unchurched a century before, and why did the Baptists, Methodists, Episcopalians, and Presbyterians in these regions split from their coreligionists in Yankeedom, the Midlands, and New Netherland? The backstory is important for understanding the geography of abortion and a whole lot of other issues besides.

In many respects, the Deep South, Tidewater, and Greater Appalachia seem about the least likely places for an evangelical Bible Belt to have formed. In the eighteenth century, Virginia, the Carolinas, and Georgia were de jure Anglican, as the Church of England was the official, taxpayer-financed church across the region. These same regions were de facto unchurched. The Southern colonies had less than half as many churches per white resident as the Midland- and Yankee-controlled ones in 1750 and in many Tidewater and Deep Southern parishes of the official

Anglican church, less than half of eligible (white) parishioners regularly attended services. Presbyterian and evangelical preachers from Yankeedom, the Midlands, New Netherland, and Great Britain followed the Scots-Irish as they pushed through the uplands of Virginia in the late 1740s, but they encountered a ribald culture where, as one reported, the Sabbath was observed by drinking, "some fighting, some swearing, some playing tricks . . . hunting, sporting, and shooting at marks, horse-racing, jumping and foot-racing." Even in the lowland parishes, church attendance was far lower than in the northern colonies, with church-going a minority activity among whites in many parishes. (Enslaved people's exposure to Christian services depended on the whims and orders of their masters.)[11]

Early evangelical missionaries had a hard go of it. They forbade drinking, gambling, swearing, fighting, and all manner of other popular activities, which didn't help recruitment, and their practices represented a potential threat to the region's power structures. Preachers welcomed women and African Americans into fellowship, cast aspersions on slavery, and encouraged followers to regard one another as family, regardless of race, class, and marital status. They encouraged intense spiritual introspection in a culture where this had not been a feature, provoking sobbing, shrieking, writhing, shouting, and other emotional displays that frightened friends and family. "Evangelicals, far from dominating the South, were viewed by most whites as odd at best and subversive at worst," wrote University of Delaware historian Christine Leigh Heyrman, whose book *Southern Cross: The Beginnings of the Bible Belt* is the foundational work on these early missionary efforts.[12]

They had a hard go of it until they adapted to the cultures around them, that is. Starting around 1800, evangelical Baptist and Methodist missionaries in these regions stopped criticizing slavery and ceased trying to monitor white men's private conduct or to interfere in their regional "culture of honor," whereby insults or slights were met with disproportionately violent responses. Clergy began asserting absolute authority over their churches—like a master over his plantation—cracking down on outspoken women and driving Black people into segregated, slave lord–approved churches. Camp meetings adopted a manly, martial vibe, with morning bugle calls, marches to the altar, and posted rules enforced by "dog whippers," guards with special insignia attached to their coats who patrolled the grounds. A few decades later, southern Baptists and Methodists would break from their northern counterparts over their support of slavery, which is where the *Southern* Baptist Convention and the Methodist Episcopal Church, *South* come from.

"It's not too much of an oversimplification to say that what happens in the South between 1780 and the Civil War is that the religion, evangelicalism, adapts to the culture," Heyrman tells me. "This is one of the things my students have a hard time wrapping their heads around: the evangelicalism in the North is in many ways a very different animal than in the evangelical South."[13]

And while northern evangelicals faced ever-increasing competition from other groups—homegrown rivals like the Mormons, Seventh Day Adventists, or Christian Scientists and immigrant-powered Catholic, Lutheran, Orthodox Christian, and Jewish congregations—to a surprising degree, their southern counterparts had the field to themselves. Most Anglican priests had fled to England when the American Revolution broke out, making westward religious expansion impossible, while the Presbyterians' reliance on university-educated clergy made them unable to keep up with denominations that made do with unlettered, barely paid itinerant pastors on the expanding frontier. The three southern regions' feudal nature repelled the immigrants of the Great Wave of 1880 to 1924, causing them to be nearly bereft of Catholics, Jews, Orthodox Christians, and other non-evangelicals until the 1980s.

It's within these regions' religious monoculture that opposition to abortion is strongest. There's no theological reason why white evangelicals should be more animated about this issue than Catholics, northern (non-Fundamentalist) Baptists, or Black evangelicals. The explanation is cultural, and specific to the southern regions. In chapter 2, I described these regions' "culture of honor," which shapes white males to respond aggressively to insults and threats, leading to white homicide rates that are three, four, and five times that of New Netherland. In addition to adapting to southern ideas about race and power, the southern evangelical churches onboarded these regional honor cultures, including fundamentalist biblical interpretations of the duty of white males to rule over women, wives, children, and enslaved people. This led millions of people who professed to follow Jesus Christ's teachings to vociferously defend slavery in the 1850s, the Southern racial caste systems in the early 1900s, segregation in the 1960s, and, more to the point of this chapter, patriarchal gender norms against the growing feminist and gay rights movements of the 1970s. "Biblical texts define an honorable male as head of the house and spiritual shepherd in the church and helped Baptists identify a two-headed dragon of feminism and homosexuality as the latest cultural and moral threat to the South just as desegregation and abolition had menaced earlier white evangelical Souths," Edward R. Crowther, emeritus professor of history at Adams State College, wrote in a study of honor and manhood among Southern evangelicals."[14]

The pivotal moment in this late-twentieth-century campaign was when a group of Deep Southern fundamentalists, led by former Houston judge Paul Pressler and Baptist college president Paige Patterson of Dallas, orchestrated a successful coup against less-extreme leaders, seminarians, and Baptist college professors at the 1980 meeting of the Southern Baptist Convention, far and away the largest and most influential institutional structure in American Evangelical Protestantism. The takeover, consolidated over the 1980s, resulted in the Danvers Statement, which asserted that God ordained that men lead church and home, and that women submit to them and stay in their prescribed childrearing and husband-supporting lanes. It also resulted in a sharp change in the SBC's position on abortion. In the 1970s, its official statements called for adherents "to work for legislation that will allow the possibility of abortion under such conditions as rape, incest, clear evidence of severe fetal deformity, and carefully ascertained evidence of the likelihood of damage to the emotional, mental, and physical health of the mother." In the years after the 1980 coup, however, new resolutions dropped all exceptions save for protecting the mother's life from "immediate threat" and tied abortion to sinful sexual ideas and practices. Christian Nationalist leaders began arguing that banning abortion was essential to America's survival. "If we expect God to honor and bless our nation," the Moral Majority founder Jerry Falwell declared in 1981, "we must take a stand against abortion." Today, when a majority of white evangelicals hold Christian Nationalist views, national polling has showed they are much more likely than other Americans to support the death penalty, political violence, bans on life-saving vaccines, and the criminal punishment of women who seek abortions. "Christian nationalism, in other words, isn't opposed to death," sociologists Andrew Whitehead and Samuel Perry wrote in 2023. "It's opposed to disorder—specifically the disruption of established hierarchies and the traditional moral order."[15]

It's not surprising, then, to find that evangelicals—the primary proponents of total abortion bans—are overwhelmingly concentrated in the southern American Nations regions.

The map on the next page, first shown in chapter 5, shows the largest religious denomination in each county as of 2020. Outside the South, Catholics are the largest single religious group, the legacy of the Great Wave immigrants between 1870 and 1924, plus ongoing immigration from Mexico and Central America, mostly to El Norte. Notice also the scattered northern Methodist belt in the Midlands. Both of these denominations are far more moderate on abortion than southern Baptists and other evangelical Protestants. Meanwhile, Mormons, depicted with hatched lines on this map and dominant in only one portion of the Far West, are second only to evangelicals in their opposition to abortion, according to PRRI's 2022 American Values Atlas, a detailed survey of 23,000 Americans. Not surprisingly, Unitarian Universalists, the inheritors of the New England Enlightenment tradition embraced by the elite circles of antebellum Mas-

Dominant Religious Denomination by County (2020)

■ Catholic Church   ▨ Southern Baptist Convention   ■ Evangelical Lutheran Church in America
▧ United Methodist Church   ▨ Nondenominational Christian Churches
▨ Church of Jesus Christ of Latter-day Saints   ▨ Other

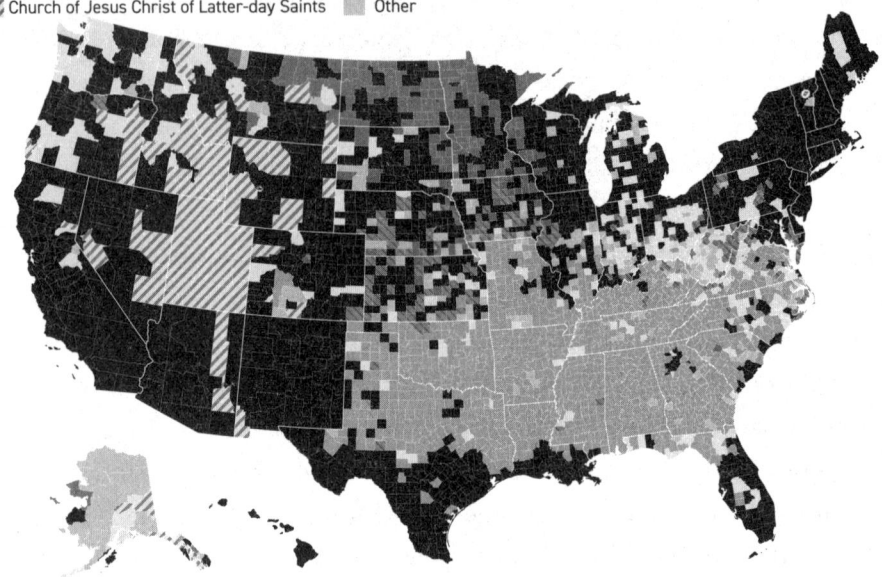

Data: Association of Statisticians of American Religious Bodies, 2020 U.S. Religion Census

sachusetts, are the most abortion-friendly denomination in the country, with 85 percent of adherents saying the procedure should be legal in most or all cases. This regional maldistribution of religious traditions has greatly increased the gap between the American Nations on reproductive rights issues.[16]

You'll have noticed that Louisiana's **New France** enclave is far and away the most conservative on this issue, despite being less than 16 percent white evangelical. This is because Catholics in this enclave are far more socially conservative than U.S. Catholics at large. As Tulane University political scientist Brian Brox told *FiveThirtyEight*, in Louisiana "Catholics are actually going to be both socially and politically closer to evangelical Protestants than a Catholic in Massachusetts or a Catholic in California." The Nationscape data showed that 33.9 percent of Catholics there supported a ban, whereas those in the other regions fell between

18.8 and 28.7 percent. The region's white evangelicals are more support-ive of a total abortion ban (47 percent of them) than even their Deep Southern (42 percent) or Greater Appalachian (44 percent) counterparts. New France's Catholics have been extremely conservative on a wide range of issues, threatening their own archbishop for his liberal stances on desegregation, racial equality, and working conditions. Many of the enclave's most successful twenty-first-century political figures, from Dem-ocratic Senator John Breaux and Governors Kathleen Blanco and John Bel Edwards to Republican Governor Jeff Landry and Senator David Vit-ter, have been abortion opponents, as are its delegations to the Louisiana state house and U.S. Congress.[17]

Tidewater, as you may have noticed, no longer allies with the Deep South and Greater Appalachia on this issue the way it did for most of the nineteenth and twentieth centuries, as it has transformed from being the capital of a white supremacist confederation to one of the most liberal and progressive regions in the country. This applies to reproductive is-sues as well, making it difficult to restrict the procedure in Delaware, Maryland, or even Virginia (which has a large, very conservative Appala-chian section that keeps the state politically competitive). Consistent with these trends, the region is now only 17.9 percent white evangelical, less even than in the Midlands.

The three other southern regions—and the two Far Western states with large Mormon constituencies—form the backbone of the abortion counterrevolution and are opposed by states controlled by Yankeedom, New Netherland, the Left Coast, Tidewater, and El Norte, where Catholic opinion is moderate, evangelicals and Mormons are few in number, and Jews, Buddhists, Muslims, and other non-Christians are not an inconse-quential part of the electorate.

This leaves the **Midlands,** whose settlement history and underlying cultural ethos presents something of a wild card in mapping abortion opinion. This region has always had an extremely heterogenous religious identity, thanks to its Quaker founders, who welcomed people of many nationalities and religious denominations—some conservative, some liberal—to their multicultural colonies on Delaware Bay. That multicultural ethos was bolstered by new streams of religious refugees in the mid to late nineteenth century. The result was that in the Midlands, more so than any other region, different ethnoreligious communities were encouraged to erect their own villages, towns, and neighborhoods and maintain their linguistic, cultural, and spiritual practices, with a lasting imprint you can see today, from Pennsylvania to Iowa.

This matters for today's abortion politics because it has made the Midlands more like a chunky stew than a melting pot. The presence of white evangelicals is still your best tool for predicting how a given Midlands county will vote, but there are concentrations of centuries-old religious communities of surprising homogeneity that sometimes have very strong opinions on abortion. That's why the Midlands band in Ohio, which features a constellation of deeply conservative German Catholic settlements combined with a percentage of white evangelicals, voted to reject the abortion initiative by seven points.[18]

But in Kansas, eight out of ten Midlanders live in metropolitan areas, and in Kansas City, Wichita, and Topeka (unlike Toledo and Youngstown in Ohio), pro-life mainline Protestants outnumber both Catholics and white evangelicals. In the 2022 vote, the Kansas Midlands *supported* abortion by double digits, spearheading its passage over the objections of the state's much less populous Greater Appalachian and Far Western sections. In this regard, the Missouri Midlands look a lot more like Kansas than Ohio and, because that section of the state makes up two-thirds of the electorate, abortion restrictions lost at the ballot box when Missourians voted on them in a state referendum at the end of 2024.

ALL OF THIS HISTORY, data, and analysis makes Arizona Republicans' recent hard-line actions on abortion all the more perplexing. Here's a politically competitive state dominated by El Norte with vanishingly few white evangelicals where only 7 percent of residents supported an abortion ban. And yet immediately after the *Dobbs* decision in 2022, Republican legislators and then Governor Doug Ducey enacted a law banning the procedure after fifteen weeks without exceptions for rape or incest. In April of that year, the Arizona Supreme Court—which Ducey had "packed," or expanded by two seats so as to create a conservative majority—ruled that an 1864 law, created by a territorial legislature a half century before Arizona became a state and decades before women could vote, was the law of the land, imposing a near-total ban on the procedure. Republican state senators then blocked a Democratic effort to put forward legislation to repeal that law, though a few GOP defectors later helped overturn the legislation. But Arizona is one of the states that allows for citizen-initiated ballot referenda, and in November 2024, voters enshrined abortion rights in their state constitution by a whopping 62–38 margin.[19]

In Florida—where six in ten people live within the Deep South—the state Supreme Court in April 2024 greenlighted a six-week abortion ban that was promptly put to the test via a constitutional amendment ballot initiative that November. While that measure won the vote count, 57–43, it fell short of the 60 percent required to implement the measure. Voters in the **Spanish Caribbean** settlement culture zone supported the measure by nearly two-to-one margins, which was consistent with its religious geography. PRRI estimates mainline Protestants outnumber white evangelicals by nearly two-to-one in this enclave, and in its biggest counties they're rivaled or outnumbered by Jews, who are overwhelmingly pro-choice. Latino Catholics, about 17 percent of the Spanish Caribbean's population, opposed an abortion ban in the Nationscape polls by more than a 30 percent margin. But abortion rights were defeated by overwhelming opposition across Deep Southern North Florida, where many counties are 30 to 50 percent white evangelical.[20]

———————

WHAT DOES THIS MEAN FOR the future of abortion in this post-*Dobbs* world? Barring a federal ban, if you live in a state that allows citizen-initiated ballot measures and constitutional amendments, abortion will likely be available in some form outside the Deep South. But that region, in particular, has long, illiberal authoritarian traditions—slavery and a racial apartheid system among them—and most states there deny this referenda power to their citizens, as do most Greater Appalachian states, meaning abortion will likely remain (or become) illegal. New Netherland, Tidewater, and parts of Yankeedom and the Midlands also frown on citizen-initiated ballot initiatives, and there are states in these regions where it's conceivable that undemocratic outcomes on the issue could prevail—including Iowa, Wisconsin, and Virginia.

In any region, citizens can theoretically vote out legislators, governors, and members of Congress for taking an abortion stand that displeases them. But in today's Manichean political environment, it's hard to imagine that happening in the Deep South and Greater Appalachia, so this issue is going to continue to corrode the ties between states and their underlying regions at a time when they're already dangerously weak.

7

CLIMATE

E very American is dependent on the planet for life support—for food, air, water, thermal regulation, and radiological protection— and yet support for environmentalism generally, and climate protection in particular, has always varied widely by region. Since the beginnings of the conservation and naturalism movements in the early nineteenth century, appreciation for the natural world and its role in keeping us healthy, happy, and alive has been overwhelmingly concentrated in Yankeedom, New Netherland, and, later, the Left Coast, the Far West, and El Norte and opposed by the political leaders of the Deep South, Greater Appalachia, and (paradoxically) the Far West.

Today, addressing climate change is rightly the most essential environmental issue, the one upon which everything else depends, from protecting biodiversity to promoting environmental justice. For decades now, bold action to address the problem has been hampered by the United States's internal divisions on the issue, wherein politicians from some regions of the country first denied global warming was taking place—Senator Jim Inhofe of Oklahoma said it was "the greatest hoax ever perpetuated against the

American people"—then accepted it was happening but claimed that humans weren't the cause and now, increasingly, admitting it is happening but arguing that it's not worth fixing. This opposition, buttressed by the fossil fuel industry, has doomed present and future generations to live in a world of superstorms, megadroughts, unprecedented wildfires, and mass extinctions.[1]

At Nationhood Lab, we wanted to know if the regional gaps might be starting to close, given that climate change effects are hitting southern and western regions particularly hard. To gauge this, we asked the Yale Program on Climate Change Communication if we could access their 2023 county-level climate opinion estimates, which took survey results from 28,000 Americans and leveraged them with detailed demographic information in a computer model. (At a county level, the model has +/- 8 percent accuracy, and within 3 percent nationally, so the American Nations model level would be in between; we dropped First Nation from our analysis because we strongly suspect there's far too little sampling to power their model.)

The Yale data—depicted in the graphic on the next page showed that supermajorities in every regional culture agree climate change is happening, from a low of just under 61 percent in Greater Appalachia to highs of about 76 percent in the Left Coast and more than 78 percent in Greater Polynesia. But when asked if humans are causing it—and there is no doubt that we are—the numbers get quite a bit softer. Only 48.2 percent of respondents in Louisiana's New France enclave—which is sinking into the sea—accept human causation compared to 64.4 percent in the U.S. portion of Greater Polynesia (Hawaii). Among large nations this range went from 47.2 percent in Greater Appalachia to 60.4 percent in the Left Coast. The results for wanting Congress to take strong action to address the issue were nearly identical—plus or minus about 1 to 5 percent in each region, with people in most regions a bit more likely to want action than to accept that humans caused the problem—though it was about 4 percent weaker in Greater Appalachia, the Midlands, and Yankeedom and 3 percent in the Far West.[2]

The same general pattern emerged from the response to a question

Climate Change Opinion in the American Nations

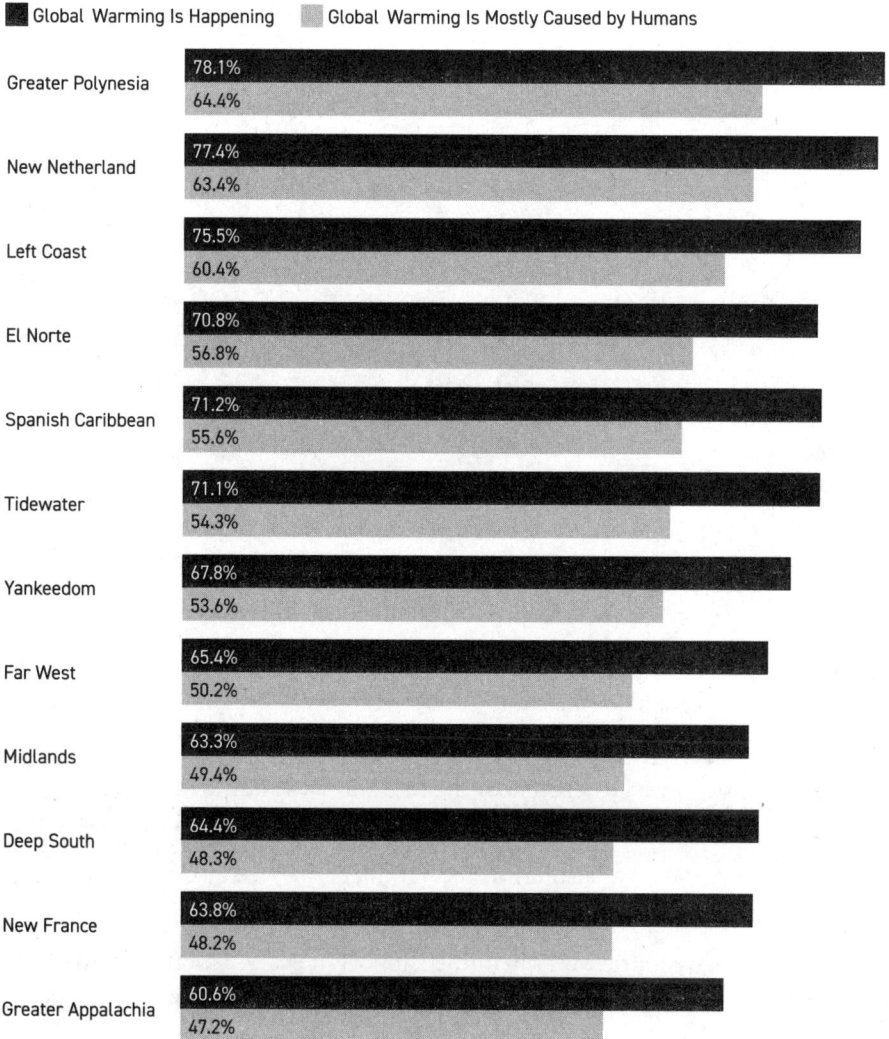

■ Global Warming Is Happening   ▨ Global Warming Is Mostly Caused by Humans

Greater Polynesia — 78.1% / 64.4%

New Netherland — 77.4% / 63.4%

Left Coast — 75.5% / 60.4%

El Norte — 70.8% / 56.8%

Spanish Caribbean — 71.2% / 55.6%

Tidewater — 71.1% / 54.3%

Yankeedom — 67.8% / 53.6%

Far West — 65.4% / 50.2%

Midlands — 63.3% / 49.4%

Deep South — 64.4% / 48.3%

New France — 63.8% / 48.2%

Greater Appalachia — 60.6% / 47.2%

Data: Yale Program on Climate Change Communication, "Yale Climate Opinion Maps 2023"

asking if most scientists believe global warming is happening (and they emphatically do). The misinformed have their strongest presence in New France, Greater Appalachia, and the Deep South and are thinnest on the ground in New Netherland, Greater Polynesia, and the Left Coast.

Do You Think Most Scientists Believe Global Warming Is Happening?

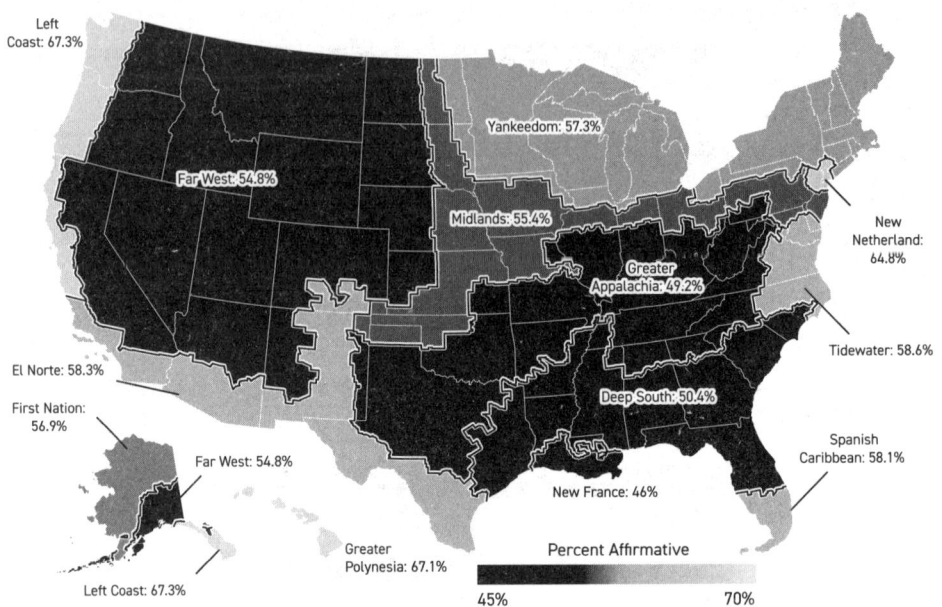

Data: Yale Program on Climate Change Communication, "Yale Climate Opinion Maps 2023"

The Yale data also showed big support in every region for regulating carbon dioxide and funding renewable energy initiatives and overwhelming opposition everywhere to drilling in National Wildlife Refuges. (Even in New France, the latter measure received only 35.3 percent support.)

To triangulate, we also crunched numbers on several climate-related questions posed by the Democracy Fund + UCLA Nationscape project. Encouragingly, we found overwhelming support in every nation for capping carbon emissions—by 25- and 30-point margins even in the least climate-conscious regions—and clear net approval for implementing a "Green New Deal" everywhere (save New France, where it was an exact tie). Americans may disagree on whether human-caused global warming is real or if we should do anything about it in the abstract, but they're almost universally in favor of creating green jobs and making power plants more efficient.

The most contentious climate-and-energy question posed in the Nationscape poll was whether authorities should lift existing barriers to oil and gas development, a measure with serious habitat protection and global warming implications. In each region at least a quarter of respondents were not sure where they stood and there were no majorities on either side of the issue. But pluralities want more drilling in New France (42.6 percent to 25.2 percent), Greater Appalachia (35.0–30.2), and the Deep South (35.7–30.8). All the other regions oppose it by varying degrees, from a point or two in New Netherland and Tidewater to nearly 20 in the Left Coast (25.6–44.2). In the Far West the net disapproval of lifting barriers was more than 4 points (31.9–36.2) and in Yankeedom more than 6 (30.0–36.3).

Should Barriers to Oil and Gas Development Be Lifted?

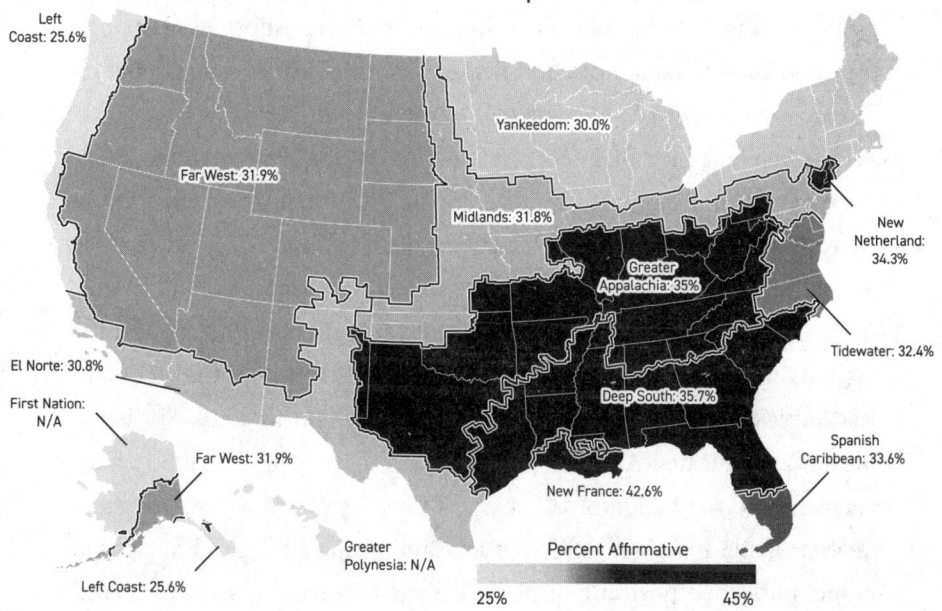

Data: Democracy Fund + UCLA Nationscape Survey (2019–2021)

Taken together, the data shows a clear pattern when it comes to public opinion on this ultimate environmental issue. The Left Coast, New Netherland, and Greater Polynesia are the most green-minded regions, with El Norte, Tidewater, and the Spanish Caribbean not far behind. The Far West and Yankeedom occupy the middle. The Midlands is pretty skeptical about climate change, and Greater Appalachia, the Deep South, and Louisiana's New France enclave (where offshore oil and gas is a major employer) are the least engaged.

THIS MATCHES PATTERNS seen throughout our history. Virtually the entire history of the environmental movement—from the writings of the Transcendentalists in the early nineteenth century to Earth Day in 1970—was driven by people and institutions in Yankeedom, New Netherland, and the Left Coast, with an occasional assist from an exiled Midlander. The Sierra Club, the continent's first grassroots environmental group, was founded in San Francisco in 1892 with substantial support from the faculty of Stanford and Berkeley, both of which were part of the mostly unsuccessful Yankee project to establish a "New England on the Pacific." George Bird Grinnell, a Yale-educated New Netherlander, fought the mass slaughter of birds by recreational hunters through the foundation of the New York–based Audubon Society in 1905. Another New Netherlander, President Theodore Roosevelt, pioneered federal involvement in environmental protection with the creation of the national forest, park, and wildlife refuge systems. His Yankee cousin Franklin Delano Roosevelt created the National Wildlife Federation in 1936. Midlands-born, Yale-educated Aldo Leopold founded the science of wildlife management and the Wilderness Society while a professor at the University of Wisconsin; his observations of the land around his rural Wisconsin home, published posthumously as *A Sand County Almanac*, is a landmark text in the green movement. From the coast of Maine, Midlands-born Rachel Carson wrote *The Sea Around Us* (1951) and *Silent Spring* (1962), which raised the ecological consciousness of millions. Two of the most prominent environmental groups that emerged in the 1960s—the Natural Resources Defense Council and the Environmental Defense Fund—were based in New Netherland. The Left Coast gave the world Greenpeace (founded in Vancouver, BC), the Sea Shepherd Society (based in

Friday Harbor, Washington), and Friends of the Earth, founded in San Francisco under the auspices of Berkeley native David Brower, who also founded the Earth Island Institute and League of Conservation Voters. The father of the Appalachian Trail, Benton MacKaye, wasn't from Appalachia at all but rather was a Harvard-educated Connecticuter whose grandparents had been prominent Yankee abolitionists.[3]

Public interest in these causes followed the same pattern, but with the addition of the Far West and Tidewater. By 1993, per capita membership in the thirteen largest national environmental organizations was overwhelmingly concentrated in Left Coast, Yankeedom, New Netherland, Tidewater, Far West, El Norte, and Spanish Caribbean counties; the Midlands occupied a middle ground; residents of Greater Appalachia, the Deep South, and New France were almost entirely absent from the environmental groups' membership rolls. Six of the top twenty-five counties in per capita membership were in the Colorado Rockies, but not one was from those three southern regions. A state-level study examining average environmental opinions from 1973 to 1982, as expressed by respondents to the National Science Foundation–funded General Social Survey, showed the strongest green values in the West Coast and northeastern states and weakest in the Deep Southern and High Plains ones. A 2024 study by researchers at the University of Michigan School for Environment and Sustainability examined millions of Twitter posts to map how climate change denialists were distributed across the nation's then-extent 3,143 counties; the same general pattern appeared, with denialism concentrated in Greater Appalachia, the Deep South, and the High Plains portion of the Far West.[4]

State environmental policies often follow this regional pattern. An especially robust examination of 256 indicators of a state's environmental record in 1991 to 1992 conducted by the Institute for Southern Studies resulted in a list with the West Coast, Yankee, and New Netherlander states occupying the top eleven positions and Deep Southern and Greater Appalachian states monopolizing the bottom eight. A 2020 ranking of the "greenest states" by the review and advice publisher Red Ventures incorporated renewable energy prevalence, open spaces, recycling, and environmental justice factors and resulted in a broadly similar list, with Pacific and New England states dominating the top of the list, Deep Southern, Greater Appalachian, and most Far Western states the bottom. (Though Florida, where 38 percent of the population lives in the green-friendly Spanish Caribbean, ranked sixth.)[5]

Who recycles the most? Maine, which reused 47.7 percent of its waste in 2023, followed by another Yankee state, Minnesota (44.8 percent), and California (controlled by the Left Coast and El Norte) at 41.8 percent. Who recycles the least? Louisiana, at only 0.5 percent, with Utah, Oklahoma, Alaska, and Mississippi just behind with between 2 and 5 percent. Who still dumps most of their waste in landfills? Alaska, Mississippi, Arizona, Georgia, Oklahoma, and Idaho, all of which bury more than 90 percent of their total. Who landfills the least? Connecticut (7.7 percent), Maine (15.1), Massachusetts (20.4), Minnesota (31.3) and New Hampshire (35.2). In early 2023, as states prepared to spend billions in Covid relief funds to upgrade infrastructure, which ones had done the most to reduce climate impacts and equity via supports for vehicle electrification, bike lanes, transit-oriented developments, "green" procurement, and other measures? California, Massachusetts, Vermont, Oregon, Washington, and New York, according to an indexing study by the Natural Resources Defense Council. Who did the least? Kentucky, Louisiana, Nebraska, Alabama, and South Carolina. In fact, not a single state in the Deep South, Greater Appalachia, or New France made the top twenty in the report's rankings, and no state run by Yankeedom, New Netherland, or the Left Coast was in the bottom fifteen. Where did the Green Party achieve its zenith of support in the early aughts, before its capture by nonenvironmental interests? In Yankee Maine, where the nation's first and only Green Party state legislator was seated in 2003, while three of his party colleagues constituted a powerful bloc on the nine-person governing council of the state's largest city.[6]

Public opinion doesn't always get matched in public policy, however. This is especially true in the **Far West**, where the public is environmentally conscious but their elected representatives are often hostile to green policies, including those centered around climate change. Martin Nie, director of the University of Montana's Bolle Center for People and Forests, wrote his dissertation on this phenomenon, which he called "the Great Divide." He found much of the political leadership's hostility to environmental regulation was wrapped up in its resentment of the federal government which, because it controls a majority of the land in many Far Western states, has an enormous say in land and resource use. "Conservative representatives in the region are often as antagonistic to the federal origins of environmental policies as they are to the policies themselves," Nie wrote back in 1998. "The question now worth asking . . . is whether or not these same political representatives will continue to favor local control when such control means environmental protections that are as stringent or even more stringent than those imposed by the federal government." The answer, thus far, appears to be yes, in that Far Western states with the "greenest" electorates—Colorado and Nevada—are generally ranked in the middle of the pack in terms of environmental policies while those with fewer environmentalists, like Utah, Idaho, and North Dakota, are at the bottom.[7]

The American Nations regions' congressional delegations have also shown remarkably consistent environmental policy voting patterns over the past century and a half. When the U.S. House was asked to endorse the creation of the first national park to protect Yellowstone in 1872, the delegations from Yankeedom, New Netherland, and the Midlands overwhelmingly agreed, with those from the Yankee-dominated states breaking 28–5 in favor. In the Deep Southern, Greater Appalachian, and Tidewater-run states the measure lost 20–26. After the first Earth Day, the League of Conservation Voters began tabulating environmental scores of 0 to 100 for each member of Congress based on the voting record at the end of each session. When graduate student Joseph Sheeran compiled the LCV's rankings for all members of the U.S. House for the period from

1973 to 1996, the top five delegations were all from New England and the top nineteen were from states controlled by communitarian Yankeedom, New Netherland, the Midlands, and Greater Polynesia. Alaska ranked worst in the country, with Deep Southern, Far Western, and Greater Appalachian states clustered at the bottom. The U.S. Senate showed a similar pattern, with those same regions failing to break the top fifteen, and states in the communitarian regions absent from the bottom ten. While Democratic House members were more supportive than Republicans in every state save Rhode Island, Republicans in nearly every Yankee- and New Netherland–controlled state had higher scores than Democrats from the Deep South, Tidewater, or Greater Appalachia. In 2023, the top scoring House delegations were all from Yankee-, Midland-, Greater Polynesian-, and El Norte–controlled states, each receiving a score of 96 to 100 from the League; the worst delegations were from Wyoming, West Virginia, Utah, Montana, Arkansas, and the Dakotas, each earning scores of between 0 and 5.[8]

WHY DO THESE GEOGRAPHICAL PATTERNS persist over decades and centuries, despite the enormous changes that have taken place? As we've seen with the Far West, culture and history play a big role.

Since the Chicano and other *Norteño* cultural movements emerged in the 1960s, **El Norte** has become one of the more pro-environment regions, largely because the region's Latinos felt their fate was linked to that of the land. From Thoreau to Muir, Yankee and Left Coast environmental thought has framed nature as something needing protection from human predation. By contrast, the Latin American tradition—including the Chicano mythology around Aztlán—saw nature as a garden, a place where people had developed ecologically appropriate ways to provide for themselves, like the traditional arid farming and open-range ranching techniques practiced by *Norteños* in the pre-American period. In this discourse, the "Anglo" colonizers were responsible for destroying the land upon which the people depended, either by polluting the neighbor-hoods where they lived, or fencing the range, or by introducing irrigation-dependent crops that depleted the region's aquifers. Environmental protection became wrapped up in the effort to cultivate *Norteño* identi-ties and to reverse the post-annexation marginalization of the region's Latinos. Social scientists have demonstrated that pro-environment atti-tudes among Mexican Americans are typically linked to traditional obli-gations to their extended family and community. "Mexican Americans tend to define nature as homeland, not natural resources or wilderness," notes anthropologist Devon G. Peña, and "emphasize local community rights and management of land, wildlife, and water." This sometimes puts them at odds with large Yankee- and Left Coast–dominated national environmental organizations.[9]

The **Deep Southern** oligarchy, past and present, has sought to build a colonial-style extractive economy founded on a compliant, low-wage work force, with few taxes or services and a weak regulatory environment that indulges polluters and disempowers public challenges to them. After the Civil War, it successfully blocked a Congressional effort to distribute public lands to formerly enslaved people, instead allowing it to fall un-der the control of industrial interests. In the twentieth century, the re-gion's leaders welcomed toxic polluters and imported huge quantities of hazardous and nuclear waste that manufacturers and energy companies found difficult or impossible to dispose of in most other regions. State governments are typically very lax in enforcing what environmental laws they have; Alabama's environmental protection department is so notori-ous that a state judge said he'd prefer to turn a court-mandated cleanup process over to the polluter. Conservation laws often have ulterior goals, like that of Alabama's "pioneering" legislation protecting fish and game from exploitation. "Negros have become completely disarmed under the game law," the state's first game commissioner, John Wallace, explained shortly after the 1907 law was passed. Pushed off public lands, subsis-tence hunters would be forced "to pursue the avocation of an honest and industrious life" under the exploitable terms of the region's Jim Crow system. Authoritarian regimes are rarely good for the environment and are hostile to notions of environmental justice, and the Deep South's have been no exception.[10]

Greater Appalachia's people have always been suspicious of government authority and regulations, including regulations protecting the environment. Destruction of natural landscapes and resources is unpopular, but the regional preference for weak (and therefore unthreatening) institutions has made it easy prey for rapacious industrial interests, from mining and timber companies to the slaughterhouses and pig farms owned by external food conglomerates. Home-grown environmental activism in the region has typically been hyper-local, typically involving a community trying to defend their own backyards against degradation or usurpation while eschewing alliances with other communities or external groups. This model, which scholars sometimes call "militant particularism," has stunted the growth of an effective environmental movement in the region, especially in situations where the threat comes from a major local employer.[11]

White evangelical Christians make up a substantial plurality of both of these regions—23.9 percent in the Deep South and 30.9 percent in Greater Appalachia—and these religious traditions have turned away from "creation care" since the 1980s. These denominations hold that the Bible is literally true and inerrant and should guide policy choices today. Many pastors look to Genesis 1:28, interpreting its directive that humans "fill the earth and subdue it" as a call to exploit and conquer nature. (Tidewater also shares this religious tradition but, as seen in almost every issue we've explored at Nationhood Lab, has undergone a dramatic cultural and ideological transformation ever since the 1970s.) On top of that, a substantial segment of the evangelical right subscribes to Reconstructionism, which can be apathetic about environmental destruction because they believe the End Times are coming. "God made the world, and it does not hang in the balance," declared D. James Kennedy, a leading Deep Southern evangelical pastor and founding member of Moral Majority, in his 2008 book *How Would Jesus Vote?*, adding that it was "human hubris" to think we could alter the atmosphere.[12]

By contrast, the **Midlands**, **Yankeedom**, and **New Netherland**, were for generations dominated by what religious scholars term "Public Protestants," as opposed to the "Private Protestantism" of the major southern denominations. Public Protestants—northern Baptists, northern Methodists, Episcopalians, Lutherans, Unitarians, Dutch Reformed, and Congregationalists among them—emphasize the salvation of society and the social gospel.[13] The world, they argue, can and should be improved, and caring for creation often follows from this. Yankeedom's Puritan founders were an extreme version of this approach, but Penn's Quakers, Joseph Smith's Mormons, and Mary Baker Eddy's Christian Scientists all shared it. Self-restraint for the common good, a deep Yankee trait, meshed with the goals of the early wildlife and land conservation movements, making Yankeedom and its emissaries in other regions the founders of the environmental movement.

As we've already seen, outside the southern regions, Protestants haven't been a hegemonic force for more than a century, if they ever were. But all of the large religious denominations in the northern and western regional cultures are much greener than the southern evangelicals. The Catholic Church is relatively environment-friendly, with a conservation ethic going back to medieval thinkers like St. Hildegard of Bingen and St. Francis of Assisi that has accelerated since the late 1980s. ("Disregard for the environment always harms human coexistence, and vice versa," Pope Benedict XVI declared in 2007. "It becomes more and more evident that there is an inseparable link between peace with creation and peace among men.") As we've already demonstrated in our examination of immigration patterns, the Great Immigration Wave of 1880 to 1924 made Catholics the largest denomination in Yankeedom, New Netherland, the Midlands, El Norte, and the Left Coast—and they still are today—but virtually no Catholics migrated to the Deep South or Greater Appalachia in this era, which is why conservative evangelical Christianity has such sway over these places today. Similarly, the vast majority of Orthodox Christians migrated to Yankeedom, New Netherland, the Midlands, and the Left Coast, and today they remain concentrated in these regions (plus in El Norte and the Spanish Caribbean). For the past two decades, the leading figure in the Orthodox world, the Ecumenical Patriarch Bartholomew I, has been aggressively promoting human stewardship of the environment, earning himself the moniker "the Green Patriarch." The Jewish tradition, whose adherents are overwhelmingly concentrated in the same regions, emphasizes the need to balance the requirements and claims of humans and nature.[14]

Religious teachings—be it from a pope, patriarch, or pastor—have a significant effect on people's environmental values. PRRI's 2023 Climate Change Survey report asked if climate change was real and caused by humans. Sixty-seven percent of Jewish respondents said "yes," along with majorities of white Catholics and mainline Protestants and both Hispanic and Black Protestants. By contrast, only 39 percent of white evangelicals agreed. Overwhelming majorities of white evangelicals (62 percent) and Black Protestants (73 percent)—the two most influential faith traditions in the Deep South and Greater Appalachia—agreed that the severity of recent natural disasters was evidence that we had entered Biblical End Times, compared to just 49 percent of Hispanic Catholics, 23 percent of white mainline Protestants, and 21 percent of white Catholics. In a 2014 survey, PRRI also surveyed Americans about whether they believed God gave humans complete dominion over the world's other species and natural resources or, alternatively, had tasked humans to steward the planet's life and resources, which were not there just for human benefit. Nearly half of white evangelicals and Black Protestants supported Dominionism, compared to just 35 percent of Catholics, 28 percent of white mainline Protestants, and 29 percent of the "unaffiliated." Because religious traditions are maldistributed across the map, all of this has increased the divide between the American Nations regions.[15]

In addition to religious influences, several of the "greenest" nations have deep, region-specific cultural attachments to the natural world that have led them to champion environmental issues, from landscape protection to climate change.

The **Left Coast**'s identity has been tied up with its landscapes since the early colonization period. In the San Francisco Bay Area, Oregon's Willamette Valley, and the Olympic Peninsula and Puget Sound regions of Washington State, prominent leaders embraced the protection of nature in the late nineteenth century. John Muir's Sierra Club was spearheaded by a group of Stanford and Berkeley professors, backed by San Francisco's business community, and led to the creation of Yosemite and Sequoia National Parks. Portland's Mazamas Club, founded by members of Oregon's elite in 1894, successfully lobbied for the creation of the Cascade Range Forest Reserve and what became Crater Lake National Park. In 1904, their Seattle subsidiary broke off to become The Mountaineers Club, whose members helped create the Mount Rainier, North Cascades, and Olympic National Parks. Scholars have described how these groups exemplify a key aspect of the region's culture: "a nature spirituality that envisions the region as both spiritually and economically productive," in the words of the Arizona State University environmental humanities professor Evan Berry. The same could be said of a series of radical communitarian colonies that cropped up on the shores of Puget Sound between 1885 and 1915—the Puget Sound Co-operative Colony, Freeland, and the Harmony, Equality, and Burley colonies—whose residents sought salvation in collectively sharing in the abundance of nature.[16]

It's this ethos that Ernest Callenbach drew on when writing his 1975 science-fiction classic, *Ecotopia*, which imagined a secessionist nation consisting of Washington, Oregon, and Northern California founded on principles of sustainability, self-sufficiency, and environmental justice, which itself influenced the environmental movement and Left Coast regional identity. A few years later, visiting *Washington Post* editor Joel Garreau declared the region to have embraced Callenbach's vision. "Ecotopia was able to catch the wave when environmental thinking became popular," Garreau reported in 1981. "This is the first region in North America in which even the middle class has moved on the idea that a person may have to lower his monetarily described standard of living in order to raise his overall quality of life. . . . In order to be better off you may have to have less money? Less production? Fewer cars? Fewer factories? Smaller farms?" By the time Garreau wrote those words, Seattle University sociologist David McCloskey had already proposed the idea that an area extending from the top of Alaska's lower panhandle in the north to Cape Mendocino, California, in the South was really a "bioregion" with a shared identity imposed by nature that transcended state and international borders. This region, Cascadia, is still promoted as a place where people seek to cooperate and live sustainably with one another and nature. "We consciously recognize the awesome influence of our natural surroundings—urban, rural, and suburban alike—and have strongly embraced a civil religion of conservation and sustainability across political ideologies," one proponent, Ryan C. Moothart, wrote in *Towards Cascadia*, in which he makes the very Turnerian argument that the land itself reshapes the people who come there. "Whatever connections to established social structures with which non-native settlers entered this region quickly dissipated and changed (when they) collided with the nature of Cascadia. The statuses quo for these individuals changed and the ethos of Cascadia held firm, unbreakable." Cascadia now has a flag, a Cascadia Independence Party, and a regional culture-building organization, Cascadia Now, all devoted to the idea of a sustainable, more enlightened society. (Even if many of their proponents cling to the idea that the Far Western parts of their states—plus Idaho and western Montana—want to come along for the ride.)[17]

Twenty-first-century tech-bro culture may have eroded some of those green-minded values, but they were values that first became mainstream in the Left Coast, and it's there, of all the big regions, they run deepest.

First Nation's people, by necessity, developed a sustainable relationship with the Arctic and sub-Arctic ecosystems they depended on, but, cruelly, the rest of the world's pollution has poisoned and destabilized their world. The Arctic was a key strategic battleground in the Cold War because it lay on the shortest route for the United States and the USSR to have launched nuclear strikes on one another. In the twenty-first century, the United States returned obsolete military sites to Greenlandic and Canadian control, but refused to clean up dump sites and contaminated buildings and couldn't find the hydrogen bomb it lost when a B-52 crashed in northern Greenland. In the 1980s, scientists discovered that persistent organic pollutants (or POPs) flowing into the world's oceans had become hyperconcentrated in the truncated Arctic food chain; Indigenous peoples in the Arctic, who hunt and consume large quantities of marine fish and mammals, had POP concentrations more than ten times that of non-Arctic people, triggering cancer, heart disease, and neurological and immune system problems. By the early 2000s it was also clear that greenhouse gas emissions were rapidly warming the Arctic climate, resulting in a massive meltdown of its tundra, sea ice, and 10,000-year old ice sheets, forcing the abandonment of Arctic Alaskan villages (due to coastal erosion) and Greenlandic sled dog traditions (because the winter sea ice was no longer sled-able).[18]

Despite their small numbers and profound marginalization, the Indigenous peoples of the Far North have organized and fought for their environments with impressive effectiveness on both the national and global stages. Up until the early 1960s, the Inupiat, Aleut, Tlingit, and other people of the north were isolated from one another by distance, language, externally imposed political boundaries, and a lack of communications and political infrastructure. All that changed dramatically after a chance 1958 encounter in the far northwest of Alaska between seal hunters and Atomic Energy Commission (AEC) engineers who were surveying the area in preparation for an outrageous demonstration project: the detonation of 2.4 megatons of thermonuclear devices to hollow out the seafloor and create a deepwater harbor. Though it had no economic rationale—there were no mineral resources in the area and the harbor would still be icebound for three quarters of the year—the AEC's project would have radioactively contaminated the sea and lichen and, in turn, the marine creatures and caribou the Inupiat ate. That nobody bothered to inform immediate residents of these plans, better yet solicit their input, prompted Indigenous leaders to create a newspaper, *Tundra Times*, to share crucial information across Alaska's First Nation section. Published in English (the lingua franca between Alaska's disparate Native peoples) and relying on reader contributions, the paper catalyzed a region-wide consciousness and efforts to organize around environmental protection, recognition of aboriginal land title, and other cultural rights issues. The paper's dispatches prompted the AEC to cancel the project in 1962 and helped facilitate the Alaska Native Claims Settlement Act of 1971, which has allowed Indigenous peoples to have a say about what industrial activities happen in their part of the country.[19]

Alaska Natives played a key role in creating the Inuit Circumpolar Council, an international body connecting the Indigenous Arctic peoples of Alaska, Greenland, the Canadian North, and, for a time after the Cold War, the Russian Far East. This First Nation–wide organization successfully pushed the persistent organic pollutant issue onto the international stage, shaping negotiations at the United Nations that resulted in the phasing out of the substances via an international convention. In the early 2000s, they did the same for climate change, which was affecting communities and ecosystems in First Nation earlier and more profoundly than any other part of the continent. "It's not just an environmental issue, it's about a people who are trying to find their rightful place in this new global order so it affords us respect and our rightful place to not only survive but to thrive," former ICC President Sheila Watt-Cloutier of Iqaluit,

Canada, told me the year before she was nominated for the 2007 Nobel Peace Prize for her work on the issue.[20]

The first settler culture of **Greater Polynesia**—in the United States, that of the Native Hawaiians—centers the sacredness of the land and the people's ties to and reciprocal relationship with it. Their spiritual beliefs and cultural practices bond land and people, and task the latter with responsibility for the natural world. "The land is our mother . . . Papahānaumoku—'She who gives birth to lands' [and] as caretakers, Native Hawaiians understand that She is the beneficent source of all living things . . . a divine living entity who gives Native Hawaiians the natural world and the resources therein," wrote Momiala Kamahele. "As human beings, we understand that our obligation is to serve Her. We do so as guardians and stewards of the land. By our service, we are assured of Her care."[21]

As among the Arctic peoples of First Nation, land and most natural resources were traditionally owned collectively by the community, and many Polynesian cultural practices and rituals involve collecting, harvesting, and honoring the living resources of their finite islands and the vast oceans connecting them. To a far greater extent than in First Nation, however, Hawaiian Polynesians have been colonized and dispossessed of their land and traditional land use, with mainland U.S. plantation, military, real estate, and tourism interests having successfully deprived them of federal land, sovereignty, and legal guarantees.[22]

Since the 1960s, however, Native Polynesians have successfully challenged colonial projects that would have destroyed landscapes and the cultural practices associated with them, including the planned destruction of a large rain forest on the Big Island (to make way for geothermal power stations) and the tourist-oriented development of unpopulated Kaho'olawe (an island the Navy had used as a bombing and missile target range.) Their efforts have been focused on returning land to Indigenous purposes, which often puts them at odds with the state's economic and political elite. The latter are not consistently reliable protectors of the land, but they have had an interest in reducing waste and pollution that might threaten the state's vital tourism sector. And all residents of Greater Polynesia constantly confront the physical and environmental limitations that come with living on small islands thousands of miles from the nearest land mass. In combination, Native cultural values, the physical constraints of the landscape, and economic self-interest have made Polynesia's Hawaiian section one of the most reliably "green" regions in the contemporary United States.[23]

In summary, there's a clear regional pattern, past and present, in how the regional cultures and their political elites look on environmental protection. The **Left Coast**, **New Netherland**, **Greater Polynesia**, and **First Nation** have the most environmentally minded publics and their political and cultural leaders have always followed suit. The public in the big communitarian regions—**Yankeedom** and the **Midlands**—isn't far behind, but their political and intellectual elite have always been at the forefront of the environmental movement. **El Norte** and the **Spanish Caribbean** lean green in both respects, while the **Far West** is unique in having a conservation-minded public represented by political leaders who are often deeply opposed to taking meaningful action on climate change, landscape protection, and other relevant issues. At the other end of the spectrum are **Greater Appalachia**, the **Deep South**, and **New France**, which have the least environmentally informed and engaged publics—though pluralities do care about the global warming—and an elite dead set against taking meaningful action to protect land, air, sea, or climate.

Given these backstories, the real surprise may not be so much that we find regional gaps on climate issues but rather that there is as much consensus as there is.

8

DEMOCRACY

America's democracy is collapsing. Part of me can't believe I'm writing those words, even though I've spent the past two decades engaged in the struggle to protect it, but they're true. At this writing, at the end of 2024, the country's democratic norms have already eroded to an alarming degree. The Supreme Court recently ruled that presidents can commit crimes with impunity, and only one in five voters now believe the court would be politically neutral if it had to resolve a contested election. A dozen states have turned into illiberal regimes to one degree or another, systematically suppressing their citizens' ability to express their political consent. The plutocrats who own the *Washington Post* and *Los Angeles Times* stopped those newspaper's supposedly independent editorial boards from endorsing the Democratic presidential nominee, Kamala Harris, apparently because they feared retaliation by her rival, former President Trump, if he regained office. Trump—a convicted felon also indicted on charges relating to absconding with highly sensitive national security documents and attempting to stay in power by supporting a violent coup attempt—has been reelected to the most powerful office on Earth despite promising to use the military against his detractors, whom he'd dubbed "enemies of the state," to prosecute and jail his political opponents, and to create internment camps for undocumented immigrants, whom he referred to as "vermin." Nearly half the American public thought it was a good idea to return him to power, apparently because they are more concerned about post-pandemic consumer price inflation than the survival of American democracy.[1]

We can still save the republic. In fact, I think we probably will, but only if we understand how we got here, the role the American Nations have played in the story, and the true nature of the threat. It is our ultimate challenge, the outcome of which will determine if we can solve or mitigate our other conflicts over immigration, climate change, guns, abortion, or social spending. The next two chapters tell this sobering story, which unfolded in two phases, like a rocket using two booster stages to achieve orbital velocity. The first, cruder phase, started in the midst of the 2008–2009 global financial crisis and raised authoritarian politics onto the state and national stages, but had appeared to have run out of fuel by 2015. The second, more dangerous act kicked to life in 2016, and is the topic of chapter 9. In the final chapter of the book, we'll show just how unpopular ethnonationalist authoritarianism really is and offer a plan for what we can all do to vanquish it, once again.

It gives me no joy that the story that follows puts the Republican Party and many of its leading figures in a bad light. It would be more comforting if the salient threats to the American Experiment really did come from extremists on "both sides," as some of our mainstream media institutions bend over backward to imply. It would make Nationhood Lab's mission to build a trans-partisan, supermajority coalition to defend the American Experiment much easier. But it simply isn't the case. Left-wing illiberalism exists, of course, but it is largely confined to some college campuses and a small cadre of progressive activists who seek to achieve justice and equality by silencing and punishing people with other points of view. As threats go, it's a paper tiger. But the threat on the right is very real, and it's seized the Republican Party, much to the horror of the many millions of Republicans who care about the American Experiment. Some have sacrificed their political futures and put their lives and property at risk to stand up to the threat, including die-hard conservatives like House Republican Conference Chair Liz Cheney of Wyoming, Senator Jeff Flake of Arizona, Trump's former chief of staff, John Kelly, and his former vice president, Mike Pence. Their numbers are small, but pro-democracy conservatives are vital to returning our democracy to health. This crisis won't end until we again have a healthy, democratic, center-right party on the national stage.

To UNDERSTAND WHAT'S HAPPENED TO our country, it's helpful to start with a thought experiment.

Imagine you're a leader of a political movement that's just won power in your state and you've decided you're willing to do whatever it takes to make sure you'll never have to surrender it, even if your citizenry wants to be rid of you. How would you do it without falling afoul of the law and getting yourself imprisoned?

If you'd taken power just before the full results of the decadal U.S. Census were released, you'd seek to draw new electoral district lines so as to ensure your party could win a majority of the legislative seats even in an election where most people voted for your opponents. (The process is called gerrymandering, named after one of its first practitioners, the early nineteenth-century Massachusetts Governor Elbridge Gerry, who used it to keep the state senate in the hands of his party despite a popular vote loss in the election of 1812.) But because you've taken power in the 2010s, you have access to new computer technologies and databases that allowed you to identify exactly who your supporters were and were not, letting you draw those lines with a level of accuracy Governor Gerry could never have dreamed possible. If you were really ruthless—and you lived in a state that allowed the majority party free reign—you could conjure a legislative supermajority from an essentially tied election result. Instead of voters picking their political leaders, you and your colleagues will get to pick your voters. Until 2019 you might have wanted to avoid being too obvious in your pressing for partisan advantage because of the equal protection clause of the Fourteenth Amendment, which makes it unconstitutional to treat one individual differently under the law than another. But in their ruling in *Rucho v. Common Cause*, your partisan allies on the U.S. Supreme Court relieved you of these concerns in declaring that federal courts aren't allowed to judge partisan gerrymandering.[2] Phew.

But what if state courts were to get in the way of your plans? If you live in one of the thirty-six states with elected judges the solution is obvious: ruthlessly gerrymander the *judges'* electoral districts. And if you're worried that a judicial candidate might not back you and your movement over constitutional or democratic principles, be sure to pull out all the stops come election time—attack ads, floods of lies and disinformation on social media, and bucketloads of campaign cash—to make sure a reliable loyalist wins your party's primary. If you did your gerrymandering right, the general election should be in the bag.

You can also gerrymander the congressional district lines to ensure a majority of your state's delegation backs you up in the U.S. House. Unfortunately, you can't use this tactic to win the statewide offices that are often the most powerful ones of all: governor, U.S. senator, and, in many states, the lieutenant governor, the attorney general (who is the state's top prosecutor), and the secretary of state (who oversees elections). To secure these statewide offices, you won't be able to simply pick your voters, so you'll have to prevent your opponent's voters from casting ballots. If you don't care about democracy—and let's assume you don't—you'll just spread made-up claims of widespread voter fraud, even though numerous studies have shown the rate of fraud at U.S. ballot boxes is essentially zero.[3] You'll use these baseless claims as cover to pass laws that make it harder or impossible for the many who will likely oppose your movement to participate in the election. You'll require specific forms of identification they won't be likely to have (like a passport, driver's license, or a gun permit) and reject forms they probably do possess (like a university ID card). You'll have far fewer polling stations per capita in areas where unfriendly voters are, so they'll have to stand for hours in line to cast their ballot, because you've also cleverly banned or severely restricted early, absentee, or mail-in voting. Since those voters might be standing outside in oppressive heat or bitter cold, you might even criminalize handing out water, hot drinks, or snacks to people waiting in line. Since your potential opponents include a lot of infrequent voters—the poor, young, and disengaged—you could work with your secretary of state to regularly purge the voter rolls of people who haven't cast a ballot in nearly every recent election (and maybe tens of thousands of people who have, because "mistakes" happen). As educated young people as a group really don't seem to like your goals—from letting climate change run amok to transferring the tax burden from the super-rich to the middle and working classes—you'll also want to intimidate college and university students from voting in your state, where they now live and pay taxes.

That'll all help, but what if voters are so upset with your nakedly authoritarian policies that they manage, despite all your hard work, to eke out a narrow win in some electoral contest? It'd be best if you've already seized control of the electoral system, changing laws and personnel to ensure that your agents are the ones who will oversee the vote, adjudicate election disputes, and officially certify the results. Unlike most other democracies, the United States doesn't have a centralized election administration agency; with your control of the state legislature, you have the power to pass laws to govern elections for local, state, and even federal offices, which is why you got to gerrymander everything in the first place. You'll want to rewrite things so as to give yourself ample opportunities to annul any results you don't like, though you might make sure you've subdued the judicial and executive branches ahead of time. And if your state allows citizen-initiated ballot measures, you'll want to try to do away with those, too, as they give the public an avenue to interfere with the consolidation of your regime.

Finally, if somehow the opposition captures the governorship or secretary of state's office, you can always tell the voters to go pound sand by passing laws that take power away from those positions. If they win a majority on the state supreme court you could simply impeach the newly elected judge—no legitimate reason required if you have a supermajority—or, if judges are appointed in your state and you have the governor's mansion, simply add however many seats it takes to restore your majority.

Take all these steps and you'll have created an autocracy, a system in which the people have no say over who governs them or what policies are enacted by the regime. You'll have betrayed the Declaration of Independence and popular sovereignty and all the tenants of democracy. But you'll have all the state-level power, including the ability to throw your state's Electoral College votes in the next presidential election. And if your allies in enough other states do what you did, you could control the federal government and rule the country forever.

THIS PLAN MIGHT SOUND FAR-FETCHED, but it is exactly what a right-wing authoritarian movement has tried to accomplish across the United States starting in 2010, when the Tea Party movement first exploded onto the national stage. In the end, the Tea Party achieved few of its aims on the *national* stage, but it had enormous success at the state level in certain regions of the country, laying the foundations for the autocratic threat to come.

At its core, the Tea Party movement was a national effort operating from a centralized playbook. Between 2010 and 2016 it was deployed in almost every part of the country, from California to Maine, harnessing legitimate popular anger about the misgovernment of the country to an authoritarian agenda set by cynical elites, many of them based in Washington and working on behalf of reactionary corporate interests. While this effort had some early successes in a few Yankee- and Midland-controlled states, its program to create authoritarian, one-party regimes in all the American states was stopped in its tracks in most of the regions of the country during this six-year time period. But it was disturbingly successful in Greater Appalachia, the Deep South, and New France, regions where authoritarianism, not liberal democracy, have been the norm throughout most of U.S. history. The states controlled by these regions, University of Buffalo Law School professor James A. Gardner observed in 2021, "bear a close resemblance to countries like Hungary and Turkey, which seemed for a while to have made the transition to liberal democracy, but in which democratic backsliding has been so severe as to call into question the degree to which liberalism ever took root." Those southern states, he added, "may be in the process of severing their relatively recent—and it turns out, shallow—ties to the family of liberal democracies."[4]

This illiberal restoration has dangerous implications for all of us. The states controlled by the Deep South, Greater Appalachia, and New France together hold 28 senate seats, more than 150 seats in the U.S. House, and 181 Electoral College votes. That alone gives an authoritarian alliance the ability to block the certification of a presidential election and the peaceful transfer of power, to filibuster an opposition party's agenda, and to dominate the Republican caucus of the U.S. House. Potentially joining them are the states they control together with the Midlands—or which are dominated by the Midlands, a region that's proved susceptible to twenty-first-century authoritarianism. This brings another 9 states—with 18 Senate seats and 79 Electoral College votes—into play. That's a massive authoritarian bloc, which, in alliance with more traditional conservatives in the Far West, could force a fascist regime on the rest of the country. It would be like Reconstruction in reverse, with the former Confederacy forcing illiberal authoritarianism on Yankeedom, New Netherland, the Left Coast, and other parts of the country. Understanding what's happened is essential to countering the threat it poses.

———

THE CURRENT AUTHORITARIAN MOVEMENT has its origins in the 2008 global financial collapse, the George W. Bush administration's multi-trillion-dollar rescue of the banking system, and the election of the country's first Black president that November. The Great Recession that followed the crisis, the most severe economic downturn since the Great Depression, wiped out 5.5 million American jobs, $7.4 trillion in stock value, $3.4 trillion in real estate holdings, and $648 billion in economic growth in a single year. Politically it marked the final verdict on Bush's laissez-faire regulatory policies, but it also resulted in a shock to closet white supremacists, who saw the inauguration of the country's first Black president as a sign they were losing control of the country to the "others." Tens of millions of people were furious at elected officials from both parties for letting the unscrupulous bankers who'd caused the catastrophe escape legal consequences, and using the public's money to bail them out of any financial or professional consequences, as well. Particularly aggrieved, research later revealed, were reasonably comfortable, middle-aged white people who felt their hard-earned money was being given away to the undeserving. In the summer of 2009, the pent-up anger exploded on the American political scene.[5]

It's forgotten now, but the Tea Party's real ignition point was in March 2009, when the public learned that part of their $170 billion bailout of AIG, the world's largest insurance group, would be spent paying $165 million in bonuses to the very executives whose greed and irresponsibility had helped cause the financial crisis and bring down the firm. Spooked by death threats, several senior managers of the firm resigned, while guards were posted around the firm's Connecticut headquarters to protect the rest. "Never before or since have I seen vehement universal public anger reach such a white-hot level," Representative Barney Frank, then chair of the House Financial Services Committee, later recalled. "I feared we were in danger of losing our capacity to govern—not just to enact a national financial reform bill but also to pass any legislation that required public trust in elected officials."[6]

The motivations of individual rank-and-file Tea Party activists were diverse, but powerful forces quickly swooped in to redirect their anger away from the financiers and toward the government. The key entity was FreedomWorks, a DC-based advocacy organization founded by conservative billionaire brothers Charles and David Koch and run by former House Majority Leader Dick Armey (R.–Deep South). FreedomWorks jumped in to educate Tea Party participants in the Kochs' laissez-faire capitalist agenda and then mobilize them to engineer a hostile takeover of the GOP. "By seizing control of the party, we can spend our time focused on ideas and use the party infrastructure that has been built over the past 156 years," Armey counseled in his self-described "Tea Party Manifesto," published in the summer of 2010. In alliance with Fox News, he started acting as a spokesperson for the movement, and paid more than $1 million to conservative media personality Glenn Beck to, as Armey later put it, say "nice things about FreedomWorks on the air." What emerged over the coming years was a two-headed beast. Freedom-Works's leadership urged followers to set aside social issues and embrace a libertarian economic platform, summed up in the group's motto: "Lower Taxes, Less Government, More Freedom."[7] Glenn Beck's primary contribution was to tirelessly promote the works and ideas of the late W. Cleon Skousen, a right-wing conspiracist who argued that the U.S. Constitution was inspired not by the Enlightenment philosophers but by the Old and New testaments; that its divinely inspired authors believed in a minimal, laissez-faire state and a merging of church and state; and all the tropes of the Lost Cause myth, including that slaves had enjoyed enslavement.[8] Suddenly Skousen's long-forgotten books were on the bestseller lists, propelled by bulk orders from local Tea Party groups. These two heads— one theocratic, the other more classically libertarian—shared a body of laissez-faire economic assumptions indistinguishable from those held by establishment Republicans like House Speaker Paul Ryan or Federal Reserve Chair Alan Greenspan.[9]

Not surprisingly, polls, interviews, and intensive scholarly studies revealed a bifurcated Tea Party movement, with social conservatives like Beck and former Alaska Governor Sarah Palin's variety dominant in the Deep South, Tidewater, and Greater Appalachia, and libertarians of the Ron Paul and FreedomWorks variety holding the upper hand in the Far West and Yankeedom. Many local Tea Party groups experienced power struggles between these factions, especially in Yankeedom and the Far West, where libertarians often struggled to keep Christian conservatives from splitting the movement with regionally unpopular policies. Researchers from Texas's Sam Houston State University studied 2010 polling data and found dramatic differences between movement supporters across the four traditional U.S. census regions. In the "Northeast," supporters were mostly motivated by economic issues; in the "Midwest," it was almost entirely anti-government sentiment; the "West" was the only region where immigration concerns dominated; while the "South" and West were the only regions where supporters cared about "traditional values." The movement was regionally fractured.[10]

Members of both the libertarian and social conservative factions had a number of characteristics in common which would become far more obvious at the end of the decade. They were overwhelmingly white, over forty-five years old, comfortably middle class, and described themselves as "extremely conservative." Polling and research showed the typical Tea Partier had a social Darwinist view of society that pit the worthy and hardworking (themselves) against the lazy and undeserving (the poor, the young, the uninsured). The rank and file disagreed with Beck, Skousen, and FreedomWorks in that they felt the "deserving" were justly entitled to the big-government benefits of the New Deal and Great Society: Social Security, Medicare, and Veterans Affairs. In their view, they'd worked for these programs, they'd earned them, and the nation should provide them. But they did not want to be taxed to pay for entitlements to be handed out to people they found undeserving, entitlements such as student loans for the young, health insurance for the poor, or mortgage relief for recent homebuyers caught up in the subprime mortgage scam that had triggered the Great Recession. Polls also showed they believed Blacks and whites already had equal opportunities to be successful, implying institutionalized racism couldn't exist.[11] By 2010, the compost from which Trumpism would spring was already thick on the ground.

For all its fury, the Tea Party phase of the authoritarian movement had limited success on the national stage. In 2010, it took over many state and local Republican party organizations, and helped the GOP retake the House with a net sixty-three-seat gain. But they also caused Republicans to lose what should have been easy Far West and Midlands Senate pickups by helping nominate extremists in Delaware, Colorado, and Nevada, and they ultimately failed to derail either establishment Republican Mitt Romney (from winning the party's 2012 nomination) or President Obama (from winning a second term in the White House). By the end of 2012, even as its grip on the national Republican Party strengthened, the Tea Party's popular influence in Yankeedom, New Netherland, and the Left Coast had melted away because their laissez-faire economic agenda was anathema to the centuries-old social, political, and cultural traditions of those regions. Of the sixty members of the first, heady Tea Party caucus, only three hailed from Yankeedom and not one came from the Left Coast or New Netherland. Republicans were swept out of New England in the 2012 midterms, losing every one of the region's twenty-one U.S. House seats, five contested U.S. Senate races, and all of its Electoral College votes, as well as the lower chamber of the New Hampshire State House and both legislative houses in Maine. Republicans lost every other Senate race in Yankeedom and a majority of the Yankee-controlled state House seats in Illinois, Minnesota, Ohio, Iowa, and New York. In New Netherland, Republicans were left with just a tenth of the region's forty-odd House seats, and in the Left Coast, just one in twenty. Across these three "northern alliance" nations, with a combined population of 90 million, the Tea Party remained a force in only Wisconsin and Michigan, and then only barely. A movement advocating libertarian economics and Christian conservative social policy just wasn't tenable in these communitarian-minded regions.

By contrast, the Tea Party encountered little resistance to its agenda in the three Dixie bloc nations and New France's Louisiana enclave, as it offered a carbon copy of the Deep Southern program of the last two centuries: reduce taxes for the wealthy and services for everyone else; crush the labor unions, public education, and the regulatory system; suppress voter turnout; and make Evangelical Protestantism the de facto religion of the land. These four nations accounted for fifty-one of the sixty members of that first House Tea Party caucus—or 85 percent of them—with the Deep South alone accounting for twenty-two. In 2011, sixty-six House Republicans shocked the nation by refusing to support a final compromise on raising the ceiling on the national debt so as to authorize payment of spending Congress had already approved, a move that could have sent the U.S. into default and triggered another 2008-scale global financial crisis. Fifty-three of the debt ceiling hardliners were from the same four regions. So, too, were most of the Tea Party's most influential politicians, including Senators Jim DeMint (Deep South), Mike Lee (Far West), and Rand Paul (Greater Appalachia), former Governor Sarah Palin (Far West), secessionist-minded Governor Rick Perry (Greater Appalachia), and FreedomWorks boss Dick Armey (Deep South). Tea Party activists could be found most anywhere in the country, but only within this four-nation bloc did they have significant and sustained political success. In these regions, Trumpism would be able to build on solid foundations.

IN RETROSPECT, the most powerful legacy of the 2010–2012 Tea Party surge was something few people paid much attention to at the time: It had allowed radicals to take over state legislatures just as they were preparing to draw new district boundaries using 2010 census data. In 2010, Republicans gained a total of 721 state legislative seats, flipping control of 20 legislative chambers and tying for control of the Oregon House. They controlled the entire legislative branch in 25 states—11 more than they had before the election—the highest number since 1952. Political junkies knew this meant that 195 of 495 U.S. House districts would be redrawn in states where Republicans controlled the legislature and governor's office and had, under state law, full authority to redraw the lines that would be used for the 2012, 2014, 2016, 2018, and 2020 elections. Few thought about the implications of the fact that in all of those states, legislative lines could also be radically redrawn to further their majorities. In 23 states where legislatures had free hands to control redistricting—most but not all of them in the Deep South, Greater Appalachia, and the Far West—Republicans were now in full control of the process. In states that were still competitive, they moved aggressively to insulate themselves from the popular will.[12]

The subset of states in 2010 that were both potentially competitive and allowed for gerrymandering broke into three groups. First, there were Yankee states where right-wing extremists knew their grip on power was extremely tenuous: New Hampshire, Michigan, and Wisconsin. They were only slightly more secure in a second group of states that Midlanders and Greater Appalachians controlled together: Pennsylvania, Ohio, Indiana, and Missouri, all of which had been swing states just ten years earlier. In a third group of Greater Appalachian and Deep Southern states, Tea Partiers were in friendly territory, but they recognized an opportunity to restore the authoritarian-style regimes that had been toppled in the 1960s; this category included Alabama, Georgia, North Carolina, Florida, Tennessee, and Texas. (Democrats had few opportunities to gerrymander because most of the states where they still had full control were in the Left Coast or Yankeedom and had independent or bipartisan redistricting commissions that produced maps fair to both sides.) The maps the Tea Party–inflected legislatures in these states produced would have lasting consequences for democracy.

Some of the most aggressive gerrymanders occurred in the Yankee states where Republican's long-term position was weakest. Wisconsin's new maps were the most notoriously antidemocratic. In the 2012 election, the majority of voters cast ballots for Democratic state assembly candidates—52.4 percent—and yet Republicans came away with sixty of the ninety-nine assembly seats. These maps were still in place in 2018 when Democrats won every statewide race and 53 percent of the legislative vote and yet wound up with only thirty-six of the ninety-nine seats. Republicans won a similar assembly majority in 2020, as well, which meant they would lead the redistricting process for the 2020 cycle, too.[13] In Michigan, an independent analysis found that in a tied election, gerrymandering would give Republicans 15.2 percent more of the seats in the state senate; this helped them retain a 22–16 majority in that chamber after the 2018 election during which Democrat Gretchen Whitmer won the governorship by nearly ten points.[14] In New Hampshire, Republicans had controlled the legislature (and, thus, redistricting) for decades, but they upped their gerrymandering game after 2010 to maintain a built-in 10 percent advantage in state senate races in a now-purple state; in 2012 they retained a 13–11 majority despite losing the popular vote for that chamber by 4 percent.[15]

In the Midland- and Greater Appalachian–controlled states, Republicans sought to amplify rightward electoral trends. In Missouri in 2012, their maps allowed Republicans to secure 72 percent of the state house seats with 59 percent of the vote.[16] In Ohio, Republican candidates for the lower legislative chamber won 55,000 fewer votes than Democrats, but earned sixty of ninety-nine seats, giving them a veto-proof supermajority.[17] Democrats had controlled the lower house in Indiana up until 2010, but by 2018, Republicans were able to win 67 percent of those seats and 80 percent of the upper chamber in an election where their four candidates for statewide office won only 51 to 59 percent of the vote.[18] Republicans also sought to aggressively gerrymander Pennsylvania's legislative map, but were stymied by that state's supreme court.

It was on friendlier turf that the Tea Party right had lasting influence. In the states controlled by the Deep South and Greater Appalachia, the 2010 surge had returned many state houses and governorships to solid, one-party control for the first time in decades, completing the decades-long transition from rule by Southern white supremacist Democrats to rule by Southern "anti-woke" Republicans. With that partisan identity shift completed—Richard Nixon's "Southern Strategy" finally triumphant—the possibility of restoring the region's old authoritarian, one-party regimes returned.

Recall that the Deep South, most of Greater Appalachia, old Tidewater, and the New France enclave were all slaveholding societies until the Confederate defeat and the passage of the Thirteenth Amendment. From the 1870s to the 1960s every state controlled by these regions—including Missouri, Indiana, Kentucky, West Virginia, Maryland, and the Oklahoma Territory—passed and enforced Jim Crow laws that made it a crime for Blacks and whites to marry one another or go to school together, or for bars, hotels, restaurants, railways, and streetcar companies to not segregate their patrons. They all embraced the Lost Cause mythology surrounding the Civil War and suppressed the political and citizenship rights of non-whites via laws, lynchings, and murderous pogroms. The Deep South was generally worst in all these respects, extending formal oppression to poor whites as well as to Blacks, but even northern parts of Greater Appalachia differed only in their degree of repression and autocratic behavior. Most states in these regions also altered their constitutions in the 1890s and early 1900s to limit poor and minority participation in elections via poll taxes, literacy tests, property qualifications, and whites-only primaries (the only elections that mattered in a one-party state). They were, by any definition of the term, illiberal autocracies. In the 2010s, the new ruling party started taking steps toward making them so again.

Gerrymandering was the first step. It was implemented most aggressively in North Carolina, a state that had become increasingly competitive as the Tidewater and Research Triangle cities liberalized in the early twenty-first century. Their maps were so racially inspired that they were eventually found unconstitutional, but not until after they'd been used in three gerrymandered elections, the last of which gave Republicans veto-proof legislative majorities—62 percent of the House and 70 percent of the Senate—with just 53 and 55 percent of the votes.[19] In Oklahoma, state law limited the degree of tinkering that could be made to the state's forty-eight senate districts, but Republicans made sure to redraw them in such a way as to cut the hometowns of three Democratic incumbents out of their previous districts.[20] In Florida, Rick Scott narrowly won the 2010 governor's race with 47.8 percent of the vote, but a statistical analysis showed that under the new legislative maps, his ballots would have won in 26 of 40 senate and 73 of 120 house districts.[21] Georgia's majority Republicans terminated the legislature's long-term map-drawing partnership with the University of Georgia's nonpartisan Carl Vinson Institute of Government and gerrymandered legislative districts in both 2011 and 2015 to great effect: In the 2016 election, 46 percent of Georgians voted for the Democratic presidential candidate, Hillary Clinton, but Democrats won only 35 percent of the seats in the State House.[22]

In all of these states, gerrymandering was also applied to U.S. House districts, giving Republicans far larger Congressional caucuses than America's voters intended them to have. In 2012, Pennsylvania Republicans won 72 percent of the state's House seats with 49 percent of the statewide vote. Ohio's got 62.5 percent of them with less than half the vote, Missouri's took 75 percent of seats with a 58 percent vote share, and, in 2018, North Carolina's claimed 77 percent of seats with 50.3 percent of ballots. Statisticians at the University of Vermont found that the combined effect of these gaps was a net Republican overrepresentation in Congress of twenty-eight House seats in 2012, twenty in 2014, and twenty-five in 2016. These were significant boosts in Republican power but, unlike the situation in many State House chambers, not enough to have determined partisan control in and of itself in any of those Congresses.[23]

The Tea Party gerrymanders proved short-lived in states controlled by Yankeedom and the Midlands, where they clashed with regional democratic norms and encountered powerful pushback from institutions and civil society. In Michigan, Republicans tried to block a 2018 citizens' referendum to end gerrymandering but were rebuffed by courts; it went on to pass with 61 percent of the vote, resulting in maps for the 2020 census cycle independent experts described as among the fairest in the nation.[24] In Ohio, separate citizen ballot initiatives to create independent redistricting commissions for legislative and Congressional races won in 2015 and 2018 with three-to-one margins. When Republicans found loopholes to seize control of the commissions anyway, the biased maps they produced were thrown out by the state court and citizens' groups gathered signatures to pass a constitutional amendment to ensure independence. Wisconsin voters put Democrats in charge of statewide offices and, in a 2023 election, broke conservative Republican control of their supreme court, which then ruled that the state's radically gerrymandered maps were unconstitutional and prompting a fair redrafting.[25] In 2020, a ballot initiative allowed Missouri voters to force lawmakers to draw districts that are compact, contiguous, and avoid splitting municipalities. New Hampshire doesn't allow citizen ballot measures, but lawmakers themselves passed a bipartisan bill to turn redistricting over to an independent commission; Republican Governor Chris Sununu used his veto powers to stop the reform from going through, leaving his state the only one in New England to enter the 2020 census cycle with gerrymandered maps.[26]

The gerrymanders have stuck in states under Deep Southern and Greater Appalachian control, in large part because few of those states allow citizens to intervene via ballot measures. Some states doubled down for the 2020 census cycle. In 2021, North Carolina's Republican lawmakers created a Congressional map so egregious the state supreme court threw it out and redrew lines that were used in the 2022 midterms, resulting in a U.S. House delegation that was evenly split between the parties, like the electorate itself. But in those midterms, Republicans won control of that same court, which then allowed them to go ahead with a wildly redrawn map for 2024 that statisticians demonstrated would likely give them eleven of fourteen U.S. House seats and allow them to maintain a State House supermajority while winning just half the votes cast.[27] Florida's new state house maps for 2022 received a grade of F for partisan fairness from the Princeton University Gerrymandering Project, which compares each enacted map to a million alternatives generated by a computer algorithm. Texas's house and senate maps both received a C. At the Congressional level, the Princeton project assigned As and Bs across the Democratically controlled states in Yankeedom and even the Republican-controlled ones in the Far West. In the "blue" regions, only Oregon (dominated by the Left Coast) and Illinois (by Yankeedom and the Midlands) received failing grades, though New York State lawmakers' original maps probably would have as well had they not been thrown out and replaced with ones created by a special ombudsman as per that New Netherland–dominated state's laws. By contrast, most Deep Southern and Greater Appalachian states received an F.[28]

THE TEA PARTY WAVE BOOSTED Republican legislative strength and got hundreds of right-wing extremists into positions of power in their states. But what did they do with their newfound influence, and how did their policy efforts fare across the American Nations? As with the effort to cement themselves in power, the authoritarian legislative drive had little to no success in states under New Netherland and Left Coast influence, struck powerful headwinds in Yankeedom, hit speed bumps in the Midlands, and passed largely unobserved in the Far West. But they scored major successes in the Deep South and Greater Appalachia.

The authoritarian's main policy vehicle was a group called the American Legislative Exchange Council. While ALEC claimed to be a nonpartisan professional association for state legislators, it was really a corporate-funded conduit to allow businesses to write legislation for compliant state lawmakers. Virtually all of its funding came from its corporate members—private prison companies, for-profit virtual school behemoths, gunmakers, big oil, pharma, telecom, and tech—who had collective veto power over the text of the self-serving model bills it produced, which covered everything from union-crushing right-to-work labor laws to death-inducing "stand your ground" gun laws. They had drafts of laws to prevent towns and cities from building public broadband networks or regulating pesticides, to channel taxpayer education dollars to massive for-profit virtual education companies, and to penalize homeowners who installed solar panels. The corporate members provided "scholarships" to fly Republican legislators to luxury hotels far from their home states for secret, closed-door meetings, where they were given model bills to take home, call their own, and introduce at their state capitols. In 2012 and 2013, when the organization's secret membership lists leaked, every member of Arizona's Republican legislative leadership was on them along with almost half of all legislators in that state. Maine's past and present members included the sitting education commissioner, the governor's top policy advisor (who was still employed as a corporate lobbyist for many ALEC member companies), and the Republican Senate majority leader, who also served on ALEC's national board. Ohio's members included the governor, Senate majority leader, and future House Speaker. Iowa's legislative leaders were all members, and they proactively signed up every member of their caucus to the group, requiring them to opt out if they didn't want to be included. Wisconsin's Tea Party governor, Scott Walker, was a past member, as was former Governor Tommy Thompson and the party's 2012 U.S. Senate nominee. In all, one third of all state legislators in the country—2,000 lawmakers—were members of ALEC in 2014.[29]

Most of the model bills they handed off to lawmakers were written in the interests of the group's corporate members, but they included several measures to further one-party control in each state. This was because their plans to rig the market, labor rules, tax code, and regulatory environment in their favor were incredibly unpopular most everywhere and would likely have damaged the electoral prospects of politicians who implemented them. To decrease the chance their agents would lose reelection, one of these bills required anyone seeking to register to vote to present their U.S. passport, birth certificate, or other documentation of citizenship, documents that many poorer, naturally born Americans don't possess and which are expensive and time-consuming to acquire. After Kansas implemented such a law in 2013, 20 percent of new registrants were suspended under its provisions. Independents were suspended at a rate almost twice that of their share of the state's electorate, Republicans at a rate less than half of theirs.[30] Even though voter fraud has been repeatedly shown to be effectively nonexistent in the United States, another ALEC bill required registered voters to present an unexpired state- or federally issued photo identification card before they could cast their ballots.[31] Other model bills targeted potential sources of organized opposition, such as labor unions, by illegalizing union shops (where employees have to become union members) and prohibiting collective bargaining by the public sector unions representing teachers, university professors, and civil servants. To ensure a generally supportive demographic's turnout, another model bill departed with the group's fiscal austerity stance to require state authorities to express-mail or courier absentee ballots to military personnel overseas within four days.[32]

Authoritarian-minded Republicans made a full-court press to pass these laws in the Yankee states they gained control over after the 2010 election: Wisconsin, Michigan, New Hampshire, and Maine. Despite governing with trifectas in three of these four states, they came up short. Under Tea Party Governor Paul LePage, Maine Republican leaders tried to impose voter identification requirements, end same-day voter registration, and eliminate union shops with an ALEC right-to-work bill. Angry voters restored same-day voting just months later via ballot measure by a 60–40 margin, while the other two measures couldn't even muster enough Republican support to become law.[33] New Hampshire's new GOP supermajorities passed a voter ID law in 2012, but had to water it down to avoid a veto by the state's Democratic governor; their right-to-work bill was vetoed in 2011 and a reprise in 2024—when the state finally had a Republican trifecta—failed to garner enough GOP support.[34] Michigan's Republican governor, Rick Snyder, vetoed his own party's newly passed voter ID law; their right-to-work law, passed amid street protests during a lame-duck session in 2012, became the first such legislation to be over-turned in nearly sixty years after Democrats achieved a governing trifecta in 2023, a result enabled by the independent redistricting commission vot-ers had forced through five years earlier.[35] The movement's agenda in Wisconsin faced unprecedented resistance. At one point, Tea Party Gov-ernor Scott Walker ordered state troopers to arrest the entire state senate Democratic caucus, who had fled to Illinois to deny Republicans a quo-rum to pass a law restricting public-sector union bargaining; after a two-week standoff, Republicans found a technical workaround, but it required them to restore the union's right to negotiate on wages (but not on work conditions) and passed the revised bill amid the chants of 100,000 pro-testers participating in the capital's largest demonstration in history. This episode, coupled with Republican passage of right-to-work and voter ID laws, spurred recall elections in 2012 that Walker and his lieutenant gov-ernor barely survived and three of his senate allies did not, briefly flip-ping control of that chamber to Democrats. By the end of 2024, Walker had lost the governorship, key parts of the public-sector union bill had been thrown out as unconstitutional (because their carve-outs for law enforcement personnel violated the equal protection clause), and the right-to-work law had been overturned by the state supreme court, where Re-publicans had lost their majority. If Wisconsin allowed citizen-initiated ballot measures, it's clear the rollback of these unpopular measures would have been much swifter.[36]

This agenda encountered headwinds in Midlands-dominated states, as well. Iowa legislators repeatedly rejected an ALEC-modeled voter ID bill, Pennsylvania's was thrown out by the state courts, and a similar measure was rejected by voters in a 2012 ballot measure by eight points.[37] Missouri voters overturned their legislature's new right-to-work law in 2018 by a 2–1 majority.[38] In Ohio, a state whose Midland section acts as a kingmaker by aligning with either the Yankee Western Reserve or the Appalachian southern tier, voters in 2011 repealed that state's new right-to-work law 61–39, prompting the chastened Republican governor, John Kasich, to say he respected the decision that "requires me to take a deep breath and to spend some time to reflect on what happened here." Voters themselves didn't fare as well. Ohio Republicans instituted a strict voter ID law, cut back the early voting and absentee voting periods, and commenced a draconian purge of voter rolls that fell hardest on that state's Yankee section; Cuyahoga County lost 220,000 voters, 20 percent of its total.[39] Only in Kansas, whose Midland section accounts for more than 80 percent of the population, did the agenda encounter little resistance.

In the Deep South and Greater Appalachia, the plans went just fine. Almost every state in these regions already had right-to-work laws by the time the Tea Party came along and Georgia and Indiana had voter ID requirements. After 2010, Tennessee, Alabama, Mississippi, and Texas added photo ID requirements and, along with Florida, West Virginia, and North Carolina, reduced early voting hours. Alabama, Georgia, and Tennessee also required official documents to prove citizenship before registering to vote. The Brennan Center for Justice estimated Alabama's voter ID law reduced the voter pool by 250,000 to 500,000 votes (8 to 16 percent of the electorate) while North Carolina's early voting reduction likely suppressed enough votes to allow Republican Thom Tillis to win the 2014 U.S. Senate race by a 1.5 percent margin.[40] These states went beyond the ALEC agenda, too. A new 2012 Florida law imposed onerous fines on civic groups engaged in voter registration drives if they failed to turn in forms within forty-eight hours of collection, forcing the League of Women Voters and Rock the Vote to suspend their work in the state. A 2011 Texas law said only officially sanctioned individuals could participate in such campaigns and that they had to be Texas residents and eligible voters and take a training course that was rarely offered. Between 2010 and 2014, Florida, Georgia, North Carolina, Tennessee, and West Virginia also reduced early and absentee voting, which were most popular with demographic groups likely to oppose the Tea Party's goals. During the same period, North Carolina ended same-day registration and the preregistration of sixteen- and seventeen-year-olds in high schools.[41]

Arizona also became a battleground in the Tea Party era. As noted before, it's a state that currently defies American Nations political analysis. The "first effective settlers" of the area around Phoenix were from El Norte, but since World War II, the city has grown explosively via massive in-migration from the Deep South. Whereas in the nineteenth century, the vast majority of Arizona in-migrants were from Mexico, in the early twentieth century they were matched by those from Texas, Arkansas, and Oklahoma, all of which had Greater Appalachian majorities in that era. In the late twentieth and early twenty-first centuries, southern California and northern Illinois became major sources of the state's population growth, almost all of which has occurred in Greater Phoenix, which is the fifth-largest city in the country and home to the vast majority of Arizonans. Phoenix is in Arizona's El Norte section, but it doesn't behave as such. The net result is that Tea Party and Trumpist politics have been contentious, creating a situation similar to that in the Midland states described above.[42]

At the dawn of the Trump Era, it had become clear that the awkward Tea Party coalition of small government conservatives and the Christian Right was doomed to be a regional movement, not a national one.

Then Donald Trump came along.

9

AUTHORITARIANISM

W hen Donald Trump crashed onto the scene in 2015, he gave the authoritarian project a vital upgrade. Trump didn't care about the Koch brothers or the Republican Party establishment's laissez-faire agenda. Economically, he campaigned on the most progressive agenda of any Republican nominee since Richard Nixon or possibly Dwight Eisenhower. He would protect social security, not privatize it. He'd throw up trade barriers to protect American manufacturing jobs, not lower them to usher jobs overseas. He'd repeal Obamacare and replace it with something cheaper and better. He'd revitalize the Rust Belt via presidential fiat, a promise that would have required a New Deal–scale intervention. In office, he would betray many of these pledges, but the agenda that allowed a washed-up reality television star and serial adulterer with no political or governmental experience to win the presidency was a rebuke to Koch, Armey, and forty years of GOP politics.

Relieved of the unpopular aspects of the Tea Party agenda, Trump was able to double down on what had always been its core appeal: ethnonationalist authoritarianism. On the 2016 campaign trail, he called for a religious test for citizenship; he encouraged supporters to get in physical altercations with protesters; he promised when elected that he would jail his opponent, Hillary Clinton, weaken free press protections, and give the *Washington Post* "problems." He declared in advance that the election would be "rigged" if he did not win it. He brushed off criticism about his serial sexual assaults on women, attacked the parents of a decorated soldier killed in battle, and praised Russia's despotic president, Vladimir Putin, whose intelligence services leaked documents to help his victory. At the time, most mainstream U.S. political reporters and editors failed to understand that Trump was following the playbook of European right-wing nationalists, advocating government activism on behalf of "good" citizens and state-sponsored retribution against internal enemies, for whom constitutional protections might not apply. The political class failed to understand that democratic "norms" have no power over the aspiring autocrat, and that without them, institutions—from the Department of Justice to the Supreme Court to the Joint Chiefs of Staff—mean nothing. When Trump, against the wishes of the party establishment, clinched the Republican Party nomination, a Rubicon was crossed. Authoritarianism was no longer a fringe movement in U.S. politics, but a serious ideological competitor to liberal democracy. A collapse into autocracy was now very much a possibility, though it would take years for most pundits, political reporters, and opposition politicians to understand this, even after Trump shocked the world (and probably himself) by winning the presidency that November.

Trump's support, however, was and would remain regionally varied, following the same geographic contours as the Tea Party's support had, but with amplified strength. He won Greater Appalachia by 25 points, New France by 22, and the Deep South and the Far West by 9. He lost the Spanish Caribbean by 14, El Norte by 19, New Netherland by more than 25, and the Left Coast by a staggering 34-point margin. Tidewater, continuing its rapid transition, went for his opponent by 14 points. But his populist rhetoric and abandonment of Koch-style laissez-faire capitalism gave him big gains in rural parts of Yankeedom and the Midlands, with their communitarian outlook. Scores of largely white, rural counties that had gone for Barack Obama by large margins in 2008 and 2012 flipped to Trump by wide margins in 2016, with dramatic implications. Whereas the previous, conventional establishment Republican nominee, Mitt Romney, had lost the Midlands by 5 and Yankeedom by 16, Trump lost them by only 0.4 and 8 percent respectively. On the Electoral College map, this white rural surge in these two regions is what made all the difference, allowing Trump to squeeze out the narrowest of victories in Wisconsin, Michigan, and Pennsylvania and to move Ohio and Midlands-dominated Iowa into the Republican camp for the first time since 2004.

2016 Presidential Election

Data: MIT Election Data and Science Lab, "County Presidential Election Returns 2000-2020."

Why the regional variations?

One reason harkens back to the religious geography we shared in chapters 5 and 6, specifically the dominance of the white evangelical religious denominations in Greater Appalachia, the Deep South, and

Tidewater, and *nowhere else*. This is important because white evangelicals emerged as the most important bloc of support for Trumpism, a fact explained by the emergence of white Christian Nationalism. White Christian nationalists believe God ghostwrote the 1789 Constitution, intending it to make the United States into His kingdom. Christian Nationalism is a political project rather than a religious one, indeed one that has diverted followers from their spiritual mission to the pursuit of Earthly power, the conquering of their own Kingdom, the United States. "We can serve and worship God or we can serve and worship the gods of this world," journalist Tim Alberta, a devout evangelical and son of an evangelical pastor, wrote in *The Kingdom, the Power and the Glory*. "Too many American evangelicals have tried to do both."[1]

To be clear, white Christian Nationalism isn't "Christian"; it's a dangerous autocratic ideology camouflaged as a faith movement. Adherents see the United States as a Christian nation founded by and for white Christians and they seek to refound the country for themselves. In 2023, 77 percent of white evangelicals said the founders intended the United States to be a Christian nation and 54 percent said that God intended America to be a new promised land for "Euro-Christians."[2] They see "white Christian Evangelical" as an ethnicity, the "real Americans" to whom the country belongs. They believe their Bible, an English translation created by order of King James I of England in 1604, is God's infallible law and should become the basis of government, criminal statute, and all institutions, public or private. In 2024, 64 percent of white evangelicals said that when the Bible and "the will of the people" conflict, the Bible should carry the day under the law.[3] Their literal and selective reading of this Bible sanctions discrimination against women, LGBTQ people, and non-Christians; rejects the Declaration's propositions about human equality, self-government, and freedom to pursue happiness; and seeks to remake the United States as an absolute monarchy. "Christian nationalists with apocalyptic views tell us that they want a theonomic state," Paul A. Djupe, who studies religion and politics at Denison University, told a reporter. "That is, they want rule by religious law."[4]

In Trump, despite his lack of religious or moral convictions, they saw their savior. He was likened to the kings of the Old Testament whom God chose to further his plans for his chosen people, King David of Israel and the Persian Emperor Cyrus the Great, who punished the Ancient Jews' enemies. David was an adulterer who had a cuckolded husband killed, who found blind and crippled people so unsightly he ordered his soldiers to slaughter them, and who oversaw the arbitrary executions of tens of thousands of civilians in the towns and cities he conquered. But he was also the person who unified the Kingdom of Israel, brought the Ark of the Covenant to Jerusalem, and planned the erection of Solomon's Temple. Cyrus was pagan, but when he conquered Babylon, he released the Jews from captivity and allowed them to rebuild the Temple. Prominent evangelicals have made explicit comparisons between Trump and these kings, including former Housing and Urban Development Secretary Ben Carson, Liberty University President Jerry Falwell Jr., former Texas Governor Rick Perry, and Texas preacher Lance Wallnau, who's been called the Father of Dominionism. "They think that politics is a form of spiritual warfare and believe that God is using Donald Trump to help wage this war," John Fea, a professor of evangelical history at Messiah University, told the *New York Times*.[5]

Christian nationalists are a subset of white evangelicals. The Public Religion Research Institute found in 2024 that two-thirds of white evangelicals are Christian nationalists and that Christian nationalists (white or not) were most concentrated in Deep Southern and Greater Appalachian states. Alabama was the most Christian nationalist state (at 23 percent of the population), followed by Mississippi, Tennessee, and Kentucky (all 19 percent), South Carolina, Louisiana, Oklahoma, and West Virginia (at 18 percent). The least Christian nationalist states were all in or dominated by Yankeedom, New Netherland, and the Left Coast: Connecticut (2 percent), Maine and Washington (both 4 percent), Massachusetts, Oregon, New York, and New Jersey (all 5 percent).[6] This geographic pattern is a great part of the reason why the modern authoritarian movement has been most successful in the southern regions.

A SECOND REASON for the regional variations in authoritarians' prospects is that the authoritarian mindset is also more common in some regions than in others.

We learned this after fielding a nationwide survey in 2024 that asked 1,700 registered voters a series of questions from a well-established academic test of right-wing authoritarian attitudes. This was the Authoritarianism-Conservatism-Traditionalism (ACT) model—developed by political psychologists John Duckitt of the University of Auckland, Boris Bizumic of Australian National University, and their coauthors—which holds that right-wing authoritarian attitudes flow from three distinct, though related, ideological attitudes: authoritarian *Aggressiveness* (a desire for strict, tough, harsh, punitive, coercive social control), *Conservatism* (which is about uncritical, respectful, obedient, submissive support for existing societal or group authorities and institutions), and *Traditionalism* (a desire for traditional, old-fashioned social norms, values, and morality.)[7]

We took the percentage of people with high scores in each of these ACT categories and subtracted the percentage of people with low scores to get a net figure. We then compared this figure for each regional culture to that of the United States as a whole, revealing the relative levels of A, C, and T for each nation in a way that allowed side-by-side comparisons of the three factors. (We didn't have enough respondents to assess two low-population nations—First Nation and Greater Polynesia—which are not included in this analysis.)

Here's what we found:

Authoritarian Mindset Scores: Deviance from U.S. Average

■ Deep South ▨ Yankeedom ■ Midlands ▦ Greater Appalachia ▨ Far West
▦ New Netherland ▦ El Norte ▦ Tidewater ▦ Left Coast

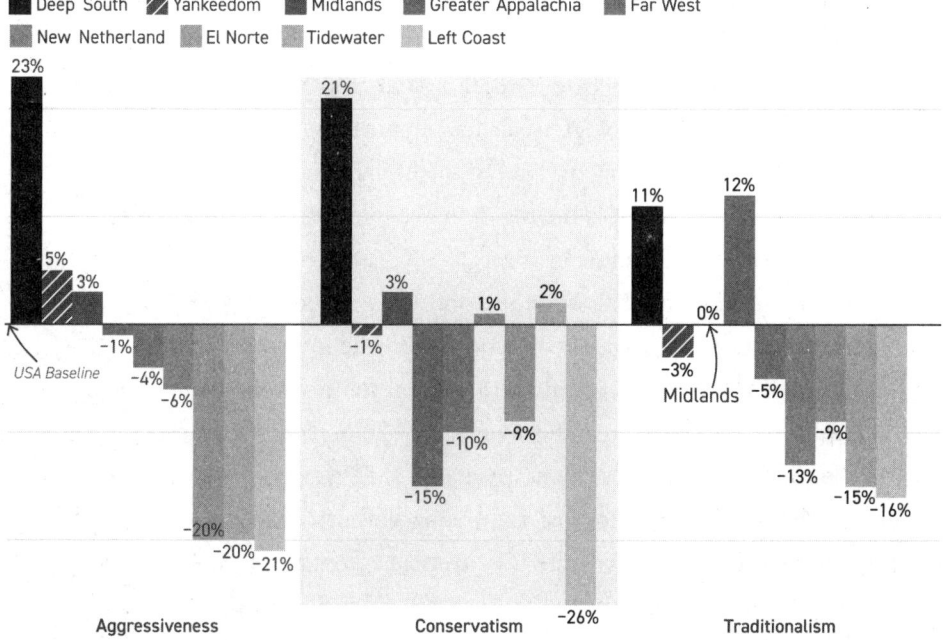

Data: Nationhood Lab/Embold Research national poll, April 2024, n=1567.

One clear takeaway is that the **Deep South** is in a class by itself, with net 23 percent more high Aggressiveness respondents than the U.S. average, 21 percent more high Conservatism respondents, and 11 percent more high Traditionalism respondents. These were also by far the highest Aggressiveness and Conservatism scores of any region and a very close second for Traditionalism. This is an authoritarian's trifecta, a population with lots of people who favor punitive law enforcement, uncritical respect for authority, and defense of traditional mores. **Greater Appalachia**—the region most enthusiastic about Trumpism—has a different mix. Readers should not be in the least surprised to see it has the second-lowest net Conservatism result of all the regions (–15), reflecting its people's historic refusal to submit to authority. But it also scores slightly below the U.S. average on Agressiveness—the desire to harshly punish rulebreakers—which may tie into that distrust of established authority, apparently to include law enforcement and the courts; this may have worked in Trump's favor as he regularly evaded serious consequences for his crimes, from sexual assault to trying to overthrow the republic. Yet in psychological terms, support for Trumpism may best be understood by the region having the highest Traditionalism levels in the country, meaning it is the region most committed to stopping social, cultural, and demographic change.

Consistent with what we've seen on the ground, the **Left Coast** is a massive outlier in the other direction, with the lowest scores of any nation in all three categories: net –16 percent for Traditionalism, –21 percent for Aggressiveness, and a staggering –26 percent for Conservatism, 11 points lower than its closest competitor. **El Norte**'s population is the second least disposed toward right-wing authoritarianism, one of only three regions to fall below the U.S. average across all three ACT factors, and is especially resistant to the Aggressiveness factor (at –20). For a region that started with a patron-peon socioeconomic system and spent much of the nineteenth and twentieth centuries under an externally-imposed Jim Crow–style caste system, this is a remarkable testament to the tolerance and openness of the region's people. **Tidewater**, once again, is shown here to now be one of the most liberal parts of the federation, with the second-lowest net Traditionalism (–15 percent), and is tied with El Norte for the same honors in regards to Aggressiveness (–20).

Despite being regarded as a "red" region, the **Far West** is inhospitable turf for right-wing authoritarians. It's one of only three regions to be under the U.S. average across all three ACT mindsets and, at –10 percent, its net Conservatism score (submissiveness to authority) is the third lowest among the regions. **New Netherland** is also a tough environment for would-be dictators, with low net Aggressiveness (–6) and very low net Traditionalism. Curiously, it's a hair keener on Conservatism (+1) than the national average, which perhaps explains how they've tolerated having so many terrible early-twenty-first-century mayors.

The **Midlands**, true to form, is very close to the national average across all three factors, with a net +3 in Authoritarianism and Conservatism and a net zero in Traditionalism. Overall, this means it's only slightly more susceptible to a right-wing authoritarian takeover than the United States as a whole, which matches what we've seen since 2010. As for **Yankeedom**, perhaps the most intriguing finding is that four centuries after the Puritans showed up, the region still has the second-highest net Aggressiveness score at +5 percent. Yankees still want transgressors roundly punished. It's also only slightly below the U.S. average in Conservatism and Traditionalism, at –1 and –3 percent respectively. This is also consistent with twenty-first-century experience: Yankeedom may be well inoculated against libertarianism, but its historical experience and cultural attributes don't provide it with particularly strong antibodies in a fight against ethnonationalism.

As Trump took control of the White House in 2016, he could count on only a few regions of the country to embrace his desire to consolidate an authoritarian regime, a few others to resist it, and a few to be battlegrounds.

UNPREPARED AND UNSUITED FOR public office, Trump's first administration was chaotic, incompetent, and disorganized, unable to effectively implement its agenda. But this agenda was even more autocratic and ethnonationalist than his campaign had intimated. He tried to ban entry to visitors on the basis of their (Muslim) religion. He took thousands of babies, toddlers, and small children from their asylum-seeking parents, kept them in detention-camp cages, and didn't bother to create records to ensure they could one day be reunited with their now-deported parents. He refused to condemn torch-bearing neo-Nazi marchers. He embraced the dictators of North Korea, Russia, and Saudi Arabia while burning bridges with the leaders of the United States's longtime liberal democratic allies. He demonized Mexicans as disease-carrying rapists and Africans as denizens of "shithole countries," while lamenting we didn't welcome more immigrants from Norway. He said native-born U.S. House Representatives of African descent should "go back home." He claimed the election he had just won had been rigged against him—because he had lost the popular vote—and that he wouldn't accept the results of future elections if he hadn't won them. He wanted to order active-duty military units to attack peaceful protesters, but was prevented by more constitutionally minded military leaders.[8]

Trumpism draws strength from the Great Replacement Theory, which claims there is a liberal conspiracy to replace white people with non-white immigrants who share their political views. Trump himself repeatedly proclaimed that unauthorized migrants constituted an "invasion" that would "pour into and infest" the United States. Trumpian propagandist Tucker Carlson told television viewers that "Democrats know if they keep up the flood of illegals into the country, they can eventually turn it into a flood of voters for them. . . . Their political success does not depend on good policies, but on demographic replacement." Another top ally, Laura Ingraham, told her followers that Democrats want "to replace you, the American voters, with newly amnestied citizens and an ever-increasing number of chain migrants."[9] And these lies worked. A 2022 Yahoo News/ YouGov poll found a shocking 61 percent of Donald Trump's supporters subscribed to this replacement theory, while only 24 percent disagreed with it. In 2024, the Pew Research Center found four in ten Trump supporters hold to a central tenet of this theory: that the decline of the proportion of people who are white is bad for society, compared to just one in ten Joe Biden supporters. Furthermore, when political scientist Robert Pape's team at the University of Chicago's Project on Security and Threats carefully studied the beliefs and attitudes of the January 6 insurrectionists, they found fears of the "Great Replacement" were the most consistent factor, tripling the likelihood of someone having joined the coup attempt.[10]

In Greater Appalachia, with its historical mythos about being home to a "real American" ethnic group, this thinking may be the most important element of Trumpism's appeal. The region experienced the largest drop in the proportion of people who identify as white, falling from 75 percent to 68 percent in the ten years leading up to the 2020 census. Our Nationhood Lab analysis of the geography of immigration found the proportion of foreign-born people in that region has more than doubled since 1900, at the height of the great 1880–1924 immigration wave, from 3.5 to 8.2 percent, a period when the proportion in Yankeedom more than halved. The region's high Traditionalism score suggests this sort of transformation, disrupting cultural and demographic norms, may have been especially unwelcome.

Trump sought to consolidate support among white ethnonationalists by championing the thousands of monuments white supremacists had erected to Confederate heroes in public spaces across the Deep South, Tidewater, and Greater Appalachia in the early and mid-twentieth century. The neo-Nazi marchers he praised as "fine people" had been protesting the planned removal of the statue to slaveholder Robert E. Lee in Charlottesville, Virginia. Black Lives Matter, the protest movement that gained international attention in 2020 after the brutal police murder of an African American man, George Floyd, drew attention to the Lost Cause monuments, which had been erected in part to intimidate and humiliate Jim Crow–era African Americans. As governors, cities, and citizens across these regions took action to remove these ethnonationalist symbols, Trump expressed outrage. The protesters "hate our history, they hate our values, and they hate everything we prize as Americans," he told a mostly white audience at an evangelical megachurch in Phoenix. "Our country didn't grow great with them. It grew great with you and your thought process and your ideology. The left-wing mob is trying to demolish our heritage, so they can replace it with a new oppressive regime that they alone control." He issued an executive order that directed prosecutors to deal harshly with anyone who damaged monuments on federal property and withheld federal funding to cities and local law enforcement agencies that had "surrendered to mob rule" by not defending the statues.[11]

At the time, at least ten U.S. military installations were named for Confederate officers, including Pierre Beauregard, who opened fire on federal troops at Fort Sumter, and Louisiana slave lord Braxton Bragg, widely regarded as one of the war's worst generals, whose men saw him as "a merciless tyrant." When Trump learned the Pentagon leadership was considering renaming these bases for people who hadn't committed treason, he forcefully intervened. "My Administration will not even consider the renaming of these Magnificent and Fabled Military Installations," he tweeted. "Our history as the Greatest Nation in the World will not be tampered with. Respect our Military!" In one of his last acts in office, he vetoed the entire $740 billion bipartisan defense funding bill because it directed the military to rename the bases. The Republican-controlled congress overrode his veto, the only time they did so in his four years in office.[12]

ETHNONATIONALISM HELPED TRUMP WIN OFFICE, but his betrayal of most of his populist economic promises doomed his first reelection bid. He didn't restore manufacturing to the heartland or replace Obamacare with something better, but he did stock his cabinet with corporate CEOs and signed an enormous tax giveaway to the super-wealthy. As a result, the gains his movement made for Republicans in rural Yankeedom and the Midlands fell back in both the 2018 midterms and his 2020 reelection bid. In 2018, half of the forty-one U.S. House seats Democrats picked up were in Yankeedom and the Midlands, and they flipped state legislative chambers in Maine, New Hampshire, Connecticut, Minnesota, and New York. In the 2020 presidential contest, Democrats boosted their margins by 3.5 points in Yankeedom and 2.5 in the Midlands, tipping Michigan, Wisconsin, and Pennsylvania back to their camp.[13]

This loss prompted Trump's most autocratic move yet: an attempt to

2020 Presidential Election

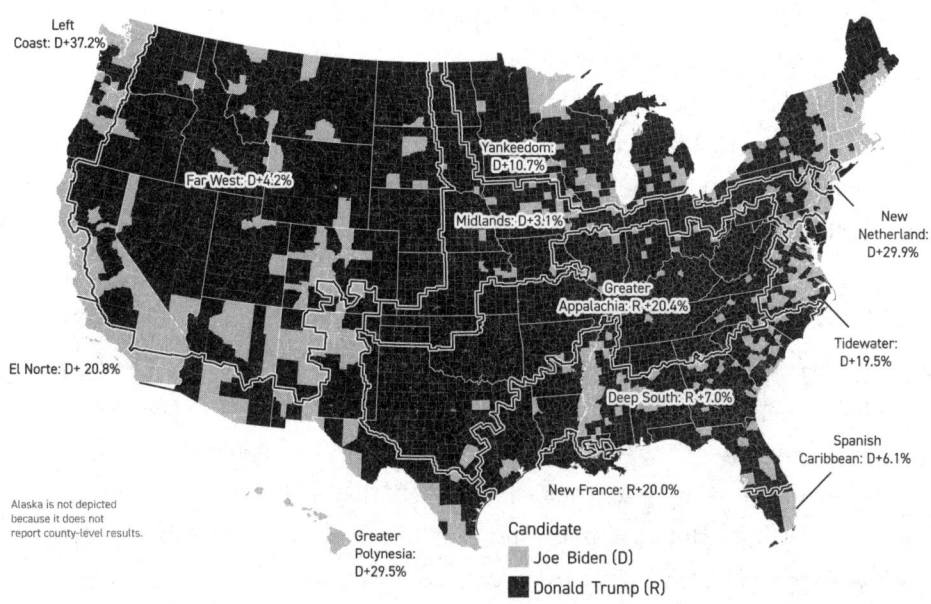

Left
Coast: D+37.2%

Yankeedom:
D+10.7%

Far West: D+4.2%

Midlands: D+3.1%

New
Netherland:
D+29.9%

Greater
Appalachia: R+20.4%

Tidewater:
D+19.5%

El Norte: D+ 20.8%

Deep South: R+7.0%

Spanish
Caribbean: D+6.1%

New France: R+20.0%

Alaska is not depicted
because it does not
report county-level results.

Greater
Polynesia:
D+29.5%

Candidate

Joe Biden (D)

Donald Trump (R)

Data: MIT Election Data and Science Lab, "County Presidential Election Returns 2000–2020."

overturn the results of a free and fair election so as to stay in power. He first cast evidence-free aspersions on the election results, undermining faith in democracy and institutions, and then held a series of phone calls and meetings to pressure state-level officials and lawmakers in Michigan, Arizona, and Georgia to replace Biden's electors with ones who would vote for Trump. He pressured Georgia's top elections official, Republican Secretary of State Brad Raffensperger, to "find 11,780 votes" that would give him the state's electoral college votes, threatening that it was "a criminal offense" not to do so. He was spurned by Republican officials, who exposed themselves to death threats to uphold democracy and the rule of law. "I voted for you. I worked for you. I campaigned for you," Arizona House Speaker Rusty Bowers told him. "I just won't do anything illegal for you." Trump then pushed his attorney general, Bill Barr, and other senior Justice Department officials to open criminal investigations into his invented allegations of fraud; they, too, refused. On Christmas Day,

Trump started insisting Vice President Mike Pence should refuse to carry out his purely ceremonial role of counting the certified electoral college ballots, scheduled for January 6, an entirely lawless and unconstitutional act the heretofore loyal Pence also refused to commit.[14]

Trump tried to remain in power by force via the attempted coup of January 6, 2021. He called tens of thousands of supporters to the National Mall and, knowing some had weapons, directed them to the Capitol building as Congress gathered to certify the election results, telling them to "fight like hell." When an aide reported that some in the crowd were armed, Trump told her, she later testified, "I don't effing care that they have weapons. They're not here to hurt me. Take the effin' mags [magnetic sensors for detecting weapons] away. Let my people in. They can march to the Capitol from here." For more than three hours, Trump sat in the White House dining room watching Fox News' coverage of the beating of police officers, the breach of the Capitol, the frantic evacuation of Congress, and the sacking of the Senate chambers. He made no calls for help—not to the Pentagon or Homeland Security or the Justice Department—despite pleas by his aides and by the vice president, the House Speaker, the Senate Majority Leader, and others sheltered in basement bunkers. When he finally issued a video telling the insurrectionists— who included men in riot gear bearing hog ties and protesters carrying signs saying "Hang Mike Pence"—to stand down, he added they were "very special" to him.[15]

When the Capitol was finally secured in the wee hours of the morning of January 7, shell-shocked congresspeople convened to certify the results. Despite everything that had happened, 7 Republican senators[16] and 138 Republican representatives[17] voted to reject the entirely legitimate and already certified electoral college votes of contested states, siding with Trump over democracy and the rule of law. They were soon aptly named the "Sedition Caucus." The Senate members were all from states controlled by some combination of the Deep South, Greater Appalachia, and the Midlands.[18] Less than a third of the House Republican caucus voted for democracy, the constitution, and the rule of law that night, but the patriots included a majority of the caucus from districts in Yankeedom and the Far West, as well as the Left Coast's lone Republican, Jaime Herrera Beutler of Washington; out of dozens of Deep Southern Republicans, only nine had the courage not to betray their country.[19]

TRUMP WAS VOTED OUT of power in 2020, but Trumpism remained a dangerous and corrosive force in Greater Appalachia, the Deep South, and parts of the Far West and Yankeedom.

In these regions, authoritarians redoubled their efforts to make sure they, not the public, determined the results of future elections. In the three years following the 2020 election, Republicans introduced more than six hundred bills in state legislatures that would increase the possibility of such election subversion, with sixty-two becoming law by the end of 2023. These laws aimed to give Republican-controlled legislators or state officials direct control over election outcomes; created obstacles to the smooth operation of election administration so as to create excuses for intervention; introduced penalties or criminalized inadvertent mistakes committed by election workers; or shifted election administration from nonpartisan actors to Republican controlled positions. But despite introducing such bills in nearly every state, not a single one became law in states controlled by Yankeedom, the Midlands, New Netherland, or the Left Coast, with the exception of Wisconsin. Reports by a coalition of nonpartisan organizations monitoring such laws show them to have been overwhelmingly concentrated in the Deep South, Greater Appalachia, and the Far West, with Florida, Texas, Georgia, and North Carolina the most egregious.[20]

Despite myriad efforts to suppress their voters, Democratic candidates won the governorships of North Carolina in 2016 and Michigan and Wisconsin in 2018. Immediately after those elections, Republican-controlled legislatures held lame-duck sessions in those states to pass new laws stripping powers from the incoming governors. In North Carolina, they cut the number of gubernatorial appointees from 1,500 to 300, required cabinet appointees to be approved by the Republican-controlled state senate, reduced the governor's appointments to the state Board of Education and UNC boards of trustees, and changed the makeup of state and county election boards so that Republicans, instead of the governor's party, would have a majority in every election year. In Wisconsin, they curtailed the governor's oversight of a controversial economic development board and prevented him from making changes to any program for which Wisconsin had received a waiver from federal requirements, so as to stop him from reversing Governor Walker's imposition of drug testing for food stamps recipients and work requirements to receive health care via Medicaid. Michigan Republicans used their lame-duck session to pass laws that would have allowed the legislature to hire lawyers to intervene in court cases, circumventing the Democratic attorney general, and to take control of a key campaign finance regulating body; but they were stymied by that state's outgoing, moderate, Yankee Republican governor, Rick Snyder, who vetoed the bills before leaving office. "This is a textbook example of how democracies die," Michael Wagner, associate professor of political science at the University of Wisconsin, said at the time. "When norms about the peaceful transfer of power are violated, we are in trouble."[21]

At Nationhood Lab we worked with the Cornell Institute of Politics and Global Affairs and their Deputy Director, political scientist Douglas Kriner, to parse polling data they collected in late 2022 around Americans' concerns about the various assaults on their democracy. Not surprisingly, we found significant differences in public opinion between the American Nations. For instance, nationwide, a narrow majority— 51 percent—said the January 6 attack was a major threat to the country. But there was a 22-point gap between respondents in the Deep South (42 percent of whom saw the attack as a major threat) and the Left Coast (64 percent). Greater Appalachia—the region most supportive of Trump in both of his presidential bids—also discounted the danger, with only 46 percent regarding it as a major threat, while residents of Tidewater, the Midlands, and New Netherland were more concerned than the national average. The regional gap was also great among January 6 threat deniers, with one in five respondents in Greater Appalachia saying the attacks represented no threat at all, compared to just 5.6 percent of Left Coasters and 9 percent of Yankees.[22]

Respondents were also asked to assess the threat posed by state legislators trying to change voting laws to prevent people of color from voting or making it harder for them to vote. Again, 51 percent of Americans overall said this was a major threat. In the Deep South, Greater Appalachia, and El Norte, only 46 to 48 percent shared this view, while in the Left Coast, Tidewater, and the classic swing region of the Midlands, the rate topped 60 percent. Similarly, the percentage of Greater Appalachians who regard this as no threat at all (17.9) was more than double that of Left Coasters and Yankees (both 7.6). There was a similar pattern of concern with voter fraud, which has repeatedly been shown to be effectively nonexistent. The bottom line is that large numbers of Americans everywhere recognize the true source of the threat to American democracy, but that in the aggressively individualistic nations they don't constitute a majority.

THE NAZI POLITICAL THEORIST Carl Schmitt, who helped create Hitler's Reich, argued that politics was ultimately about having an enemy, and who that enemy was would determine who your friends were. He defined such political enemies thusly: "He is the other, the alien, and it suffices that in his essence he is something existentially other and alien in an especially intensive sense."[23] With the advent of Trumpism, U.S. authoritarians found coalition-building utility in stepping up attacks against LGBTQ people, especially those who identify as transgender or nonbinary. "For the good of society," the conservative commentator

Michael Knowles told the audience at the Conservative Political Action Conference in 2023, "transgenderism must be eradicated from public life entirely." From the stage of the 2024 Republican National Convention, Representative Marjorie Taylor Greene of (Appalachian) Georgia said politicians had been "selling us out" by recognizing transgender people. "Let me state this clearly, there are only two genders, and we are made in God's image." North Carolina Lieutenant Governor Mark Robinson, a self-declared "Black Nazi" whom Trump affectionately called "Martin Luther King Jr. on steroids," has said: "There's no reason anybody anywhere in America should be telling any child about transgenderism, homosexuality—any of that filth." That state's Republican electorate then nominated him to be their party's 2024 gubernatorial nominee.[24]

The authoritarians have had an uphill struggle. The Nationscape surveys showed that in 2020 and early 2021 most people in every region had overwhelmingly favorable opinions of "gays and lesbians" and approved of transgender people serving in the military. But at the same time, the vast majority of people said there are only two genders, male and female, with wide variance across the regions. This suggested attitudes toward transgender people were tolerant but not fully accepting. The Trumpists have sought to change this while social attitudes remained plastic, especially in the southern regions where tolerance was scarcer.

The drive to "other" transgender people has been extremely aggressive in some regions and a failure in others. A notorious 2016 law passed by North Carolina's Republicans overturned and banned local laws that prohibited discrimination against LGBTQ people in workplaces and public accommodation and passed new legislation that forced transgender people to use bathrooms corresponding with the gender on their birth certificate.[25] By 2024, six states had implemented "bathroom laws" that applied to some or all government buildings as well as public schools: five Deep Southern states and Utah. Eight more had such laws for public schools alone, all of them in states controlled by the Far West, Greater Appalachia, the Deep South, or the Midlands. No state under Yankee,

Transgender People Should Be Allowed to Serve in the Military

■ Agree ▦ Disagree ▫ Not Sure

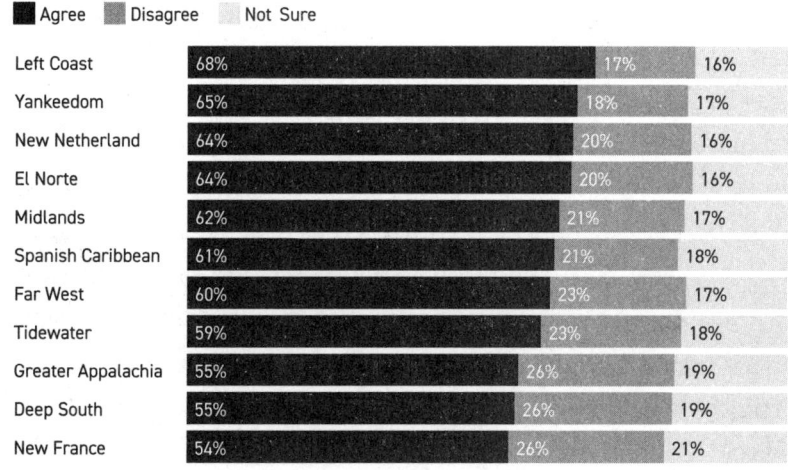

	Agree	Disagree	Not Sure
Left Coast	68%	17%	16%
Yankeedom	65%	18%	17%
New Netherland	64%	20%	16%
El Norte	64%	20%	16%
Midlands	62%	21%	17%
Spanish Caribbean	61%	21%	18%
Far West	60%	23%	17%
Tidewater	59%	23%	18%
Greater Appalachia	55%	26%	19%
Deep South	55%	26%	19%
New France	54%	26%	21%

Data: Democracy Fund + UCLA Nationscape Survey (2019–2021)

There Are Only Two Genders: Male and Female

■ Agree ▦ Disagree ▫ Not Sure

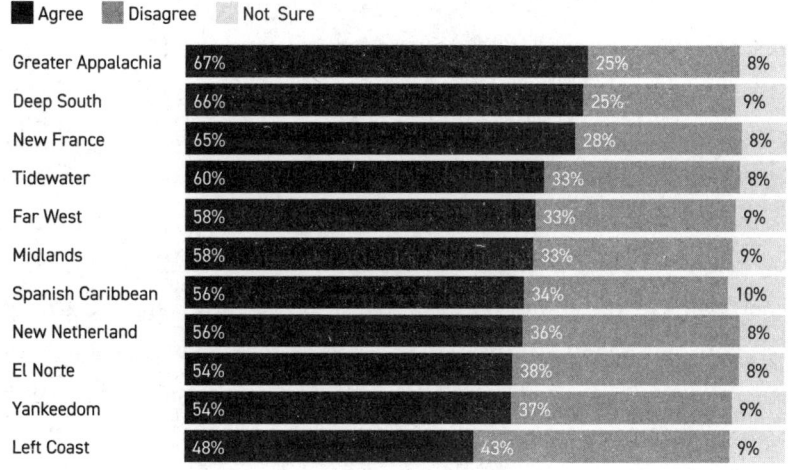

	Agree	Disagree	Not Sure
Greater Appalachia	67%	25%	8%
Deep South	66%	25%	9%
New France	65%	28%	8%
Tidewater	60%	33%	8%
Far West	58%	33%	9%
Midlands	58%	33%	9%
Spanish Caribbean	56%	34%	10%
New Netherland	56%	36%	8%
El Norte	54%	38%	8%
Yankeedom	54%	37%	9%
Left Coast	48%	43%	9%

Data: Democracy Fund + UCLA Nationscape Survey (2019–2021)

Left Coast, New Netherland, or El Norte control had such laws. Seven states passed strict "don't say gay" laws that prohibited public school teachers from speaking about their gender or sexual identities, all of them in the Deep South, Greater Appalachia, and the Midlands. Eight states passed laws requiring school staff to "out" LGBTQ children if asked by their parents, all of them controlled by these three regions and the Far West. Utah passed a 2024 law requiring prisoners to be housed with cellmates based on their gender at birth while Tennessee prohibited jailed and imprisoned transgender people from receiving their hormone treatments. Idaho had new laws that year requiring public employees, including school teachers, to use only students' legal names and the titles and pronouns corresponding to their biological sex. Sixteen states provided no protection against employment discrimination based on sexual orientation or gender identity, every one of them in Greater Appalachia, the Deep South, the Far West, the Midlands, or combinations thereof. Every state controlled by Yankeedom, the Left Coast, El Norte, Tidewater, New Netherland, or combinations thereof had laws explicitly protecting against discrimination for either orientation or identity.[26]

Efforts to ban books from school and public libraries have seen a dramatic explosion in the Trump era. One of the prime targets has been books centering LGBTQ experiences. At the end of 2023, the anticensorship nonprofit PEN America found such titles accounted for 26 percent of all banned books, including the two most banned book of all, *Gender Queer*, Maia Kobabe's award-winning memoir about being nonbinary, and Mike Curato's *Flamer*, an autobiographical young adult graphic novel about trying to be closeted, Catholic, and queer at a Boy Scout camp in the mid-1990s. Successful book bans were overwhelmingly concentrated in just five states, Texas, Florida, South Carolina, Missouri, and Utah, all of which are controlled by some combination of the Deep South, Greater Appalachia, the Midlands, and the Far West. Texas's book bans alone outnumbered those of the other forty-five states combined. In late 2023, Sarah Kate Ellis, the president and CEO of the LGBTQ advocacy group GLAAD, told CNN that the bans furthered "othering" and were building "this culture that LGBTQ people, queer people, don't belong and should be on the margins of society."[27]

Authoritarians often turn to immigrants and foreigners in their effort to create a "hated other," and as the Trumpist movement became more clearly fascistic in the early 2020s, rhetoric against both groups became increasingly extreme. Trump's successful 2024 campaign for a second term in the White House centered almost entirely on hatred of immigrants, whom he blamed for everything from housing shortages to nonexistent crime waves. He and his vice presidential candidate, a U.S. senator from the Appalachian section of Ohio, J.D. Vance, used national debate stages to spread a completely made-up story that legal Haitian immigrants in Ohio were eating their neighbors' house pets. He's repeatedly told his followers that he'd save them from non-white immigrant "animals," "vermin," and "stone-cold killers," who had "bad genes" and were the "enemy from within." He promised to accomplish this clean-up with military force and deportation camps. "What is so jarring to me is these are not just Nazi-like statements. These are actual Nazi sentiments," Robert Jones, founder of PRRI and the author of *The Hidden Roots of White Supremacy*, told *Politico* in late 2024. "Hitler used the word vermin and rats multiple times in *Mein Kampf* to talk about Jews. These are not accidental or coincidental references. We have clear, 20th century historical precedent with this kind of political language, and we see where it leads."[28]

As of this writing, the United States approaches its 250th anniversary. The long-term survival of its experiment in democratic self-government is very much in doubt. Trump, who was facing multiple criminal indictments for trying to overthrow the 2020 election, is returning to the White House. Right-wing leaders in the Deep South, with its deep authoritarian traditions, are joined by those in Greater Appalachia, with its surfeit of Christian Nationalism and "Great Replacement" anxieties, to further his effort to remake the United States on illiberal, ethnonationalist grounds. This project receives significant but not always reliable support from political leaders within parts of the Far West and the Midlands and has made forays into Yankeedom, from which it is usually repulsed. It is soundly rejected by most people in the Left Coast, New Netherland, Greater Polynesia, Tidewater, and El Norte, regions whose people again voted against Trump by substantial margins while voters in the Deep South and Greater Appalachia backed him by double digits.[29] The country is cracking to a degree not seen since the 1860s.

What had been an authoritarian movement in the 2010s has become a textbook fascist one by 2024. "Fascist" is, of course, a provocative word, commonly associated with Hitler and his genocidal Nazi Party. However, it is a word with an actual meaning, describing a particular ideology that was first packaged by the Italian dictator Benito Mussolini and his ally, the political philosopher Giovanni Gentile, in the 1920s. Back in 2004— when Trump supported Democrats and nobody would have dreamed he could become president—political scientist Ken Paxton defined fascism as having nine mobilizing passions. They were:

- A sense of overwhelming crisis beyond the reach of traditional solutions;

- The primacy of the group, for which one has duties superior to every individual or human right, and the subordination of the individual to it;

- The belief that one's group has been victimized, a sentiment justifying any action, unburdened by legal or moral limits, against the group's internal and external enemies;

- Dread of the group's decline under the corrosive effects of individualistic liberalism, class conflict, and alien influences;

- The need for closer integration of a purer community, by consent if possible, or by exclusionary violence if necessary;

- The need for authority by natural chiefs (always male), culminating in a national chieftain who alone is capable of incarnating the group's historical destiny;

- The superiority of the leader's instincts over abstract and universal reason;

- The beauty of violence and efficacy of will, when they are devoted to the group's success;

- And the right of the chosen people to dominate others, unrestrained by any human or divine law, justified by the group's Darwinian prowess.

Fascists, the late Carleton College historian Diethelm Prowe wrote in 1994, are also typically led by a charismatic leader, a "saviour" said to have a deep intuitive understanding of the people and their destiny, whom they promise to champion against an allegedly corrupt and parasitic elite. Fascistic leaders promise to eliminate this elite, uniting the nation around his own person in what Dennis Tourish, professor of leadership studies at the University of Sussex, describes as "a crusade against hated enemies and behind a project of national renewal."

Trump and Trumpism check every one of these scholars' boxes.[30]

At the dawn of 2025, our regional divides have brought us to the edge of fascism. Many people wonder what can be done to bring us together again, and back from the abyss.

10

HOLDING THE COUNTRY TOGETHER

Alexander Hamilton had no illusions about what would happen to Americans if the United States collapsed.

If we failed to ratify the newly drafted constitution, he warned in 1787, we would quickly fall upon one another in a "War between the States" that, because it would be fought by irregular armies across unfortified borders, would be nastier and more destructive than European conflicts. Large states would overrun small ones. "Plunder and devastation" would march across the landscape, reducing the citizenry to "a state of continual danger" that would nourish authoritarian, militarized institutions. "If we should be disunited, and the integral parts should either remain separated, or . . . thrown together into two or three confederacies, we should be, in a short course of time, in the predicament of the continental powers of Europe," he continued in *Federalist* No. 8. "Our liberties would be a prey to the means of defending ourselves against the ambition and jealousy of each other."[1]

Now the U.S. Constitution is again under siege, with a third of the American citizenry and a majority of the members of Congress from one of our political parties happy to end democracy if it kept their candidate in power. A sitting president called forth a violent insurrection against our government—the very definition of treason—and yet not only escaped criminal accountability, but was reelected to the office via the overwhelming support of voters in the Deep South, Greater Appalachia, the Far West, and New France and over the objection of large majorities in Yankeedom, El Norte, New Netherland, the Left Coast, and Greater Polynesia. The stakes are at least as high as they were in Hamilton's time.

It's been obvious for more than a decade that the bonds holding the United States have been weakening, but the events of the early 2020s have exposed just how bad the rot is, leaving many Americans with a growing fear that there's precious little still holding us together as a people. The union Abraham Lincoln called "the last best hope on Earth" is stepping close to collapse. If we want this republic to survive—and given the risks of dissolution Hamilton pointed to, we certainly should—we must rediscover and reinvigorate our lost story of shared national purpose. Because of the special characteristics of our federated nation, we can't long survive without one.

MAINTAINING A SHARED SENSE OF nationhood has always been a special challenge for the United States, arguably the world's first civic nation, one defined not by organic ties, but by a shared commitment to a set of ideals. It came into being not as a nation, but as a contractual agreement, a means to an end for thirteen disparate rebel colonies facing a common enemy. Its people lacked a shared history, religion, or ethnicity, with Pennsylvania having a German plurality in 1776 and South Carolina an enslaved African majority. Americans didn't speak a language uniquely their own and most of its people hadn't occupied the continent long enough to imagine it as their mythic homeland, occupied since the dawn of time, and they'd cleansed or killed the people who could make such a claim. Its component states had been founded by completely different groups of settlers with often incompatible political, economic, ethnographic, and religious characteristics and so they had no shared story of who they were and what their purpose was. In short, they had none of the foundations of a nation-state.

I want to emphasize how important such stories are for cultivating national identity. Nations are ultimately abstractions, "imagined communities" in the oft-quoted words of the late Anglo-Irish political scientist Benedict Anderson. That's not to say they're not real, but they are socially constructed, and they further not just the objectives of elite state builders, but also the cognitive and psychological need for a shared social identity passed down to each and every one of us by the forces of evolutionary biology. Our ancestors had already been living in small bands for more than a million years by the time the first recognizable *Homo sapiens* appeared on the scene 300,000 years ago. We were genetically hardwired to be tribal, to join groups, and, having done so, to consider them superior to others. Indeed, it's one of our crowning adaptations that led to our eventual conquest of the entire planet.

We've always competed for survival and reproduction within groups, but we came to dominate this planet because our groups—camps, bands, tribes, societies, nations—competed against one another for dominance, with individuals sometimes willingly giving their lives for their group. We're the product of 1.8 million years of evolution selecting for the ability to build and maintain ever more sophisticated coalitions with unrelated individuals and complete strangers. This is astounding, because we're the only species on the planet with this capacity—to scale trust among strangers. In order to form the trust necessary to share resources and engage in collective projects with people we don't know or haven't even met, humans developed an instinctive drive to form social identities: memberships in groups that bond through symbols, rituals, and stories that reinforce a collective identity. David Samson, associate professor of anthropology at the University of Toronto, Mississauga, calls this our tribe drive. "A tribe is a network of intersubjective belief where symbols serve as tokens of identity, signaling membership," Samson, author of *Our Tribal Future:*

How to Channel our Foundational Human Instincts Into a Force for Good, tells me. "This network facilitates cooperation among strangers by embedding them within a shared mythology, functioning as a covert society. The signals of coalitionary alliances act as 'secret passwords,' granting access to the rights, responsibilities, and benefits of the collective 'imagined order.'"[2]

We're each members of lots of "tribes" simultaneously, which can include everything from our racial, ethnic, class, professional, or religious identity to being a devoted fan of an athletic team, musician, or political figure. The nation is one of the largest and perhaps most consequential of our social identities. This group identity idea emerged with the collapse of dynastic kingdoms and empires and the rise of the printing press in seventeenth-century Europe, spread and consolidated in the Americas in the late eighteenth and nineteenth centuries, and was adopted and forced on most everyone else on the planet during the twentieth century. National identity fulfills a range of human cultural, economic, political, and defensive needs while giving members belonging, security, and, if successful, prestige and self-esteem. Constructing a sense of nationhood has always been an exercise in storytelling, in mythmaking if you will, to provide a basis for collective belonging. It may spotlight things that foster unity and forget facts and events that don't, but that doesn't mean it's all a lie. "Myth cannot be constructed purely out of false material; it has to have some relationship with the memory of the collectivity that has fashioned it," the late Hungarian historian György Schöpflin once wrote. "It is hard to see how the Czechs and Slovaks, say, could define their mythopoeias by inventing a strong seafaring tradition." Because they meet a deep, evolutionary, human need, these national narrative stories aren't optional. A society without one, historian William McNeill warned back in 1982, "soon finds itself in deep trouble, for in the absence of believable myths, coherent public action becomes very difficult to improvise or sustain." People need such stories and, as Harvard University historian Jill

Lepore has put it, "they can get it from scholars or they can get it from demagogues, but get it they will."[3]

ALEXANDER HAMILTON'S PLEA WAS SUCCESSFUL, of course, in that we indeed ratified a new, stronger constitution in 1789. But we still hadn't agreed on why it was we had come together and what defined us as a people. For a time, the citizens of the new federation tried to get by on having won the American Revolution together and by beatifying George Washington as the father of the nation and model of republican virtue. But by the 1830s, the generation who had fought the Revolution had departed from the scene, and the identity crisis could no longer be papered over. Armed Appalachian settlers in western Pennsylvania and Virginia had contemplated secession in 1794, as had New England statesmen during the War of 1812. Slavery, which many of the Founders had regarded as an embarrassing anachronism that would fade away on its own, was fortifying its hold on the Deep South and Tidewater, whose leaders had begun arguing it was a positive good, increasing tension between the regions. Americans needed a story of United States nationhood if their experiment were to survive.

The first person to come to the rescue, to package and present a national story for the United States, was the historian-statesman George Bancroft, whom we met in chapter 4. On his return from his doctoral studies and intellectual adventures in Europe in 1822, he failed in bids to be a poet, professor, prep school master, and preacher. But in 1832, at age thirty-two, he began what would prove his life's work: to give his young nation a history that would answer those great questions: Who are we? Where did we come from? Where are we going?[4]

Bancroft's vision—laid out over four decades in his massive ten-volume *History of the United States of America*—combined his Puritan intellectual birthright with his German mentors' notion that nations developed like organisms and from a plan history had laid out for them. It held that Americans had been charged by Providence to implement the next stage of the progressive development of human liberty, equality, and freedom, and that this promise was open to people everywhere. "The origin of the language we speak carries us to India; our religion is from Palestine," Bancroft told the New York Historical Society in 1854. "Of the hymns sung in our churches, some were first heard in Italy, some in the deserts of Arabia, some on the banks of the Euphrates; our arts come from Greece; our jurisprudence from Rome." It was a civic national vision that defined an American as being a person devoted to the ideals set down in the Preamble to the Declaration of Independence: equality, liberty, the pursuit of happiness, self-government, and the natural rights of all people to these things.

Bancroft's version had its questionable parts, too: that the Founders were guided by God, that we were a chosen people destined to spread across the continent, that our success was all but preordained, a vision that prompted one of his journalistic fans to opine about the country's "manifest destiny." These ideas—which Bancroft clung to despite the Civil War, the failure of Reconstruction, and the restoration of authoritarian white supremacist regimes across half the federation—undermined the struggle to make the Declaration's promise a reality by fostering complacency rather than vigilance, and justifying imperial conquests that violated every natural rights principle in that document.

Abraham Lincoln knew Bancroft's work, had met the historian on multiple occasions before and during the war, and understood its shortcomings. So when he stood on the edge of Gettysburg's Evergreen Cemetery in 1863, surrounded by fields pockmarked with thousands of temporary graves of American soldiers killed fighting one another weeks earlier, the president didn't present this civic national myth—"a new nation, conceived in Liberty, and dedicated to the proposition that all men are created equal"—as our destiny. Rather, Lincoln said it was an ideal that had not yet been achieved and, if not fought for, might perish from the Earth. A U.S. president had, for the first time in our history, tasked the country with making good on the Declaration's promise. Had he not been assassinated, Lincoln might have been able to deliver. Instead, the promise would be betrayed.[5]

The former slave Frederick Douglass—who had traveled to the wartime White House to persuade Lincoln to take a stand for the Declaration's ideals—picked up and carried the civic nationalist torch through the dark days of the 1870s and 1880s, when its prospects seemed hopeless. In these decades, northern and southern whites agreed to put aside the Declaration's commitments to human equality in favor of sectional unity, even though it meant accepting death squads in the Deep South, Tidewater, and Greater Appalachia; the creation of a racial apartheid system; and the judicial nullification of the Fourteenth and Fifteenth Amendments, without which the Declaration's promises were nearly impossible to protect. "I want a home here not only for the negro, the mulatto and the Latin races; but I want the Asiatic to find a home here in the United States, and feel at home here, both for his sake and for ours," Douglass said in an 1869 speech that summarized U.S. civic nationalism as well as anyone ever has. "We shall spread the network of our science and civilization over all who seek their shelter . . . [and] all shall here bow to the same law, speak the same language, support the same Government, enjoy the same liberty, vibrate with the same national enthusiasm, and seek the same national ends."[6]

The discomforting truth is that Bancroft's version of our national myth was challenged from the outset by the political and intellectual leaders of the Deep South and Chesapeake Country. These men—they were all men—had a narrower vision of who could be an American and what the United States's purpose was to be.

People weren't created equal, insisted William Gilmore Simms, the Deep South's most prominent intellectual, and the continent belonged to the superior Anglo-Saxon race. "The superior people, which conquers, also educates the inferior, and their reward, for this good service, is derived from the labor of the latter," he proclaimed in a seminal 1837 essay in the *Southern Literary Messenger*, then the South's leading journal.

While Bancroft had done his best to ignore the presence of slavery, Simms and other lowland southerners argued it was in fact one of the "greatest moral goods and blessings, and that in all ages has been found the greatest and most admirable agent of Civilization," creating a stable society with the master race in command. When the U.S. was considering whether to annex Texas in 1847, Simms urged John C. Calhoun to do it not for the good of the federation, but of Deep Southern slavery, which he expected would continue expanding southward into Mexico. "In the case of Texas, so, beyond the Rio Grande, what we once acquired would ensure to the South and to the South exclusively," Simms explained. "It might ultimately help us to a sufficiently large republic of our own etc . . . the Anglo Norman race would never forgive the public man who should fling away territory." If Mexico were conquered, he predicted, it would ensure "the perpetuation of slavery for the next thousand years."[7]

The Confederacy lost the war, of course, but they would go on to win the peace with an Anglo-Saxon supremacist agenda for the nation.

After the collapse of Reconstruction—and the systematic subjugation of non-whites in the south to a race-based caste system—Americans needed to adapt the national narrative in such a way as to find common ground between northerners and southerners, now clearly destined to live together in a strong nation-state. The compromise solution, described in detail by David Blight in *Race and Reunion*, was to tacitly accept the Deep Southern point of view on race and to systematically forget the moral content of the war: that slavery was central to the Confederate project and, thus, the conflict itself. The liberal nationalist vision of Bancroft, Lincoln, and Douglass was jettisoned in favor of what was effectively an ethnonationalist model, a model that would dominate politics, constitutional law, school texts, and the academy from the late 1870s to the early 1960s.

As related in chapter 5, this model was developed and propagated via the fiction of Thomas Nelson Page and Thomas Dixon Jr. in D. W. Griffith's blockbuster film *The Birth of a Nation* and the histories, policies, and pronouncements of their friend Woodrow Wilson, the first-ever Deep Southern president. Wilson, whose father had become the leading light of the Presbyterian Church of the Confederacy for his assertions that slavery was ordained by God, presided over the segregation of the federal government and, during the negotiations in Paris to create the League of Nations, blocked a measure introduced by Japan professing the equality of the races. Democratic self-government, he argued, was not the heritage of mankind but "the heritage of races purged alike of hasty barbaric passions and of patient servility to rulers, and schooled in temperate common counsel." He was elected and reelected to the presidency with unified support in the Deep South, Tidewater, and Greater Appalachia over the almost unanimous opposition of Yankeedom, New Netherland, and the Left Coast.[8]

It was during the Wilson administration that William Randolph Hearst began calling for an "America First" policy that specifically jettisoned the notion that the United States had an idealistic mission vis a vis humanity at large. It was in this era that the vast majority of the South's Confederate monuments were erected, each an homage to an explicitly illiberal, ethnically defined nationality. (The Robert E. Lee statue at the center of the Charlottesville "Unite the Right" rally—where torch-bearing neo-Nazis chanted "Jews will not replace us"—was erected in 1924.) The Second Ku Klux Klan, founded in Atlanta on the eve of the 1915 debut of *The Birth of a Nation* in that city, grew to a million members by 1921 and as many as five million in 1925; it sought to restore "true Americanism" by intimidating, beating, or killing African Americans, Mexicans, Asians, Catholics, Eastern Europeans, and most any other non-Anglo-Saxons. Members included a small army of future governors, senators, and big-city mayors and at least one Supreme Court justice, Hugo Black.

This was a vision of a Herrenvolk democracy, a homeland by and for the dominant ethnic group. The precise definition of who belonged in this group evolved over time, first from Anglos to other "Saxon" people, then to white Protestants and, more recently, white Catholics and Jews. Those flagged as being culturally or genetically unfit for democratic self-government once included Scots-Irish immigrants in the 1730s, Irish ones in the 1850s, Poles, Hungarians, Slovaks, Italians, and Greeks in the early 1900s, Muslims, Mexicans, and Central American immigrants, and anyone from any country the sitting president deemed a "shithole" at the end of the 2010s. It was and is an explicitly ethnonationalist and, in a country as diverse as ours, inherently authoritarian definition of American nationhood that could never bring the federation unity.

THIS ETHNONATIONALIST MODEL was itself overthrown in the 1960s, when civic nationalist conceptions returned to the fore, forged in the fires of the War to End All Wars and its even more devastating sequel. Mass conscription in both world wars produced multiethnic military units and multiracial armies, whose members felt they'd earned the rights to full citizenship and consecrated them with blood sacrifices. African, Latino, and Native American veterans of these wars would form a backbone of resistance that culminated in the civil rights movement of the 1960s, which challenged northern racism and the southern apartheid system. Ethnonationalism, which helped trigger the wars and built the industrial extermination machines of the Holocaust and the mass atrocities in Japanese-occupied Manchuria, had suffered grievous reputational damage, weakening its sway over white people in the northern and western American Nations regions. If what the Nazis and Japanese had done in service of master race ideologies was bad, how could Americans tolerate having formal racial caste systems and extralegal death squads terrorizing people of color across more than a third of their federation's territory?

As the civil rights movement gained strength, the Cold War compelled federal officials to support it at critical junctures. This was because the conflict with the USSR had become a proxy war for the hearts and minds of non-white populations in what we now call the Global South but was then called the Third World. The Soviets could accurately and effectively tell these people that if they or their country's ambassadors and diplomats traveled in four of five directions from Washington, DC, they would be denied access to beaches and restrooms, restaurants and hotels, even those hotels holding conferences to which they may have been invited to speak. They would be treated as second-class citizens, as racially inferior, and subject to vigilante violence. This, Presidents Truman, Eisenhower, Kennedy, and Johnson realized, could not stand. So commanders in chief desegregated the military and sent the 101st Airborne to escort Black children into Little Rock Central High School. Presidents introduced, backed, and signed into law the Civil Rights Act and Voting Rights Act, which made it possible for the federal government to enforce the dismantling of the Jim Crow system.[9]

The civil rights movement toppled Southern apartheid and challenged Northern racism. The feminist movement demanded social, professional, and sexual equality for a gender that comprised the majority of the population. Gays and lesbians fought the police and discriminatory ordinances. Elite colleges began partially dismantling their old boys' networks and public universities rapidly expanded to increase educational opportunities. Congress passed a new immigration law in 1965 that repealed ethnonationalist quotas, reopening America's gates to humanity at large. A new generation of historians challenged the neo-Confederate narrative of American history that had dominated scholastic textbooks for half a century, while dispelling the innocence of American colonization of the continent.

The civic national narrative finally triumphed, federation-wide, nearly two centuries after the Founders endorsed the Declaration. That's when the United States became a liberal democracy for the first time—not in the 1860s, but in the 1960s. For my generation, Generation X, who were born as these events were culminating, it seemed the change was permanent, that America's white supremacist model had been toppled forever. We went on to elect an African American president twice, after all! But it's not inevitable; it's an incredible gift that had to be fought for and continues to be fought for. Because ethnonationalism has not been vanquished. Instead, it is on the march, and its proponents have *their* narrative, the story of the kind of country they are fighting for, all worked out. They will Make America Great Again, like it was before the 1960s, before the civic national triumph. "We will root out the communists, Marxists, fascists and the radical left thugs that live like vermin within the confines of our country," Trump promised early in his 2024 bid to return to the White House, parroting the words of mid-twentieth-century white supremacists as well as Adolf Hitler, while warning that immigrants were "poisoning the blood of our country." He would "restore law and order in our nation's cities, empower our men and women in law enforcement, and stop the Radical Marxist prosecutors," he wrote in an op-ed shortly thereafter, while cutting federal funding "for any school pushing far-left content on our children," a reference to material teaching about the struggle for racial equality and civic nationhood. These are fascist promises, of blood purity and violent vengeance, censorship and dehumanization. It may be the Mussolini variant, not the Nazi one, but it is still a very bad thing, and the antithesis of the American Promise.[10]

The rest of us don't have our story worked out, the 70 or 80 percent of us who don't want to live in a fascistic world. We've lost our story, our message. Americans have never been great at talking about what the civic ideals in the Declaration mean in practice, but we stopped even trying after the Cold War, when our leaders celebrated not the triumph of liberal democracy over one-party dictatorship, but rather that of capitalism over communism. Nation-states, they claimed, were on their way to extinction, to be replaced by capital flows, multinational corporations, and technocratic trade regimes, so there was no need to bother maintaining the national stories they needed to bond their inhabitants together.

We never reassembled a coherent story of United States nationhood that incorporates all the valuable post-1960s scholarship revealing the myriad ways Americans had failed to uphold the Declaration's ideals. Post–Cold War America (and much of "the West") was left with no story at all, apart from a vague materialist argument about increasing the national GDP. A void opened up, and when globalization collided with reality—on 9/11, in America's ill-conceived Forever Wars, and with the 2008 financial collapse—demagogues stepped right in, as they always do, armed with hate, lies, and an insatiable hunger for spoils, power, and vengeance.

We need a rebooted civic national story now, the rhetorical, philosophical, and symbolic banner around which our pro-democracy supermajority can rally. This is vital not only because democracy really is better than fascism, but also because the consolidation of an ethnonationalist authoritarian regime would almost certainly trigger the physical collapse of this federation, given the antidemocratic extremes that would be required to maintain one in a country where no ethnoracial group has a majority. We're a country bonded together by commitment to ideals. Take that away while trying to impose an authoritarian regime and the regions will cleave from one another, creating a dangerous and likely deadly situation.

THAT'S THE WORK WE COMPLETED at Nationhood Lab in early 2025: the testing, polling, and crafting of a clear and emotive American story, the answer to why we should stay together, why we all belong, and where we're going. It's a story that can be used in ordinary conversations in real-world situations and can rally the latent supermajority to defend what should have been America's values for all of these past two and a half centuries. It tasks Americans with building and defending a society where the civic national values of the Declaration can be realized. Here is how we went about it and what we came up with.

We wanted to first understand what Americans already thought about the country's story so we could meet them where they are. In the spring of

2024, we hired a professional polling firm, Embold Research, to ask more than 1,500 adult Americans a series of questions about the nature of the United States. We offered statement pairs about our national purpose, American identity, and the meaning of our past. In each case, one statement was keyed off the ideals in the Declaration, while the other was rooted in more intrinsic characteristics like ancestry, heritage, character, and values, the stuff ethnonationalist narratives are constructed with. We wanted each to sound as attractive as possible. I wasn't sure what to expect, given how polarized the country has become, but my gut instinct was that the ethnonationalist-friendly versions would win out, if only because they seemed more concrete than pledging loyalty to abstract ideals. Instead, the civic nationalist ones proved far more attractive to respondents regardless of their gender, age, race, education, or American Nations region of residence.

Sixty-three percent of respondents preferred the statement that we are united "not by a shared religion or ancestry or history, but by our shared commitment to a set of American founding ideals: that we all have inherent and equal rights to live, to not be tyrannized, and to pursue happiness as we each understand it." Only 33 percent of respondents embraced the statement that said we are united "by shared history, traditions, and values and by our fortitude and character as Americans, a people who value hard work, individual responsibility, and national loyalty." That's nearly a two-to-one advantage for the Declaration-inspired version. In the table on the next page, I've shared some cross tabulations for this question. As you can see, this statement was the overwhelming favorite for most everyone with two major exceptions: Republicans and those who voted for Trump in 2020. Still, 45 percent of respondents from both those segments preferred the Declaration, joining 63 percent of independents and 79 percent of self-identified Democrats. I didn't include all the crosstabs for the regional cultures, but the civic version was favored by wide margins, from 18 points in the Deep South to 49 points in the Left Coast. Respondents from El Norte (at +37) and the Far West (+34) preferred that version by wider margins than Yankeedom (+29) or the Midlands (+20). Not sur-

Defining U.S. Nationhood: Heritage or Ideals?

Q: Are we united by commitment to the founding ideals in the Declaration or by history, traditions, values, and character?

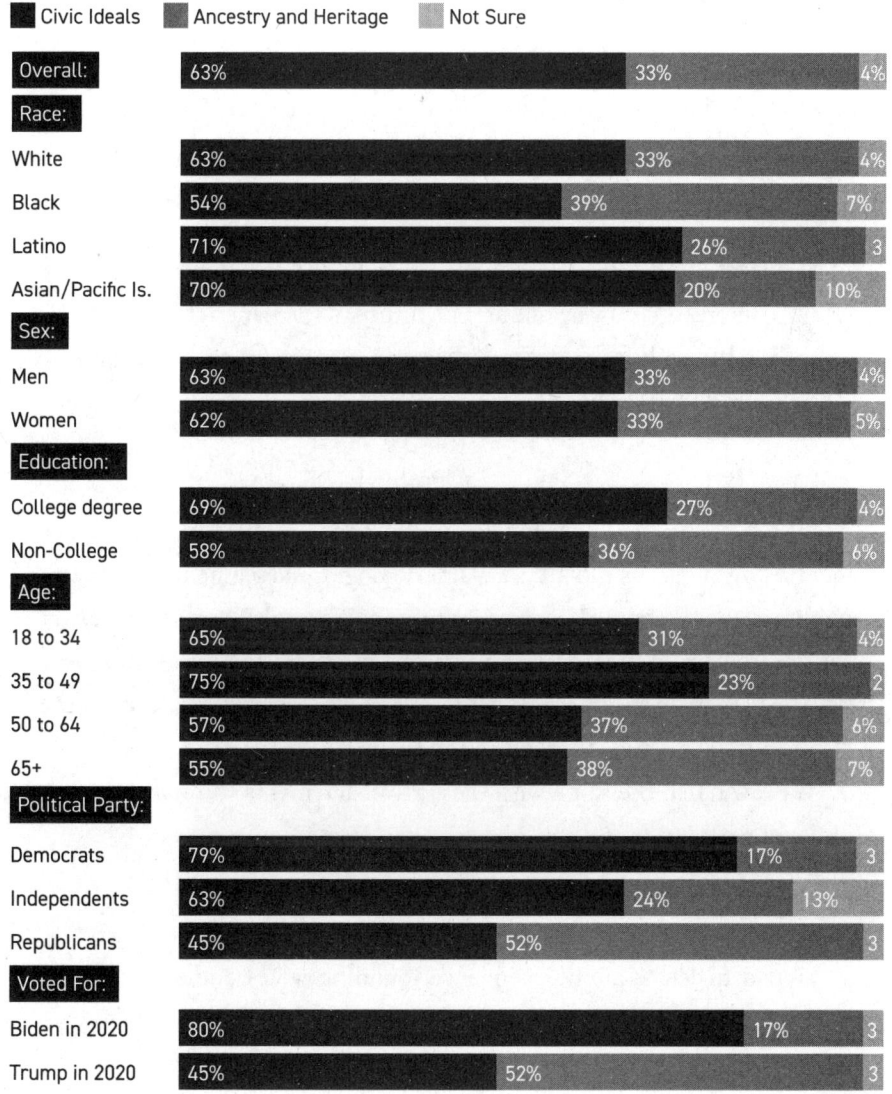

■ Civic Ideals   ▓ Ancestry and Heritage   ▒ Not Sure

	Civic Ideals	Ancestry and Heritage	Not Sure
Overall:	63%	33%	4%
Race:			
White	63%	33%	4%
Black	54%	39%	7%
Latino	71%	26%	3
Asian/Pacific Is.	70%	20%	10%
Sex:			
Men	63%	33%	4%
Women	62%	33%	5%
Education:			
College degree	69%	27%	4%
Non-College	58%	36%	6%
Age:			
18 to 34	65%	31%	4%
35 to 49	75%	23%	2
50 to 64	57%	37%	6%
65+	55%	38%	7%
Political Party:			
Democrats	79%	17%	3
Independents	63%	24%	13%
Republicans	45%	52%	3
Voted For:			
Biden in 2020	80%	17%	3
Trump in 2020	45%	52%	3

Data: Nationhood Lab/Embold Research national poll, August 2024, n=2734.

prisingly, evangelicals were far more skeptical, evenly split between the two statements.

We found a similar pattern of results with these rival statement pairs about national purpose:

Statement A: As Americans, we are duty-bound to defend one another's inherent rights. The future of the American Experiment ultimately rests on our shared commitment to building a more free, just, and equal nation.

Statement B: As Americans, we are duty-bound to defend our culture, interests, and way of life. The future of the American Experiment ultimately rests on our shared commitment to building a more free, prosperous, and secure nation.

AMERICANS OVERALL PREFERRED the civic national version (Statement A) by 56–36, as did all the major demographic segments except Republicans (with whom it lost by a 24-percent margin), Trump 2020 voters (–27 percent), and men over 65 years of age (where the statements were tied). All regions preferred Statement A, with support weakest in the Deep South (+13) and strongest in the Far West (+33).

We saw much the same with these rival statements summarizing our national past:

Statement A: America's story is our ancestral fight, at home and abroad, to defend our independence, founding values, and way of life. From the American Revolution to World War II and the Cold War, we have fought for centuries to secure and defend these birthrights.

Statement B: America's story is our ancestral fight, at home and abroad, for liberty, rights, and equality for all. From Abraham Lincoln at Gettysburg to Martin Luther King Jr. on the Washington Mall, we have strived for centuries to secure and strengthen these founding ideals.

Statement B, which evoked landmark events in securing the Declaration's promises, won 54–34 overall, and carried majorities of every segment except Republicans, Trump voters, and evangelicals, who rejected it by 30-, 28-, and 15-point margins. Those blocks might sound like "half the country," but they're not. In 2024, Gallup found only 28 percent of American adults consider themselves to be Republicans (while 43 percent are self-identified independents and another 28 percent are Democrats). Exactly the same share of the adult population—28 percent—cast votes for Trump in 2020. Evangelicals constituted less than a quarter of the population in 2021 and are on a declining trend. These three segments overlap: the overwhelming majority of evangelicals and Trump 2020 voters are Republicans.[11]

The weakest support was for the civic vision for our stance going forward (Statement A) against one evoking tradition, unity against threats, and individual liberty. The civic statement won 54–40, but lost among 50- to 64-year-olds (–8 points), seniors (–1), white men (–5), whites without college degrees (–9), mainline (–6) and evangelical (–19) Protestants, rural voters (–9), and Deep Southerners (–1). It was loathed by Republicans (–47) and Trump voters (–50).

> **Statement A:** Freedom, justice, and equality are ideals each generation must fight for. We must reckon with our shortcomings, take pride in our advances, and pledge ourselves to make our Union more perfect.

> **Statement B:** Security, individual liberties, and respect for our founding values are the heritage each generation must fight for. We must defend our nation, take pride in our history, and pledge ourselves to make our Union more perfect.

Americans were clearly open to a national narrative based on the Declaration's values, but maybe they had other ideas or actually disagreed with one or another of its central propositions. To explore this we had our pollsters conduct in-depth interviews with twenty-five representative respondents from the polls. Our strategy was to start each conversation with some open-ended questions about what they thought the country's purpose was, who could potentially belong, and what, if any, beliefs one should have to become an American; after that we would dive into detailed questions about the Declaration's assertions. To our surprise—and my personal delight—respondents from wildly different backgrounds just started referencing the Declaration unprompted to questions about what makes someone an American or what America's purpose is. Here are some responses:

> "The United States of America was formed on a very few core ideals: one was democracy, another was equality. Another one was freedom, freedom of speech, freedom of assembly, things like that. I think what really makes someone an American is that they just believe in all of those ideals and in that way of living, that way of thinking, that way of seeing the world and connecting with the rest of the world. . . . If you think that way, if you subscribe to those beliefs, I think that's probably the most important part of being an American."
>
> —*Male, 24, South Asian American urban professional, Left Coast*

> "I think people who support and believe in the founding ideals of the country and the foundations that was laid down generally for the makeup of the country, how to run it with people's rights that was afforded them at birth, not given to them by the government."
>
> —*Male, 53, white Republican health worker, rural Left Coast*

> "I think that the idea of what someone being an American should be, is, like, a person who lives in a democratic state and has a

voice and a say, and, you know, that whole everyone is free and everyone is equal, like a lot of things that are reflected in the Declaration of Independence. In an ideal world, I would say that those are the things that make people American."

—Female, 46, disabled white Democrat, Midlands

"I think you commit to the values that are implicit in the constitution that this is a representative democracy and a republic and that all people are created equal, that we must not discriminate against people based on their creed. . . . The golden rule, you know, treat others the way you would like to be treated."

—Male, 63, white Republican-turned-Democrat, Far West

"That's the beauty of America being founded that way, that the Founders understood that you have these basic what they called unalienable rights that cannot be taken away. And they just put them on paper to show how important that is."

—Female, 42, white Republican, Deep South

"I think there are freedoms that are both in our constitution and also just, like, kind of taught, like, ingrained in us. So believing in the freedom of speech, believing in people's, like, right to their life, liberty, and pursuit of happiness. I think those are things that are integral in to, like, becoming an American. Even though we disagree, I think that should be the base. If you have a view that maybe doesn't align with the traditional view of that, that's ok. But, like, that still has to be the basis of where you're coming from in my opinion. You definitely need to believe in freedom. You definitely need to believe in, like, other people's right to freedom. Yeah, I think that. That I do."

—Male, 30, African American salesperson, Democrat, Yankeedom

"We have a government that is supposed to acknowledge our inalienable rights, versus other countries that don't have that. So today we do have a lot more freedoms than a lot of other countries do." [Question: What's the United States's purpose?] The Declaration of Independence says the purpose of our government is to secure your rights."

—*Male, 38, white Republican, lower management, Greater Appalachia*

"Life, liberty, and the pursuit of happiness. I would say that's probably the purpose. To live here, to believe who you want to worship, to love who you want to love, to be left alone as long as you're not busting on someone else."

—*Female, 52, American Indian independent, Midlands*

In a subsequent national survey fielded in the late summer of 2024, we asked 2,500 American voters if they agreed with the idea of an American covenant. The Declaration tells us, the question read, that "government exists to protect the rights of people to life, liberty, and the pursuit of happiness. Do you agree or disagree that as Americans, it's our job to protect one another's rights to these things?" At this point we assumed most people would agree, but wondered if it would split on partisan lines. After all, the Declaration's explicit language to this point doesn't come until the very end of the document, after most readers' eyes have glazed over reading the long list of indictments against King George I. "And for the support of this Declaration, with a firm reliance on the protection of divine Providence," it reads, "we mutually pledge to each other our lives, our Fortunes, and our sacred Honor." The document ends with the delegates' signatures, pledging themselves and the colonies they officially represented to this sacred task. The results floored us: Americans agreed with this statement by an incredible 97–2 margin, one of the widest our pollsters had ever seen on any question. This included 95 percent of Republicans, Trump voters, evangelicals, and Democrats.

Americans appear hardwired to support the Declaration's ideals and, therefore, liberal democracy. But would they actually act to defend these ideals when the going gets tough? To "stress test" their commitments, we asked a series of questions about real-world scenarios in which the Declaration's natural rights propositions were clearly under assault. When it came to aggressive book bans—governments trying to force public libraries to remove titles some find offensive under threat of funding cuts or eviction—everyone was opposed. Same, broadly speaking, for election subversion: refusing to certify a fraud-free election because your party lost. Though, in both cases, notice in the figures below that Republicans' support for the Declaration's natural rights is substantially weaker.

Support for Government Book Banning

Q: Across the country, local and state governments have forced public libraries to remove books some people find offensive or inappropriate by withholding funding or threatening eviction. Do you support or oppose these kinds of actions?

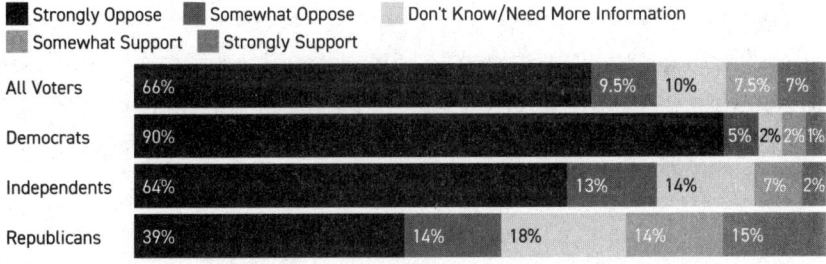

Data: Nationhood Lab/Embold Research national poll, August 2024, n=2734.

However, Republican support fell apart when people were asked if they would approve of lawmakers from their own party eliminating election day voter registration explicitly because they believed it would suppress turnout for the other party's supporters. Overall, 61 percent strongly or somewhat opposed voter suppression to secure political power. But look at the partisan splits: Republicans supported it by an 8-point margin

Support for Election Subversion

Q: Imagine there is an election where you live. Your party controls the government, but loses the election to the opposing party. There's no evidence of fraud, but officials are refusing to certify the election results. Would you support or oppose their actions?

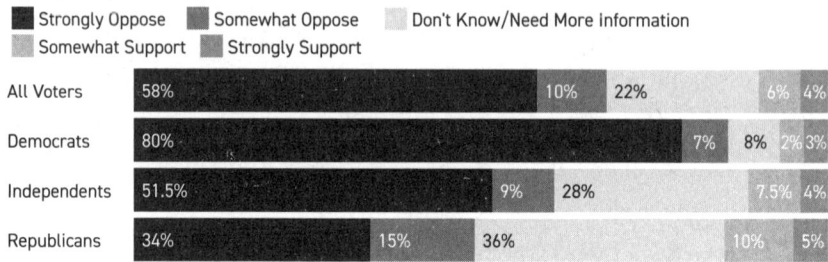

Data: Nationhood Lab/Embold Research national poll, August 2024, n=2734.

even as independents were opposed by 36 points and Democrats by 77. Even worse was the response to the Supreme Court's controversial decision that presidents can't be held accountable for crimes committed as part of an official act, a ruling that literally put presidents above the law. (Justice Sonia Sotomayor, in her dissent in this case, noted that under this definition a president would face no consequences if they ordered SEAL Team Six to assassinate their political opponents, as that would be an official act.) Republicans supported the ruling by 67–16, a staggering 51-point margin for a party that nominally fears government tyranny. Democrats opposed it by a near universal 93–3, a 90-point margin, joined by independents with a 29-point margin. Republican support is almost certainly conditioned by the fact that this ruling came from *Donald J. Trump v. United States.*[12]

To gain further insights, we conducted a separate poll of the civic nonprofit More in Common's Hidden Tribes respondents, who have been segmented based not on income, education, or race, but on their core underlying beliefs. These values-based segments, built on decades of academic work by moral and political psychologists like New York University's Jonathan Haidt and Karen Stenner of Australia's Griffith University, often more reliably predict people's policy and political opinions than conventional ones like race, income, education, ideology, or party.

In 2017, More in Common surveyed some 8,000 Americans asking about their moral values, parenting styles, ideas about personal responsibility, identity, threats, and trust. They then sorted them into seven "tribes": Progressive Activists, Traditional Liberals, Passive Liberals, Politically Disengaged, Moderates, Traditional Conservatives, and Devoted Conservatives, which they describe in detail on their website and in their reports. In 2023, we worked with them and their pollsters, YouGov, to determine how these personality archetypes are maldistributed across the American Nations regions, with Devoted Conservatives—that's the MAGA right—having twice the share of the population in the Deep South than they have in the Left Coast, for instance.[13]

In August 2024, we had YouGov ask the same Declaration "stress test" questions of 1,000 Hidden Tribes respondents. Like the Embold survey of the national population, we again found strong support for presidential immunity and partisan voter suppression among only the right-wing "tribes," and the level of support was very strong. Devoted Conservatives supported presidential immunity by a 79-point margin and voter suppression by 35 points. For Traditional Conservatives those margins of support for these illiberal, anti-democratic stances were 35 and 23 points respectively. This poll also asked if respondents supported Trump's promise to pardon convicted January 6 insurrectionists, and these two groups said "yes" by 84- and 27-point margins.

None of the other five "tribes" supported any of these measures, with the most left-wing group, Progressive Activists, opposing each by 82- to 97-point margins. Of these five groups, the softest support for the liberal democratic stance came from the two tribes in what More in Common calls the "exhausted majority" of the country, Moderates and the Politically Disengaged. For these groups, the margins of support were between 9- and 53-points depending on the question and tribe. But for both groups, significant shares of the respondents said they didn't know or needed more information, as high as 46 percent (of Politically Disengaged) in the case of the voter suppression question.

In this survey, we also posed the question about the American covenant to protect one another's natural rights. All five "liberal" and "conservative" tribes were almost universally supportive. In fact, the softest support—if you can call it that—was from the Exhausted Majority, where 5 percent of the Politically Disengaged and 8 percent of Moderates (the genuinely middle-of-the-road Americans) opposed the statement.

THE TAKEAWAY FROM ALL of this was that the Declaration's ideals are deeply revered by the vast majority of Americans outside of the most die-hard Trumpist right. A rebooted civic national story based on these ideals would be in a very strong position to gather a broad-based coalition of everyone, save the ethnonationalists, around a shared sense of purpose. If we could optimize the language to inspire and mobilize people, it might give Americans a restored sense of common purpose that holds the republic and our balkanized federation together.

I've been studying and writing about our struggles over the national narrative for the better part of a decade. With the advice and feedback of scholars, speechwriters, political practitioners, and colleagues, we've drafted potential scripts, dissected them into their component parts, and tested different ways of communicating the ideals in polls of both the national electorate and the Hidden Tribes respondents. Generally, we found little variation across demographic and regional segments, with the unsurprising exception of the ethnonationalist-oriented Trumpist ones. At the end of the process, this is what we came up with for the basic script, the messaging "cheat sheet" that educators, elected officials, politicians, business leaders, celebrities, and citizens can borrow from when articulating America's purpose:

CIVIC NATIONAL NARRATIVE

We're a nation defined not by shared bloodlines, religion, or history, but by a commitment to a set of ideals, the world-changing propositions about the inherent rights of humans set forth in our opening statement as a people, the Declaration of Independence. That every one of us has a set of intrinsic rights given to them by the universe or God or, as the Declaration puts it, Nature's God:

- *to survive;*

- *to live safe in their own person, free from domination;*

- *to live the life they choose for themselves;*

- *and to take part in determining who represents us and in holding them accountable.*

And that we, as Americans, are in a covenant to defend one another's natural rights to these things. That's the American Promise, our mutual pledge to uphold these inalienable rights. And the American Experiment is the effort—despite the despotic track record of human history—to build a nation, a society, a world where that is possible. We're a people united by our commitment to uphold and defend this experiment, lest it perish from the Earth.

These are the ideals Frederick Douglass fought for in every speech he gave. This is Lincoln at Gettysburg and Martin Luther King Jr. on the Mall. They're ideals we've spent 250 years struggling to achieve, ideals contested from the outset by those who would make our country something far less, just another nation-state built on blood—tribal kinship, inherited rule, inherited slavery, or inherited servitude—where rights are things granted by superiors when they are granted at all. Americans fought a Civil War over them at home and a World War for them abroad and advanced them at Seneca Falls, Selma, and Stonewall. They're ideals each generation must fight for and that we fight for today. We reckon with our shortcomings, take pride in our advances, and pledge ourselves to make our Union more perfect.

While this narrative was compelling across most demographic segments, we found some alternative wording more effective when communicating with uniformly right-leaning audiences. For these audiences we suggest this variant script, which fundamentally says the same thing but casts it in a different light. Be aware this script is less attractive with other, non-conservative segments of the population.

CIVIC NATIONAL NARRATIVE—CONSERVATIVE VARIANT

We're a nation defined not by shared bloodlines, religion, or history, but by a commitment to a set of ideals, the world-changing propositions about the inherent rights of humans set forth in our opening statement as a people, the Declaration of Independence. That every one of us has a set of intrinsic rights given to them by the universe or God:

- *to survive;*

- *to not be tyrannized;*

- *to live the life they choose for themselves;*

- *and to take part in determining who represents us and in holding them accountable.*

And that we, as Americans, are in a covenant to defend one another's natural rights to these things. That's the American Promise, our mutual pledge to uphold these inalienable rights. And the American Experiment is a project to protect one another's rights by governing ourselves. We're a people united by our commitment to uphold and defend this experiment, lest it perish from the Earth.

These are the ideals Frederick Douglass fought for in every speech he gave. This is Lincoln at Gettysburg and Martin Luther King Jr. on the Mall. They're ideals we've spent 250 years struggling to achieve, ideals contested from the outset by those who would make our country something far less, just another nation-state built on blood—tribal kinship, inherited rule, inherited slavery, or inherited servitude—where rights are things granted by superiors when they are granted at all. Americans fought for these ideals at Valley Forge and Yorktown, in the trenches of France and on the beaches of Normandy. They're ideals each generation must fight for and that we fight for today. We reckon with our shortcomings, take pride in our advances, and pledge ourselves to make our Union more perfect.

What to do with these words? Well for one thing, consider making use of them yourself when issues of American purpose and identity come up in interactions with your friends, family, and colleagues. I don't mean verbatim. You're probably not going to say that we need to protect our democracy "lest it perish from the Earth," but you can get across this idea in your own words—that we could lose it—and maybe even back it up with the reminder that Lincoln warned this could happen. Instead of talking about our "intrinsic rights," you might talk about rights we're all born with that can't be taken away. Rather than referring to the Declaration's "world-changing propositions" about these rights, you might evoke the Declaration's authors having recognized that God created people with these rights (if you're religious and a monotheist) or that the universe made us this way (if you're neither). These scripts are your source material to retell in your own words, with pieces that fit together like a puzzle, linking our nation's ideals with our past struggles and present purpose. Use them, adapt them, but honor what they mean.

At Nationhood Lab, we're also working on wholesaling these ideas to groups and organizations whose work can benefit from them and who have their own networks, audiences, and outreach that can amplify them. We're collaborating with people working on revitalizing civic education in U.S. schools and colleges; on weaving civic national ideals into the creative mix of filmmakers, television writers, and showrunners; on helping business leaders grapple with how much erosion of democracy and the rule of law their companies can tolerate and how to use their influence to help prevent that from happening; on helping devise the stories our diplomats abroad can use to win the hearts and minds of people in other countries tempted to align with Russian, Chinese, or Iranian autocrats; on protecting people's ability to vote and ensuring their votes will be counted; and with elected officials and politicians, Republicans, Democrats, independents, or whatever, so long as they want to defend the American Experiment. I'm writing these words at the end of 2024, and the 250th anniversary of the country and the Declaration is nigh upon us, so we're reaching out to state and local organizers of these commemorations to offer these ways of talking about the meaning of it all at a time when Americans will be prompted to do just that.

You might say you'll never convince everyone. That's true. There's that 10 or 20 percent of Americans I wrote about in chapter 9 who really are all-in on full-blown ethnonationalist authoritarianism. This small but not insignificant segment of the population genuinely relishes Trump's public promises to assign active-duty military forces to domestic law enforcement duties; to pardon convicted insurrectionists and other criminals en masse; to investigate and jail critics and political rivals on trumped up charges; to purge the civil service and stack it with people whose loyalty is to him only, not the people, country, or law; to use the Insurrection Act to crush protesters. A world where reporters, public officials, election workers, and anyone The Leader regards as "vermin" are physically threatened or attacked at his behest. A world where armed government agents permanently separate babies and toddlers from their parents with the aim of terrorizing people seeking sanctuary from murderous regimes abroad. A world where elections will no longer be settled by voters, but by the machinations of the regime. The 10 or 20 percent who genuinely support this agenda will reject the national narrative I propose precisely because they reject the American Experiment.

It's also true that many more won't want to listen or hear, committed to their tribal identity, the safety and comfort of an information bubble, or love of The Leader. But some will. And to protect democracy over the next decade, in a country poised on a knife's edge, shifting 5 or 6 or 7 percent of those asleep at the wheel, unaware of the stakes and the threat—would be decisive. And in the middle and long term I believe the wind is at our backs—the backs of the omni-partisan, antiauthoritarian majority—because there is a massive generational split in our society. The younger generations—and as I'm writing this, that's the Millennials and Generation Z—are not on board for authoritarian ethnonationalism. Polls throughout the 2016 to 2024 era showed they strongly oppose Trumpism—driven by the massive opposition of women and LGBTQ people—but our survey work also found they were massively opposed to nearly every authoritarian- and ethnonationalist-coded idea, statement, or question we offered in our various polls, even as Gen X and Baby Boomers supported them. In the 2024 election, exit polls showed that young white and Latino men shifted massively toward Trump, but also that they were overwhelmingly voting on jobs and the economy, not immigration, abortion, racism, or any of the other issues Trumpism champions.[14]

Whatever you think of "young people today," they're not the ones who've endangered the republic, and if we still have free and fair elections in the 2030s, they'll vote the authoritarians, white supremacists, and fascists (yes, we have some) right out of office. When they do, that particular threat to our country will recede, and we can move on to addressing the core problems that got us here in the first place.

THE BACKGROUND PROBLEMS ARE THESE. We're a balkanized federation, and our component regional cultures have never agreed on the big questions, from the relationship of church and state to the American Experiment itself. But as we used hard data to probe the current regional differences in policies and outcomes it became clear that the biggest driver of many of our deepest problems and regional disparities lies in some regions being overly committed to individualism at the expense of the shared infrastructure that makes it possible for most people—not just a handful of families on the top—to be healthy, wealthy, safe, satisfied, and free. From gun violence to life expectancy, poverty prevention and social resilience, from preventing climate change and diabetes to defending the republic from authoritarians and fascists, the aggressively individualistic nations have performed terribly for a quarter millennium now, repeatedly fostering the conditions for the destruction of the American Experiment. The most communitarian of the large regions—the Left Coast and New Netherland—have had the most vibrant economies, the healthiest and safest populations, the wealthiest and most democratically minded citizenries and Yankeedom, El Norte, the Midlands, and (today's) Tidewater are close behind. In its extreme form, communitarianism can become dangerous to freedom, but none of America's regional cultures are anywhere near that tipping point. Looking out on the global stage with an eye to affluence, social stability, and democratic performance, most unbiased observers would likely say the Left Coast, New Netherland, and Yankeedom could go quite a bit further before the returns for the American Experiment would start diminishing. The cult of individual freedom has, paradoxically, driven us to the brink of despotism.

In the medium and long term, the most important thing we can do to restore our democracy's civic health is to see the Deep South, Greater Appalachia, and New France begin *socially* investing in themselves and their people. We're still an incredibly wealthy country and there's no reason American children shouldn't grow up with quality schools and health care, in neighborhoods where they can find grocery stores and places to exercise and where they don't have to worry about the next-door neighbor killing everybody with their military-grade weaponry or their classmates spreading polio, the measles, or whatever plague comes next. There's no reason they should grow up to go to unsafe workplaces where they're underpaid, prevented from organizing, and can't get health insurance for their families, or that they or their spouse has to face death because the state has criminalized providing life-saving medical care during complications from pregnancy. Their children shouldn't be exposed to poisons a factory or refinery put in the air and water because it's cheaper than disposing of it properly. The American Experiment really is a shared project and ultimately we all benefit from one another being able to participate in it.

The argument for communitarian policies in individual freedom-loving regions is straightforward: Implementing them is how you, your loved ones, and your community will become and stay free. Implementing them is our sacred duty, tasked to us as Americans by the Founders in our opening statement as a people, the Declaration. It's how every one of us can have life and liberty and pursue our happiness, regardless of the circumstances of our birth. It's how we ensure this nation, so conceived and so dedicated, can long endure, that government of the people, by the people, for the people, shall not perish from the Earth.

Let's get started.

ACKNOWLEDGMENTS

I've previously written six books, but none were as much of a team effort as *Nations Apart*.

Much of the data and polling within these covers is from work I led at Nationhood Lab, the research project I founded at the end of 2022 at Salve Regina University's Pell Center for International Relations and Public Policy. I came to Salve because Jim Ludes, the Pell Center's director, had read *American Nations* and *Union* and immediately recognized and understood the importance of the work I wanted to undertake. He's been a fantastic boss, thought partner, and champion of the lab, which seeks to understand and help to solve the problems of United States nationhood, including our lost story of common purpose. Salve Regina has proved a terrific home, where I've benefited from the assistance and support of a wide range of colleagues and students, from the Pell Center's Teresa Haas, Erin Barry, and Katie Sonder to university provost Nancy Schreiber and president Kelli Armstrong. Go Seahawks.

Early on, I formed a partnership with Motivf, an Alexandria, Virginia-based geospatial consultancy that incorporates cultural factors into its work and whose founder, Jaymes Cloninger, shared my unlikely passions for vernacular architecture and the island nations of Micronesia. I collaborate and work with a lot of people at Nationhood Lab, but with nobody more regularly intensely as my counterparts at Motivf, data analyst Tova Perlman and graphic designer John Liberty. Tova's work underpins quite a few of the data projects in this book and John made most of the maps and graphics. Thanks to all of you for your stalwart work to make this analysis possible.

Early versions of some of the data analysis and polling results in *Nations Apart* first appeared on Nationhood Lab's website and in shorter companion articles I wrote for various media outlets I'd previously worked with or for in my journalism career. These included pieces on the national narrative, regional differences in gun ownership, the 2022 midterms, and our polling on national narratives for *Washington Monthly*, where my friend Paul Glastris is editor in chief; on the geography of abortion opinion for *Talking Points Memo*; and, thanks to my longtime editor Bill Duryea, on life expectancy and gun violence for *Politico*, where the latter story was one of their most read of 2023. I've also talked about the challenges facing our national narrative and the need for a new one in the pages of the *Monthly*, *Smithsonian*, the *Portland Press Herald*, the Minnesota *Star-Tribune*, and the American Enterprise Institute's Social Breakdown series.

Other data projects were undertaken with my primary academic collaborators, Ross Arena of the University of Illinois Chicago and Nicolaas Pronk, president of the Minneapolis-based HealthPartners Institute. Together with a shifting set of fellow researchers, we published twenty-one peer-reviewed scientific journal articles in as many months, including work on the regional distribution of a wide range of unhealthy living characteristics, diseases, health problems, and metrics of well-being. Ross and Nico are warmhearted and enthusiastic research partners and their expert data analysis and interpretation helped underpin the material in chapter 3. Thanks, guys. More work ahead.

Most of Nationhood Lab's polling work on the national narrative was conducted by Embold Research, the nonpartisan arm of Change Research; thanks to all the team there and especially to our analyst there, Jessica Mason. We also benefited from polling work conducted by YouGov—overseen by Marissa Shih—of More in Common's Hidden Tribes respondents; thanks to Tim Dixon, Mathieu Lefèvre, Stephen Hawking, Paul Oshinksi, Kate Carney, Daniel Yudkin, and Dan Vallone for granting us access. We also relied on data compiled and kindly shared by Democracy Fund + UCLA's Nationscape project, the Yale Program on Climate Change Communication, the Public Religion Research Institute, the Association of Statisticians of American Religious Bodies, the Columbia University Institute of Politics and Government Affairs, and the University of Wisconsin Population Health Institute's fantastic County Health Rankings & Roadmaps program, which compiles a wide range of official, county-level data on various health indices.

A number of experts generously shared their knowledge with me, including social psychologist Dov Cohen of the University of Illinois Urbana-Champaign (on the culture of honor), geographers Sam Otterstrom of Brigham Young University and Tim Anderson of Ohio University (on first settler effects), constitutional law professor Carl Bogus of Roger Williams University (on gun control), political scientists Douglas Kriner of Cornell University (on public opinion on threats to democracy) and the University of Chicago's Robert Pape (on political extremists), PRRI's CEO Melissa Deckman (on the nexus between religion and policy), University of Toronto evolutionary anthropologist David Samson (on human's tribal drive), Harvard University political philosopher Danielle Allen (on the Declaration and the national story), historian David McMahon of Kirkwood Community College (on teaching the national narrative), Balkans expert Jasmin Mujanović, and New America scholar Theodore Johnson (on national narratives).

An army of people helped me along the way with either Nationhood Lab, *Nations Apart*, or both. These include, in no particular order: Craig Varoga, Andrew Marshall, Susan Eisenhower, Derek Cholet, Anna Greenberg, Keegan Goudiss, Farah Pandith, Jim Kessler, and Nick Pennimann in Washington, DC; Steve Israel, Daniella Ballou-Aares, Clint Watts, and Ken Roberts in New York; fellow Mainers Nate Fick, Margaret Angell, Rajiv Vinnakota, Steve Greenlee, David Shaw, Donald Sussman, Bill Burgess, Tom and Rita Saliba, Jay Espy, and James Herbert; Rhode Islanders David Brodsky and Christine Stenning; Connecticut's Dan Abbasi; Tavan Pechet in Washington state; David McMahon in Iowa; Dan Carol in Michigan; Beck Carpenter and Juan Sepulveda in Texas; Michael Shrout in Maryland; Conrad Kiechel, and Steven Fish in California; and Philippe Étienne (France's former ambassador to the United States) and Andreas Michaelis (who currently has the same role for Germany).

This book wouldn't have happened without the stalwart guidance of my editor at Viking, Camille LeBlanc—thank you for guiding this to a safe landing—and my literary agent from the beginning, Jill Grinberg. At Viking thanks also to Meighan Cavanaugh for the book design, Janine Barlow and Ryan Boyle for copyedits, and Steven Leard for the cover.

And most of all, thanks to my family: Sarah, Henry, and Sadie, who saw the book to fruition, and my late father, Strohn Woodard, who sadly did not.

Finally, thanks to you, the reader, without whom all of this would be for naught.

NOTES

INTRODUCTION

1. Taylor Orth, "The States Whose Residents Are Most Likely to Support Secession: Alaska, Texas, and California," YouGov, February 14, 2024, today.yougov.com/politics/articles/48669-state-support-secession-alaska-texas-california-poll; Taylor Orth, "Two in Five Americans Say a Civil War Is at Least Somewhat Likely in the Next Decade," YouGov, August 26, 2022, today.yougov.com/politics/articles/43553-two-in-five-americans-civil-war-somewhat-likely.
2. Colin Woodard, *American Nations: A History of the Eleven Rival Regional Cultures of North America* (New York: Viking, 2011).
3. Heather Cox Richardson, *Democracy Awakening: Notes on the State of America* (New York: Random House, 2023), xii.

CHAPTER 1: NATIONS

1. Frederick Jackson Turner, "Sections and Nation," in *Frontier and Section: Selected Essays of Frederick Jackson Turner*, ed. Ray Allen Billington (Englewood Cliffs, NJ: Prentice Hall, 1961), 141–42; Colin Woodard, *Union: The Struggle to Forge the Story of United States Nationhood* (New York: Viking, 2020), 239–42, 275, 283–85, 294–96, 315–17, 355–56; Frederick Jackson Turner, "Middle Western Pioneer Democracy," *Minnesota History Bulletin* 3, no. 7 (August 1920): 405.
2. Turner, "Sections and Nation," 136–37.
3. For a detailed treatment of the American Nations model, see Colin Woodard, *American Nations: A History of the Eleven Rival Regional Cultures of North America* (New York: Viking, 2011). The model is laid out for an academic

audience in Colin Woodard, Ross Arena, and Nicolaas P. Pronk, "The American Nations Model: An Analytical Tool for Understanding the Influence of U.S. Regional Cultures on Health and the Social and Political Determinants of Health," *Progress in Cardiovascular Diseases* 89 (March/April 2025).

4. Wilbur Zelinsky, *The Cultural Geography of the United States* (Englewood Cliffs, NJ: Prentice Hall, 1973), 13–14, 38–40, 68–76; Woodard, *American Nations*, 15–19.

5. John Winthrop, "A Model of Christian Charity (1630)," in Daniel T. Rogers, *As a City on a Hill: The Story of America's Most Famous Lay Sermon* (Princeton, NJ: Princeton University Press, 2018), 307.

6. E. B. O'Callaghan, ed., "Petition of the Commonalty of New Netherland & c., to Director Stuyvesant," *Documents Relative to the Colonial History of the State of New York*, vol. 1 (Albany, NY: Weed, Parsons & Company, 1856), 550–52.

7. Robert C. Ritchie, *The Duke's Province: A Study of New York Politics and Society, 1664–1691* (Chapel Hill: University of North Carolina Press, 1977), 150–51; Thomas J. Archdeacon, *New York City, 1664–1710: Conquest and Change* (Ithaca, NY: Cornell University Press, 1979), 40.

8. David Dean Bowlby, *The Garden and the Wilderness: Church and State in America to 1789* (Lanham, MD: Lexington Books, 2013), 90–91.

9. Richard S. Dunn, "An Odd Couple: John Winthrop and William Penn," *Proceedings of the Massachusetts Historical Society*, third series, volume 99 (1987): 1–24; David Hackett Fischer, *Albion's Seed: Four British Folkways in North America* (New York: Oxford University Press, 1989), 594.

10. Jack P. Green, *Pursuits of Happiness: The Social Development of Early Modern British Colonies and the Formation of American Culture* (Chapel Hill: University of North Carolina Press, 1988), 126–27; Allan Kulikoff, *From British Peasants to Colonial American Farmers* (Chapel Hill: University of North Carolina Press, 2000), 131–33.

11. Manisha Sinha, "The Counter-Revolution of Slavery: Class, Politics and Ideology in Antebellum South Carolina" (PhD diss., Columbia University, 1994), xiv–xvi; John Locke, "The Fundamental Constitutions of Carolina (March 1, 1669)," in *The Works of John Locke*, vol. X (London: Thomas Tegg, 1823), 174–97.

12. John C. Calhoun, "Disquisition on Government," in *Works of John C. Calhoun, Volume I*, ed. Richard K. Crallé (Charleston, SC: Walker and James, 1851), 55; James Henry Hammond, *Two Letters on Slavery in the United States* (Columbia, SC: Allen, McCarter, and Co., 1845), 10.

13. David J. Weber, *The Mexican Frontier, 1821–1846* (Albuquerque: University of New Mexico Press, 1982), 15, 123; Juan Gómez-Quiñones, *Roots of Chicano Politics, 1600–1940* (Albuquerque: University of New Mexico Press, 1994), 99.

14. Weber, *The Mexican Frontier*, 25–29, 32–41; Gómez-Quiñones, *Roots of Chicano Politics*, 126.

15. Gómez-Quiñones, *Roots of Chicano Politics*, 302–306.

16. Gómez-Quiñones, *Roots of Chicano Politics*, 408.

17. John Hickenlooper, interview with the author by telephone, April 22, 2016.

18. Colin Woodard, "How Mormon Principles and Grassroots Ideals Saved Utah," *Politico*, January 18, 2017; Alan Matheson, interview with the author, December 16, 2016.

19. John Gunther, *Inside U.S.A.* (New York: Harper, 1947), 166–74; Carl B. Glasscock, *The War of the Copper Kings* (New York: Bobbs-Merrill Co., 1935); Woodard, *American Nations*, 249–51.

20. Charles Reagan Wilson, "Cajun South Louisiana," *Southern Spaces*, March 12, 2004.

21. Jon D. Olsen, *Liberate Hawai'i! Renouncing and Defying the Continuing Fraudulent U.S. Claim to the Sovereignty of Hawai'i* (Waldoboro, ME: Goose River Press, 2014), 7–34, 43–51; A Joint Resolution to Acknowledge the 100th Anniversary of the January 17, 1893 Overthrow of the Kingdom of Hawaii, and to Offer an Apology to Native Hawaiians on Behalf of the United States for the Overthrow of the Kingdom of Hawaii, Pub. L. 103–150, 107 Stat. 1510 (1993).

22. Camilla Fojas, Rudy P. Guevarra Jr., and Nitasha Tamar Sharma, *Beyond Ethnicity: New Politics of Race in Hawai'i* (Honolulu: University of Hawaii Press, 2018), 1–18.

23. Ida Altman, "Marriage, Family, and Ethnicity in the Early Spanish Caribbean," *William and Mary Quarterly* 70, no. 2 (April 2013): 225–27, 228n.

24. Kathleen A. Deagan, "The Historical Archaeology of Sixteenth-Century La Florida," *Florida Historical Quarterly* 91, no. 3 (Winter 2013): 367–68; Eugene Lyon, "Pedro Menéndez's Strategic Plan for the Florida Peninsula," *Florida Historical Quarterly* 67, no. 1 (1988): 4–10; Maria Cristina García, "Cuban Exiles and Cuban-Americans: A History of an Immigrant Community in South Florida, 1959–1989" (PhD diss., University of Texas at Austin, August 1990), 5–6, 86–122; Susan Jacoby, "The 350,000 Cubans in South Florida Make a Remarkable Success Story. Even If Castro Fell Tomorrow, Great Numbers Would Not Return," *New York Times*, September 29, 1974; Thomas D. Boswell, "The Cuban-American Homeland in Miami," *Journal of Cultural Geography* 13, no. 2 (1993): 133–48; David Rieff, *Going to Miami: Exiles, Tourists, and Refugees in the New America* (New York: Little, Brown, 1987), 224.

25. Colin Woodard, "The American Nations and the 50 States," Nationhood Lab, February 9, 2024.

26. Colin Woodard, "The American Nations and the States: Change over Time," Nationhood Lab, June 28, 2024.

27. Fred Kniffen, "Folk Housing: Key to Diffusion," *Annals of the Association of American Geographers* 55, no. 4 (December 1965): 549–77; Charles O. Paullin, *Atlas of the Historical Geography of the United States* (Washington, DC: Carnegie Institution of Washington, 1932), plates 82–88; "Lynchings & Mob Violence by Region, 1835–1964," Monroe and Florence Work Today, accessed October 20, 2024, plaintalkhistory.com/monroeandflorencework/explore.

28. Eunjung Han et al., "Clustering of 770,000 Genomes Reveals Post-Colonial Population Structure of North America," *Nature Communications* 8 (2017); Catherine A. Ball, chief scientific officer of Ancestry, interview with the author by telephone, August 23, 2017.
29. Fischer, *Albion's Seed*, 640, 794.

CHAPTER 2: GUNS

1. Dylan Lovan and Claire Galofaro, "Louisville Bank Employee Livestreamed Attack That Killed 5," Associated Press, April 11, 2023; Amanda Holpuch and Claire Fahy, "Alabama Birthday Party Shooting Leaves 4 Dead and 28 Injured," *New York Times*, April 20, 2023; Cheri Mossburg, Taylor Romine, and Steve Almasy, "White Homeowner Accused of Shooting Black Teen Who Went to the Wrong House in Kansas City Will Face 2 Felony Charges, Officials Announce," CNN, April 17, 2023; Timothy Bella, "Cheerleaders Leaving Practice Were Shot After One Got in Wrong Car, Teen Says," *Washington Post*, April 19, 2023; Jesse McKinley, Hurubie Meko, and Jay Root, "New Details Emerge in Deadly Upstate Shooting of Woman in Wrong Driveway," *New York Times*, April 18, 2023; John Terhune and Rachel Ohm, "Suspect Arrested After Shootings Leave 4 Dead in Bowdoin, 3 Wounded on I-295," *Portland Press Herald*, April 18, 2023; "A Timeline Since Wednesday's Deadly Mass Shootings in Lewiston," *Sun Journal* (Lewiston, ME), October 26, 2023.
2. Calculated from Everytown Research & Policy, "The US Gun Homicide Rate Is 26 Times That of Other High-Income Countries," Everytown for Gun Safety, November 1, 2022; this analysis used the most recent year's data for each of twenty-nine countries (ranging from 2013 to 2019).
3. Our original article on this was Colin Woodard, "The Geography of Gun Violence," Nationhood Lab, April 21, 2023. I also wrote about it in Colin Woodard, "The Surprising Geography of Gun Violence," *Politico*, April 24, 2023.
4. Colin Woodard, "The Maps That Show That City vs. Country Is Not Our Political Fault Line," *New York Times*, July 30, 2018.
5. William Yardley, "In Native Alaskan Villages, a Culture of Sorrow," *New York Times*, May 14, 2007.
6. Richard E. Nisbett, "Violence and U.S. Regional Culture," *American Psychologist* 48, no. 4 (April 1993): 441–49.
7. Dov Cohen, interview with the author by telephone, March 31, 2023; Dov Cohen et al., "Insult, Aggression, and the Southern Culture of Honor: An 'Experimental Ethnography,'" *Journal of Personality and Social Psychology* 70, no. 5 (1996): 945–59.
8. Pauline Grosjean, "A History of Violence: The Culture of Honor and Homicide in the US South," *Journal of the European Economic Association* 12, no. 5 (October 2014): 1285–316.
9. Robert D. Baller, Matthew P. Zevenbergen, and Steven F. Messner, "The Heri-

tage of Herding and Southern Homicide: Examining the Ecological Founda-tions of the Code of Honor Thesis," *Journal of Research in Crime and Delinquency* 46, no. 3 (2009): 275–300.

10. Ryan P. Brown, Lindsey L. Osterman, and Collin D. Barnes, "School Violence and the Culture of Honor," *Psychological Science* 20, no. 11 (2009): 1400–1405; Katherine S. Newman, *Rampage: The Social Roots of School Shootings* (New York: Basic Books, 2005), 15.

11. Ryan P. Brown, Mikiko Imura, and Lindsey L. Osterman, "Gun Culture: Map-ping a Peculiar Preference for Firearms in the Commission of Suicide," *Basic and Applied Social Psychology* 36, no. 2 (2014): 164–75.

12. Monroe Work Today Project, "Map of White Supremacy's History of Lynchings," plaintalkhistory.com/monroeandflorencework/explore/map1/#4/34.82/-94.95.

13. Death Policy Information Center, "Executions by State and Region Since 1976," accessed August 29, 2024, deathpenaltyinfo.org/executions/executions -overview/number-of-executions-by-state-and-region-since-1976.

14. Giffords Law Center, "Stand Your Ground," giffords.org/lawcenter/gun-laws /policy-areas/guns-in-public/stand-your-ground-laws.

15. Joseph Slaughter, interview with the author by telephone, April 3, 2023.

16. Barry Benner et al., "Positive Association between Altitude and Suicide in 2584 U.S. Counties," *High Altitude Medicine and Biology* 12, no. 1 (April 2011): 31–35.

17. Tom Rosentiel, "No Shift Toward Gun Control After Tucson Shootings," Pew Research Center, January 19, 2011; Jonathan Mattise, "Tennessee Legislature Passes Bill Further Protecting Gun Companies from Lawsuits," Associated Press, April 19, 2023.

18. The homepage of the Democracy Fund + UCLA Nationscape project, which shared their data with me, is hosted by the Democracy Fund Voter Study Group here: voterstudygroup.org/nationscape. We were able to code their respondents by which American Nations region they lived in based on their congressional district, the most specific geographical tag Nationscape assigned to them. While this was very accurate for calculating nations' rates, it prevented us from com-paring this opinion data with county-level metrics from other sources.

19. Jeffrey Butts, interview with the author by telephone, April 5, 2023.

20. Jaclyn Schildkraut, interview with the author by telephone, April 4, 2023.

21. Lawrence Hamilton, "Conspiracy vs. Science: A Survey of U.S. Public Beliefs," University of New Hampshire Carsey School of Public Policy, April 25, 2022.

22. Carl T. Bogus, interview with the author by telephone, April 3, 2023; *District of Columbia v. Heller*, 554 U.S. 570 (2008).

CHAPTER 3: HEALTH AND SURVIVAL

1. Colin Woodard, *American Character: The Epic Struggle Between Individual Liberty and the Common Good* (New York: Viking, 2016), 5–24.

2. Colin Woodard, "The Regional Geography of U.S. Life Expectancy," Nationhood

Lab, August 29, 2023; Colin Woodard, "America's Surprising Partisan Divide on Life Expectancy," *Politico*, September 1, 2023.

3. U.S. Census Bureau, "Poverty Status in the Past 12 Months," Census Table Results, Table S1701, March 17, 2022.

4. The University of Wisconsin's County Health Rankings & Roadmaps project can be found online at countyhealthrankings.org.

5. National Center for Health Statistics, "2013 NCHS Urban-Rural Classification Scheme for Counties," Vital and Health Statistics 2, no. 166 (April 2014).

6. Jennifer Malat, Sarah Mayorga-Gallo, and David R. Williams, "The Effects of Whiteness on the Health of Whites in the USA," *Social Science & Medicine* 199 (February 2018), 148–56.

7. Andre M. Perry and Jonathan Rothwell, "The Black Progress Index: Examining the Social Factors That Influence Black Well-Being," Brookings Institution, brookings.edu/articles/black-progress-index.

8. Alberto Palloni and Elizabeth Arias, "Paradox Lost: Explaining the Hispanic Adult Mortality Advantage," *Demography* 41, no. 3 (August 2004): 385–415.

9. Keith P. Gennuso, Elizabeth A. Pollock, and Anne M. Roubal, "Life Expectancy at the US-Mexico Border: Evidence of Disparities by Place, Race, And Ethnicity," *Health Affairs* 40, no. 7 (June 2021): 1038–46; Keith P. Gennuso, email interview with the author, August 5–7, 2023; Andrew Fenelon, "Rethinking the Hispanic Paradox: The Mortality Experience of Mexican Immigrants in Traditional Gateways and New Destinations," *International Migration Review* 51, no. 3 (July 2018): 567–99.

10. Gopal K. Singh et al., "Trends in Physical and Mental Health, Mortality, Life Expectancy, and Social Inequalities Among American Indians and Alaska Natives, 1990–2019," *International Journal of Translational Medical Research and Public Health* 5, no. 2 (2021): 227–53; Colin Woodard, "Unsettled" (a thirty-one-part series), *Portland Press Herald*, June 27 to August 3, 2014, pressherald.com/unsettled; Crown–Indigenous Relations and Northern Affairs Canada, "Canada's Arctic and Northern Policy Framework," Government of Canada, 2019, 22.

11. Marjory Givens, email message to author, August 7, 2023, 12:23 p.m. EST.

12. Matt Broaddus and Aviva Aron-Dine, "Medicaid Expansion Has Saved at Least 19,000 Lives, New Research Finds," Center for Budget and Policy Priorities, November 6, 2019.

13. Jeremy Ney, interview with the author by telephone, August 8, 2023; at the time of writing, Ney's American Inequality project can be found online at americaninequality.substack.com.

14. Jeanne Ayers, interview with the author by telephone, July 27, 2023.

15. Ross Arena et al., "The Geographic Distribution of Unhealthy Living Characteristics According to the American Nations Model: Cultural Factors Warranting Attention," *Progress in Cardiovascular Diseases* 79 (July–August 2023): 100–106.

16. Ross Arena, interview with the author by telephone, July 17, 2023.

17. Thomas E. Kottke et al., "The Potential Influence of Firearm Violence on Physical Activity in the United States," *American Journal of Medicine* 137, no. 5 (May 2024): 426–32.

18. Deepika Laddu et al., "Unhealthy Dietary Patterns in the American Nations: A Crisis with Cultural Distinctions," *Current Problems in Cardiology* 49, no. 6 (June 2024).

19. Ross Arena, Nicolaas P. Pronk, and Colin Woodard, "Identifying the Disability Belt and epicenters within the American Nations," *Journal of Cardiopulmonary Rehabilitation and Prevention* 44, no. 1 (January 2024); Nicolaas P. Pronk et al., "Regional Cultures and Insufficient Sleep in the United States," *Journal of Activity, Sedentary and Sleep Behaviors* 3, no. 4 (January 2024); Ross Arena et al., "Arthritis in the Regional Cultures of the American Nations: An Overlooked Component of a Larger Unhealthy Lifestyle Syndemic," *American Journal of Lifestyle Medicine* (September 2024).

20. Arena, interview, July 17, 2023.

21. Ross Arena et al., "Introducing the Lifestyle Health Index in the American Nations," *Journal of Cardiopulmonary Rehabilitation and Prevention* 44, no. 4 (July 2024): E19–20.

22. Andy Davis, "Arkansas' Mayors Denied Lockdown Power," *Arkansas Democrat Gazette*, April 8, 2020; "How We Got Here: A Timeline of Gov. Greg Abbott's COVID Policies," Houston Public Media, August 20, 2021; Josie Fischels, "Arkansas Governor Wants to Reverse a Law That Forbids Schools to Require Masks," National Public Radio, August 4, 2021; Richard Luscombe, "DeSantis Backs Florida Surgeon General in Urging Residents Against New COVID Vaccine," *The Guardian*, September 9, 2023.

23. James Glanz et al., "Where America Didn't Stay Home Even as the Virus Spread," *New York Times*, April 2, 2020; Colin Woodard, "How the Geography of the Pandemic Is Determined by Centuries-Old Regional Differences," *Portland Press Herald*, July 5, 2020.

24. The trackers, which stopped updating in October 2022, were found online here under the headline "See How Vaccinations Are Going in Your County and State": nytimes.com/interactive/2020/us/covid-19-vaccine-doses.html.

25. Aaron Ruper, "How Ron DeSantis's Covid Response Became the Model of What Not to Do," *Vox*, August 13, 2021; "How We Got Here: A Timeline of Gov. Greg Abbott's COVID Policies," Houston Public Media, August 20, 2021; Shane Goldmacher, "G.O.P. Governors Fight Mandates as the Party's Covid Politics Harden," *New York Times*, August 31, 2021; Sheryl Gay Stolberg, "G.O.P. Seethes at Biden Mandate, Even in States Requiring Other Vaccines," *New York Times*, September 12, 2021.

26. Ross Arena et al., "The Lifestyle Health Index in the Context of COVID-19 Mortality and Vaccination in the United States: A Syndemic not to be Repeated," *Current Problems in Cardiology* 49, no. 9 (September 2024).

27. Jennifer Rubin et al., "Are Better Health Outcomes Related to Social Expenditure? A Cross-National Empirical Analysis of Social Expenditure and Population Health Indices," RAND Corporation, 2016, xii, 44.

28. John F. Helliwell et al., "World Happiness Report 2024," University of Oxford: Wellbeing Research Centre; Kelsey J. O'Connor, "Happiness and Welfare State Policy Around the World," *Review of Behavioral Economics* 4 (2017): 297–420.

CHAPTER 4: HISTORY WARS

1. Edmund S. Morgan, *The Challenge of the American Revolution* (New York: W. W. Norton, 1978), ix.

2. George Orwell, *Nineteen Eighty-Four* (Oxford, UK: Oxford University Press, 2021), 192; Jade McGlynn, *Memory Makers: The Politics of the Past in Putin's Russia* (London: Bloomsbury Academic, 2023), 40–44.

3. Patrick Heuveline, "'Between One and Three Million': Towards the Demographic Reconstruction of a Decade of Cambodian History (1970–79)," *Population Studies* 52, no. 1 (1998): 49–65.

4. Daniel T. Rodgers, *As a City on a Hill: The Story of America's Most Famous Lay Sermon* (Princeton, NJ: Princeton University Press, 2018), 44–45, 50–55, 139; Thomas Hooker, "Mr. Hooker's Farewell Sermon on His Departure from England [July 1633]," in *The Danger of Desertion Or A Farewell Sermon of Mr. Thomas Hooker* (London: G.M., 1641), 4; William Plumer Jr., *An Address Delivered at Portsmouth, New Hampshire on the Fourth of July, 1828* (Portsmouth, NH: T. H. Miller and C. W. Brewster 1828), 23.

5. Sargent Bush Jr., "America's Origin Myth: Remembering Plymouth Rock," *American Literary History* 12, no. 4 (Winter 2000): 745–56; Harlow Elizabeth Walker Sheidley, "Sectional Nationalism: The Culture and Politics of the Massachusetts Conservative Elite, 1815–1836" (PhD diss., University of Connecticut, 1990), 270–72.

6. William Tudor, *The Life of James Otis, of Massachusetts* (Boston: Wells and Lilley, 1823), 467; Sheidley, "Sectional Nationalism," 260–65, 283.

7. Edward Brown, *Notes on the Origin and Necessity of Slavery* (Charleston, SC: A. E. Miller, 1826), 1–2, 24.

8. Reginald Horsman, *Race and Manifest Destiny: The Origins of American Racial Anglo-Saxonism* (Cambridge, MA: Harvard University Press, 1981), 160–61; David Hackett Fischer, *Albion's Seed: Four British Folkways in North America* (New York: Oxford University Press, 1989), 207–27; Mark Twain, *Life on the Mississippi* (New York: Grosset & Dunlap, 1917), 375–76.

9. William Gilmore Simms, "The Morals of Slavery," in *The Pro-Slavery Argument* (Philadelphia: Lippincott, Grambo, 1853), 264–73.

10. James Henry Hammond, *Gov. Hammond's Letters on Southern Slavery* (Charleston, SC: Walker & Burke, 1845), 4–6; "Sketch of the Corner-Stone Speech"

in *Alexander H. Stephens in Public and Private*, ed. Henry Cleveland (Philadelphia: National Publishing Company, 1866), 721.

11. J. William Frost, "William Penn's Experiment in the Wilderness: Promise and Legend," *The Pennsylvania Magazine of History and Biography* 107, no. 4 (October 1983): 580–81, 585; William Penn to Thomas Janney, London, June 21, 1681, in Penn Family Papers, Historical Society of Pennsylvania.

12. Penn to Janney; Evan Haefeli, "The Pennsylvania Difference: Religious Diversity on the Delaware before 1683," *Early American Studies* 1, no. 1 (Spring 2003): 28–29; Colin Woodard, *American Nations: A History of the Eleven Rival Regional Cultures of North America* (New York: Viking, 2011), 92–100.

13. Russell A. Kazal, "The Lost World of Pennsylvania Pluralism: Immigrants, Regions and the Early Origins of Pluralist Ideologies in America," *Journal of American Ethnic History* 27, no. 3 (Spring 2008): 7–11.

14. Horace M. Kallen, "Democracy Versus the Melting-Pot, Part Two," *The Nation*, February 25, 1915, 220.

15. Kallen, "Democracy Versus the Melting-Pot," 220; U.S. Census Bureau, "Population: Pennsylvania," *Fourteenth Census of the United States—1920 Bulletin* (Washington: Government Printing Office), 2.

16. For examples of twenty-first-century Midland pluralism, see Ferro Trabalzi and Gerardo Sandoval, "The Exotic Other: Latinos and the Remaking of Community Identity in Perry, Iowa," *Community Development* 41, no. 1 (March 2010): 76–91; A. G. Sulzberger, "Reviving Faded Towns on the Plains," *New York Times*, November 14, 2011; John Hinshaw, "The Growing Puerto Rican Presence in the Pennsylvania Dutch Country," *Pennsylvania Magazine of History and Biography* 140, no. 3 (October 2016): 365–92.

17. David Hackett Fischer, *African Founders: How Enslaved People Expanded American Ideals* (New York: Simon & Schuster, 2022), 128–30; Joyce Goodfriend, *Before the Melting Pot: Society and Culture in Colonial New York City, 1664–1730* (Princeton, NJ: Princeton University Press, 1992), 10.

18. Russell Shorto, *The Island at the Center of the World* (New York: Doubleday, 2004), 317.

19. Benjamin B. Roberts, *Sex, Drugs and Rock n' Roll in the Dutch Golden Age* (Amsterdam: Amsterdam University Press, 2017), 12–13, 16–18, 21.

20. Michael Moon, "'The Gentle Boy from the Dangerous Classes': Pederasty, Domesticity, and Capitalism in Horatio Alger," *Representations* 19 (Summer 1987): 88–90.

21. Horace Kephart, *Our Southern Highlanders* (New York: Outing Publishing Co., 1913), 17–18.

22. William Goodell Frost, "Our Contemporary Ancestors in the Southern Mountains," *Atlantic Monthly*, March 1899, 2–4.

23. Mrs. S. M. Davis, "The 'Mountain Whites' of America," *The Missionary Review of the World*, old series 8, no. 6 (June 1895), 422–26.

24. Ellen Churchill Semple, "The Anglo-Saxons of the Kentucky Mountains: A Study in Anthropogeography," *Geographical Journal* 17, no. 6 (June 1901): 592.

25. Jerry Falwell's 1993 sermon quoted in Alan Dershowitz, *Blasphemy: How the Religious Right is Hijacking the Declaration of Independence* (Hoboken, NJ: John Wiley & Sons, 2007), 48.

26. Joy S. Kasson, *Buffalo Bill's Wild West: Celebrity, Memory, and Popular History* (New York: Hill & Wang, 2000), 13–91, 161–219.

27. On Frederick Jackson Turner and the frontier myth, see Colin Woodard, *Union: The Struggle to Forge the Story of United States Nationhood* (New York: Viking, 2020), 228–32, 240–42, 254–58, 273–76, 282–86, 294–97, 313–18, 354–56.

28. Charles Fletcher Lummis, *The Spanish Pioneers and the California Missions* (Chicago: A. C. McClurg, 1930), 303–304.

29. David G. Gutierrez, "Significant to Whom? Mexican Americans and the History of the American West," *Western Historical Quarterly* 24, no. 4 (November 1993): 522–24.

30. Charles Yves Grandjeat, "Nationalism, History and Myth: the Masks of Aztlán," *Confluencia* 6, no. 1 (Fall 1990): 19–22.

31. Lloyd Arthur Hunter, "The Sacred South: Postwar Confederates and the Sacralization of Southern Culture" (PhD diss., Saint Louis University, 1988), 166.

32. Hunter, "The Sacred South," 205; Robert Lang, ed., *The Birth of a Nation* (New Brunswick, NJ: Rutgers Films in Print, 1994), 134.

33. David Blight, *Race and Reunion* (Cambridge, MA: Harvard University Press, 2022), 282.

34. Jonathan Zimmerman, *Whose America? Culture Wars in the Public Schools* (Cambridge, MA: Harvard University Press, 2022), 34–35.

35. Susan Pendleton Lee, *New School History of the United States* (Richmond, VA: B. F. Johnson, 1900), 262.

36. Lee, *New School History*, 357.

37. Woodard, *Union*, 183–84, 208–14, 290–93.

38. "Muzzey's History False and Slanderous," *Charlotte Observer*, October 8, 1921.

39. Associated Press dispatch of June 23, 1932, appeared as "Virginia Elected by Confederates as 1933 Chieftain," *The Times-Picayune* (New Orleans), June 24, 1932, 28.

40. Jacob F. Lee, "Unionism, Emancipation, and the Origins of Kentucky's Confederate Identity," *The Register of the Kentucky Historical Society* 111, no. 2 (Spring 2013): 201–205, 231–33; Aaron Astor, "Belated Confederates: Black Politics, Guerrilla Violence, and the Collapse of Conservative Unionism in Kentucky and Missouri, 1860–1872" (PhD diss., Northwestern University, 2006), 283–86, 314, 331–32; John C. Inscoe, *Race, War, and Remembrance in the Appalachian South* (Lexington: University Press of Kentucky, 2008), 28–33.

41. Adam Wesley Dean, "'Who Controls the Past Controls the Future': The Virginia History Textbook Controversy," *The Virginia Magazine of History and Biography* 117, no. 4 (2009): 318–55; Francis B. Simkins, Spotswood H. Jones,

and Sidman P. Poole, *Virginia: History, Government, Geography* (New York: Scribner & Sons, 1951), 376.

42. *Loewen v. Turnipseed*, 488 F. Supp. 1138 (N.D. Miss. 1980).

43. Rashawan Ray and Alexandra Gibbons, "Why Are States Banning Critical Race Theory?," Brookings Institution, November 2021.

44. "Special Committee Report on Florida," Association of American University Presidents, December 2023, 32–35.

45. Zimmerman, *Whose America?*, 247–49.

46. "Joint Statement on Legislative Efforts to Restrict Education About Racism and American History," PEN America, June 16, 2021.

47. Robert Doar, "Work Is Essential to the American Dream," AEI Ideas, American Enterprise Institute, May 4, 2023; Julia Limitone, "American Dream Still Within Reach: Michael Milken," FOX Business, August 23, 2018.

48. Zimmerman, *Whose America?*, 218–19; Astrid Galvan, "Judge: Racism Behind Arizona Ban on Mexican-American Studies," Associated Press, August 22, 2017.

49. Meryl Kornfield, "California Becomes First State to Require Ethnic Studies for High School Graduation," *Washington Post*, October 9, 2021; Cedar Attanasio, "New Mexico Increases Focus on Race in K-12 Despite Backlash," Associated Press, March 4, 2022; "New Mexico Social Studies Standards," New Mexico Public Education Department, February 2022, 76.

50. Lionel Sheldon, "Arizona and New Mexico Statehood Bill in Congress," *Los Angeles Herald*, March 18, 1906.

CHAPTER 5: BELONGING

1. Yascha Mounk, *The Great Experiment: Why Diverse Democracies Fall Apart and How They Can Endure* (New York: Penguin Press, 2022), 7; for my take on Mounk's overall argument, see Colin Woodard, "Can Diverse Democracies Survive?," *Washington Monthly*, April/May/June 2022.

2. Joshua Miller, "Direct Democracy and the Puritan Theory of Membership," *Journal of Politics* 53, no. 1 (February 1991): 57–74; Thomas Hooker, *A Survey of the Summe of Church-Discipline* (London: A. M. for John Bellamy, 1648), part I, 14, and part III, 13; Carla Gardina Pestana, "The City Upon a Hill Under Siege: The Puritan Perception of the Quaker Threat to Massachusetts Bay, 1656–1661," *New England Quarterly* 56, no. 3 (September 1983): 323–53.

3. Clifford Shipton, "Immigration to New England, 1680–1740," *Journal of Political Economy* 44, no. 2 (April 1936), 225–39; "To the profound Dr. Janus," *New-England Courant*, December 16, 1724, 1–2.

4. Hector St. John de Crevecoeur, *Letters from an American Farmer* (Dublin: John Exshaw, 1782) 42.

5. Thomas Mann, "Tenth Annual Report," in *The Republic and the School: Horace Mann and the Education of Free Men*, ed. Lawrence Cremin (New York: Macmillan, 1846), 58; John Dewey, "Schools, Democracy and Education" in

Americanization: Principles of Americanism, 2nd ed., ed. Winthrop Talbot (New York: H. W. Wilson Co., 1920), 203–204; H. H. Wharton, "Education of Immigrants" in *Americanization,* ed. Winthrop Talbot, 207; Peter D. Salins, *Assimilation, American Style* (New York: Basic Books, 1997), 46.

6. Richard C. Rohrs, "Exercising Their Right: African American Voter Turnout in Antebellum Newport, Rhode Island," *New England Quarterly* 84, no. 3 (September 2011): 402; Christy Clark Pajura, "Contested: Black Suffrage in Early Wisconsin," *Wisconsin Magazine of History,* Summer 2017, 26–27; Reginald Horsman, *Race and Manifest Destiny: The Origins of American Racial Anglo-Saxonism* (Cambridge, MA: Harvard University Press, 1981), 182–85.

7. Robert Bruce Slater, "The Blacks Who First Entered the World of White Higher Education," *Journal of Blacks in Higher Education* 1, no. 4 (Summer 1994): 47–56.

8. Fred Arthur Bailey, "Thomas Nelson Page and the Patrician Cult of the Old South," *International Social Science Review* 72, no. 3/4 (1997): 110–21; Thomas Nelson Page, "The Old South" (1892), in *The Novels, Stories, Sketches and Poems of Thomas Nelson Page,* vol. 12 (New York: Charles Scribner's Sons, 1908), 321–26.

9. Colin Woodard, *Union: The Struggle to Forge the Story of United States Nationhood* (New York: Viking, 2020), 330, 340.

10. David A. Reed, "America of the Melting Pot Comes to an End," *New York Times,* April 27, 1924.

11. Rowland T. Berthoff, "Southern Attitudes Toward Immigration, 1865–1914," *Journal of Southern History* 17, no. 3 (August 1951): 328–60.

12. Berthoff, "Southern Attitudes," 343–46.

13. *The South in the Building of the Nation,* vol. 6 (Richmond, VA: Southern Publication Society, 1909), 584.

14. Hamilton Fish Armstrong, "New York Looks Abroad," *Foreign Affairs* 19, no. 3 (April 1941): 564–66.

15. Billy G. Smith and Paul Sivitz, "Identifying and Mapping Ethnicity in Philadelphia in the Early Republic," *Pennsylvania Magazine of History and Biography* 65, no. 3 (October 2016): 393, 411.

16. Benjamin Franklin to Peter Collinson, Philadelphia, May 9, 1753, New York Public Library.

17. Smith and Sivitz, "Identifying and Mapping," 403.

18. Arnold Leibowitz, "Educational Policy and Political Acceptance: The Imposition of English as the Language of Instruction in American Schools," Center for Applied Linguistics, March 1971, 9–15; Heinz Kloss, "German-American Language Maintenance Efforts" in *Language Loyalty in the United States,* ed. Jonathan Fishman et al. (The Hague: Mouton & Co., 1966), 240–46; Colin Woodard, "Yes, Iowa Still Matters," *Politico,* December 2, 2015; John Gunther, *Inside U.S.A.* (New York: Harper, 1947), 334.

19. "Mapping the Second Klan," Virginia Commonwealth University, labs.library

.vcu.edu/klan/; "Sundown Towns Map," interactive graphic based on the work of James W. Loewen of Tougaloo College, justice.tougaloo.edu/map.

20. Colin Gordon, "Race in the Heartland: Equity, Opportunity, and Public Policy in the Midwest," Iowa Policy Project, October 2019; Kim Norvell, "Midwest Among the Worst Place for Blacks to Live, New Report Says," *Des Moines Register*, October 12, 2019.

21. African American populations calculated from U.S. Census Bureau, *Negro Population 1790–1915* (Washington DC: Government Printing Office, 1918), 45; "West Virginia Population by Race," West Virginia Archives and History, archive.wvculture.org/history/teacherresources/censuspopulationrace.html.

22. C. G. Belissary, "Tennessee and Immigration, 1865–1880," *Tennessee Historical Quarterly* 7, no. 3 (September 1948): 229.

23. Ronald L. Lewis, "Peasant to Proletarian: The Migration of Southern Blacks to the Central Appalachian Coalfields," *Journal of Southern History* 55, no. 1 (February 1989): 77–102; Belissary, "Tennessee and Immigration," 229–48; Kenneth R. Bailey, "A Judicious Mixture: Negroes and Immigrants in the West Virginia Mines, 1880–1917," in *Blacks in Appalachia*, ed. William H. Turner and Edward J. Cabbell (Lexington: University Press of Kentucky, 1985), 117–22.

24. Bailey, "A Judicious Mixture," 128–30; U.S. Census Bureau, *Negro Population 1790–1915*, 44–45; Lewis, "Peasant to Proletarian."

25. On Turner's thesis, see Woodard, *Union*, 228–32, 240–42, 254–58.

26. Colin Woodard, *American Nations: A History of the Eleven Rival Regional Cultures of North America* (New York: Viking, 2011), 216–23; David George Herman, "Neighbors on the Golden Mountain: The Americanization of Immigrants in California" (PhD diss., University of California, Berkeley, 1991), 9–16, 242–48.

27. Kevin White, "The Forgotten History of the Western Klan," *The Atlantic*, April 6, 2021.

28. Ana Maria Alonso, *Thread of Blood: Colonialism, Revolution, and Gender on Mexico's Northern Frontier* (Tempe: University of Arizona Press, 1995), 15–70; Pablo Yankelevich, "Mexico for the Mexicans: Immigration, National Sovereignty and the Promotion of *Mestizaje*," *The Americas* 68, no. 3 (January 2012): 405–36; Pablo Vila, *Crossing Borders, Reinforcing Borders: Social Categories, Metaphors and Narrative Identities on the U.S.–Mexico Frontier* (Austin: University of Texas Press 2000), 21–48.

29. Kristina Campbell, "Rising Arizona: The Legacy of the Jim Crow Southwest on Immigration Law and Policy After 100 Years of Statehood," *Berkeley La Raza Law Journal* 24, no. 1 (2014): 105–10.

30. W. J. Cash, *The Mind of the South* (New York: Knopf, 1941), 297–98.

31. Clifford Grammich et al., "2020 U.S. Religion Census," Association of Statisticians of American Religious Bodies, 2023.

32. "Threats to American Democracy Ahead of an Unprecedented Presidential

Election: Findings from the 2023 American Values Survey," Public Religion Research Institute, October 25, 2023, 34; Samuel Stroope, Heather Rackin, and Paul Froese, "Christian Nationalism and Views of Immigrants in the United States: Is the Relationship Stronger for the Religiously Inactive?," *Socius* 7 (2021): 1–14; Michael Luo, "How White Christian Nationalists Seek to Transform America," New Yorker Radio Hour, newyorker.com/podcast/politics -and-more/how-white-christian-nationalists-seek-to-transform-america.

33. Zachary D. Broeren and Paul A. Djupe, "The Ingroup Love and Outgroup Hate of Christian Nationalism: Experimental Evidence About the Implementation of the Rule of Law," *Politics and Religion* 17, no. 1 (March 2024): 40–57; Darren E. Sherkat and Derek Lehman, "Bad Samaritans: Religion and Anti-Immigrant and Anti-Muslim Sentiment in the United States, *Social Science Quarterly* 99, no. 5 (November 2018): 1791–804; Eric L. McDaniel, Irfan Nooruddin, and Allyson F. Shortle, "Divine Boundaries: How Religion Shapes Citizens' Attitudes Toward Immigrants," *American Politics Research* 39, no. 1 (2011): 205–33.

34. "Modern Immigration Wave Brings 59 Million to U.S., Driving Population Growth and Change Through 2065," Pew Research Center, September 28, 2015; Jeffrey S. Passel et al., "How the Origins of America's Immigrants Have Changed Since 1850," Pew Research Center, July 22, 2024.

35. Jamie Winders, "Bringing Back the (B)order: Post-9/11 Politics of Immigration, Borders, and Belonging in the Contemporary US South," *Antipode* 39, no. 5 (November 2007): 920–42.

36. For example: Raymond A. Mohl, "Globalization, Latinization, and the Nuevo New South," *Journal of American Ethnic History* 22, no. 4 (2003): 31–66.

37. Bradley Jones, "Majority of Americans Continue to Say Immigrants Strengthen the U.S.," Pew Research Center, January 31, 2019.

38. Robert Mackey, "The Deep Comic Roots of 'Self-Deportation,'" *New York Times*, February 1, 2012.

39. Benjy Sarlin, "How America's Harshest Immigration Law Failed," *NBC News*, December 16, 2023.

40. U.S. Attorney's Office for the Northern District of Alabama, "Alabama's Immigration Law Permanently Blocked In Justice Department Lawsuit," U.S. Attorney's Office, Northern District of Alabama, press release, November 25, 2023.

41. Margaret M. Commins and Jeremiah B. Wills, "Restrictive Immigrant Policies in New South Legislatures: Understanding Regional Variations in State-Level Policymaking," *The Latin Americanist* 674, no. 2 (June 2020): 200–222.

42. Goleen Samari, Amanda Nagle, and Kate Coleman-Minahan, "Measuring Structural Xenophobia: US State Immigration Policy Climates over Ten Years," *SSM - Population Health* 16 (2021).

43. "Migrants Flown to Martha's Vineyard by Florida Gov. Ron DeSantis Can Sue

Charter Flight Company," Associated Press, April 1, 2024; Seth Freed Wessler, "Bused From Texas to Manhattan, an Immigrant Struggles to Find Shelter," ProPublica, February 7, 2024; Kevin McGill, "Appeals Court Keeps Texas' Migrant Arrest Law on Hold," Associated Press, March 27, 2024; "Louisiana Lawmakers Approve Bill Similar to Texas' Embattled Migrant Enforcement Law," Associated Press, May 22, 2024.

44. "State Map on Immigration Enforcement 2023," Immigrant Legal Resource Center, ilrc.org/state-map-immigration-enforcement.

45. "Prosecuting People for Coming to the United States," American Immigration Council, August 23, 2021.

46. "Senate Border Negotiations Forge Ahead Despite Pressure from Trump," *All Things Considered*, National Public Radio, January 25, 2024; Danielle Kurtzleben, "Why Trump's Authoritarian Language About 'Vermin' Matters," National Public Radio, November 17, 2023.

CHAPTER 6: ABORTION

1. Colin Woodard, "Abortion's Regional Divide," Nationhood Lab, May 24, 2024; Colin Woodard, "The Perplexing Geography of Abortion Opinion," *Talking Points Memo*, May 27, 2024.

2. Colin Woodard, "Ohio's Abortion Vote and the American Nations," Nationhood Lab, November 27, 2023.

3. Karen Morin, "Political Culture and Suffrage in an Anglo-American Women's West," *Women's Rights Law Reporter* 19, no. 1 (Fall 1997): 17–37.

4. Laura M. Moore, "Multi-Level Analysis of Attitudes Regarding Women and Politics: Why Is the South Different?" (PhD diss., University of Maryland, College Park, 1999), 13–18; Jennifer Di Noia, "Indicators of Gender Equality for American States and Regions: An Update," *Social Indicators Research* 59 (July 2002): 35–77.

5. "The 2020 PRRI Census of American Religion," Public Religion Research Institute, July 8, 2021.

6. "The 2020 PRRI Census of American Religion: County-Level Data on Religious Identity and Diversity," Public Religion Research Institute, July 8, 2021.

7. Rebecca Sager and Keith Bentele, "Coopting the State: The Conservative Evangelical Movement and State-Level Institutionalization, Passage, and Diffusion of Faith-Based Initiatives," *Religions* 71 (2016), 71–96.

8. Christopher Scheitle, interview with the author by telephone, January 31, 2024.

9. The Church of Jesus Christ of Latter-day Saints, "Abortion," newsroom .churchofjesuschrist.org/official-statement/abortion; "Abortion Attitudes in a Post-Roe World," Public Religion Research Institute, February 2023, 7.

10. Jennifer Holland, interview with the author by telephone, February 5, 2024.

11. Patricia U. Bonomi and Peter R. Eisenstadt, "Church Adherence in the

Eighteenth-Century British American Colonies," *William and Mary Quarterly* 39, no. 2 (April 1982): 245–86; Christine Leigh Heyrman, *Southern Cross: The Beginnings of the Bible Belt* (New York: Knopf, 1997), 8–11, 45–47.

12. Heyrman, *Southern Cross*, 6.

13. Christine Leigh Heyrman, interview with the author by telephone, February 9, 2024; Heyrman, *Southern Cross*, 138–42, 223, 230–52.

14. Edward R. Crowther, "Iron Chests: Honor and Manhood in Southern Evangelicalism," in *The Field of Honor: Essays on Southern Character and American Identity*, ed. John Mayfield and Todd Hagstette (Columbia: University of South Carolina Press, 2017), 276–91; "The Danvers Statement," Council on Biblical Manhood and Womanhood, December 1987, accessed March 15, 2025, cbmw.org/about/the-danvers-statement.

15. "Resolution on Abortion," Southern Baptist Convention, June 1, 1971, sbc.net/resource-library/resolutions/resolution-on-abortion; this moderate resolution was reaffirmed in 1974, 1976, and 1979; compare with "Resolution On Encouraging Laws Regulating Abortion," Southern Baptist Convention, June 1, 1989, sbc.net/resource-library/resolutions/resolution-on-encouraging-laws-regulating-abortion; and "On Thirty Years Of Roe V. Wade," Southern Baptist Convention, June 1, 2003, sbc.net/resource-library/resolutions/on-thirty-years-of-roe-v-wade. See also Andrew Whitehead and Samuel Perry, "White Christian Nationalism Isn't Pro-Life. It's Pro-Order," Religion News Service, January 19, 2023.

16. Mark W. Harris, "A Faith for the Few?," *UU World*, Spring 2011; "Abortion Attitudes in a Post-Roe World: Findings From the 50-State 2022 American Values Atlas," Public Religion Research Institute, February 23, 2023.

17. Micah Cohen, "Political Geography: Louisiana," *FiveThirtyEight*, March 24, 2012.

18. Colin Woodard, "Ohio's Abortion Vote and the American Nations," Nationhood Lab, November 27, 2023.

19. "Abortion Attitudes in a Post-Roe World," Public Religion Research Institute; "Arizona Attorney General Mark Brnovich Says New State Abortion Law Will Go Into Effect in About 90 Days," KNXV-TV, June 24, 2022; Mary Jo Pitzl and Reagan Priest, "Arizona House GOP Halt Democrats' Effort to Overturn Civil War Era Law in Chaotic Session," *Arizona Republic*, April 10, 2024.

20. Arek Sarkissian, "Florida Supreme Court Upholds Strict Abortion Bans While Giving Voters a Say in November," *Politico*, April 1, 2024.

CHAPTER 7: CLIMATE

1. "Climate Impact Map: Historical 1986–2005," Climate Impact Lab, impactlab.org/map/#usmeas=absolute&usyear=1986-2005&gmeas=absolute&gyear=1986-2005&tab=united-states; Suzanne Goldenberg, "Republicans' Leading Climate Denier Tells the Pope to Butt Out of Climate Debate," *The Guardian*, June 11, 2015.

2. The Yale climate opinion estimates can be found here: Jennifer Marlon et al., "Yale Climate Opinion Maps 2023," Yale Program on Climate Change Communication, December 13, 2023, climatecommunication.yale.edu/visualizations -data/ycom-us.

3. Colin Woodard, *American Nations: A History of the Eleven Rival Regional Cultures of North America* (New York: Viking, 2011), 282; Colin Woodard, "Geography of Environmentalism, Climate Action, and Climate Denial," Nationhood Lab, July 29, 2024.

4. Sung Eun Kim and Johannes Urpelainen, "Environmental Public Opinion in U.S. States, 1973–2012," *Environmental Politics* 27, no. 1 (2018): 89–114; Dimitrios Gounaridis and Joshua P. Newell, "The Social Anatomy of Climate Change Denial in the United States," *Scientific Reports* 14 (2024).

5. Bob Hall and Mary Lee Kerr, *1991–1992 Green Index: A State-by-State Guide to the Nation's Environmental Health* (Washington, DC: Island Press, 1991); "The Greenest States in America 2020," MPHOnline.org/green-states.

6. Kathryn Parkman, "Greenest States in the U.S.," *Consumer Affairs*, June 12, 2024; John Bailey and Dave Grossman, "Getting Transportation Right: Ranking the States in Light of New Federal Funding," Natural Resources Defense Council, 2023.

7. Martin A. Nie, "Green Sagebrush: The American West, Political Culture, and Environmental Politics" (PhD diss., Northern Arizona University, 1998).

8. Kenneth Charles Martis, "The History of Natural Resources Roll Call Voting in the United States House of Representatives: An Analysis of the Spatial Aspects of Legislative Voting Behavior" (PhD diss., University of Michigan, 1976), 176–77; Joseph Robert Sheeran, "How Green is Congress? An Analysis of Congressional Voting Behavior on Environmental Issues from 1973–1996" (master's thesis, California State University, Fullerton, 1997), 184–85; "2023 National Environmental Scorecard: First Session of the 118th Congress," League of Conservation Voters, 5.

9. Barbara Deutsch Lynch, "The Garden and the Sea: U.S. Latino Environmental Discourses and Mainstream Environmentalism," *Social Problems* 40, no. 1 (February 1993): 108–24; Devon G. Peña, *Mexican Americans and the Environment: Tierra y Vida* (Tempe: University of Arizona Press, 2005), xxxii, 110–23; Sarah Marie Naiman, "La Familia, La Identidad, y El Ambientalismo: Understanding the Motivators of Latine Environmentalism" (PhD diss., Cornell University, August 2022).

10. Ellen Griffith Spears, "(Re)Writing Histories of Environmentalism in Alabama," *Alabama Review* 70, no. 2 (April 2017): 171–88.

11. Jennifer Rice and Brian Burke, "Building More Inclusive Solidarities for Socio-Environmental Change: Lessons in Resistance from Southern Appalachia," *Antipode* 50, no. 1 (January 2018): 212–32; Philip Lewin, "'I Just Keep My Mouth Shut': The Demobilization of Environmental Protest in Central Appalachia," *Social Currents* 6, no. 6 (December 2019): 534–52.

12. Julie Ingersoll, "The Christian Reconstruction Movement in U.S. Politics," in *Oxford Handbook Topics in Religion*, online edition, Oxford Academic, February 3, 2014.

13. Martin E. Marty, *Righteous Empire: The Protestant Experience in America* (New York: Dial Press, 1970).

14. "Message of His Holiness Pope Benedict XVI for the Celebration of the World Day of Peace," Vatican Dicastery for Communication, January 1, 2007; Alexi Krindatch, "Putting American Orthodox Churches on the Map: Geography of Parishes and Members 2010–2020," Orthodox Reality, orthodoxreality.org /wp-content/uploads/2021/04/ReportOnOrthodoxGeographyWithMaps.pdf; Colin Woodard, "An Orthodox Odyssey," *Bulletin of the Atomic Scientists*, January/February 1988, 9–11; Colin Woodard, "Orthodox Leader Blesses Green Agenda," *Christian Science Monitor*, July 24, 2003; David Vogel, "How Green Is Judaism? Exploring Jewish Environmental Ethics," *Business Ethics Quarterly* 11, no. 2 (April 2001): 349–63.

15. "The Faith Factor in Climate Change: How Religion Impacts American Attitudes on Climate and Environmental Policy," Public Religion Research Institute, 2024, 5, 9; Daniel Cox and Joanna Piacenza, "Majority of Catholics for Religious Stewardship, One-Third Say God Gave Humans Dominion Over Earth," Public Religion Research Institute, June 17, 2015.

16. Charles Pierce LeWarne, *Utopias on Puget Sound, 1885–1915* (Seattle: University of Washington Press, 1995), 3–14, 227–42; Ingeborg Husbyn Aarsand, "Imagining Cascadia: Bioregionalism as Environmental Culture in the Pacific Northwest" (master's thesis, University of Oslo, 2013), 34–38.

17. Ernest Callenbach, *Ecotopia* (New York: Bantam Books, 1975); Joel Garreau, *The Nine Nations of North America* (New York: Houghton Mifflin, 1981), 261–62; Ryan C. Moothart, *Towards Cascadia* (Minneapolis: Publish Green, 2015), chapter 2; Brandon Letsinger, founder of Cascadia Now, interview with the author by telephone, April 12, 2018; Colin Woodard, "Where Do You Draw the Line?" Medium, May 10, 2018.

18. Colin Woodard, "U.S. Cold War Waste Irks Greenland," *Christian Science Monitor*, August 22, 2008; Saranya Palaniswamy et al., "Environmental Contaminants in Arctic Human Populations: Trends over 30 Years," *Environment International* 189 (July 2024); Colin Woodard, "In Greenland, Potatoes Thrive as Seal Hunting Wanes," *Christian Science Monitor*, October 1, 2007.

19. Elizabeth James, "Toward Alaska Native Political Organization: The Origins of Tundra Times," *Western Historical Quarterly* 41, no. 3 (Autumn 2010): 285–303; Stephen Haycox, *Battleground Alaska: Fighting Federal Power in America's Last Wilderness* (Lawrence: University of Kansas Press, 2016), 64–81.

20. Sheila Watt-Cloutier, interview with the author by telephone, December 19, 2006.

21. Momiala Kamahele, "'Īlio'ulaokalani: Defending Native Hawaiian Culture," in *Asian Settler Colonialism: From Local Governance to the Habits of Everyday*

Life in Hawai'i, ed. Candace Fujikane and Jonathan Y. Okamura (Honolulu: University of Hawaii Press, 2008), 79–82.

22. Mililani Trask, "Native Hawaiian Historical and Cultural Perspectives on Environmental Justice," *Race, Poverty & the Environment* 3, no. 1 (Spring 1992): 3–6.

23. Kamahele, "'Īlio'ulaokalani," 77–78, 81–95; Melody Kapilialoha MacKenzie, Susan K. Serrano, and Koalani Laura Kaulukukui, "Environmental Justice for Indigenous Hawaiians: Reclaiming Land and Resources," *Natural Resources & Environment* 21, no. 3 (Winter 2007): 37–42, 79.

CHAPTER 8: DEMOCRACY

1. "Harris, Trump Voters Differ Over Election Security, Vote Counts and Hacking Concerns," Pew Research Center, October 24, 2024.

2. *Rucho v. Common Cause*, 588 U.S. __ (2019).

3. Justin Levitt, "The Truth About Voter Fraud," Brennan Center for Justice, November 9, 2007; Justin Levitt, "A Comprehensive Investigation of Voter Impersonation Finds 31 Credible Incidents Out of One Billion Ballots Cast," *Washington Post*, August 6, 2014; Sharad Goel et al., "One Person, One Vote: Estimating the Prevalence of Double Voting in U.S. Presidential Elections," *American Political Science Review* 114, no. 2 (2020): 456–69; Christopher Famighetti, Douglas Keith, and Myrna Pérez, "Noncitizen Voting: The Missing Millions," Brennan Center for Justice, May 5, 2017.

4. James A. Gardner, "Illiberalism and Authoritarianism in the American States," *American University Law Review* 70 (2021): 909.

5. Phillip Swagel, "The Cost of the Financial Crisis: The Impact of the September 2008 Economic Collapse," Pew Financial Reform Project, April 28, 2010.

6. Brandy Dennis and David Cho, "Rage at AIG Swells as Bonuses Go Out," *Washington Post*, March 17, 2009; Russell Goldman, "Employees Fear for Their Lives: The Other AIG Outrage," ABC News, March 27, 2009; Barney Frank, *Frank: A Life in Politics from the Great Society to Same-Sex Marriage* (New York: Macmillan, 2015), 298–301.

7. Theda Skocpol and Vanessa Williamson, *The Tea Party and the Remaking of Republican Conservatism* (New York: Oxford University Press, 2013), 104–105; Joe Strupp, "Dick Armey Dishes on FreedomWorks' Deals with Beck & Limbaugh," Media Matters, January 4, 2013.

8. W. Cleon Skousen, The American Heritage & Constitution Study Course (Provo, UT: Freeman Institute, c. 1980); Alexander Zaitchik, "Meet the Man Who Changed Glenn Beck's Life," *Salon*, September 16, 2009; Kate Zernike, *Boiling Mad* (New York: St. Martin's Press, 2010), 73–77; Sean Wilentz, "Confounding Fathers," *New Yorker*, October 18, 2010.

9. Colin Woodard, *American Character: The Epic Struggle Between Individual Liberty and the Common Good* (New York: Viking, 2016), 227–32.

10. Nate Silver, "Were the Tea Parties Really a Libertarian Thing?," FiveThirtyEight,

April 26, 2009; Colin Woodard, "The Soul of the Tea Party," *Newsweek*, December 1, 2010; Stacy G. Ulbig and Sarah Macha, "It's Tea Time, but What Flavor? Regional Variation in Sources of Support for the Tea Party Movement," *American Review of Politics* 33 (Summer 2012): 95–121.

11. Skocpol and Williamson, *The Tea Party and the Remaking of Republican Conservatism*, 56–61; Lisa Disch, "A 'White Citizenship' Movement?," in *Steep: The Precipitous Rise of the Tea Party*, ed. Lawrence Rosenthal and Christine Trost (Berkeley: University of California Press, 2012), 136–37, 143.

12. Tim Storey, "Legislature Landslide," *Sabato's Crystal Ball*, The Center for Politics at the University of Virginia, December 9, 2010; Dan Balz, "The Republican Takeover in the States," *Washington Post*, November 14, 2010; "Redistricting Commissions: Legislative Plans," National Conference of State Legislatures, 2009.

13. "Redistricting Reform in Wisconsin," *Marquette Law Review* 101, no. 233 (2017): 249–250.

14. David Eggert, "Michigan Redistricting Panel OKs US House, Legislative Maps," Associated Press, December 28, 2021.

15. Rebecca Lavoie and Dan Barrick, "As New Hampshire Shifts to a Swing State, Why Do Legislative Lines Still Favor Republicans?," New Hampshire Public Radio, April 20, 2016, www.nhpr.org/politics/2016-04-20/as-new-hampshire -shifts-to-a-swing-state-why-do-legislative-lines-still-favor-republicans.

16. Joseph Findley, "Partisan Gerrymandering and the Show Me State: Applying the Standard in *Whitford v. Gill* to the Contest of Missouri's State and Congressional Districts," *UMKC Law Review* 88, no. 1 (Fall 2019): 181.

17. Richard Gunther, "Ohio Strikes Blow Against Gerrymandering," *The Conversation*, November 4, 2015.

18. Chris Sikich, "Critics: Redistricting Bill Falls Short: Say It's Unlikely to End Indiana Gerrymandering," *Journal & Courier* (Lafayette, IN), February 25, 2019.

19. Jason DeBruyn, "How Gerrymandered Districts Helped GOP Keep Veto-Proof Majority," North Carolina Public Radio, November 11, 2016; Van R. Newkirk II, "The Supreme Court Finds North Carolina's Racial Gerrymandering Unconstitutional," *The Atlantic*, May 22, 2017.

20. Adam Krejci, "Welcome to the Jungle: Gerrymandering and Oklahoma's Journey into the Redistricting Thicket in *Wilson v. State ex rel. State Election Board*," *Oklahoma City University Law Review* 38, no. 1 (Spring 2013): 149–50.

21. Jordan Lewis, "Fair Districts Florida: A Meaningful Relationship Reform?," *University of Miami Race & Social Justice Law Review* 5, no. 1189 (2015): 205–208.

22. Thomas Wheatley, "How Redrawing Districts Has Kept Georgia Incumbents in Power," *Atlanta Magazine*, January 12, 2018; Sue Sturgis, "Extreme Partisan Gerrymandering Sent Marjorie Taylor Greene to Congress," *Facing South*, Institute for Southern Studies, February 12, 2021.

23. Nick Kato, "Pennsylvania Freedom of Expression Clause and Partisan Gerrymandering," *Temple Law Review* 91, no. 2 (Spring 2019): 365–66; Findley, "Par-

tisan Gerrymandering and the Show Me State," 181–202; Jacob M. Grumbach, "Laboratories of Democratic Backsliding," *American Political Science Review* 117, no. 3 (2023): 974; Jeffrey S. Buzas and Gregory S. Warrington, "Gerrymandering and the Net Number of US House Seats Won Due to Vote-Distribution Asymmetries," unpublished manuscript, August 8, 2017, gswarrin.w3.uvm.edu/research/seats.pdf, 1.

24. Nick Corasaniti, "Ungerrymandered: Michigan's Maps, Independently Drawn, Set Up Fair Fight," *New York Times*, December 29, 2021; Eggert, "Michigan Redistricting Panel OKs US House, Legislative Maps."

25. Gunther, "Ohio Strikes Blow Against Gerrymandering"; Jessie Balmert, "'The Way Our Districts Are Drawn Is BS': Ohio Redistricting Effort Moves Toward Fall Ballot," *Columbus Dispatch*, July 1, 2024; Molly Beck, Eva Wen, and Andrew Hahn, "Gov. Tony Evers Signs New Election Maps, Ending Wisconsin Republicans' Grip on Legislative Power," *Milwaukee Journal Sentinel*, February 19, 2021.

26. David A. Lieb, "Missouri Republicans Are Split over Changes to State Senate Districts," Associated Press, February 1, 2024; Jane C. Timm, "New Hampshire Governor Vetoes Bipartisan Bill to Ward Off Gerrymandering," NBC News, August 9, 2019.

27. Maggie Astor, "North Carolina Republicans Approve House Map That Flips at Least Three Seats," *New York Times*, October 26, 2023; Jonathan Mattingly, "Newly Proposed NC Maps Are More Gerrymandered and Less Responsive than Maps Struck Down in 2021," Quantifying Gerrymandering, Duke University, October 20, 2023, sites.duke.edu/quantifyinggerrymandering/2023/10/20/newly-proposed-nc-maps-are-more-gerrymandered-and-less-responsive-than-maps-struck-down-in-2021.

28. "Redistricting Report Card," Gerrymandering Project, Princeton University, gerrymander.princeton.edu/redistricting-report-card.

29. Lewis A. Freeland, "The Laboratory for Oligarchy," in *Education for Democracy: Renewing the Wisconsin Idea*, ed. Chad Alan Goldberg (Madison: University of Wisconsin Press, 2020), 232; Colin Woodard, "Bill Seeks to Restrict Maine Towns' Efforts to Build High-Speed Internet Networks," *Portland Press Herald*, May 2, 2017; Colin Woodard, "LePage's Koch Brothers Connection Revealed," *Portland Phoenix*, September 7, 2011; Colin Woodard, "The Profit Motive Behind Virtual Schools in Maine," *Maine Sunday Telegram*, September 2, 2012; Colin Woodard, "The Lobbyist in the Henhouse: Whose Interests Is Maine's DEP Commissioner Serving?," *Maine Sunday Telegram*, June 16, 2013; David Pepper, *Laboratories of Autocracy: A Wake-Up Call from Behind the Lines* (Cincinnati, OH: St. Helena Press, 2021).

30. "Taxpayer and Citizen Protection Act" (model bill text), American Legislative Exchange Council, approved June 2008, alecexposed.org/wiki/Taxpayer_and_Citizen_Protection_Act_Exposed; "Expert Report of Dr. Michael P. McDonald," *Fish v. Kobach*, 189 F. Supp. 3d 1107 (D. Kan. 2016), aclukansas.org/sites

/default/files/field_documents/fish_v._kobach_-_expert_report_of_dr._michael_
mcdonald.pdf.

31. "Voter ID Act" (model bill text), American Legislative Exchange Council, approved July 2009, alecexposed.org/w/images/d/d9/7G16-VOTER_ID_ACT _Exposed.pdf.

32. "Right to Work Act" (model bill text), American Legislative Exchange Council, approved 1995, alecexposed.org/w/images/c/c8/1R10-Right_to_Work_Act _Exposed.pdf; "Express Delivery for Military Ballots Act" (model bill text), American Legislative Exchange Council, approved August 27, 2009, alecexposed .org/w/images/3/3f/7G0-ALEC_Express_Mail_Delivery_for_Military_Ballots _Act_Exposed.pdf.

33. Eric Russell, "Mainers Vote to Continue Election Day Registration," *Bangor Daily News*, November 9, 2011; "Maine Republicans Try Again to Push Through 'Right-to-Work' Legislation," Maine Public Broadcasting Network, March 12, 2015.

34. Amanda Gokee and Annmarie Timmins, "House Defeats Right-to-Work Legislation," *New Hampshire Bulletin*, June 3, 2021.

35. Dave Murray, "Gov. Snyder Vetoes Election Bills Denounced as 'Voter Suppression' by Critics," *Grand Rapids Press*, July 3, 2012; Nick Niedzwiadek, "Michigan Strikes Right-to-Work Law Detested by Unions," *Politico*, March 24, 2023.

36. Mary Spicuzza and Dee Hall, "Senate Orders Arrest of Missing Democrats," *Wisconsin State Journal*, March 3, 2011; James B. Kelleher, "Up to 100,000 Protest Wisconsin Law Curbing Unions," Reuters, March 12, 2011; Jessie Opoien and Laura Schulte, "Dane County Judge Strikes Down Elements of Wisconsin's Act 10 Law That Curbed Public Unions," *Milwaukee Journal Sentinel*, July 3, 2024; Scott Bauer, "Unions Score a Major Win in Wisconsin with a Court Ruling Restoring Collective Bargaining Rights," Associated Press, December 2, 2024.

37. Andrew Cohen, "The Uncertain Future of Voter ID Laws," *The Atlantic*, January 18, 2014; Jim Ragsdale, "Voter ID Drive Rejected," *Star Tribune*, November 7, 2012.

38. Ian Kullgren, "Unions, Citing 'Buyer's Remorse,' Score Major Win in Missouri," *Politico*, August 8, 2018.

39. Reginald Fields, "Ohio Voters Overwhelmingly Reject Issue 2, Dealing a Blow to Gov. John Kasich," *Plain Dealer*, November 9, 2011; Pepper, *Laboratories of Autocracy*, Kindle location 3079.

40. Jasmine C. Lee, "How States Moved Toward Stricter Voter ID Laws," *New York Times*, November 3, 2016; Pepper, *Laboratories of Autocracy*, Kindle location 3301; Wendy Weiser, "How Much of a Difference Did New Voting Restrictions Make in Yesterday's Close Races?," Brennan Center for Justice, November 5, 2014.

41. Gardner, "Illiberalism and Authoritarianism in the American States," 900–904.

42. On Arizona's sources of in-migrants, see Colin Woodard, "The American Na-

tions and the States: Change Over Time," Nationhood Lab, June 28, 2024;
James Gregory, "Arizona's Migration History, 1860–1918," America's Great
Migrations Project, Civil Rights and Labor History Consortium, University of
Washington, depts.washington.edu/moving1/Arizona.shtml.

CHAPTER 9: AUTHORITARIANISM

1. Philip Gorski, "White Christian Nationalism and the Threat to American Democracy," *Hambach Democracy Paper* 1/23 (2023), 1–5; Tim Alberta, *The
Kingdom, the Power, and the Glory: American Evangelicals in an Age of Ex-
tremism* (New York: Harper, 2023), 12.
2. "Threats to American Democracy Ahead of an Unprecedented Presidential
Election: Findings from the 2023 American Values Survey," Public Religion
Research Institute, October 25, 2023, 34.
3. Michael Rotolo, Gregory A. Smith, and Jonathan Evans, "8 in 10 Americans Say
Religion is Losing Influence in Public Life," Pew Research Center, March 15,
2024, 45–47.
4. Chauncey Devega, "Apocalypse Now: Donald Trump Dons the 'Armor of
God'—and Pushes for Theocracy," *Salon*, February 22, 2024.
5. Philip Gorski, "Why Evangelicals Voted for Trump: A Critical Cultural Sociol-
ogy," *American Journal of Cultural Sociology* 5, no. 3, 347–48; Anugrah Kumar,
"Jerry Falwell Jr. Compares Trump to Bible's King David, 'a Man After God's
Own Heart;' Russell Moore Responds," *Christian Post*, March 14, 2016; Justin
Rohrlich, "Ben Carson Compares Donald Trump to King David in Fox News
Interview," *Daily Beast*, January 15, 2024; "Rick Perry's Belief that Trump Was
Chosen by God Is Shared by Many in a Fast-Growing Christian Movement,"
The Conversation, December 1, 2019; Chrissy Hallowell, Arden Farhi, and
Clare Hymes, "Evangelical Leader Lance Wallnau Pitches Trump to Followers
as Divinely Chosen for Presidency," CBS News, September 4, 2024; Thomas
Edsall, "The Deification of Donald Trump Poses Some Interesting Questions,"
New York Times, January 17, 2024.
6. "Support for Christian Nationalism in All 50 States: Insights from PRRI's 2024
American Values Atlas," Public Religion Research Institute, February 28,
2024, 3, 36–37.
7. John Duckitt et al., "A Tripartite Approach to Right-Wing Authoritarianism: The Authoritarianism-Conservatism-Traditionalism Model," *Political
Psychology* 31, no. 5 (2010): 685–715; Colin Woodard, "Survey Results: Authoritarian Mindsets and the American Nations Regions," Nationhood Lab, August 29, 2024.
8. Piper French, "Left Apart," *New York*, February 27, 2024; Alan Fram and Jonathan Lemire, "Trump: Why Allow Immigrants from 'Shithole Countries'?,"
Associated Press, January 12, 2018; John Wagner and Seung Min Kim, "Trump
Accuses Four Minority Congresswomen of Being 'Very Racist' and 'Not Very

Smart,'" *Washington Post*, July 22, 2019; Michel Martin and Tinbete Ermyas, "Former Pentagon Chief Esper Says Trump Asked about Shooting Protesters," *All Things Considered*, National Public Radio, May 9, 2022; "Trump Threatens to Deploy Military amid National Unrest," *Axios*, June 1, 2020.

9. Peter Baker and Michael Shear, "El Paso Shooting Suspect's Manifesto Echoes Trump's Language," *New York Times*, August 4, 2019; Tucker Carlson, *Tucker Carlson Tonight*, Fox News, December 20, 2017, transcript available through Media Matters, mediamatters.org/tucker-carlson/tucker-carlson-democrats-want-demographic-replacement-flood-illegals-create-flood; Laura Ingraham, *The Ingraham Angle*, Fox News, October 16, 2018, transcript available through Media Matters, mediamatters.org/laura-ingraham/laura-ingraham-vote-republican-or-you-will-be-replaced-immigrants?redirect_source=/video/2018/10/16/laura-ingraham-vote-republican-or-you-will-be-replaced-immigrants/221711.

10. Andrew Romano, "Poll: 61% of Trump Voters Agree with Idea Behind 'Great Replacement' Conspiracy Theory," Yahoo News, May 24, 2022; "Cultural Issues and the 2024 Election," Pew Research Center, June 6, 2024, 16; Robert A. Pape, "Understanding American Domestic Terrorism," Chicago Project on Security and Threats, April 6, 2021.

11. Brian Bender and Matthew Choi, "In Arizona, Trump Has a Redo of His Oklahoma Rally," *Politico*, June 23, 2020; Riley Beggin, "Trump Signs an Executive Order on Prosecuting Those Who Destroy Monuments," *Vox*, June 27, 2020.

12. Ty Seidule, *Robert E. Lee and Me: A Southerner's Reckoning with the Myth of the Lost Cause* (New York: St. Martin's Press, 2020), 144–45; John Ismay, "The Army Was Open to Replacing Confederate Base Names. Then Trump Said No," *New York Times*, June 10, 2020; Donald J. Trump (@realDonaldTrump), series of posts on Twitter (now X), June 10, 2020, 2:40 p.m. EDT; Philip Ewing, "Congress Overturns Trump Veto On Defense Bill After Political Detour," National Public Radio, January 1, 2021.

13. Colin Woodard, "The Midterms Highlighted America's Dangerous Regional Divides," *Washington Monthly*, November 14, 2018; Colin Woodard, "How Centuries-Old Regional Differences Explain the 2020 Presidential Election," *Maine Sunday Telegram*, November 15, 2020.

14. Lazaro Gamio and Karen Yourish, "Trump's Pattern of Pressure to Overturn the 2020 Election," *New York Times*, January 8, 2024; Michael Shear and Stephanie Saul, "Trump, in Taped Call, Pressured Georgia Official to 'Find' Votes to Overturn Election," *New York Times*, January 3, 2021.

15. "From 'an Attempted Coup' to Chaos, Searing Moments of Jan. 6," Associated Press, July 23, 2022.

16. U.S. Senate Roll Call Vote, January 7, 2021, senate.gov/legislative/LIS/roll_call_votes/vote1171/vote_117_1_00002.htm?congress=117&session=1&vote=00002.

17. U.S. House of Representatives Roll Call Vote, January 7, 2021, clerk.house.gov /Votes/202111.

18. For the record, they were Ted Cruz of Texas, Josh Hawley of Missouri, Cindy Hyde-Smith of Mississippi, Cynthia Lummis of Wyoming, Roger Marshall of Kansas, Rick Scott of Florida, and Tommy Tuberville of Alabama.

19. An analysis of the House roll call that night cross-referenced with each House district and which nation had a majority of that district's population during the 117th Congress's apportionment yielded the following tally of "anti-sedition" Republicans: eleven Far Westerners, twelve Midlanders, fifteen Greater Appalachians, twelve Yankees, two from El Norte, and one each from New Netherland and the Left Coast.

20. "Democracy Crisis in the Making: How State Legislatures Are Politicizing, Criminalizing, and Interfering with Election Administration," States United Democracy Center, Protect Democracy, and Law Forward, reports of December 2021, May 2022, June 2023, and December 2023.

21. Tara Golshan, "North Carolina Republicans' Shocking Power Grab, Explained," *Vox*, December 16, 2016; Tara Golshan, "How Republicans Are Trying to Strip Power from Democratic Governors-Elect," *Vox*, December 14, 2018; Mitch Smith, "Fears of Republican Power Grab in Michigan Fade as Governor Vetoes Bill," *New York Times*, December 28, 2018; Matthew Rozsa, "Election Expert: Wisconsin GOP's Power Grab Is 'a Textbook Example of How Democracies Die,'" *Salon*, December 8, 2018.

22. Douglas L. Kriner and Colin Woodard, "Regional Differences in Perceptions of the Threats to U.S. Democracy," Nationhood Lab, March 27, 2023.

23. Richard Wolin, "Carl Schmitt, Political Existentialism, and the Total State," *Theory and Society* 19, no. 4 (Aug. 1990): 406.

24. Lauren Gambino, "Anti-Trans Rhetoric Took Center Stage at Cpac amid Hostile Republican Efforts," *The Guardian*, March 7, 2023; Megan Lebowitz, "Anti-LGBTQ Rhetoric Plays a Prominent Role in First Night of RNC," NBC News, July 15, 2024; Kate Sosin and Barbara Rodriguez, "At the RNC, a Party That Called for Unity Also Verbally Attacked Trans People," The 19th, July 18, 2024; Matt Lavietes, "RNC Speakers Lean Into Homophobic and Transphobic Rhetoric," NBC News, July 18, 2024.

25. German Lopez, "HB2, North Carolina's Sweeping Anti-LGBTQ Law, Explained," *Vox*, March 30, 2017.

26. Active state laws as of September 2024 from "Snapshot: LGBTQ Equality by State," Movement Action Project, lgbtmap.org/equality-maps; see also Utah State Legislature, Sex-Based Designations for Privacy, Anti-Bullying, and Women's Opportunities, H.B. 257 (2024); Utah State Legislature, Inmate Assignment Amendments, H.B. 316 (2024); Tennessee General Assembly, S.B. 2861 (2024); and Legislature of the State of Idaho, Relating to Civil Rights, H.B. 538 (2024).

27. Kasey Meehan and Jonathan Friedman, "Banned in the USA: State Laws

Supercharge Book Suppression in Schools," PEN America, April 20, 2023; Elizabeth Wolfe, "Book Bans Are Harming LGBTQ People, Advocates Say. This Online Library Is Fighting Back," CNN, December 16, 2023.

28. Myah Ward, "We Watched 20 Trump Rallies. His Racist, Anti-immigrant Messaging Is Getting Darker," *Politico*, March 12, 2024; Adam Wren, "'Springfield, Ohio, Is Caught in a Political Vortex, and It Is a Bit Out of Control,'" *Politico*, September 15, 2024.

29. Colin Woodard, "The American Nations and the 2024 Presidential Election," Nationhood Lab, December 4, 2024.

30. Robert Paxton, *The Anatomy of Fascism* (New York: Knopf, 2004), 219–20; Diethelm Prowe, "'Classic' Fascism and the New Radical Right in Western Europe: Comparisons and Contrasts," *Contemporary European History* 3, no. 3 (November 1994): 293; Dennis Tourish, "It Is Time to Use the F Word About Trump: Fascism, Populism and the Rebirth of History," *Leadership* 20, no. 1 (February 2024): 9–32.

CHAPTER 10: HOLDING THE COUNTRY TOGETHER

1. Alexander Hamilton, *Federalist* No. 8, November 1787, in *The Papers of Alexander Hamilton*, vol. 4: January 1787–May 1788, ed. Harold C. Syrett (New York: Columbia University Press, 1962), 326–32.

2. Benedict Anderson, *Imagined Communities: Reflections on the Origin and Spread of Nationalism* (New York: Verso, 1983); E. O. Wilson, *The Social Conquest of Earth* (New York: Liveright, 2011), 31, 42–47, 226–27, 243; Robert Sapolsky, *Behave: The Biology of Humans at Our Best and Worst* (London: Vintage, 2018), 385–424; Pascal Boyer and Pierre Liénard, "Ingredients of 'Rituals' and Their Cognitive Underpinnings," *Philosophical Transactions of the Royal Society B* 375 (2020); David Samson, email message to author, October 10, 2024.

3. Daniel Druckman, "Nationalism, Patriotism, and Group Loyalty,: A Social Psychological Perspective," *Mershon International Studies Review* 38, no. 1 (April 1994): 43–45; George [György] Schöpflin, "The Functions of Myth and a Taxonomy of Myths," in *Myths and Nationhood*, ed. George Hosking and George [György] Schöpflin (New York: Routledge), 1992; William H. McNeill, "The Care and Repair of the Public Myth," *Foreign Affairs* 61, no. 1 (Fall 1982): 1; Jill Lepore, *This America: The Case for the Nation* (New York: Liveright, 2019), 3–4.

4. The story of Bancroft, Simms, Douglass, Wilson, and the battle to create a U.S. national narrative is told in Colin Woodard, *Union: The Struggle to Forge the Story of United States Nationhood* (New York: Viking, 2020).

5. Abraham Lincoln, "Address at Soldiers' National Cemetery," Gettysburg, PA, November 19, 1863.

6. Frederick Douglass, "Our Composite Nationality: An Address Delivered in

Boston, Massachusetts on 7 December 1869," in *The Frederick Douglass Papers: Series One: Speeches, Debates and Interviews, Volume Four: 1864–1880,* ed. John W. Blassingame (New Haven: Yale University Press, 1991), 242–59.

7. William Gilmore Simms to James Henry Hammond, March 29, 1847, in *The Letters of William Gilmore Simms, Volume 2: 1845–1849,* ed. Mary C. Oliphant et al. (Columbia: University of South Carolina Press, 1953), 288–89; Simms to Hammond, July 13, 1847, in *The Letters of William Gilmore Simms,* 333.

8. Woodrow Wilson's white supremacist worldview and role in national narrative construction is discussed in detail in Woodard, *Union,* 183–84, 208–14, 233–39, 287–93, 298–313, 319–53; Wilson's quotes are from Woodrow Wilson, "The Character of Democracy in the United States," *The Atlantic,* November 1889, 582.

9. For a detailed account of how Cold War national security concerns prompted federal interventions on behalf of civil rights, see Thomas Borstelmann, *The Cold War and the Color Line: American Race Relations in the Global Arena* (Cambridge, MA: Harvard University Press, 2001).

10. Zachary B. Wolf, "Trump's Rhetoric in Final Campaign Sprint Goes to New Dark Extremes," CNN, December 18, 2023; Katie Sullivan, "Trump's Anti-Immigrant Comments Draw Rebuke," CNN, October 6, 2023; Donald Trump, "Donald Trump: I Will Make America Great Again for Young People," *Newsweek,* November 29, 2023.

11. "Party Affiliation" (data table), Gallup, news.gallup.com/poll/15370/party-affiliation.aspx; "About Three-in-Ten U.S. Adults Are Now Religiously Unaffiliated," Pew Research Center, December 14, 2021.

12. Dissent of Justice Sonia Sotomayor, *Trump v. United States,* 603 U.S.__(2024), 29.

13. Stephen Hawkins et al., *Hidden Tribes: A Study of America's Polarized Landscape* (New York: More in Common, 2018); Colin Woodard, "The Hidden Tribes and the American Nations," Nationhood Lab, November 16, 2003.

14. "The Youth Vote in 2024," Center for Information and Research on Civic Learning and Engagement, Tufts University, November 2024, circle.tufts.edu/2024-election.

INDEX

Page numbers in *italics* refer to maps and figures.

Winthrop, John, 20, 109
Wisconsin, 18, 93, 148, 149, 204, 236, 237,
    238, 241, 243–45, 251,
    260, 263, 264
women, 252, 283
  abortion rights for, *see* abortion
  religion and, 196–99
  sexism and, 187–89, *189*, 198
  voting rights for, 187
workers, 159–61, 172
  labor unions, 236, 244, 245
  right-to-work laws, 245, 246
World Happiness Reports, 105, 106
World War I, 28, 157, 282
World War II, 39, 108, 282
Wyoming, 38, 187, 214

Yale Program on Climate Change
    Communication, 206–8
Yankeedom, 24–25, 29, 49–50, 52, 69, 84,
    132, 151, 160, 161, 281
  abortion and, 182, 183, 191–95, 201, 204
  African Americans in, 149–52
  Deep South and, 33
  defining characteristics of, 18–20
  democracy and authoritarianism and, 231,
    234, 235, 237, 238, 241, 242, 244, 250,
    251, 257, 260, 263, 265–68, 270, 274

demographics of, 18
environmental issues and, 205, 206,
    209–15, 217, 224
executions in, 72
guns in, 60, 62–69, 72–78
health in, 84, 85, 87–90, 93, 98–104, 106
historical narrative of, 109–13, 131,
    137, 143
immigration and belonging in, 146–50,
    167, 168, 172, 175–76, 178, 179,
    217–18, 259
Left Coast and, 33, 37, 38, 162, 163
in maps, *13, 15*
national narrative and, 286
New Netherland and, 21, 33
philosophical orientation of, 18, 79, 80,
    81, 84, 302
population and density of, 18
religion in, 19, 20, 109–12, 116, 146–47,
    195–96, 201, 217–18, 254
women's rights and, 187–88
Yellowstone National Park, 213
Youngkin, Glenn, 139
Yugoslavia, 4–5
Yukon, 43

Zelinsky, Wilbur, 14
Zul, Esteban, 174

100 YEARS of PUBLISHING

———◇———

Harold K. Guinzburg and George S. Oppenheimer founded Viking in 1925 with the intention of publishing books "with some claim to permanent importance rather than ephemeral popular interest." After merging with B. W. Huebsch, a small publisher with a distinguished catalog, Viking enjoyed almost fifty years of literary and commercial success before merging with Penguin Books in 1975.

Now an imprint of Penguin Random House, Viking specializes in bringing extraordinary works of fiction and nonfiction to a vast readership. In 2025, we celebrate one hundred years of excellence in publishing. Our centennial colophon features the original logo for Viking, created by the renowned American illustrator Rockwell Kent: a Viking ship that evokes enterprise, adventure, and exploration, ideas that inspired the imprint's name at its founding and continue to inspire us.

———◇———

For more information on Viking's history, authors, and books, please visit penguin.com/viking.